Schleiermacher, the Study of Religion,
and the Future of Theology

Theologische Bibliothek Töpelmann

Herausgegeben von
O. Bayer · W. Härle · F. Nüssel

Band 148

Walter de Gruyter · Berlin · New York

Schleiermacher, the Study of Religion, and the Future of Theology

A Transatlantic Dialogue

Edited by
Brent W. Sockness and Wilhelm Gräb

Walter de Gruyter · Berlin · New York

∞ Printed on acid-free paper which falls within the guidelines of the ANSI
to ensure permanence and durability.

Library of Congress Cataloging-in-Publication Data
A CIP catalogue record for this book is available from the Library of Congress.

ISSN 0563-4288

ISBN 978-3-11-048851-7

Bibliographic information published by the Deutsche Nationalbibliothek

The Deutsche Nationalbibliothek lists this publication in the Deutsche Nationalbibliografie;
detailed bibliographic data are available in the Internet at http://dnb.d-nb.de.

© Copyright 2010 by Walter de Gruyter GmbH & Co. KG, 10785 Berlin

All rights reserved, including those of translation into foreign languages. No part of this book may be reproduced or transmitted in any form or by any means, electronic or mechanical, including photocopy, recording or any information storage and retrieval system, without permission in writing from the publisher.

Printed in Germany
Cover design: Christopher Schneider, Laufen

For
B. A. Gerrish

Contents

Preface xi

Abbreviations xv

Keynote Address

Richard Crouter
A Precarious Journey: The Art of Translating Schleiermacher 1

Schleiermacher and the Study of Religion Today

Andrew Dole
Schleiermacher and Religious Naturalism 15

Wayne Proudfoot
Immediacy and Intentionality in the Feeling of
Absolute Dependence 27

Theodore Vial
Anschauung and Intuition, Again
(Or, "We Remain Bound to the Earth") 39

Notger Slenczka
Religion and the Religions:
The Fifth Speech in Dialogue with Contemporary Conceptions
of a "Theology of Religions" 51

Volkhard Krech
Schleiermacher's Contested Place in Religious Studies Today 69

Georg Pfleiderer
"Theologie als Universitätswissenschaft":
Recent German Debates and What They (Could) Learn from
Schleiermacher 81

Schleiermacher and the Prospects for a Transcendental-Anthropological Theory of Religion

Sergio Sorrentino
Feeling as a Key Notion in a Transcendental Conception
of Religion 97

Peter Grove
Symbolism in Schleiermacher's Theory of Religion 109

Jacqueline Mariña
Schleiermacher, Realism, and Epistemic Modesty:
A Reply to My Critics 121

Franklin I. Gamwell
Schleiermacher and Transcendental Philosophy 135

Jörg Dierken
Transcendental Theories of Religion: Then and Now 151

David E. Klemm
Mediating Schleiermacher: The Prospects for a Transcendental-
Anthropological Theory of Religion 165

Schleiermacher and the Future of Historical-Empirical Dogmatics

Dietrich Korsch
Dogmatics of Redemption: The Nature and Status of
Christian Doctrine within the *Glaubenslehre* 179

Walter E. Wyman, Jr.
The Cognitive Status of the Religious Consciousness:
The Nature and Status of Dogmatic Propositions in
Schleiermacher's *Glaubenslehre* 189

Arie L. Molendijk
"Non-Binding Talk": The Fate of Friedrich Schleiermacher's
Concept of Historical-Empirical Dogmatics 203

Kevin W. Hector
Attunement and Explicitation:
A Pragmatist Reading of Schleiermacher's "Theology of Feeling" . 215

Julia A. Lamm
Schleiermacher on "The Roman Church":
Anti-Catholic Polemics, Ideology, and the Future of
Historical-Empirical Dogmatics 243

Elisabeth Gräb-Schmidt
Schleiermacher's Original Insight:
Infinite Inwardness as Consciousness of Freedom and its
Consequences for Theology as Encyclopedia 257

Schleiermacher and the Hermeneutics of Culture

Brent W. Sockness
Schleiermacher's "Essentialist" Hermeneutics of Culture 273

Arnulf von Scheliha
Sources of Normativity in Schleiermacher's Interpretation
of Culture 285

Michael Moxter
Schleiermacher and Contemporary Theories of Culture 299

James M. Brandt
Interpretation of Culture in Schleiermacher's *Christian Ethics* 311

William Schweiker
Schleiermacher's Ethics: Humanistic Premise and
Ecological Promise 323

Wilhelm Gräb
Schleiermacher's Conception of Theology and Account of Religion
as a Constitutive Element of Human Culture 335

Schleiermacher Studies in Germany: New Avenues and Vistas

Andreas Arndt
Schleiermacher:
Dialectic and Transcendental Philosophy, Relationship to Hegel .. 349

Eilert Herms
Schleiermacher's Encyclopedia, Philosophical Ethics,
Anthropology, and Dogmatics in German Protestant Theology ... 361

Cornelia Richter
Friedrich Schleiermacher: Symbol Theory, Hermeneutics,
and Forms of Religious Communication 375

Contributors 391

Index of Authors 393

Preface

The past three decades have witnessed a significant transatlantic and transdisciplinary resurgence of interest in the early nineteenth-century Protestant theologian and philosopher Friedrich Schleiermacher (1768–1834). As the first major Christian thinker to theorize religion in a post-Enlightenment context and re-conceive the task of theology accordingly, Schleiermacher holds a seminal place in the histories of modern Christian thought and the modern academic study of religion alike. Whereas his "liberalism" and humanism have always made him a controversial figure among theological traditionalists, it is only relatively recently that Schleiermacher's understanding of religion has become the target of polemics from Religious Studies scholars keen to disassociate their discipline from its partial origins in liberal Protestantism. This book documents a historic meeting in the history of Schleiermacher studies at which leading scholars from Europe and North America gathered in equal numbers in order to interpret and probe the viability of central features of Schleiermacher's theological and philosophical program in light of its contested place in the study of religion.

The main venue for this three-day conference, held October 29–November 1, 2008, was Swift Hall of the University of Chicago Divinity School, an institution long known for its insistence that theological studies be pursued within the context of the academic study of religion and that inquiry—be it historical, social scientific, humanistic, or philosophical in nature—into the phenomena of religion comply with the highest standards of the modern research university. Such an institutional ethos—whatever its complex origins in European and distinctly American intellectual traditions—is fully in the spirit of Schleiermacher, who, by making the Christian religious community's "way of believing" (*Glaubensweise*)—rather than God or scripture—the primary object of theological reflection, helped pave the way for the emergence of *Religionswissenschaft* in the second half of the nineteenth century and "Religious Studies" in the twentieth. For this reason it was likewise fitting that a conference of this nature be brought to a conclusion at the Annual Meeting of the American Academy of Religion (AAR), the world's largest association of scholars and teachers of religion. The papers found in the first five parts of this volume, then, began as lectures delivered in the stately third floor lecture hall of Swift Hall to an audience of Schleiermacher specialists, students and faculty from the Divinity School and surrounding Hyde Park seminaries, and interested scholars of religion travelling to Chicago for the AAR Annual Meeting. The research reports that comprise the final, sixth part of the volume were delivered in the Waldorf Room of the Chicago Hilton to a fraction of the some 5000 AAR members in attendance at the early November meeting.

Readers of this volume will find a wide variety of perspectives on key aspects of Schleiermacher's religious, theological, and philosophical thought. Indeed, the "conflict of interpretations" present in these pages is one of the book's most striking features. In order to see this, one need only compare Richard Crouter's (chapter 1) warning about the dangers of too eagerly pressing Schleiermacher into contemporary service with Eilert Herms' (chapter 27) insistence that detailed historical reconstructions of the sort favored by Crouter quickly confront a law of diminishing returns and only acquire their real import to the degree that they are able to inform and illuminate current theological questions. Alternatively, one might read part three with a close eye on the remarkably different understandings of "transcendentality" more (Gamwell, Dierken, Klemm) or less (Sorrentino, Grove, Mariña) explicitly held by that part's six contributors. Even a category as basic to Schleiermacher's conception of religion as "feeling" seems quite up for grabs with respect to its precise place in Schleiermacher's understanding of selfhood and its relation to the cognitive and social dimensions of religion. This largely tacit disagreement over *Gefühl* is discernible across the entire volume.

While it of course belongs to a classic thinker to generate a plurality of interpretations, a brief surmise as to a few likely sources of disagreement might prove helpful, especially to non-specialist readers. Three present themselves as most salient: First, the continued expansion of the Schleiermacher *Kritische Gesamtausgabe* (1980–) has gradually but decisively broken through the old "canon within a canon" of available and frequently studied sources. The result has been a shakeup and reassessment of some of the most familiar territory in Schleiermacher studies as even the most canonical of works (e.g., the *Speeches*) suggest new readings in light of the expanded constellation of texts in relation to which such worked-over classics stand. Second, the disciplinary background and institutional placement of the various contributors clearly exercise a considerable influence upon the approaches adopted, specific themes developed, and the evaluative judgments tendered by each author. And while the majority of conference participants belong to departments of Religious Studies or theological faculties/schools, this bipolar distribution belies a far more complex disciplinary pluralism within which philosophical, historical, ideology-critical, and more conventional ecclesial-theological interests compete. Third, the transatlantic dimension of the volume is perhaps its most interesting feature, since the papers are not only colored by pre-understandings supplied by different disciplinary orientations and institutional contexts, but also by the broader intellectual traditions, trends, and academic discourses found on either side of the Atlantic. So, for instance, the impact of analytic philosophy of religion (Dole, Proudfoot, Mariña), pragmatism (Hector), and process theology (Gamwell) are palpable on the American side. By contrast, on the German-dominated European side, one can discern strong echoes of the recent Cassirer renaissance (Moxter, Richter), a pronounced emphasis—indebted to Habermas and Apel—on the communicative aspects of Schleiermacher's theory of religion, and the prominence of what might be called a neo-idealist impulse inspired by the work Dieter Henrich (Grove, Dierken, Gräb-Schmidt; with a mild protest from Arndt). Such broad and diffuse "atmospheric" differences help explain why American disputes over Schleiermacher's theory of religion are often carried out in terms (e.g., "naturalism" or "realism") quite foreign, even jarring, to German researchers immersed in the discourses of communicative rationality and *Subjektivitätstheorie*.

The editors wish to thank, first and foremost, William Schweiker, Director of the Martin Marty for the Advanced Study of Religion, and Richard Rosengarten, Dean of the Divinity School of the University of Chicago, for so enthusiastically hosting the conference behind this volume. Thanks to their generous financial and organizational support, two very full days of lectures and discussions in Swift Hall proceeded without a hitch. Susie McGee, Project Assistant for the Marty Center, attended to the many on-site logistical details. For her extensive assistance, we express our sincere thanks. Absent from this volume are four conveners who moderated the discussions surrounding the book's four central parts: Friedrich Wilhelm Graf (University of Munich), Francis Schüssler Fiorenza (Harvard University), Dawn DeVries (Union Theological Seminary and Presbyterian School of Christian Education), and Kathryn Tanner (University of Chicago). For their "Vermittlung" of the real-time dialogue these papers engendered, our thanks go as well.

Preparation of these pages involved the sustained effort of three graduate students in religion on both sides of the Atlantic. At Stanford, Noreen Khawaja and Peter Woodford dedicated many hours to copy editing the manuscripts behind the chapters to follow. This work included assisting Brent Sockness in the "precarious art of translation" required in order to refine the English translations supplied by the non-native speaking authors. Roughly half of the chapters to follow are the result of a happy cooperation between the European contributors, who went to considerable effort to provide a readable English manuscript, and the informed and judicious interventions of the "Stanford team." In Berlin, Nathan Vanderpool likewise assisted Wilhelm Gräb with all matters concerning the layout and formatting of the volume. He also prepared the name index. The editors could not have wished for a more patient, competent, and cheerful editorial staff.

At the Press, we wish to thank the series editors, Prof. Dr. Oswald Bayer, Prof. Dr. Wilfried Härle, and Prof. Dr. Friederike Nüssel for their support of the kind of international work on Schleiermacher that this volume represents. Special thanks go to Dr. Albrecht Döhnert, Editorial Director of the Theology, Judaism, and Religion division at Walter de Gruyter, for his initial interest in the yield of this conference and his expert assistance at every stage.

The following organizations and institutions underwrote the conference's significant budget: the Deutsche Forschungsgemeinschaft, the Stanford University School of Humanities and Sciences and Department of Religious Studies, the Martin Marty Center of the Divinity School, the Deutscher Akademischer Austauschdienst, and the Schleiermacher-Gesellschaft. International bridge building in the academy is absolutely dependent upon the generous support of such institutions.

Stanford and Berlin, November 2009

Brent W. Sockness
Wilhelm Gräb

Abbreviations of Schleiermacher's Collected Works

Friedrich Daniel Ernst Schleiermacher. *Kritische Gesamtausgabe* (KGA). Edited by Hans-Joachim Birkner et al. Berlin: Walter de Gruyter, 1980–.

KGA I/1	*Jugendschriften 1787–1796*, ed. Günter Meckenstock (1984)
KGA I/2	*Schriften aus der Berliner Zeit 1796–1799*, ed. Günter Meckenstock (1984)
KGA I/5	*Schriften aus der Hallenser Zeit 1804–1807*, ed. Hermann Patsch (1995)
KGA I/6	*Universitätsschriften, Herakleitos, Kurze Darstellung des theologischen Studiums*, ed. Dirk Schmid (1998)
KGA I/7	*Der christliche Glaube nach den Grundsätzen der evangelischen Kirche im Zusammenhange dargestellt (1821/22)*, vols. 1 and 2, ed. Hermann Peiter (1980)
KGA I/10	*Theologische-dogmatische Abhandlungen und Gelegenheitsschriften*, ed. Hans-Friedrich Traulsen (1990)
KGA I/11	*Akademievorträge*, ed. Martin Rössler (2002)
KGA I/12	*Über die Religion (2.–)4. Auflage, Monologen (2.–)4. Auflage*, ed. Günter Meckenstock (1995)
KGA I/13	*Der christliche Glaube nach den Grundsätzen der evangelischen Kirche im Zusammenhange dargestellt*, 2 vols., ed. Rolf Schäfer (2003)
KGA I/14	*Kleine Schriften 1786–1833*, ed. Matthias Wolfes and Michael Pietsch (2003)
KGA II/8	*Vorlesungen über die Lehre vom Staat*, ed. Walter Jaeschke (1998)
KGA II/10	*Vorlesungen über die Dialektik*, 2 vols., ed. Andreas Arndt (2002)
KGA V/1	*Briefwechsel 1774–1796*, ed. Andreas Arndt and Wolfgang Virmond (1985)
KGA V/5	*Briefwechsel 1801–1802*, ed. Andreas Arndt and Wolfgang Virmond (1999)

Keynote Address

A Precarious Journey

The Art of Translating Schleiermacher

RICHARD CROUTER

We gather here this evening as the heirs of a complex scholarly tradition that surrounds the name of Friedrich Daniel Ernst Schleiermacher.[1] Today the significance of Schleiermacher as theologian, philosopher, translator, ethicist, preacher, educator, and political reformer is widely recognized in Germany and throughout the world of human letters. Yet fundamental questions regarding his legacy remain unsettled. What is the proper understanding of Schleiermacher in his own day? Or, for that matter, in ours? How does his place among the early Romantics and German idealists relate, if at all, to contemporary debates within philosophy of language, theology, or philosophy of religion? If such questions are difficult within the German setting, they are all the more problematic on the wider world stage.

Tonight I want to suggest that the study of Schleiermacher is more precarious, the paths forward more uncertain, than we often admit in public. To study Friedrich Schleiermacher well requires that one combine the tedium of philology with the logical clarity of philosophy and the imaginative flare of the Romantics. To study Schleiermacher with the aim of translating him, literally and culturally, into very different times and places poses a daunting challenge. This is true for native German speakers, who are neither his contemporaries nor automatically his kindred spirits, as well as for those of us in the Schleiermacher diaspora. Today we seek to analyze and interpret his thought through a lens, often with assumptions, alien catchwords, and intentions that are well removed from his original setting.

It is not my intent to trace the history of Schleiermacher studies as shaped in our own day. To do so would rehearse the pioneering work of Hans-Joachim Birkner and scores of others, both in and beyond Germany. Implicit in the work of this conference is the fact that, since

---

1 The conversational tone of the original address has been largely retained.

its founding in 1994, the Schleiermacher Gesellschaft has been linked to the production of volumes in the *Kritische Gesamtausgabe*. Yet the fact that a Schleiermacher Gesellschaft first came into being so recently suggests that our professional work is very much still in process. Compared to other German scholarly societies (Kant, Goethe, Hegel or Nietzsche), professional academic concern with Schleiermacher has been belated, despite a decided upswing of interest in his place within theology and the human sciences.

Tonight I wish to speak about the study of Schleiermacher as a precarious undertaking, an open-ended journey that involves us in the thorny decisions of verbal and cultural translation. Like any kind of performance, the art of translating is more complex than meets the eye. To talk about it is to talk about the modern preoccupation with language, its relation to reality, and how a view or philosophy of language impinges upon our ability to understand historical texts. Translation is central to the task of communicating with one another as philosophers, theologians, ethicists, and historians of thought. Hermeneutics and theories of communication lie at the heart of the work of Schleiermacher as well as the wider world of human letters.

For Schleiermacher, literary and academic translating (the art of *übersetzen* that has to do with *Kunst* and *Wissenschaft*) are higher and more reflective than the oral or written interpreting (*dolmetschen*) that occurs in the everyday worlds of business, law, and affairs of state. Like Schleiermacher, I am primarily concerned not with the rendering of meaning in the languages of commerce or statecraft, but with a higher form of literary-aesthetic translating that has to do with artistic or philosophical-theological texts. To translate the latter sorts of texts requires us to make decisions based upon discriminating judgments. Schleiermacher's theory of translation serves as a prism that points to his lifelong concern with hermeneutics, dialectics, ethics, a sense of history, and a sense of the subjectively existing individual in human community.

Allow me to insert a personal word. I am drawn to this topic both from my experience in rendering the original 1799 *Über die Religion: Reden an die Gebildeten unter ihren Verächtern* into English as well as having examined the academic mores and distinctive submissions by German- and English-speaking scholars to the *Journal for the History of Modern Theology/Zeitschrift für Neuere Theologiegeschichte*. But all of us gathered here today know something of the joys and perils of translating. I sometimes think that such work resembles the pleasure and the satisfactions of doing crossword puzzles. Both have linguistic ingenuity, a sense of structure, and clues to be deciphered. But the analogy doesn't work. Unlike translations, crossword puzzles have explicit right and wrong answers that remain under the strict control of their maker. By contrast, with translations only an author who is still living can occasionally oversee and sometimes intervene in the process. It would be instructive if Schleiermacher, like Umberto Eco in his 2001 title, *Experiences in Translation*,[2] might return to take stock of the pitfalls of translation by directly examining the linguistic trade-offs and choices faced by his modern translators. In such a fantasy, I am quite certain that Schleiermacher would take little pleasure in some aspects of the dissemination of his thought.

But these remarks are mere stage setting for the matter at hand. We will do well to let Schleiermacher speak for himself, drawing from his well-known 1813 lecture "On the Different Methods of Translation" ("Über die verschiedenen Methoden des Übersetzens").[3]

1. The Lecture on Translating

In a letter to his young wife, Henriette, on summer holiday with the children on the Baltic island of Rügen, dated Monday, June 21, 1813, Schleiermacher states, "Today I have begun work on a lecture that I am to read in the Academy on Thursday."[4] Then, as now, pressure in the face of a writing deadline appears to have fostered intellectual productivity. The lecture in question, "On the Different Methods of Translation," some thirty pages in length, is not among the main works that capture the attention of philosophers and theologians, even if its ideas mirror its author's lifelong concerns. Four days later, after delivering the paper, Schleiermacher again wrote to Henriette. On Thursday, June 24th he reported back on the lecture on translating: "It is a rather trivial piece [*ziemlich triviales Zeug*], but precisely for this reason people took it to be clever and nice, and asked me to read it in the public session. I didn't want to refuse the request, since I haven't given anything public at all, and they would have taken it for false modesty (24 June 1813)."[5] Despite Schleiermacher's modest disclaimer, giving the lecture to the Academy came off fairly well. Its non-technical formulation speaks of immediate problems in the life of the mind. In fact, the piece is any-

---

2   Umberto Eco, *Experiences in Translation*, trans. Alastair McEwen (Toronto: University of Toronto Press, 2001).
3   Friedrich Schleiermacher, "Über die verschiedenen Methoden des Übersetzens," in KGA I/11, 65-93.
4   KGA I/11, xxxii. Unless otherwise noted, translations from German are my own.
5   Ibid., xxxiii.

thing but trivial. It raises perplexing questions that go to the heart of our collective work.

At age forty-five Schleiermacher had considerable experience behind him as a translator of English and of Greek. Along with Henriette Herz he had translated much of David Collins' account of the transport of British convicts, along with their keepers, to the English colony in New South Wales, thus contributing to the Berliners' passion for travel literature and anthropological lore. At the behest of his ecclesiastical mentor, F.S.G. Sack, Schleiermacher had published two volumes of the English sermons of the Scottish Enlightenment preacher, Hugo Blair. His multi-volume Plato translation, the epitome of a literary-philosophical project that combines *Kunst* and *Wissenschaft*, was well underway. Even more auspicious is the fact that since 1804 in Halle he had been lecturing on hermeneutics.

To enter this debate properly requires us to review the definitions and arguments within Schleiermacher's treatise on translating. Roughly one-third of the way into the lecture, the text states its central concern in the form of a well-known, often-cited Either-Or dilemma: "Either the translator leaves the author in peace, as much as possible, and moves the reader towards him; or he leaves the reader in peace, as much as possible, and moves the author towards him."[6] Simply put, for Schleiermacher, a translator must choose between taking the reader back to the original source or bringing the original source to the reader. Each horn of the dilemma receives roughly ten pages in the lecture. While never pretending that the task can be done with perfection, Schleiermacher insists on defending the first alternative of taking a reader back to the author. On his view the second alternative—bringing the original author to today's reader—rests on a set of dubious if not impossible assumptions.

Just *why* Schleiermacher prefers the first alternative and *what follows* from that decision are matters that concern us here. It behooves us to attend to the lecture with care in order to discern *why* Schleiermacher takes the position that he does and *how* this stance—the necessity of coming to know individual minds amid their own history—mirrors the larger predilections of his work on hermeneutics, dialectics, ethics, and the human subjectivity that informs these fields.

---

6   Schleiermacher, "On the Different Methods of Translating," trans. André Lefevere in *German Romantic Criticism*, ed. Amos Leslie Willson (New York: Continuum, 1982), 9; KGA I/11, 74; also available in André Lefevere, *Translating Literature: The German Tradition from Luther to Rosenzweig* (Assen: Van Gorcum, 1977), 66-89. Subsequent references to this lecture will be given in text, with the page number of Lefevre's translation in Willson's volume, followed by the corresponding page in KGA I/11.

Yet before stating his dilemma Schleiermacher offers some preliminary reflections. Happily for us who are meeting in Chicago, he observes that translation allows people to be in cultural contact with one another on opposite sides of the earth. He quickly acknowledges the wide range of meaning and nuances of translation, including the fact that translation can and does occur within the same basic language. Translation within a single language system, he says, takes place when (a) local dialects are related to a dominant or national discourse, (b) when different social classes need to communicate with each another, (c) when we sometimes translate the speech of another person for ourselves, even if he is our social equal. In addition, (d) we must sometimes translate our own words, as he puts it, "when we want to make them really our own again" (2; 67). This thinking of oneself as a "foreign country" points to Schleiermacher's belief in the intimacy between language and thinking, the process of gaining clarity and depth of reflection through reformulation. Presumably this is what we do in a good conversation and in the tedious editing of our own ideas. The activity of rethinking and reformulating constitutes a self-translation within our own thought processes. Yet such a self-dialogue differs from the proper topic at hand, the translations of texts that originate in a foreign language. In the example of a self-dialogue no rules can be promulgated "except to keep a purely ethical mood" for oneself so that our "receptivity for the less congenial remains open" (2, trans. altered; 68). I seize upon this "purely ethical mood" (*reine sittliche Stimmung*) in the formulations of our self-musing, since if ethics is alive there, it is also alive in our choices within the wider art of translating. It is alive when we embrace more fully the incongruities of history and culture in order to disseminate words and the meaning of original texts to a new audience.

As Schleiermacher moves into his topic, he touches upon two other methods by which we pass along to others the meaning of a work in a foreign language. These methods, which augment, and sometimes distort, more faithful acts of translating, he calls "paraphrase" and "imitation." The two categories are well known and practiced—sometimes unintentionally—in our day. In its brevity paraphrase conveys content more summarily, while imitation leaps forward boldly to communicate something of an original text's qualities and meaning in a wholly new, often transformed, manner. In both instances, paraphrase and imitation, something less than actual translation is substituted for the original.

Contemporary examples of paraphrase and imitation come readily to mind. Paraphrase typically occurs when summaries of classic texts are provided in the form of prose. Versions of Bible stories for children come to mind, as do those of the *Iliad* or *Odyssey* for young schoolchildren. Or, we might take a British example, Charles and Mary Lamb's one-volume *Tales from Shakespeare: For the Use of Young Readers*, begun in 1807 and republished ever since, a book that renders each of Shakespeare's plays in the form of a short story.[7] In the deft hands of the Lambs, Shakespeare's plays are transformed into memorable fairy tales.

Imitation differs from paraphrase by being even freer in rendering the past for the sake of the present. Imitation occurs when a writer seeks to capture the essence of an earlier work by wholly transforming it into an idiom that will do something like the original for a contemporary audience. In a radical form, like putting the story line of the *Iliad* into a contemporary comic strip, Umberto Eco would call it "transmutation." Less radically, it would be imitation, not paraphrase, if I were to recast the arguments of *On Religion: Speeches to its Cultured Despisers*, while substituting contemporary American religion despisers and spiritual seekers for the cultural catchwords and allusions of the German original. My favorite example of imitation is the philosophical book by the Kierkegaard-influenced American novelist, the late Walker Percy. His work *Lost in the Cosmos: The Last Self-help Book* satirizes the self-help movement of religiosity by reformulating the basic arguments of Kierkegaard's 1849 title *The Sickness unto Death* in an American idiom.[8] In his wisdom, Percy apparently knew that few Americans could be lead back to the permanent despair and angst of the original text. Instead, he tries to slip something of that text into their consciousness, as it were, through a kind of literary stealth. It is a fine book, but it probably only works for those who know the original text's power well enough to savor Walker Percy's imaginative efforts at cultural translation. As we see, paraphrase and imitation can be useful—but they are not translations.

As I have stated, Schleiermacher views translating as divided into two approaches that appear to be irreconcilable because they move in opposite directions.

> Either the translator leaves the author in peace, as much as possible, and moves the reader towards him; or he leaves the reader in peace, as much as possible, and moves the author towards him. The two roads are so completely separate from each other that one or the other must be followed as closely as possible, and that a highly unreliable result would proceed from

---

7   Charles and Mary Lamb, *Tales from Shakespeare* (Washington, DC: Folger Shakespeare Library, 1979).

8   Walker Percy, *Lost in the Cosmos: The Last Self-help Book* (New York: Farrar, Straus & Giroux, 1983).

any mixture, so that it is to be feared that author and reader would not meet at all. (9; 74)

For Schleiermacher the two paths are so completely separate from each other that "one or the other must be followed as closely as possible." In the first example, the translator "tries to communicate to the reader the same image, the same impression, he himself has gained—through his knowledge of the original language. . . ." In this instance a translator tries to move a reader towards a point of view that is foreign. In contrast, in the second example, which brings the original author to the reader, a Latin author would not only know German well but have to have changed himself into a German speaker. Not a trace of a foreign element in syntax, style, or tone will any longer cling to the work in question.

I am aware that KGA editor Martin Rössler holds that we cannot be sure of the target of Schleiermacher's critical theory of translation. At the same time, Rössler notes its juxtaposition with Goethe's February 1813 elucidation of two patterns of translation, expressed in a tribute to the poet and writer Christoph Martin Wieland (1733-1813).[9] In contrast with Schleiermacher, Goethe inverts the order of the two options and writes:

> There are two translation maxims: the one requires that the author from a foreign nation be brought over to us in such a way that we are able to view him as one of us; the other by contrast puts the demand on us that we should go over to the foreigner and find ourselves in his circumstances, his manner of speaking, and his peculiarities. The advantages of each are well enough known to educated men through masterful examples. Our friend [Wieland], who here sought the middle way, sought to connect both, yet as a man of feeling and good taste he preferred the first maxim in doubtful cases.[10]

In sharp contrast with Schleiermacher—who allows no middle ground—Goethe first recommends that we combine the two approaches to translation and then suggests a preference on the side of modernizing, i.e., on the side of aesthetics, felicity, and reader accessibility. Since Goethe seems commonsensical in what he says, we are pressed all the more to ask why Schleiermacher is so insistent upon the aim of taking a reader back to an original author.

In proceeding to explicate the two paths, Schleiermacher wishes "to show what the peculiar advantages and disadvantages of each are, as

---

9 Wolfgang Goethe, "Wieland's Andenken in der Loge Amalia zu Weimar gefeiert den 18. Februar 1813," cited in KGA I/11, xxxiv n. 113.
10 Translated from Hans Joachim Störig, ed., *Das Problem des Übersetzens* (Stuttgart: Henry Goverts Verlag, 1963), 35.

well as the limits of their applicability, and in what respect each best attains the goal of translation" (11; 76). In taking a reader to the author—his preferred pattern—two false tendencies (one timid, the other reckless) are to be avoided. The first of these is hesitant, ill-informed, and piecemeal, concentrating on individual terms in a school-child manner that lacks full experience with the original language, while the second leaps into the original language as if the translator could truly "go native" in a foreign world, while forgetting or ignoring his mother tongue (11; 77). Both alternatives misconstrue the distance between translator and source text, the first by being too awestruck by the original to render it properly and the second by imagining there is no distance at all. As we might put the matter: the first translator clings to a dictionary from inexperience and a fear of the divide, while the second suffers the illusion of thinking that there is no divide and hence does not feel "any incommensurability between [his] thinking and the language in which [he] read[s]" (12; 77).

Standing between these two extremes, the proper art of translating aims at giving a "reader the same image and the same delight which the reading of the work in the original language would afford any reader" (12; 77), while being aware that part of the knowledge of a foreign language is knowing that it will always remain foreign. Like languages themselves, the knowledge of foreign languages is also historical. Schleiermacher reflects upon the ability of the German language in his era to encapsulate the Western classics, Hölderlin on Sophocles, Voss on Homer, Wieland, A. W. Schlegel, and Tieck on Shakespeare, Humboldt's Latin version of the Bhagavad Gita, and his own German rendering of Plato. "Language," he writes, "is an historical fact, there can be no right sense for it without a sense of history. Languages are not invented, and all arbitrary work in them and on them is stupid; but they are gradually discovered, and scholarship and art are the powers through which this discovery is promoted and brought to fulfillment" (13; 78). Having this sense of history, the sense of the past's contingencies and of one's present historicity, decisively informs Schleiermacher's theory of translation, just as it does his overall work in philosophy and theology.

In expositing on the theme of taking a reader back to an original author Schleiermacher notes that imperfections and "insurmountable difficulties" must be faced. Odd things transpire when we enter the past for the sake of the present. A freshly coined word or expression in the original language may best correspond to an older, even antiquated expression in the translator's language. In words that rival the *Sprachgefühl* of a multi-lingual Umberto Eco, Schleiermacher writes:

If one considers the word-shaping work produced by a master in its totality, his use of related words and roots of words in a whole number of interrelated writings: how does the translator propose to find a happy solution here, since the system of concepts and their signs in his language is totally different from that of the original language, and since roots of words do not cover each other in parallel, but rather cut through each other in the most amazing directions.

He adds that it is "impossible for the translator's use of language to be as coherent as that of his author ... he will have to be content to achieve in particular what he cannot achieve in general" (14; 79). Such problems, he acknowledges, are even more pronounced in the fields of poetry and artistic prose. A translator may be forced to choose between logical clarity and the tone of a work. Being inclined to high ethical sensitivity may detract from an ability to capture the metrical elements and music of an original text.

Defending his preferred method, Schleiermacher challenges us to ask how we can render something that is at once both familiar and foreign, a body of work that captures the beauty and idiom of the translator's mother tongue, while revealing the same qualities in the original language, when, as is the case, these qualities have a different form. His respect for history makes him want to keep Plato a Greek, not a German, just as our respect for history ought to make us want to keep Schleiermacher German, while presenting him in English. We walk the finest of lines, he says, in our "attempts to keep the tone of the language foreign," while recognizing that "everyone draws that line a little differently" (16; 81). A nimble and inventive use of a translator's language may stretch the language's natural proclivities. Hence, the ideal way of translating, to take a reader back to the original author, requires a level of education, the development of an ear and feeling for language that is not to be found everywhere. Overall, however, the emphasis is on building a bridge that mediates for today something of the original authenticity and the otherness of classical texts.[11]

In turning to the second method, which brings an original author to the reader's "immediate proximity," Schleiermacher acknowledges that

---

11 Including his remarks on the first mode of translating, Schleiermacher writes: "These are the difficulties that beset this method and the imperfections essentially inherent in it. But once we have conceded them, we must acknowledge the attempt itself and cannot deny its merit. It rests on two conditions: that understanding foreign works should be a thing known and desired and that the native language should be allowed a certain flexibility. Where these conditions are fulfilled this type of translation becomes a natural phenomenon, influencing the whole evolution of a culture and giving a certain pleasure as it is given a certain value" ("On Translating," 19; KGA I/11, 83-84).

the task initially seems more straightforward. Here the aim is to "show the work as it would have been if the author himself had originally written it in the reader's language" (19; 84). Tacitus *auf Deutsch* must somehow speak the way he would have spoken, had he been born German. On this model Schleiermacher must speak the way he would have if he had been born, for example, British or American (and, as we know, the two are not the same). Such an imagined ideal does, of course, quicken the mind and stimulate thought, even if it relies on a cultural fiction. The goal of this second method of translating is clearer and less ambiguous. Here the ubiquity, power, and perfection of the translator's mother tongue rules supreme.

What, then, are the arguments against this second mode of translating? Not surprisingly, they have been implied in the assumptions that guide Schleiermacher's preference for the first method. At its core, the second model, for him, rests on a kind of magical, i.e., unbelievable conviction. Only if we can think that a person can be severed from the language he or she was born into, can we think that individuals or their train of thought "could be one and the same in two languages." His argument, which has deep implications for our own work, rests on the irreducibility of individual subjectivity. Schleiermacher's conviction also rests on the view that "everyone produces original work in his mother tongue only, so that the question cannot even be raised of how he would have written his works in another language" (21; 85). Schleiermacher's claim reflects commitments that we associate with early German Romanticism, especially the organicism of our being, the subjectivity of the self, and the inherently complex, finally unknowable, aspect that clings to our sense of selfhood and trumps the categories of a uniform rationalism.

It follows, we might think, that on Schleiermacher's account there is no way of accounting for a Vladimir Nabokov, who writes so originally and brilliantly in English as a second language. Perhaps Goethe has the last word after all. Schleiermacher's argument may fail from an inability to imagine the kind of linguistic transmigration and enrichment brought about by the forced migrations of the twentieth century and globalizing cultural systems of our day. At the same time, if Nabokov does transcend cultural-linguistic divides, the passage of his name through foreign ports of articulation—whether he is known in a given culture as *Nab*-o-kov, Nab-*o*-kov. Nah-bo-*kov*—can only be amusing and argues on the side of Schleiermacher's linguistic pluralism.

In fact, Schleiermacher acknowledges the possibility that, under certain conditions, distinguished multilingual figures have done the thing he decries. In the cases of Grotius and Leibniz, Latin was still at least nominally a mother tongue for philosophical thought. In the example of the Prussian King Friedrich, a conscious effort was made to produce in French in accord with perceptions of the world of courtiers and political affairs of his day. Schleiermacher thinks of Friedrich der Große alongside those diplomats and courtiers who are able to say "sweet nothings and dainty phrases" with excellence in many languages, and all with great ease. Of course, such linguistic gifts serve a useful purpose. They are required by the affairs of the world, both in the era of European Enlightenment and today. But this type of speech does "not belong in the realm in which thoughts grow forcefully from the deep root of a particular language" (22; 87). For Schleiermacher we contradict the deep structure of our mother tongue at our peril. I suspect he would have smiled at the fact that Heidegger could write in German that "die griechische Sprache, und sie allein, ist *logos.*"[12] His uttering this in the German language awakens self-referential suspicion, even as it seems to denigrate and to belittle Heidegger's *Muttersprache.*

Two further arguments are made against the second method of translation. First, just as Schleiermacher does not believe in religion-in-general but only in embodied religion that takes root in the messiness of human history, he does not believe in an idealized dream of a common language that unites all humanity. Citizens of the world lose their bearings if they are not anchored firmly with a sense of their own origins in time and place.[13] Second, for Schleiermacher the rarity of being able to write compellingly in a foreign language should give pause to anyone who imagines this sort of thing, or further imagines that his or her own translation could ever possibly assume the actual voice of the original author. Why this is so rests on the point, brought up earlier in the tract, that no translation consists merely of its semantic parts, as a mere matching up of words, but invariably reflects and assumes a place within the semiotic system where it originated. Even the greatest conceptual abstractions, words such as "God" and "is," are for Schleiermacher only understood through the interplay of the parts with the whole of a linguistic and cultural system (25; 89).

When Schleiermacher finally argues that we ought to shun the effort to breathe the spirit of a language that is alien into an original work he is making the same point. He insists that a sense of incommensurability, foreignness, traces of alienation, must survive the process of

---

12 Martin Heidegger, *What is Philosophy?* trans. Jean T. Wilde and William Kluback (New York: Twayne Publishers, 1958), 44.
13 "Just as a man must decide to belong to one country, just so he must adhere to one language, or he will float without any bearings above an unpleasant middle ground" (Schleiermacher, "On Translating," 23; KGA I/11, 87).

translating texts. Such awareness must be present in order for the task of higher literary or philosophical translation to do its proper work.

2. Some Concluding Remarks

Allow me a few words of summation, for I have dwelt more on Schleiermacher's theory of translation than on its implications for the work that stands before us. If I have rightly grasped his thought, and if we wish not just to think *about* but to think *with* and *out of* his legacy, then the ideas I have sketched have implications that need our attention.

At least three theses drawn from Schleiermacher's 1813 lecture on translation apply to the work of this conference, and to our ongoing endeavors as his interpreters in today's world.

First: Given Schleiermacher's acute sense of history, including the historicity of the past and of ourselves as interpreters, as cultural ambassadors, we need to respect his work in the first instance for its own sake, i.e., in its own setting, as a potential corrective for lifting him prematurely into an alien world of today, whether in the U.S., Deutschland, or elsewhere in the world.

Second: If Schleiermacher has correctly placed priority on one's mother tongue (and by extension on our own scholarly and cultural-linguistic enclaves), we are required to be as nimble and self-aware as possible about our interpretive language, its hidden assumptions and pitfalls that may be read back into original texts, especially when the meaning of those texts—as is the case with Schleiermacher—is almost never immediately transparent.

Third: If Schleiermacher's own era witnessed the flowering of translated insight into classical texts from the past, we must ask whether we who are non-native speakers of German are properly upholding the bargain with history and the stake that we have in his legacy. It is doubtful whether the true depths of Schleiermacher's thought are even now adequately appreciated in the Anglophone world owing, among other things, to the limited number of his serious works that have gained a footing in our cultural setting.

The potential intellectual yield of this conference is great indeed. Yet the way forward in the conference and beyond remains precarious. To be blunt: An unbiased observer might view the topics of this conference as tilting toward present-mindness. They seem to invite reflection about the bearing of Schleiermacher with respect to today's marketplace of ideas: Schleiermacher and the Study of Religion Today,

Schleiermacher and the Prospects of a Transcendental-Anthropological Theory of Religion, Schleiermacher and the Future of an Historical-Empirical Dogmatics, and Schleiermacher and the Hermeneutics of Culture.

If an entire conference can be seen as a work of translation, what kind of translators do we wish to be? What lasting products and directions do we wish to leave for the next generation that is already taking up these problems? When are we willy-nilly doing the work of imitation? When are we paraphrasing in the interest of agendas and intellectual problems that are peculiar to our own cultural and linguistic situations?

The implications of all this for the work of this conference takes the question of the art of translating onto a wider hermeneutical stage. I believe that an ethics of inquiry and of historically sensitive knowing lie at the heart of Schleiermacher's work. Elsewhere I have argued in defense of Wilhelm Dilthey's view that biography, i.e., a sense of thought as contextualized and embodied, is crucial to a proper understanding of Schleiermacher's thought.[14] To say that is merely to assert that at the heart of all our scholarly pursuits lie the claims of individual persons in their existence.

---

14 Richard Crouter, *Friedrich Schleiermacher: Between Enlightenment and Romanticism* (Cambridge: Cambridge University Press, 2005), 21-38.

Schleiermacher and the Study of Religion Today

Schleiermacher and Religious Naturalism

ANDREW DOLE

1. Introduction

In this brief essay I will argue that the mature Schleiermacher should be regarded as a religious naturalist in a specific and non-trivial sense of the term. I will also argue that he put religious naturalism to work in a particular way within *The Christian Faith*, for particular reasons. I think Schleiermacher's embrace of religious naturalism marks a noteworthy episode in the history of the academic study of religion, and by the end of the essay I will stake a claim as to why contemporary scholars of religion should regard his project as an interesting one.[1]

The point of my paper has to do with the place Schleiermacher occupies in English narratives concerning the history of the study of religion. The Anglophone literature that addresses Schleiermacher's relationship to religious naturalism is both slender and equivocal. At least four scholars within the last generation have addressed the subject: Wayne Proudfoot in *Religious Experience* (1985), Peter Byrne in *Natural Religion and the Nature of Religion* (1989), Walter Capps in *Religious Studies: The Making of a Discipline* (1995), and James Thrower in *Religion: The Classical Theories* (1999).[2] Of these four, two (Byrne and Capps) classify Schleiermacher as a species of religious naturalist and two (Proudfoot and Thrower) place Schleiermacher on the opposite side of the fence from religious naturalism. Byrne identifies substantive continuities between Schleiermacher's approach to religion and that of the naturalistically-inclined Deists; Capps assimilates Schleiermacher to the

---

[1] The arguments I present in this essay draw upon material presented at greater length in my forthcoming book, *Schleiermacher on Religion and the Natural Order* (Oxford: Oxford University Press, 2009). In this paper I do not touch on the primary project of the book, which is a reconstruction of Schleiermacher's account of religion.

[2] Wayne Proudfoot, *Religious Experience* (Berkeley: University of California Press, 1985); Walter Capps, *Religious Studies: The Making of a Discipline* (Minneapolis: Fortress Press, 1995); Peter Byrne, *Natural Religion and the Nature of Religion* (London: Routledge, 1989); James Thrower, *Religion: The Classical Theories* (Washington, DC: Georgetown University Press, 1999).

"enlightenment paradigm" of "reconceptualizing religion on a natural base."[3] By contrast, Proudfoot argues that Schleiermacher's "description of the religious consciousness is formulated in order to preclude the reduction of that consciousness and thus to rule out as illegitimate several kinds of criticism of religious doctrine and belief" and thus associates him with the position that "the distinguishing mark of the religious is that it is assumed to elude natural explanation";[4] and Thrower distinguishes "religious" theories of religion from "naturalistic" theories and assigns Schleiermacher firmly to the former category.[5] So today I hope to bring some clarity to a disagreement within the existing literature.

My focus in what follows will be on the second edition of *The Christian Faith*, largely because this text can be regarded as the articulation of a discrete project. That project, of course, is that of advocating an "eternal covenant between the living Christian faith and completely free, independent scientific inquiry, such that faith does not hinder science and science does not exclude faith."[6] While much of what I will claim regarding Schleiermacher's position is true (in my view) of the young Schleiermacher as well, here I will be concerned with Schleiermacher the mature academic theologian, dedicating his magnum opus to the cause of the peaceful coexistence of religious faith and scientific inquiry.

2. Schleiermacher's Religious Naturalism

"Religious naturalism" can be understood in a variety of ways, and I think there are at least three interesting senses in which one can be a religious naturalist. Religious naturalism might be understood, first, as a commitment to the non-existence of anything other than that which constitutes the natural order (Wesley Wildman, for example, has recently unpacked his self-description as a religious naturalist in these

---

3   Byrne, *Natural Religion*, 8-10, 161; Capps, *Religious Studies*, 11, 16.
4   Proudfoot, *Religious Experience*, 38, 217.
5   Thrower, *Religion*, 3, 49. It is worth noting that Thrower acknowledged that the designations "religious" and "naturalistic" are not mutually exclusive and have overlapped in the work of some theorists. He does not include Schleiermacher among these (ibid., 3).
6   Friedrich Schleiermacher, *On the Glaubenslehre: Two Letters to Dr. Lücke*, trans. James Duke and Francis Fiorenza (Atlanta: Scholars Press, 1981), 64.

terms).⁷ Second, one might understand religious naturalism as the position that religion is a "product of human nature" rather than a purely cultural and thus historically accidental phenomenon; this is roughly the sense D. Jason Slone has given the term.⁸ Fairly uncontroversially, Schleiermacher does not qualify as a religious naturalist in the first sense (setting aside for the moment the question of pantheism) and does qualify as a religious naturalist in the second sense. But it is a third sense of religious naturalism in which I am interested.

According to this third sense, religious naturalism is the position that religion is a product of the workings of the natural order. In this sense it contrasts with what might be termed "religious supernaturalism," the position that what makes religion distinctive is the fact that it (or some essential component of it) results from the influence of entities or agents that are not themselves natural. Thus Wildman would be a religious naturalist in this sense (since he believes that there are no entities that are not natural) and Rudolf Otto a nonnaturalist, inasmuch as Otto's position was that "religious phenomena are due to the action of some Transcendent being."⁹ It should be apparent that this third form of religious naturalism is neutral with respect to the other two forms: embracing the idea that religion is a product of the natural order does not generate any obligation either to affirm or deny the existence of anything outside that order and is compatible with either affirming or denying that religion is a "product of human nature."

It is a commitment to this form of religious naturalism that I attribute to Schleiermacher, a commitment that he expressed in causal language. Precisely expressed, I attribute to him the position that religion is a *naturally caused* rather than supernaturally caused phenomenon, the position that the efficient causes of religion are to be found within the natural order or *Naturzusammenhang* rather than outside that order. On this position the one who seeks after the causes of religion will not discover within that phenomenon any events that result directly from the activity of supernatural beings, and the one who refuses to

---

7   In a recent essay Wildman has noted his agreement with the view that "supernatural beings do not interfere in natural processes. In my case, this is because I believe that supernatural beings do not exist (i.e., I am a religious naturalist)." Wesley Wildman, "The Significance of the Evolution of Religious Belief and Behavior for Religious Studies and Theology," in *Where God and Science Meet: How Brain and Evolutionary Studies Alter our Understanding of Religion*, vol. I, ed. Patrick McNamara (Westport, CT: Praeger, 2006), 268.

8   D. Jason Slone, *Theological Incorrectness: Why Religious People Believe What They Shouldn't* (Oxford: Oxford University Press, 2004), 14.

9   This is how David Bastow describes the "theory-claim" articulated by Otto's *The Idea of the Holy* in "Otto and Numinous Experience," *Religious Studies* 12 (1976): 173.

entertain the possibility of supernatural influence in investigating religion does not thereby incur any risk of failing to identify correctly the causes of religiously significant events.

Now it is not simply his embrace of religious naturalism in this sense that makes Schleiermacher interesting; as Byrne noted, this embrace simply locates Schleiermacher downstream, historically speaking, from the naturalism of the deists. But before moving on I want to offer some support for my claim that this was his position. The textual basis for my ascription of religious naturalism to Schleiermacher is the discussion of God's eternity and omnipotence in §51-54 of the second edition of *The Christian Faith*, and specifically the way finite causality and the divine causality are distinguished in this discussion. Because the divine causality is simple and eternal, it does not operate at discrete locations within the natural order, but rather operates upon that order as a whole. The *Naturzusammenhang* itself is a nexus of particular or finite causes, "nothing but the twofold reciprocally determined totality of the finitely causing and the finitely caused."[10] Thus the divine causality is "equivalent in compass" to the entire system of finite causality, but it "can never in any way enter as an addition, as it were, to the natural causes in their place; for then like these it would have to work temporally and spatially."[11] It follows from this that no event within the natural order will be caused solely by the divine causality, and all events will have a discrete natural cause or set of natural causes, which the eternal and simple divine causality orders and sustains. Thus "everything which happens temporally and spatially has its determinations in the totality of that which is outside it [in space] and before it [in time], however much these may be hidden from us, and in this way come under the ordered power [of the divine causality]; if some, to the exclusion of others, were to be traced back to [its] immediate power, all natural order would be overturned."[12]

The path from this position to religious naturalism should be fairly clear. If any event within the temporal order will have one or more finite causes and none will be caused discretely by the divine causality, the same will be true of the range of events which constitute religion: both outward religion (acts of religious communication and worship,

---

10 Friedrich Schleiermacher, *Der christliche Glaube nach den Grundsätzen der evangelischen Kirche im Zusammenhange dargestellt* (1830/31), in KGA I/13.1, 325 (§54.1), henceforth CG; *The Christian Faith*, ed. H.R. Mackintosh and J.S. Stewart (Edinburgh: T&T Clark, 1928; repr. 1989), 211, henceforth CF. Translations will be those of Mackintosh et al. unless otherwise noted; here the translation is mine.
11 CG, 325-26 (§54.1); CF, 212 (my translation).
12 CG, 329 (§54.4); CF, 215 (translation modified).

the formation of religious communities, the formulation of doctrines) and inward religion (pious feelings, attitudes, beliefs and so on), inasmuch as these are complexes of events or states of affairs occurring within the stream of time, will have discrete finite causes. In no case will one of these lack such finite causes and instead be caused directly by God. Thus when Schleiermacher remarks, following his argument against belief in miracles, that "everything—even the most wonderful thing that happens or has happened—is a problem for scientific research," this remark should be understood as equivalent to the claim that the events that constitute religion are no less natural than any other events.[13]

It is also worth noting that in paragraph §47—where what is at issue is the question of whether God ever brings about events within the natural order, as it were, directly—Schleiermacher extends the argument to the question of the cause of the feeling of absolute dependence itself. A miraculous event would be "something . . . which is not to be comprehended through the totality of finite causes." If in order to account for such events "we have to admit the entrance of a divine efficacy without natural causes," we must then grapple with the question of whether events of this sort could possibly have been brought about naturally. If we answer yes, then in postulating a direct causal efficacy of God we are supposing that "God deliberately did not so order the system of nature that his whole will should be accomplished through it" even though he could have done so. But to say that the events in question could *not* have been produced by natural causes is tantamount to claiming that "what is to be comprehended through the natural order can never rightly (*mit Recht*) arouse within us the feeling of the absolute dependence of the finite."[14] These two alternatives constitute a *reductio ad absurdum* of the idea of miracles, and thus the conclusion is, I think, inescapable that on Schleiermacher's understanding the feeling of absolute dependence is itself naturally caused: it is "aroused" through avenues that are themselves "to be comprehended through the natural order." This should not be surprising, since here Schleiermacher was simply being consistent.

There are strands of argumentation in the *Glaubenslehre* that are not easily reconciled with religious naturalism as I have described it. One such strand is Schleiermacher's account of the appearance of the Redeemer (specifically, the appearance of perfectly powerful God-

---

13 CG, 286 (§47.3); CF, 184.
14 CG, 282-83 (§47.2); CF, 182 (translation modified). Mackintosh et al. render *zu begreifen ist aus* as "can be explained by."

consciousness in a member of the human species).[15] Another is the awareness that Schleiermacher attributes to Christians of a "particular divine impartation" within the divine causality oriented towards specific events within the natural order.[16] I believe he can be interpreted so that he remains internally consistent on these questions—and, to be sure, a full defense of my position would require such an interpretation—but I do not have time to pursue the matter here.[17]

3. Religious Naturalism in Context

In a recent essay responding to an argument by the psychologist Paul Bloom that religious belief is an "evolutionary accident," the philosopher Peter van Inwagen observes that "[a]ny naturalistic explanation of any phenomenon can be incorporated without logical contradiction into a "larger," more comprehensive supernaturalistic explanation of that phenomenon. A theist (or other "supernaturalist") may therefore accept any naturalistic explanation of supernaturalistic belief (or of any other phenomenon) without logical contradiction."[18] This point, acknowledged by Van Inwagen as "trivial," accounts for a central structural characteristic of *The Christian Faith*. As Schleiermacher describes it, religion is the result of the dynamics of cause and effect that are internal to the *Naturzusammenhang*; but this understanding is itself placed into the context of a "broader" account that ascribes the existence and persistence of the natural order as a whole to God's activity, i.e. the divine causality.

Taken as a whole, then, the *Glaubenslehre* describes religion as a product of the workings of the natural order in the same sense as any other historical phenomenon, but positions God's activity as the ultimate source of the natural order's existence and character. There is a sense in which religion is also a product of divine activity, in that the divine causality is responsible for the existence and preservation of the natural order as a whole and thus is responsible for religion as something that unfolds within that order. But the same can be said, of

---

15 CG, 106-14 (§13) and CG (vol. 2 = KGA I/13.2), 21-27 (§88); CF, 62-68, 361-65.
16 See, for example, CG, 486ff. (§§79-80); CF, 325ff.
17 I discuss these issues in chapter 4 of *Schleiermacher on Religion and the Natural Order*.
18 Peter Van Inwagen, "Explaining Belief in the Supernatural: Some Thoughts on Paul Bloom's 'Religious Belief as an Evolutionary Accident,'" in *The Believing Primate: Scientific and Philosophical Perspectives on the Evolution of Religion*, ed. Jeffrey Schloss and Michael Murray (Oxford: Oxford University Press, 2009), 134-35. I thank Michael Murray for access to manuscript versions of chapters from this work.

course, for any other phenomenon within space and time; on this view religion is not made distinctive by a connection to the divine causality that other natural phenomena lack. In Schleiermacher's dogmatics, religious naturalism, in the sense I have given to the term, is integrated into an ultimately theistic account of the overall natural order, in such a way that it informs the work of dogmatic theology.

Why did Schleiermacher incorporate religious naturalism into his dogmatics in this way? In his open letters to Lücke, Schleiermacher spoke of the eventual attainment by the sciences of "comprehensive knowledge of the world," a state of affairs that he thought would involve the falsification of many claims commonly regarded as essential to the Christian faith.[19] In these letters Schleiermacher described his dogmatics as an attempt to set out an understanding of Christianity that would "avoid entanglements with science." It matters for this "mediating" project that religion be understood as naturally caused for two reasons. First, the thought that religiously significant events are not naturally caused is both vulnerable to empirical falsification and anathema to science in general as Schleiermacher understood it. And second, his position seems to have been that once religious naturalism is accepted as a general postulate, the kind of more specific information that "comprehensive knowledge of the natural order" would provide—say, information concerning the specific causes of religiously significant events—would have relatively little impact on religious faith.[20] Premising a theological account of Christianity on religious naturalism, then, was a strategy for ensuring religion's ongoing compatibility with scientific knowledge, and with scientific knowledge concerning religion in particular.

What I think makes Schleiermacher interesting has to do with this project of putting religious naturalism to work in the service of the reconciliation of faith and science. But to grasp the distinctiveness of his project requires an appreciation of the cultural and political context of his theological work.

Schleiermacher's description of a positive and peaceful relationship between religion and science was not a prophecy or a prediction, but a *proposal* intended to counter the rush of history towards an alternative,

---

19 Schleiermacher, *On the Glaubenslehre*, 60-61.
20 "[I]t is obviously incorrect," Schleiermacher remarked in §46, "to claim, as if on the basis of a general experience, that that which is uncomprehended as such always stimulates pious feeling more than that which is understood . . . even the greatest confidence with which we accept any particular hypothetical explanation of these phenomena does not overturn that feeling" (CG, 266 [§46.1]; CF, 171-72, my translation).

and disastrous, state of religious affairs. Now one could be forgiven for taking away from the bulk of the English literature the view that Schleiermacher feared above all the triumph of secularism—that it was his view that Christianity required protection from criticism because without such protection it would wither and die in the face of advancing knowledge. But in fact secularism was not the worry that animated Schleiermacher's theological work. The alternative to his vision of an "eternal covenant" was not a future in which advances in the sphere of the intellect would drive Christianity to extinction.[21]

The English literature has in general made little of the tensions between Schleiermacher and the "awakened" pietism of early 19th century Prussia.[22] This movement constituted a rising power during the decades of Schleiermacher's maturity and formed the political background of a good deal of his activities. It was the "neo-pietists" who were responsible for the dismissal of his Berlin colleague Wilhelm De Wette from his post in 1819 and who eventually secured his vacant chair in biblical studies for Wilhelm Ernst Hengstenberg, a convert to the movement without adequate scholarly training but with ambition

---

21 In fact, it would be silly to ascribe to Schleiermacher the view that advancing scientific or philosophical knowledge could lead to such a result. On his view, beliefs of the sort that are vulnerable to empirical falsification or philosophical criticism are relatively superficial components of religion, which at its core is a matter of feeling. Furthermore, like many contemporary evolutionary- and cognitive-psychological theorists of religion, Schleiermacher did not consider religion to be a purely accidental phenomenon such that developments within the sphere of culture could eliminate it once and for all. Rather, religion predictably emerges out of collective human life in all but extraordinary cultural circumstances, assuming different forms under different historical conditions. In addition, the material I describe in the remainder of the paper—Schleiermacher's worries about the growing cultural influence of neo-pietism—make it clear that his understanding of the cultural dynamics of religion allowed for the persistence of 'retrograde' forms of religion in cultural backwaters isolated, by design or accident, from developments within the intellectual sphere. This is not to say, however, that Schleiermacher ascribed a kind of invincible flexibility to religion. In the third of the *Speeches*, for example, he lamented the effects of bourgeois culture on religious development, describing a "forcible suppression" of the religious instinct from childhood on as one concomitant of contemporary life among "prudent and practical" people. There were cultural circumstances that could lead to the at least temporary suppression of religion in his view; but these were not primarily a matter of advances in the sphere of knowledge.

22 Thomas Howard's recent book *Protestant Theology and the Making of the Modern German University* (Oxford: Oxford University Press, 2006) discusses this historical episode at some length. For English speakers a primary source of information on Prussian church politics remains Robert Bigler, *The Politics of German Protestantism: The Rise of the Protestant Church Elite in Prussia, 1815-1848* (Berkeley: University of California Press, 1972).

and connections. It was Hengstenberg who after 1827 edited the *Evangelische Kirchen-Zeitung*, the house-organ of the neo-pietist movement remembered at midcentury by Adolf Hilgenfeld primarily for its "anathematization of all true science."[23] And it was Hengstenberg who, from the mid-1820s on, spearheaded efforts to expose "unbelief . . . which encourages disrespect for heavenly and worldly order" within the academy.[24] A notorious episode of this program was his orchestration of a public attack by Ludwig von Gerlach on the Halle theologians Gesenius and Wegscheider in 1830, which Hengstenberg would later describe as an attempt to "carry the fight from the lecture hall to the Protestant church . . . from the field of scholarship into public life."[25]

It was for these neo-pietists that Schleiermacher reserved some of the most stinging rhetoric of his mature corpus. In his preface to the 1821 edition of the *Speeches* he remarked that one who wanted to write on the topic of religion in the current context "might rather find it necessary to write speeches to the sanctimonious and to the slaves of the letter, to those unknowing and unloving superstitious and hyperbelieving persons" than to his original religiously skeptical audience, "who seem no longer to be there at all."[26] More pointed still is a passage from the "explanations" appended to the third speech: "The intolerant lovelessness of our newly pious, which is not content with drawing back from that which is opposed to it but uses every social connection for vilification, which may soon render all free spiritual life hazardous; the anxious listening for particular expressions according to which they characterize one person as white and another as black . . . and the general fear of all science—these are no signs of an open sense, but rather of a deeply rooted diseased condition, which must be treated with love but also with strict firmness if the detriment to the whole of society which grows out of this is not to be greater than the spiritual profit which the awakened religious life brings to individuals."[27]

The alternative to Schleiermacher's vision of a positive and productive relationship between faith and science was not secularization, but rather the flourishing of a defensively anti-intellectual and politically muscular Christianity, championed by "those who can hack away at science with a sword, fence themselves in with weapons at hand to

---

23 Adolf Hilgenfeld, "Die wissenschaftliche Theologie und ihre gegenwärtige Aufgabe," *Zeitschrift für wissenschaftliche Theologie* I (1858): 11.
24 Bigler, *The Politics of German Protestantism*, 102.
25 Ibid., 103.
26 KGA I/12, 10.
27 Ibid., 178. Cf. Friedrich Schleiermacher, *On Religion: Speeches to its Cultured Despisers*, trans. John Oman, 3rd ed. (Louisville: John Knox Press, 1994), 144-45.

withstand the assaults of sound research and behind this fence establish as binding a church doctrine which appears to everyone outside as an unreal ghost."[28] Although Schleiermacher decried the "intellectual starvation" that such an outcome would produce for adherents of such forms of Christianity, his broader worries concerned the effects that efforts by the leaders of such defensively oriented sects to protect their convictions from change would have on the rest of society. The dismissal of De Wette made it clear by 1820 that "awakened" pietism and its alignment with politically reactionary forces posed real threats to intellectual freedom, and to the freedom of research into the nature and history of Christianity in particular. And when it is recalled that Schleiermacher regarded "church," "state," and "academy" as three of the fundamental forms of human association, the interrelationship of which constitutes society as a whole, it should be evident that in opposing an arrangement whereby the *church* aligns itself as closely as possible with the *state* in order to dictate to the *academy* what lines of research it can and cannot pursue, he was attempting to promote the flourishing of both church and academy in independence from the state, and in fact to promote the general goal of social harmony.

In short, the "detriment to society" that the "newly pious" threatened was that of cultural polarization. Schleiermacher foresaw a future in which Prussian society would be divided into two warring camps, with those interested in the pursuit of knowledge on one side and the faithful on the other; and in his vision the primary agents of this polarization would be the religious, driven by the conviction that the survival of Christianity requires its protection from criticism and eager to make use of state power in suppressing threats to the faith. His "eternal covenant" was an attempt to forestall this polarization through the advocacy of an understanding of religion which would preserve claims essential to a Christian self-understanding while offering no resistance to the advance of knowledge, thus undercutting the idea that Christianity requires protection from criticism.

4. Conclusions

What makes Schleiermacher interesting in relation to the history of the academic study of religion lies not in the fact that he developed a naturalistic understanding of religion, nor in the fact that he embedded this understanding within a theological account of God's providential supe-

---

28 Schleiermacher, *On the Glaubenslehre*, 60.

rintendence of the natural order. Neither does it lie in the fact that he employed this understanding of religion to conduct a far-reaching critical examination of the traditional stock of Protestant doctrines, thus carrying out what Capps described as the "reconceptualization" of Christianity "on a natural base." Schleiermacher did do all of these things. But to my mind what makes his project historically noteworthy for those interested, as I am, in the historical fortunes of religious naturalism is the fact that *The Christian Faith* constitutes an attempt to apply and transmit religious naturalism outside the realm of scholarship and beyond the walls of the academy.

The success of the "eternal covenant" would require more than the assent of scholars to Schleiermacher's proposal. It would require broad acceptance of his model of religion, in at least its broad outlines, among clergy, agents of the state, and laypeople—among all of those groups otherwise vulnerable to the appeal of the neo-pietists' warnings about the perils of impious criticism. His dogmatics, in other words, was an attempt to disseminate an understanding of Christianity premised on religious naturalism into a Christian population in the interests of influencing religious attitudes and behaviors, particularly behaviors towards those engaged in the pursuit of knowledge. Describing religion as a naturally caused phenomenon open to investigation by the full range of the natural and human sciences constituted for Schleiermacher the central component of a strategy for influencing the direction of religious life in Prussia, and thereby for intervening in the large-scale dynamics of Prussian society in response to the threat of cultural fragmentation.

In historical retrospect, Schleiermacher's anticipation of cultural polarization (and his view of religion's role therein) seems as prescient as his proposed remedy seems overly optimistic. The sharp divide between the neo-pietists and the "scientific theologians" that had become all too evident by the middle of the nineteenth century is a recognizable antecedent of the North American culture wars, the effects of which are still felt both in the academy and in the public sphere. Whether the kind of work that scholars of religion do can, or even should, have an impact beyond the walls of the academy is still being debated; at least some such scholars still feel a responsibility to engage in projects of "mediation" to some degree.[29] And if the withdrawal of many Ameri-

---

[29] In the final chapter of *Schleiermacher on Religion and the Natural Order*, I examine three essays that grapple with this issue. These are Carl Raschke, "Religious Studies and the Default of Critical Intelligence," *Journal of the American Academy of Religion* 54 (1986): 131-38; Burton Mack, "Caretakers and Critics: On the Social Role of Scholars who Study Religion," *Bulletin of the Council of Societies for the Study of Religion* 30

can religionists behind intellectual and institutional fortifications has for some time been not a looming possibility but a simple historical fact, it is not clear that there is no point to such efforts.

If one day the history of attempts to apply the benefits of religious naturalism to the religious condition of particular societies is traced, Schleiermacher's dogmatics will deserve treatment as an early and eminent example of this project. And contemporary scholars of religion—particularly those who themselves identify with religious naturalism—who hope to address their work to the public sphere have an important historical resource in Schleiermacher: for in his work we have the record of a perhaps uniquely prominent and at least partially successful attempt at premising an understanding of religion shared by scholars, clergy, and ordinary religious adherents alike on the idea that religion is a natural phenomenon.

(2001): 32-38; and Russell McCutcheon, "A Default of Critical Intelligence? The Scholar of Religion as Public Intellectual," *Journal of the American Academy of Religion* 65 (1997): 443-468.

Immediacy and Intentionality in the Feeling of Absolute Dependence

Wayne Proudfoot

One of many benefits of the renewed interest in Schleiermacher is an appreciation of the fact that neither philosophy of religion nor theology can be done adequately without attention to religion. Neo-orthodox thinkers and some contemporary philosophers of religion have tried to distance themselves from the study of religion and scholars of religion have often ignored philosophy and theology. Schleiermacher not only took the study of religion to be central for the philosophy of religion, but he was attentive to the social and cultural dimensions of religion as well as to its transmission and development in history.

In *Religious Experience* I introduced an analysis of some of the problems that arise in attempts to describe and to explain religious experience by a brief interpretation of Schleiermacher's account of piety in the *Reden* and in *Der christliche Glaube*.[1] I argued there that Schleiermacher tries unsuccessfully to identify a moment of unmediated experience that is independent of thought. This account of piety served better to capture what he took to be its distinguishing mark than accounts that identify religion chiefly with belief or action, and it also served to preclude any conflict between religious doctrine and scientific beliefs about the world.

Schleiermacher, I wrote, characterizes the common element in religion as a moment of intuition or feeling that is immediate in a way that renders it independent of concepts or thought. "Consequently, it remains unscathed by Kant's contention that our experience is structured by the categories and thoughts that we bring to it and thus that we produce rather than reproduce the world we think we know."[2] I said that Schleiermacher was committed to holding both that the distinguishing moment in religion is unmediated in the sense of being inde-

---

[1] Wayne Proudfoot, *Religious Experience* (Berkeley: University of California Press, 1985).
[2] Ibid., 2.

pendent of thought and that it can be specified only by reference to its grammatical object, and that these two requirements are incompatible. If the common element in piety is characterized as sense and taste for the infinite, as in the *Reden*, or as a feeling of absolute dependence directed toward a co-determinant specified only as a "whence," as in the introduction to *Der Christliche Glaube*, then that intuition or sense or feeling cannot be independent of thought, even though both "infinite" and "whence" are indeterminate terms.

I continue to think that Schleiermacher regarded the distinctive moment in piety as one that is unstructured by the Kantian forms and categories, but I am now unsure whether or not he regarded it as independent of concepts. The feeling or consciousness of absolute dependence seems to assume at least the concept or category of causality, a concept that is central both for Schleiermacher's philosophical account of religion in the introduction to *Der christliche Glaube* and for his theological accounts of Christian doctrine in the body of that work. He is clear both in the *Reden* and in *Der christliche Glaube* that religious doctrine, rightly construed, cannot conflict with the deliverances of science. In this paper I want to look more closely at the passages in the introduction to the latter in which Schleiermacher clarifies what he means by immediate self-consciousness and describes the feeling of absolute dependence.

1. Immediacy

Ted Vial rightly remarks that for Schleiermacher all experience is shaped by language.[3] My claim that the distinctive moment in piety, especially as described in *Der christliche Glaube*, is independent of thought, was ambiguous between meaning that it is pre-linguistic or that it is nonconceptual. I had avoided using the term "pre-linguistic" for some of the same reasons that Vial gives, though for Schleiermacher language and thought are correlative. I had not attended to Schleiermacher's elucidation of the term "immediacy" as he uses it in this context as without self-reflection.

Vial argues that Schleiermacher's use of the terms "intuition" and "feeling" to characterize religion in the *Reden* is not an attempt to remove piety from the arena of human experience, and, in particular, from the recognition that all experience is shaped by language.

---

3   See Ted Vial's contribution to this volume, "Anschauung and Intuition, Again (Or, 'We Remain Bound to the Earth')."

Schleiermacher's use of the term, he says, stands within the Kantian tradition, and we should therefore look to Kant for clues about how it is to be understood. He quotes Kant's definition of intuition from the *Prolegomena* as "a representation of the sort which would depend immediately on the presence of an object."[4] For Schleiermacher as well as for Kant, Vial writes, intuition is the product of an action on us by something external to us. It is, for Schleiermacher, the objective side of experience, and feeling is the subjective side, the change that occurs in us because of this action. Religion is a product of human nature. Schleiermacher writes: "All intuition proceeds from the influence of the intuited on the one who intuits, from an original and independent action of the former, which is then grasped, apprehended, and conceived by the latter according to one's own nature."[5] This apprehension is shaped by language, culture, and individuality. Neither intuition nor feeling is pre-linguistic for Schleiermacher.

Vial suggests that in the introduction to *Der christliche Glaube* Schleiermacher means by "immediate self-consciousness" what he means by "intuition" in the *Reden*. He describes it differently, but there also he refers to the influence of an independent and original source of activity, which is imagined and conceived according to one's own nature and culture.

Philosophy of religion, Schleiermacher writes in that introduction, can distinguish the permanently identical from the changeable elements in religious societies in a way analogous to the manner in which a philosophy of right can set out a critical conception of the state.[6] He begins his account by distinguishing piety, which is the basis of all religious communions, from both knowing and doing. It is a modification of feeling, or of immediate self-consciousness. Piety cannot be identified either with religious knowledge or with moral virtue. The fact that someone is proficient in theology and the history of religious thought does not, by itself, settle the question of whether or not he or she is a pious person. The same question can be asked about someone who is morally admirable. Piety is related to both knowing and doing, but it is

---

4   Immanuel Kant, *Prolegomena to Any Future Metaphysics*, ed. and trans. Gary Hatfield (Cambridge: Cambridge University Press, 1997), 33; *Prolegomena zu einer jeden künftigen Metaphysik*, in vol. 4 of *Gesammelte Schriften*, ed. Königlich Preußische Akademie der Wissenschaften (Berlin: Georg Reimer, 1903), 282. See Vial, "Anschauung and Intuition," sect. 2.

5   Friedrich Schleiermacher, *On Religion: Speeches to its Cultured Despisers*, trans. Richard Crouter (Cambridge: Cambridge University Press, 1996), 24-25; *Über die Religion*, in KGA I/2, 213-14. Quoted in Vial, "Anschauung and Intuition," sect. 2.

6   Friedrich Schleiermacher, *The Christian Faith*, ed. H.R. Mackintosh and J.S. Stewart (New York: Harper and Row, 1963), §2.2. Henceforth CF.

not to be identified with belief, as some Enlightenment theorists tried to do, or with particular actions; nor does it arise exclusively out of the moral life, as it does for Kant. It occupies a mid-point, or indifference point, on a spectrum between those moments in which either knowing or doing is dominant.

The distinguishing mark of piety is a feeling, Schleiermacher writes, that is immediate in the sense that it is not mediated by self-reflection. Feeling, he says, has long been associated in common parlance with piety. He remarks that he calls it "self-consciousness" to ensure that feeling not be so broadly construed as to include unconscious states. He adds the qualifier "immediate" (*unmittelbar*) to distinguish it from a kind of self-consciousness that is not feeling at all, "as, e.g., when the name of self-consciousness is given to that consciousness of self which is more like an objective consciousness, being a representation of oneself, and thus mediated by self-contemplation."[7] He offers joy and sorrow as examples of genuine states of feeling, as contrasted with self-approval and self-reproach, which are not immediate in the sense used here. At one point, though, Schleiermacher seems to go further and to say that genuine feeling, properly understood, is not representation at all.[8]

For Schleiermacher, "immediate" means non-reflexive, not mediated by self-representation. That need not imply that such states are independent of thought. I suspect that he would agree that joy and sorrow are not to be equated with pleasure and pain. Joy is usually joy in something, as in my joy at seeing my friend after a long absence or in having solved a problem on which I have been working. Sorrow is sorrow over something or someone in some respect. In each case, the feeling assumes concepts and thoughts, often but not always including thoughts about oneself. Perhaps the difference between my joy at having solved a problem and my joy at the fact that it was I who solved the problem would capture the distinction Schleiermacher is drawing. Joy and sorrow, in this sense, need not be self-reflective but they assume concepts and beliefs. In this construal a feeling is an intentional state that is identified under a description that includes reference to an object and to conceptual content, as in my joy at seeing my friend or at having solved the problem.

As examples of feelings that are pious in themselves apart from any consequences that might proceed from them and prior to any self-

---

7 CF §3.2.
8 "Jenes eigentliche unvermittelte Selbstbewusstsein aber welches nicht Vorstellung ist sondern im eigentliche Sinne Gefühl, ist keinesweges immer nur begleitend . . . " (ibid). It is difficult to tell whether Schleiermacher means here that real feeling is without representation of self or without representation of any sort.

reflection, Schleiermacher mentions penitence, confidence, and joy in God.[9] It is difficult to see how these rather complex feelings could be pre-reflective. It is possible that he doesn't regard them as immediate in his sense of the word, though he has said that genuine feelings are immediate. In any case, they are not independent of thought.

Genuine feelings are not reflexive. This is not merely a phenomenological distinction for Schleiermacher, but an analytic one. Feeling belongs chiefly to the realm of receptivity. Manfred Frank characterizes intuitions in the *Reden* as immediate and individual representations of the world that are "maximally 'passive'" in comparison with concepts, which have a higher degree of spontaneity.[10] In describing piety as a modification of immediate self-consciousness, Schleiermacher wants to emphasize its receptive character. Genuine states of feeling or of immediate self-consciousness are pre-reflective and more receptive than are states that include self-reflection.

2. Intentionality

The common factor in piety, and its distinguishing mark for Schleiermacher, is the consciousness of absolute dependence, which is the same, he says, as being in relation to God. That consciousness seems to presuppose, and tacitly to ascribe to the subject, at least concepts of dependence and its correlative, freedom.[11] Even more clearly than joy and sorrow, this feeling or consciousness is identified under a particular description, one that assumes concepts and reference to an intentional object. In this case, as Schleiermacher makes clear, the object is not given in the feeling or consciousness. But the description under which the consciousness is identified is one with a direction, a causal arrow clarifying the direction of the dependence. Schleiermacher marks this grammatically with the word "whence" (*Woher*), which stands as a placeholder for the object of the dependence. How can a consciousness that assumes concepts and is grammatically structured be an immediate self-consciousness? As we have seen, "immediate," as Schleiermacher is using the term, means non-reflective and maximally recep-

---

9   CF §3.4.
10 Manfred Frank, "Metaphysical Foundations: A Look at Schleiermacher's *Dialectic*," in *The Cambridge Companion to Friedrich Schleiermacher*, ed. Jacqueline Mariña (Cambridge: Cambridge University Press, 2005), 28.
11 Schleiermacher holds that a feeling of absolute dependence requires for its possibility a feeling of freedom (CF §4.3), but it is not clear that he takes the concepts of freedom and dependence to be assumed by either of these.

tive. With this use of the term, even a feeling as conceptually and grammatically articulated as the consciousness of absolute dependence can be described as immediate.

The other, the co-determinant, that is implied in the consciousness of absolute dependence is to be construed as the whence of our active and receptive existence. This whence, Schleiermacher says, "is to be designated by the word 'God' and this is for us the truly original meaning of the word."[12] By "original" Schleiermacher does not mean temporally prior. He is making a normative claim, not an historical one. But what is the basis for its authority?

Andrew Dole argues that Schleiermacher's proposal that the word "God" shall mean this co-determinant of the consciousness of absolute dependence is stipulative.[13] Dole is right that Schleiermacher stipulates that this is what the term shall mean "for us," and that this restriction is an important critical tool that Schleiermacher uses throughout the book in his project to reform Christian doctrine. He is also right that the term as Schleiermacher stipulates it is purely formal before it is given content shaped by the specifically Christian pious self-consciousness. The identification of the term "God" with the object of the feeling of absolute dependence, an object that is not given in the feeling and that cannot be identified with the world of natural causes or any part of it, ensures that the term designates something other than that world.

Schleiermacher's stipulation that the content of the word "God" be restricted to its designation of the co-determinant in the feeling of absolute dependence is closely connected with his identifying description of that feeling. That feeling, which is the essence or distinguishing mark of piety, is distinct from all other feelings. "Our proposition," he writes, "is intended to oppose the view that this feeling of dependence is itself conditioned by some previous knowledge of God."[14] There may or may not be knowledge of God from some source other than the feeling of absolute dependence, but if there is it has nothing directly to do with piety and is therefore irrelevant for a system of Christian doctrine. This feeling is not influenced by any possible speculative knowledge of God. Claims to such conceptual knowledge arise out of almost total freedom, in contrast to the receptive character of the feeling of absolute dependence.

---

12   CF §4.4.
13   Andrew Dole, "Schleiermacher and Otto on Religion," *Religious Studies* 40 (2004): 401. Dole's article shows clearly the sharp differences between Schleiermacher's view of religion and that of Rudolf Otto, differences that I neglected to address in *Religious Experience*.
14   CF §4.4.

The common factor in different forms of piety, or the essence of piety, Schleiermacher says, the feeling of absolute dependence, comes from a source that is independent of knowledge or concepts of God that are not themselves derived from that feeling. Both the feeling and the term "God" that is used to designate it are expressions and products exclusively of the consciousness of absolute dependence. If, he writes, the term "God," like all terms, assumes an idea or representation (*Vorstellung*), then this idea is nothing more than the expression of and direct (*unmittelbarste*) reflection on the feeling of absolute dependence and is conditioned only by that feeling.[15]

Whether or not Schleiermacher's argument for the consciousness of absolute dependence is viewed as a transcendental one, the formal and apparently empty content of the terms "whence" and "God" are central to his description of that consciousness. Schleiermacher's stipulation of the way "God" is to be used sets it and its object apart. The object of the feeling of absolute dependence is not given in the feeling, but what is given is that the object is not the world or anything in it and is a source on which all of our activity and the entire causal nexus is dependent. It is specified in such a way that the object could not be the nexus of natural causes taken as a whole. In respect to that whole, as to any part of it, Schleiermacher says, we still have some slight modicum of freedom.

While the object is not given in the feeling of absolute dependence, the feeling, and the term "God" that is associated with it, are identified, in part, by reference to its cause. The co-determinant of the feeling, and the whence of the dependence, is something other than the totality of natural causes. Any further content of the idea of God must be developed out of this.[16] This idea is conditioned only by the feeling of absolute dependence and is independent of any knowledge apart from it. As Robert Adams points out, Schleiermacher employs the way of causality (*via causalitatis*) in the body of the work to explicate the divine attributes, and in this respect he stands in a long tradition of theologians.[17] Schleiermacher says that "all the divine attributes to be dealt with in *Glaubenslehre* must go back in some way to the divine causality, since they are only to elucidate the feeling of absolute dependence."[18] Both the feeling of absolute dependence and the idea of God are speci-

---

15 Ibid.
16 Ibid.
17 Robert Merrihew Adams, "Faith and Religious Knowledge," in Mariña, *Cambridge Companion to Schleiermacher*, 44. Schleiermacher mentions Albertus Magnus, and Adams adds Maimonides and Thomas Aquinas.
18 CF §50.3. Quoted in Adams, "Faith and Religious Knowledge," 43-44.

fied by reference to a causal source that is independent of the nexus of natural causes.

Schleiermacher writes of the idea of God that "The feeling of absolute dependence becomes a clear self-consciousness only as this idea (*Vorstellung*) comes simultaneously into being."[19] He says that the development of both assumes both animal consciousness and its eclipse by the sensible consciousness that arises with the development of language and concepts of relations to others. Here and in other works he emphasizes the social character of individuals and their development. The clarification of the pious self-consciousness and of the idea or representation of God are achieved through social and linguistic development in particular institutional and cultural contexts. But the distinguishing core of that self-consciousness and its representation are uninfluenced by and are in that sense independent of other feelings and ideas. They are apprehended and conceived in different ways by different individuals and communities, but it is still possible for philosophy of religion to distinguish, in principle, a modification of self-consciousness and a representation of it that are unshaped by social and cultural causes that are not themselves derivative from the consciousness of absolute dependence.

3. Revisions

Robert Adams has proposed an extension of the concept of intentionality and Kevin Hector a redescription of the idea of immediacy that are meant to clarify the relation between the intentionality of the feeling of absolute dependence and its immediacy in Schleiermacher's account.[20]

Adams begins with the assumption that Schleiermacher held that the religious consciousness is independent of concepts, in the sense of not being structured by concepts. He argues that this is consistent with at least an implicit intentionality. The essential element in the religious consciousness is a consciousness of oneself as absolutely dependent, or, as in relation with God. This seems to bear the marks of intentionality, Adams writes, but it is not clear that this consciousness has an intentional object because Schleiermacher states that the object is not itself given in the consciousness. Yet it would not be accurate to say of

---

19 CF §4.4.
20 Adams, "Faith and Religious Knowledge," 35-51; Kevin Hector, "Attunement and Explicitation: A Pragmatist Reading of Schleiermacher's 'Theology of Feeling,'" in this volume.

Schleiermacher's account that God is not an intentional object of the religious consciousness but only of our thoughts reflecting on it. Adams proposes a two-step distinction in Schleiermacher's account between the religious consciousness and his description of it, on one hand, and the inference that can be drawn from that description, on the other.

First, according to Adams, Schleiermacher's description of the distinguishing element in piety as a feeling of absolute dependence is an interpretation. Drawing a parallel between Schleiermacher's accounts of the feeling of absolute dependence in CF §4 and of Christian doctrine in CF §15, Adams describes Schleiermacher's account as an interpretation of a religious state of mind set forth in speech. It is an interpretation of the religious consciousness as a feeling of absolute dependence. The feeling is intentional in that it can only be specified in terms of such concepts as dependence and relative as compared to absolute dependence. Second, though Schleiermacher makes clear that the object itself is not given in the feeling, this interpretation of the religious consciousness prompts an inference to a whence or source of the dependence and this issues in a representation or concept of God. The intentional object is arrived at only by an inference from the feeling of absolute dependence, which is itself an interpretation of the religious mind.

Adams asks whether this implicit intentionality is consistent with what he takes to be Schleiermacher's account of the religious consciousness as independent of concepts. That depends, he says, on whether there can be and are states of consciousness that are not conceptually structured but are best understood by us by analogy with the intentionality of conceptual thought.[21] If there were such states, then Schleiermacher's account of the feeling of absolute dependence could be understood as a feeling that is best interpreted as of absolute dependence, leading to an inference to a whence, or God, as its intentional object. That would allow the religious consciousness to be nonconceptual, though its best interpretation, the most direct reflection on it, would require concepts. Only the religious feeling would be related directly or immediately to God, but not either the interpretation or the inference.

While the feeling of absolute dependence is not structured by concepts for Schleiermacher, Adams says, it is not causally independent of conceptual thought. As we have seen, Schleiermacher holds that the feeling comes to full self-consciousness only after the acquisition of language and the emergence of sensible self-consciousness out of animal consciousness. But Adams's distinction between the development

---

21 Adams, "Faith and Religious Knowledge," 38.

of language and thought as a causal condition or as a conceptual condition for the feeling of absolute dependence is not convincing. Language learning and the sensible self-consciousness require training in grammatical rules and in the practice of drawing inferences. The development of a consciousness of freedom, for instance, which is required for a feeling of dependence, is not a causal condition if that is to be distinguished from logical or conceptual conditions. We assume conceptual relations when we ascribe feelings to others. This is a logical or conceptual matter and not merely a causal one. Schleiermacher's account of the different stages is not only a causal account of the use of concepts but also a story of conceptual development.

While Adams proposes to reconcile immediacy and intentionality by revising the concept of intentionality, Hector suggests a different way of understanding immediacy. The observation, "That is red," is immediate in that it is usually direct, non-inferential, and does not require explicit reflection, but it assumes concepts of color and redness and training in the ability to use these and other concepts in accordance with the relevant rules. All experience presupposes the prior development of linguistic and inferential categories. It does not require subscribing to what Wilfrid Sellars calls "the myth of the given," the idea that some object of experience can be given independently of concepts and beliefs.[22]

Hector uses this rejection of the myth of the given to offer what he takes to be a pragmatist reading of Schleiermacher's concept of feeling. For Schleiermacher, feeling is an immediate self-consciousness, without self-reflection or representation. It is the mediating link between knowing and doing. Hector proposes that this idea of feeling be understood as a non-reflective attunement that is the result of participation in social practices and the internalization of custom.[23] Feeling is a non-discursive responsive disposition that is itself a product of discursive practice. Reliable dispositions to respond in certain ways under appropriate conditions are produced either by explicit training or by less explicit internalization of custom and practice. Understood in this way, feeling is immediate in the sense that it is pre-reflective, non-inferential, and could be described as non-conceptual, but as a product of discursive social practices it is not independent of concepts and beliefs. Feeling, in Schleiermacher's sense of the term, on this view, is not only a causal

---

22   Wilfrid Sellars, *Empiricism and the Philosophy of Mind* (Cambridge: Harvard University Press, 1997).

23   Hector uses the word "attunement" because it is a common English translation of Heidegger's concept of *Befindlichkeit*, which he reads as similar to his own construal of Schleiermacher's idea of feeling.

product of concepts and beliefs, but the result of having been trained in their proper use.

An issue that might arise on this view of immediacy is that with proper training almost anything could be made habitual, non-inferential, and thus immediate. Just as an experienced physician might diagnose a particular condition immediately and without inference, an individual might directly experience the presence of the Holy Spirit or of other spirits, depending on the cultural background and the dispositions cultivated by particular social practices. Hector addresses this issue by arguing that criteria can be developed that are internal to piety as a social practice but irreducible to it and thus provide norms by which it can be judged.

Hector offers a plausible interpretation of what it is for a feeling to be both immediate and dependent upon concepts and beliefs, but he doesn't account for Schleiermacher's insistence that the feeling of absolute dependence is unconditioned by any concept or knowledge that is not itself derivative from that feeling. To achieve this, Schleiermacher seems to require reference to a cause of the feeling that is distinct from the web of natural causes, including the cultivation of social practices.

4. Conclusion

Schleiermacher says that he uses the term "immediate" to exclude forms of self-consciousness that are self-reflective, include representations of self, and therefore are not real feelings at all. If this is all the term excludes I was wrong to say in *Religious Experience* that the portrayal of the feeling of absolute dependence as an intentional state, identified under a conceptual description, was inconsistent with his claim that the feeling is immediate. At times, though, he does seem to say that the feeling is independent of representation of any sort, and not only of representations of the self.

Schleiermacher makes clear that the object of the feeling of absolute dependence is not given in the feeling itself. But his description of that feeling includes an important constraint on how that object is to be identified. The co-determinant of the feeling, the whence that is the sole designate of the term "God," cannot be identified with the world as the total causal nexus or with any part of that world. Both the world and its parts are objects in relation to which we have at least a modicum of freedom and therefore they cannot be co-determinants in a consciousness of absolute dependence. This restriction is an important part of Schleiermacher's criteria for identifying the essence of piety.

Anschauung and Intuition, Again

(Or, "We Remain Bound to the Earth")

THEODORE VIAL

What does Friedrich Schleiermacher mean when he calls the essence of religion "intuition and feeling" and says that where there is religion there is "an astonishing intuition of the infinite"?[1] It is common in recent books in English on the field of religious studies to make passing remarks on Schleiermacher on the way to making proposals to improve the study of religion. Russell McCutcheon traces the "dominant stance" of scholars in the American Academy of Religion back to Schleiermacher. Schleiermacher, he writes, reconceives of religion "as a non-quantifiable individual experience, a deep feeling, or an immediate consciousness."[2] Such a move makes religion internal and ineffable and protects it from explanation. Eric Sharpe mentions Schleiermacher only briefly, writing that "the 'romantic revival' did supply the West with a sense of history, and with a feeling for the irrational in religion," and continuing that Herder and Hegel are responsible for the first (sense of history), Schleiermacher for the second (feeling for the irrational).[3] Wal-

---

1   I here cite from Richard Crouter's English translation: Friedrich Schleiermacher, *On Religion: Speeches to its Cultured Despisers* (Cambridge: Cambridge University Press, 1988), 22, 13. For all German sources in this paper I note the available English translation. I indicate translations that are my own. In all other cases I have checked the available translation against the German original, in this case, *Über die Religion: Reden an die Gebildeten unter ihren Verächtern*, in KGA I/2.
2   Russell McCutcheon, *Critics Not Caretakers* (Albany: State University of New York Press, 2001), 4.
3   Eric Sharpe, *Comparative Religion: A History* (New York: Charles Scribner's Sons, 1975), 20, 160, and 164. Discussing Otto, Sharpe writes: "Another term used by Otto to describe 'the faculty, of whatever sort it may be, of genuinely cognizing and recognizing the holy in its appearances' is 'divination'—normally used in the more specific sense of receiving communications from the supernatural world. This Otto specifically describes as a 'theological discovery,' and refers back to the classical Christian doctrine of the witness of the Holy Spirit . . . , the theology of Schleiermacher, and the doctrine of Ahnung as found in J. F. Fries." Sharpe's pairing of

ter Capps, in a section entitled, "Schleiermacher's Shift to the Aesthetic Mode," argues that Schleiermacher defines religion as a kind of feeling or quality, "something akin to a deep sensitivity. Feeling connotes a manner of inwardness, an interior self-consciousness, an awareness of the kind we speak of when we say that something 'moves' us deeply."[4]

One can easily trace a genealogy of this reading of Schleiermacher backwards from McCutcheon (2001), Capps (1995), and Sharpe (1975) to Wayne Proudfoot's *Religious Experience* (1985) and George Lindbeck's *The Nature of Doctrine* (1984), to Mircea Eliade's *The Sacred and the Profane* (1957), where Eliade claims to be extending the work of Rudolf Otto's *The Idea of the Holy* (German 1917). We come full circle with Otto's (in)famous dis-invitation: "whoever knows no such moments in his experience is requested to read no further."[5]

My thesis in this paper is a simple one, and a simply historical one: this is a bad reading of Schleiermacher.[6] Andrew Dole has provided a major service in his careful disentangling of Schleiermacher and Otto.[7] If, as Dole shows, Schleiermacher is not doing the same thing Otto is, then what is he doing? We ought to interpret Schleiermacher on reli-

---

Schleiermacher's theology and Fries's *Ahnung* in his summary of Otto is something we will have to return to below. Sharpe also traces modern hermeneutics back to Schleiermacher (225), another point to which we will return. Sharpe's analysis of hermeneutics is far less hostile than McCutcheon's.

4   Walter Capps, *Religious Studies: The Making of a Discipline* (Minneapolis: Fortress Press, 1995), 13. Schleiermacher is not mentioned at all in Daniel Pals' *Seven Theories of Religion* (New York: Oxford University Press, 1996). The other textbook frequently assigned to students of religion in the United States is Ivan Strenski's *Thinking About Religion: An Historical Introduction to Theories of Religion* (Malden, MA: Blackwell Publishing, 2006). Strenski focuses on Schleiermacher's hermeneutics, and correctly attributes to Wilhelm Dilthey the standard interpretation of Schleiermacher as emphasizing empathy (44-46).

5   Rudolf Otto, *The Idea of the Holy* (Oxford: Oxford University Press, 1958), 8. There is a real irony to this reading of Schleiermacher. As Francis Schüssler Fiorenza has argued, much of the theological critique of Schleiermacher has been precisely that religion as defined by Schleiermacher "fail[s] to take into account the primacy of divine revelation, divine activity, and the specificity of Christian identity." See "Religion: A Contested Site in Theology and the Study of Religion," *Harvard Theological Review* 93, no. 1 (2000): 13.

6   Rudolf Otto, a careful reader of Schleiermacher, is quite clear in pointing out the profound differences between himself and Schleiermacher, and therefore his preference for Jacob Friedrich Fries. The very problems Otto sees in Schleiermacher (especially that Schleiermacher's feeling of absolute dependence refers to no supernatural object outside the self) run against the view of Schleiermacher held by present day critics. See Otto, *Idea of the Holy*, 10.

7   Andrew Dole, "Schleiermacher and Otto on Religion," *Religious Studies* 40 (2004): 389-413.

gion not looking back through Eliade and Otto, but in the context described by Charles Taylor of the post-Kant generation whose central problem was subjectivity and its relationship to the world. Taylor argues that this entire generation was driven by the need to overcome the oppositions they inherited from the Enlightenment in general and from Kant in particular. Herder, Fichte, Schiller, and Hegel all strove to "surmount . . . the opposition between thought, reason, morality, on one side, and sensibility on the other; the opposition between the fullest self-conscious freedom, on one side, and life in the community, on the other; the opposition between self-consciousness and communion with nature; and beyond this the separation of finite subjectivity from the infinite life that flowed through nature, the barrier between the Kantian subject and the Spinozist substance. . . ."[8] If Taylor has accurately described the context in which Schleiermacher is working, then the best interpretation of Schleiermacher will place his use of technical vocabulary on the field of discourse influenced by Kant. This is precisely how I propose to interpret Schleiermacher's use of "intuition" (*Anschauung*), among other terms.

1. What They're Saying About Schleiermacher

The two most influential interpreters of Schleiermacher on the American scene, on whom non-Schleiermacher specialists rely, have been the theologian George Lindbeck and the philosopher of religion Wayne Proudfoot.[9] Most English language textbooks in religious studies cite

---

8   Charles Taylor, *Sources of the Self: The Making of Modern Identity* (Cambridge: Harvard University Press, 1989), 368-90; and Taylor, *Hegel* (Cambridge: Harvard University Press, 1977), 3-50. The quote is from *Hegel*, 36. It must be noted that Taylor miscategorizes Schleiermacher. The way that Taylor formulates the category, Schleiermacher belongs with Taylor's three great "expressivists," Hegel, Herder, and Humboldt. It is certainly not accurate to claim, as Taylor does, that like other "Romantics" (Friedrich Schlegel, Novalis), Schleiermacher begins as a pantheist and ends as an orthodox theist (*Hegel*, 46).
9   I should note that there is much that I agree with in both of these critics. I am in sympathy with Proudfoot's criticism of the way much of English language work in the history of religions has relied on unhelpful ideas about religious experience. His analysis of mysticism, and his distinction between explanatory and descriptive reductionism, have stood the test of time. I am also in sympathy with Lindbeck's arguments about the role our cultural contexts play in shaping the very ideas and experiences that are possible for us. But in neither case is the Schleiermacher they use as their foil an accurate historical reconstruction. I should also note that they did not originate this cluster of mis-readings, but inherited it from Schleiermacher's late nineteenth- and early twentieth-century reception history in Germany.

one or both of these sources when discussing Schleiermacher. From the theological side, George Lindbeck names Schleiermacher as the originator of what he calls the "experiential-expressivist" theory of doctrine, which, he argues, "interprets doctrines as noninformative and nondiscursive symbols of inner feelings, attitudes, or existential orientations."[10] Lindbeck also offers a genealogy that begins with Schleiermacher, and includes Otto and Eliade.[11] Despite differences in this experiential-expressivist camp, Lindbeck argues that they all "locate ultimately significant contact with whatever is finally important to religion in the prereflective experiential depths of the self and regard the public or outer features of religion as expressive and evocative objectifications (i.e., nondiscursive symbols) of internal experience."[12] One reason for this move, according to Lindbeck, is that it opens up the possibility that a Buddhist and a Christian, for example, "might have basically the same faith, although expressed very differently."[13] For such a thing to be possible, of course, the inner experience would have to be free of external influence, such as the shaping by language and culture.[14]

Wayne Proudfoot concurs with Lindbeck on many points: Schleiermacher inaugurates a tradition of seeing "religious belief and practice as expressive of an autonomous moment of human experience."[15] This tradition in Proudfoot includes Eliade and Otto, as well as William James. Proudfoot's reading is far more extensive and penetrating than Lindbeck's, but it boils down to the same fundamental claim:

(1) the distinctive moment in the religious consciousness is radically independent of concepts and beliefs;

---

10 George A. Lindbeck, *The Nature of Doctrine: Religion and Theology in a Postliberal Age* (Louisville: Westminster John Knox Press, 1984), 16. Other exemplars of the experiential-expressivist theory are Rudolf Otto and Mircea Eliade (21), and Paul Tillich and Bernard Lonergan (31).

11 Lindbeck focuses primarily on Lonergan.

12 Lindbeck, *Nature of Doctrine*, 21.

13 Ibid., 17.

14 The classic refutation of Lindbeck's reading of Schleiermacher comes in B. A. Gerrish's review, "The Nature of Doctrine," *Journal of Religion* 68, no. 1 (1988): 87–92. The discussion is complex, but Gerrish argues that "in Schleiermacher's view, doctrines do not express a prelinguistic experience but an experience that has already been constituted by the language of the community" (90) and concludes that "[Lindbeck] should count himself among Schleiermacher's friends" (92).

15 Wayne Proudfoot, *Religious Experience* (Berkeley: University of California Press, 1985).

(2) that moment is best described as a sense of the infinite or a consciousness of absolute dependence; and

(3) religious language and doctrines are properly viewed, not as assertions or judgments, but as extensions of the natural and spontaneous expressions of this sense or consciousness.[16]

Proudfoot also agrees with Lindbeck (in more specific reference to the history-of-religions tradition of religious studies in the United States rather than the ecumenical dialogue tradition that is Lindbeck's main concern) that "[o]ur knowledge of our own affective states enables us to understand the linguistic expressions of the emotions of others."[17]

2. Anschauung and Intuition, Again

My argument rests on the fundamental claim that Schleiermacher has been mis-read on the topic of intuition. A full defense of my argument would require a discussion of Schleiermacher's hermeneutics.[18] For Schleiermacher humans are to their core linguistic beings. For him, thought is the inside of language, language the outside of thought.[19] A full defense would also require an account of the changes in language in Schleiermacher's writing on religion over time (the relative downplaying of the word "intuition" and emphasis of the word "feeling," as well as the shift in *The Christian Faith* to the language of "absolute dependence").[20] In this paper I will not trace these shifts in language. I

---

16   Ibid., 31.
17   Ibid., 24.
18   Here the argument rests on showing that, just as Schleiermacher is not Otto on religion, neither is he Dilthey on interpretation. In the same way that scholars have read into the word "intuition" things unintended by Schleiermacher, so they have read into the "psychological" part of interpretation, and especially the "divinatory" moment, things other than what Schleiermacher is careful to state on the page.
19   "Speech is admittedly also mediation of thought for the individual. Thought is prepared by inner discourse, and to this extent discourse is only the thought itself which has come into existence." Friedrich Schleiermacher, *Hermeneutik und Kritik*, ed. Manfred Frank (Frankfurt: Suhrkamp, 1977), 76. I quote from the English translation: *Hermeneutics and Criticism and Other Writings*, ed. and trans. Andrew Bowie (Cambridge: Cambridge University Press, 1998), 7. The point that, for Schleiermacher, humans are linguistic beings to their very core was nicely reiterated by Richard Crouter in his opening address at this conference, "A Precarious Journey: The Art of Translating Schleiermacher."
20   American scholars have fallen into two camps, arguing either that Schleiermacher downplays "intuition" to distinguish his position from the positions of Schelling and Fichte, which gain prominence after the first edition of the Speeches—see Richard B.

will instead focus on Schleiermacher's language in the first edition of the *Speeches,* and then conclude with some brief remarks on the Introduction to *The Christian Faith.* I will agree with Lindbeck and Proudfoot that religion as intuition and feeling and religion as absolute dependence mean roughly the same thing for Schleiermacher, though I will not agree on what that is.

In reading Schleiermacher in his more immediate post-Kantian context rather than through the eyes of Otto, it is important to recall Kant's definition of *Anschauung,* most often translated into English as "intuition." "An intuition is a representation of the sort which would depend immediately on the presence of an object."[21] This is almost the precise opposite of the normal English connotation of inexplicable, non-rational knowledge, or a hunch. It is easy for English speakers to allow "intuition" to take on connotations much closer to the German *Ahnung,* which Kant (and Schleiermacher) clearly do not mean. For Kant, of course, our experience is shaped by the a priori forms of intuition (space and time) and therefore we have no direct access to things-in-themselves; we always experience things as they appear to us. The complaints against Schleiermacher boil down to the accusation that he is attempting to pierce this Kantian veil, to give us direct access to the infinite in the finite prior to any shaping by the structure of our minds or by language, and thus Schleiermacher attempts to protect religion from the Kantian critique. My claim is not that Schleiermacher means exactly the same thing as Kant (he does not). Rather, my claim is that one can better understand what Schleiermacher means if one begins with Kant. One must attend carefully to what Schleiermacher says he means by the words "intuition" and "infinite."

Schleiermacher himself takes care to signal the Kantian context in which he is working (sometimes against Kant, but in this context nonetheless). In the first *Speech* he writes: "You are well disposed to these our brothers and might like it if they were also addressed on other higher subjects, on morality and law and freedom, and so at least for individual moments their individual striving would be raised to better

---

Brandt, *The Philosophy of Schleiermacher* (New York: Harper and Brothers, 1941), 95-144; and Van A. Harvey, "On the New Edition of Schleiermacher's Addresses On Religion," *Journal of the American Academy of Religion* 39, no. 4 (December 1971): 488-512 — or that "feeling" is a more comprehensive term that includes within it the work done by the word "intuition," and so that once this case has been made by Schleiermacher he need not make much use of the word "intuition" — see Terrence N. Tice, "Schleiermacher's Conception of Religion: 1799 to 1831," *Archivio di Filosofia* 52, nos. 1-3 (1984): 333-56.

21 Immanuel Kant, *Prolegomena to Any Future Metaphysics,* ed. and trans. Gary Hatfield (Cambridge: Cambridge University Press, 1997), 33.

things and an impression of the dignity of humanity awakened in them."[22] The sentence drips with self-conscious Kantian language.

Like Kant, Schleiermacher claims that the rudiment of religion will come from human capacities: "I wish to show you from what capacity of humanity religion proceeds. . . ."[23] "If one considers religion from its center according to its inner essence, it is a product of human nature, rooted in one of its necessary modes of actions or drives. . . ."[24] Unlike Kant, religion will not for Schleiermacher be a by-product of our moral lives; rather, it is a necessary presupposition of our cognition, in which for Schleiermacher (as for Kant) intuition plays a key role.

This intuition "is and always remains something individual, set apart, the immediate perception, nothing more."[25] Schleiermacher argues that intuition is the product of an action on us by something external to us. His examples are the action of light on us, and the pressure and weight on the tips of our fingers when we touch things. Intuition is the mechanical and chemical impact of our experience on us, of our interaction at our physical limits with the world. And Schleiermacher is very clear that intuition is not a matter of tearing aside the veil and peering into things-in-themselves: "and what you thus intuit and perceive is not the nature of things, but their action upon you. What you know or believe about the nature of things lies far beyond the realm of intuition."[26] In fact, such "knowledge" or "belief" about "the nature of things" lies in the realm of "empty mythology."

---

22 ". . . von Sittlichkeit und Recht und Freiheit geredet, und so auf einzelne Momente wenigstens ihr inneres Streben dem besseren entgegengehoben, und ein Eindruck von der Würde der Menscheit in ihrem geweckt werden" (Schleiermacher, *Über die Religion*, 191; *On Religion*, 10). Crouter (Ibid., 26 n. 11) also cites the phrase "sinnliche Anschauung" and Schleiermacher's reference to the "bewunderten und gefeierten Sternenhimmel [celebrated starry sky]" in the second speech (*Über die Religion*, 215) as obvious Kantian references.

23 *Über die Religion*, 197; *On Religion*, 10-11.

24 ". . . so ist es ein Produkt der menschlichen Natur, gegründet in einer von ihren nothwendigen Handlungsweisen oder Trieben . . ." (*Über die Religion*, 198; *On Religion*, 12).

25 "Anschauung ist und bleibt immer etwas einzelnes, abgesondertes, die unmittelbare Wahrnehmung, weiter nichts" (*Über die Religion*, 215; *On Religion*, 26). Note the similarities to Kant's definition, quoted above: "An intuition is a representation of the sort which would depend immediately on the presence of an object."

26 ". . . und was Ihr also anschaut und wahrnehmt, ist nicht die Natur der Dinge, sondern ihr Handeln auf Euch. Was Ihr über jene wißt oder glaubt, liegt weit jenseits des Gebietes der Anschauung" (*Über die Religion*, 214; *On Religion*, 25). The key paragraph *in toto*: "I entreat you to become familiar with this concept: intuition of the universe. It is the hinge of my whole speech; it is the highest and most universal formula of religion on the basis of which you should be able to find every place in religion,

One may think of intuition as the objective side of experience, the action of the world on us. Feeling, for Schleiermacher, is not emotion or an aesthetic category. Feeling is the subjective side, the change in us that occurs because of contact. "[E]very intuition is, by its very nature, connected with a feeling. Your senses mediate the connection between the object and yourselves; the same influence of the object, which reveals its existence to you, must stimulate them in various ways and produce a change in your inner consciousness."[27]

Without undertaking a thorough comparison of Kant's and Schleiermacher's philosophy of language, it is nevertheless important to point out that Schleiermacher indicates that none of this is pre-linguistic. I take this to be the force of the important clause at the end of his statement: "All intuition proceeds from an influence of the intuited on the one who intuits, from an original and independent action of the former, which is then grasped, apprehended, and conceived by the latter *according to one's own nature*."[28] Pace Kant, we will not experience the world the same way because our natures are not completely universal. This is a point Schleiermacher shares with Herder.[29]

Some support for my interpretation, in addition to Schleiermacher's *Hermeneutics*, comes from the notes he prepared for the lectures on *Dialectic* most proximate to the first edition of the *Speeches*. In this admittedly opaque text, Schleiermacher posits the influence of "national reason" in his discussion of induction. "Above all the co-existing difference is not error, rather relative knowing. National reason relates to human reason as human reason to general reason. Each has something that it presents itself, everything else is presented in relation to the way humans in general relate to the earth."[30]

---

from which you may determine its essence and its limits. All intuition proceeds from an influence of the intuited on the one who intuits, from an original and independent action of the former, which is then grasped, apprehended, and conceived by the latter according to one's own nature."

27 *Über die Religion*, 218; *On Religion*, 29.
28 *Über die Religion*, 213-14; *On Religion*, 24-25 (emphasis added).
29 Eric Sharpe ought more properly to group Schleiermacher with Herder as supplying a sense of history. See my opening remarks on Sharpe above.
30 "Zuerst die coexist*irende* Differenz ist nicht Irrthum sondern [relativirtes] Wissen. Die NationalVernunft verhält sich zur menschli*chen*, wie die menschli*che* zur allgemeinen. Jede hat etwas was sie an sich darstellt, alles andre aber in Bezug hierauf, wie der *Mensch* überhaupt alles in Bezug auf die Erde[.]" Schleiermacher, "Aufzeichnung zum Kolleg 1811," KGA II/10.1, 58. The translation is mine, in consultation with the English by Terrence N. Tice: *Dialectic or, the Art of Doing Philosophy: A Study Edition of the 1811 Notes* (Atlanta: Scholars Press, 1996), 57.

What we can know will be shaped by our idea of the world. "So the idea of the world determines also the boundary of our knowing. We are bound to the earth. All operations of thinking as well as the forming of our concepts must be grounded therein."[31] This is precisely why we will not have the same religious ideas. "Our knowledge of God is first completed with our worldview. As soon as a trace of the latter is present the groundwork of the former makes an appearance."[32] Worldview is informed by language and culture. The kinds of religious ideas it is possible for us to have are therefore not universal, but at least in part cultural. Thus Lindbeck is not correct that for Schleiermacher one can assume that there is a pre-linguistic experience that a Buddhist and a Christian (for example) would have in common. To determine the similarities and difference between their "faiths," the only recourse the Buddhist and the Christian have is a lengthy dialogue, which would unfold with all the opportunities and challenges Schleiermacher so carefully sets out in his hermeneutics.

If intuition is a matter of normal experience rather than "weird knowledge" (so far with Kant), and if intuition is shaped by our culture and language (a departure from Kant), what does it mean to say that the essence of religion is an intuition of the infinite? Here again one must attend carefully to Schleiermacher's words, lest one read back into him an Ottonian *mysterium tremendum*. In the second Speech Schleiermacher writes, "Everything finite exists only through the determination of its limits, which must, as it were, 'be cut out of' the infinite."[33] By this I take Schleiermacher to be saying that when we experience any object, we also experience the way that object is what it is by virtue of the fact that it is not any other object in the universe, and by virtue of the fact that the object has been shaped more or less by every other object in the universe. By infinite, then, he means something like the natural causal nexus. This is why, far from an attempt to protect religion from critical science, Schleiermacher believes that science can be a boon to religion. For science, in showing us the law-like connections between things, makes our experience of the infinite keener. "Certainly a greater yield is vouchsafed to us who have been permitted by a

---

31 "So bestimmt die Idee der Welt auch die Grenze unseres Wissens. Wir sind an die Erde gebunden. Alle Operationen des Denkens auch das ganze System unserer Begriffsbildung muss darin gegründet sein" (Schleiermacher, "Kolleg 1811," 48; *Dialectic*, 43).

32 "Unser Wissen um Gott ist also erst vollendet mit der Weltanschauung. Sobald von dieser eine Spur ist finden sich auch die Grundzüge von jener ein" (Schleiermacher, "Kolleg 1811," 38; *Dialectic*, 31).

33 *Über die Religion*, 213; *On Religion*, 24.

richer age to penetrate deeper into nature's interior. Its chemical powers, the eternal laws according to which bodies themselves are formed and destroyed, these are the phenomena in which we intuit the universe most clearly and in a most holy manner."[34] If one wants to draw parallels to followers of Schleiermacher, one would better look to a definition of the infinite like Feuerbach's at the beginning of the *Essence of Christianity* than to Otto or Eliade.[35]

I want finally to offer some brief evidence that Schleiermacher's basic view of religion remains largely the same in the second edition of the *Christian Faith*, though the language is not identical. In §3 he defines piety as "a determination [*Bestimmtheit*] of feeling, or of immediate self-consciousness."[36] Self-consciousness refers both to the feeling of our action on the world, and to the feeling of the world's action on us. Here Schleiermacher uses "feeling" (*Gefühl*) for our consciousness of our action on the world (*das Gegenständliche*) and "intuition" (*Anschauung*) for our consciousness of the world's action on us (*das In-sich-Zurückgehende*).[37] Our self-consciousness, our world, is made up entire-

---

34 *Über die Religion*, 227; *On Religion*, 36.
35 Feuerbach perhaps goes further than Schleiermacher in his definition of infinity when he writes, "The leaf on which the caterpillar lives is for it a world, an infinite space." Ludwig Feuerbach, *The Essence of Christianity*, trans. George Eliot (Buffalo, NY: Prometheus Books, 1989), 8. The point is that, by "infinite," Schleiermacher does not mean something beyond possible human experience. Rather, he means the limits and/or totality of what we can experience.
36 Friedrich Schleiermacher, *Der christliche Glaube nach den Grundsätzen der evangelischen Kirche im Zusammenhange dargestellt*, ed. Martin Redeker (Berlin: Walter de Gruyter, 1999), 14 (§3). I also provide the page number to the English translation, *The Christian Faith*, ed. H. R. Mackintosh and J. S. Stewart (Edinburgh: T. & T. Clark, 1986), though I do not rely on this translation.
37 Schleiermacher, *Der christliche Glaube*, 31 (§5.1); *Christian Faith*, 18. Note that the English here translates *Anschauung* with "perception." The English translation states further: ". . . while in our wide-awake hours feeling and perception [*Anschauung*] are clearly distinct from each other, and thus make up the whole wealth of man's sensible life, in the widest sense of the term. In that term we include (speaking simply of consciousness, and leaving out action proper), on the one hand, the gradual accumulation of perceptions [*Wahrnehmungen*] which constitute the whole field of experience in the widest sense of the word, and, on the other hand, all determinations of self-consciousness which develop from our relations to nature and man . . ." (Ibid., 19). Note that "perception" is used for both *Anschauung* and *Wahrnehmung*. Thus in the English it is difficult to grasp what Schleiermacher means by self-consciousness, and to trace the relationship of the way he uses "feeling" (subjective side of experience) and "intuition" (objective side of experience) in the *Speeches* to the way he uses "feeling" (awareness of our activity) and "intuition" (awareness of our passivity) in the *Christian Faith*. Despite the subtle shift in usage, the process of normal human experience is largely the same in both.

ly of this back and forth of activity and receptivity, along with the awareness that our activity itself depends on a world not of our making ("the feeling of absolute dependence"). This I take to be, in its essential elements, largely the same account of nature as a mutually determining causal nexus that we found in Schleiermacher's definition of the infinite in the *Speeches*.

But what should we make of the modifier "immediate" (*unmittelbaren*) in the phrase "immediate self-consciousness"? It is this modifier to a large extent that leads to interpretations in the English secondary literature that Schleiermacher intends a pre-linguistic, non-conceptual, and mystical point of contact with the divine. Proudfoot writes that the sense of the infinite or the feeling of absolute dependence "seems unmediated by linguistic representation."[38] Lindbeck (discussing Lonergan) does not use the word "immediate," but writes of the experience at issue that it "seems to be prior to all conceptualizations or cognition."[39] "Immediate" is often used in philosophical discourse to mean something like "pre-linguistic" or "pre-conceptual." In these senses it would appear that Schleiermacher's talk of immediate self-consciousness would mean something like direct access to the thing-in-itself in the experience of introspection that he commends to his readers in the second speech. This would be precisely a piercing of the Kantian veil to get to God, which is the heart of the accusations leveled at him by Proudfoot and Lindbeck.

But Schleiermacher is quite careful to define precisely the sense in which he uses the term "immediate" here. "Once more, the modifier 'immediate' is attached to the expression 'self-consciousness' so that no one thinks of such a self-consciousness that is not a feeling, as when one means self-consciousness in the sense of consciousness of oneself which is more like an objective consciousness, a representation of oneself and as such mediated by observation of oneself."[40] In other words, Schleiermacher intends with "immediate self-consciousness" to denote what he denoted by "intuition" in the *Speeches*, in distinction to another sense of self-consciousness in which we become aware of ourselves as

---

38   Proudfoot, *Religious Experience*, xiv.
39   Lindbeck, *Nature of Doctrine*, 32.
40   Schleiermacher, *Der christliche Glaube*, 16 (§3.2); *Christian Faith*, 6. "Wiederum ist dem Ausdruck Selbstbewusstsein die Bestimmung unmittelbar hinzugefügt, damit niemand an ein solches Selbstbewusstsein denke, welches kein Gefühl ist, wenn man nämlich Selbstbewusstsein das Bewusstsein von sich selbst nennt, welches mehr einem gegenständlichen Bewusstsein gleicht, und eine Vorstellung von sich selbst und als solche durch die Betrachtung seiner selbst vermittelt ist."

though we are observing ourselves (Schleiermacher's examples of this latter sense are self-approval and self-reproach).[41]

The account of religion in *The Christian Faith* remains largely in continuity with the account in the first edition of the *Speeches*. In each experience, we "intuit" or are conscious of things in the world, and have available to us consciousness of the fact that each thing we experience is determined by the totality of the natural causal nexus (the infinite). We may not agree with Schleiermacher's account of human experience, but we ought not continue to misread him as saying that religion is some strange flight from normal experience, and as such is deeply internal and unavailable for critical investigation. In the early and late Schleiermacher we remain "bound to the earth."

---

[41] In a note (*Der christliche Glaube*, 17; *Christian Faith*, 7), Schleiermacher states that he means by "determination of feeling or immediate self-consciousness" precisely what Henrich Steffens means by "feeling" in *Von der falschen Theologie und dem wahren Glauben: Eine Stimme aus der Gemeinde* (Breslau: Josef Max, 1823), 99-100. It is worth citing the relevant Steffans passage in full: "Was wir hier Gefühl nennen, ist die unmittelbare Gegenwart des ganzen, ungetheilten, sowohl sinnlichen als auch geistigen Daseins, der Einheit der Person und ihrer sinnlichen und geistigen Welt. Es verhält sich zum höhern Erkennen, das es begreifen möchte, wie die sinnliche Empfindung [sensation, sense perception] zum Verstande."

Religion and the Religions

The Fifth Speech in Dialogue with Contemporary Conceptions of a "Theology of Religions"[1]

NOTGER SLENCZKA

A public dialogue usually involves two parties whose positions are to be presented to an audience. In the present case, the two interlocutors are the "pluralistic theology of religion," on the one hand, and Schleiermacher's view of religions as presented in the fifth speech of his *On Religion: Speeches to its Cultured Despisers*, on the other. Because this is a dialogue between centuries as well as individuals, a moderator is needed. In taking on this role at a conference dedicated to the study of Schleiermacher, I will outline the position of recent pluralistic theologies of religion only briefly before attending in a more detailed manner to Schleiermacher's fifth speech; the constraints of time (and space) do not permit the presentation of a complete picture of each position. Thus, I intend first to concentrate on one problem that arises in the pluralistic theology of religion; then, in the second section, I will endeavor to show how Schleiermacher deals with this problem in his fifth speech. In the final and shortest section, I will summarize the previous sections by way of a short comparison and present three theses for discussion.

1. The Conception of Religions in the Pluralistic "Theology of Religions"

a. The Program of a "Theology of Religion"

The term "pluralistic theology of religion" encompasses positions represented, for example, by John Hick, the late Wilfred Cantwell

---

[1] I am grateful to Jacob Corzine, M.Div., who edited and corrected the English text.

Smith, and Raimon Panikkar;[2] in the German speaking realm, by Gustav Mensching and—from the current generation—Reinhold Bernhardt and the former Catholic theologian, Perry Schmidt-Leukel.[3] All of these theologians and philosophers are opposed to the mutually exclusive truth claims made by specific religious traditions and are united in their aim to find a non-exclusivist understanding of religion. In the following remarks, I will focus on one of them, John Hick, along with his student, Perry Schmidt-Leukel.[4]

The context of John Hick's argument is an apologetic one.[5] He points out that all religions are faced with the challenge of modern atheism; all of them are involved in a debate with a "naturalistic" alternative that interprets the religious claim of living in the presence of a transcendent reality as a projection or delusion. One of the arguments this naturalistic alternative brings forward is the diversity and apparently irreconcilable conflict between and within the different religions with regard to their construal of the divine. According to the naturalists, the very fact that the religions offer up a variety of conceptions of the transcendent indicates that their conceptions of God are lacking in "reality-relatedness."[6]

Hick, however, tries to convert this argument against the reality-relatedness of religious concepts into an argument in favor of the reality of something like "God." He suggests that the indisputable differences in conceptualizing the transcendent reality across a variety of religious doctrines and conceptions of God are responses to the one transcendent reality, in whose presence all religions claim to live. This one transcendent reality is symbolized in mediums that are culture-

---

2   John Hick, *An Interpretation of Religion: Human responses to the Transcendent* (London: Macmillan, 1989); Wilfred Cantwell Smith, *Faith and Belief* (Princeton: Princeton University Press, 1979); John Hick and Paul Knitter, eds., *The Myth of Christian Uniqueness: Towards a Pluralistic Theology of Religions* (Maryknoll, N.Y.: Orbis Books, 1987); Raimon Pannikkar, *The Intrareligious Dialogue* (Mahwah, N.J.: Paulist Press, 1999).

3   Gustav Mensching, *Toleranz und Wahrheit in der Religion* (Heidelberg: Quelle & Meyer, 1955); Reinhold Bernhardt, *Der Absolutheitsanspruch des Christentums: Von der Aufklärung bis zur pluralistischen Religionstheologie* (Neukirchen: Neukirchener Verlag, 1991); Perry Schmidt-Leukel, *Theologie der Religionen: Probleme, Optionen, Argumente* (Neuried: Ars una, 1997).

4   As regards Perry Schmidt-Leukel, I will concentrate on his most recent book, *Gott ohne Grenzen: Eine christliche und pluralistische Theologie der Religionen* (Gütersloh: Gütersloher Verlagshaus, 2005).

5   For the following, see Hick, *An Interpretation of Religion*, 7-9, 111-25, 210-30.

6   Ibid., 7-9, 12-15.

dependent and therefore distinct from each other. Such mediums include persons, ministries, rites, and ways of life.[7]

> A contemporary apologetic for belief in the transcendent, then, must start from the new situation revealed by our modern awareness of religious plurality and conceptual relativity. It must see religious thought and experience as a global continuum containing an immense variety of forms in a history moving from archaic beginnings to the present still evolving state of the great world traditions. It must recognise . . . the full . . . presence of culture-relative projection and symbolisation within this long history. *And it must show reason to believe that this vast and multifarious field of human faith is nevertheless not wholly projection and illusion . . . but constitutes our variously transparent and opaque interface with a mysterious transcendent reality.*[8]

Thus it is evident that the pluralistic theology of religion, as presented by Hick, has an apologetic background and intent. This is also the reason why at the core of his position there lies the question of whether the concept of God refers to a delusion or whether it signifies a reality that exists.

b. The Soteriological Experience and its Different Symbolizations

According to Hick, a religion is not merely a set of insights referring to a transcendent reality. Following Karl Jaspers and Robert Bellah, he distinguishes "archaic" from "postaxial" religions.[9] For the purpose of this paper, I will focus on his characterization of the latter. All postaxial religions are essentially focused on a soteriological insight: human beings are regarded as being in need of redemption. At the core of these religions lies the concept of a "human transformation" from "self-centredness" to "Reality-centredness." To live in the presence of God means to be centered in reality instead of in oneself:

> The great post-axial traditions . . . exhibit in their different ways a soteriological structure which identifies the misery, unreality, triviality and perversity of ordinary human life, affirms an ultimate unity of reality and value in which or in relation to which a limitlessly better quality of existence is possible, and shows the way to realise that radically better possibility. . . . The generic concept of salvation/liberation, which takes a different specific form in each of the great traditions, is that of the transformation of human existence from self-centredness to Reality-centredness.[10]

---

7   Ibid., 233-51.
8   Ibid., 9 (emphasis mine).
9   Ibid., 21-35.
10 Ibid., 36, cf. 299-303.

At the core of the postaxial religions lies a soteriological experience, a transformation of the structure of human existence. All dogmatic and ethical conventions are nothing more than means of eliciting and symbolizing this experience. The existing positive religions are "human responses" to the experience of a transcendent reality.

The plurality of existing religions is the result of the fact that this transformation and its framework are mediated by different experiences and therefore symbolized differently in different cultural contexts. According to Hick, the followers of the different religious traditions should distinguish their own symbolization of an ultimate reality upon which life is to be focused from this reality itself. In order to distinguish the ultimate reality, which he calls "the Real," from the variety of culturally conditioned concepts of God employed by the particular traditions, Hick turns to Kant's distinction between noumenon and phenomenon (that is, between the *Ding an sich* and its appearance).[11] The Real, then, is something beyond personal or impersonal concepts of God in the particular religious traditions. The religious traditions become means of encountering the transforming influence of this "reality beyond reality," and thereby means of being in the presence of the ultimate. But no religion should confuse its set of concepts, rites, and visualizations of the ultimate with the ultimate itself.[12]

This distinction between the ultimate and its symbolization in the different religions, together with the distinction between religious concepts and the soteriological effects of religions, makes it possible for Hick to treat all religions as individuals of a common species, religion, the function of which is to orient the life of believers toward an ultimate reality, albeit under different names. As the title of one of his first books puts it: "God has many names." Hick writes:

> It is in relation to different ways of being human, developed within the civilisations and cultures of the earth, that the Real, apprehended through the concept of God, is experienced specifically as the God of Israel, or as the Holy Trinity, or as Shiva, or as Allah, or as Vishnu . . . And it is in relation to yet other forms of life that the Real, apprehended through the concept of the Absolute, is experienced as Brahman, or as Nirvana, or as Being, or as Sunyata . . .[13]

---

11   Ibid., 241-51.
12   Ibid., 246-77.
13   Ibid., 245 (ellipses are Hick's).

c. A Fellow Traveler: Wilfred Cantwell Smith

This is, of course, a very abridged version of the basic argument of one of the most influential representatives of a pluralistic theology of religion. Hick's distinction between the Real and the specific personal or impersonal concepts of an ultimate entity is comparable to the distinction Smith makes between belief as "doctrinal opinion" or "being convinced that . . ." and faith in the sense of "trust."[14] Smith, too, argues that religion is essentially faith, by which he means a pre-theoretical "human orientation to transcendence" that is independent of particular beliefs in the sense of "being convinced that . . ." Such an orientation does not presuppose particular convictions, but it is, according to Smith, a transcendental anthropological category, a "capacity of faith" that finds its concrete form and expression in different religious beliefs. Because religions tend to make the affirmation of particular theoretical convictions or opinions a condition of faith as trust, doctrinal beliefs are a continuous danger to the existential meaning of religion as an act of faith or way of trusting in an ultimate reality.[15]

I think it is obvious that recent "pluralistic theologies" do not achieve the level of sophistication of Schleiermacher's conception of religion. The former lack Schleiermacher's elaborate theory of subjectivity, which provided a foundation for his theory of religion. Nevertheless, all of these "religious pluralists" are looking for a conception of religion or of faith that is not inseparably linked to being convinced that a certain doctrine is true or that a set of religious rites exclusively conveys salvation. In other words, they are seeking, as Schleiermacher once did, a concept of religion beyond "knowing" and "doing."

d. Religion and Religions

Now for the problem I promised to demonstrate (two problems actually): I have referenced Smith because in his thought the main theoretical move of some of the representatives of a pluralistic theology of religion can be identified most clearly: the concept of "faith" is a generic concept arrived at by an act of abstraction. This is true of most theories of religion that merely hover over the "positive religions."[16] Yet the fol-

---

14 Smith, *Faith and Belief*, 105-72, esp. 128-58; cf. Andreas Grünschloss, *Religionswissenschaft als Welt-Theologie: Wilfred Cantwell Smiths interreligiöse Hermeneutik* (Göttingen: Vandenhoeck & Ruprecht, 1994).
15 Smith, *Faith and Belief*, 129-36.
16 Ibid., 128-42.

lowing question must be raised regarding the role or function of the positive religions: why are there religions apart from religion, why do we have gods as forms of the Real, and why beliefs in addition to faith? Hick argues that all positive religions and concepts of God are culturally conditioned realizations of the orientation toward the Real, i.e., of the Reality-centredness of human existence. Living in different cultural contexts, human beings then use the means available within these contexts to express their relation to the Real. Accordingly, they also have different religious convictions, rites, doctrines, concepts of God (Hick) and beliefs (Smith), which are forms of being related to the ultimate reality of the Real beyond the Gods (Hick) or expressions of the attitude of faith. But the question remains: Why does religion (Reality-centredness or faith) incarnate itself in different religions and their denominations? Is it impossible to be related to the Real without being a member of one of these positive religions, and if so, why? Why is it—as it seems—essential for Reality-centredness to divide itself into subspecies and denominations and into individual religious conceptions? Is that merely an accidental fact contingent upon the different cultural conditions in which human beings live, or is it a fact that belongs to the essence of religion, and if so, why?

And that raises a second question: Where does this generic concept of faith or of religion or of the Real come from? This question is relevant because the generic concept is not only derived by abstraction from all existing religions, but is fundamental to the criticism of such existing religious convictions. According to Hick, not all doctrines are equally acceptable. A religion that promotes the mutilation of women, the sacrifice of human beings, or warfare as an instrument of mission is, according to Hick or Schmidt-Leuckel, not a legitimate form of the orientation toward God or the Real.[17] Obviously, this concept of "religion beyond the Gods" is not gained simply by abstraction but is a normative concept; it implies ethical criteria not derived from but to be met by all existing religions. Like Hick, Schmidt-Leukel also holds that these criteria are gained from the soteriological experience that lies at the core of religions. This implies, according to Schmidt-Leukel, that these criteria are derived from the specific soteriological experience of the one specific religion in which the interpreter participates—in his case, Christianity. For Schmidt-Leukel, this soteriological experience and the fundamental attitude derived from each religion's specific experience of salvation is the criterion by which these religions evaluate the truth claims of other religious convictions. He argues that, on the

---

17 Hick, *An Interpretation of Religion*, 299-315, cf. 316-42.

basis of the compatibility of these soteriological concepts, these religious traditions, notwithstanding their differences on the level of dogmatic convictions, can mutually acknowledge each other as being of equal intrinsic value. They aim at an identical soteriological transformation (Reality-relatedness instead of self-relatedness) and at compatible existential and ethical effects of that transformation.[18] In this way, a pluralistic theology of religion aims at the dialogue between different religious traditions not in order to seek a conformity of doctrines or material convictions, but rather to seek a conformity in the structure of life determined by the soteriological experience of "being in the presence of the Real" that results from participation in these religious traditions. But this implies that the starting point of a generic concept of religion is one particular religious tradition, and such a generic concept is inevitably shaped by this starting point. There is no religion *an sich* apart from the actual positive religions; rather, religion is always realized in certain convictions, rites, and concepts of salvation. The generic concept of religions is derived from the perspective of the one religion in which the interpreter participates.

That there is no "religion *an sich*" apart from the "positive religions," and that to be religious means to participate in one specific, positive religion—this is precisely the position Schleiermacher defends in his fifth speech, entitled "On the Religions." Focusing now on this text, we will see that Schleiermacher already had his finger on this problem.

2. Schleiermacher's Conception of Positive Religions

The systematic center of Schleiermacher's debate with the "cultured despisers" of religion is undoubtedly at first sight the second speech and its description of the "essence of religion." Yet, as far as I can see, Schleiermacher does not actually reach his goal until the fifth speech. Clearly, the third and fourth speeches, in addition to the fifth, develop the implications of the conception of religion outlined in the second speech, and in so doing they shed additional light on the essence of religion. In this section, I have a very limited aim: First, I will try to reproduce the argument of the fifth speech. Second, I will comment briefly on the systematic position of the fifth speech in the *Religionsschrift* as a whole, arguing that the fifth speech is, in fact, the key to interpreting the *Speeches*. Finally, returning to the remarks on the recent theologies

---

18 Schmidt-Leukel, *Gott ohne Grenzen*, 250-69.

of religion, I will spell out some consequences for the hermeneutics of a theory of religion.

a. The Theme of the Fifth Speech

It is well known that the subject of the fifth speech is the relation between the conception of religion developed in the second speech and the "positive" religions given in history (Buddhism, Christianity, Islam, Judaism, etc.).[19] Given Schleiermacher's definition of religion as "intuition of the universe," and given that this is the very core of religious consciousness and the very "essence" by which religions are religions, which stance does Schleiermacher take towards these positive religions? Would it not be most consistent for him to attempt to show that at the bottom of all of the particular ideas, rites, and commandments of the various religious traditions one finds the conception of religion outlined in the second speech, namely, one that reflects the unity of religions beneath their differences? In this case, the idea of "natural religion" would be the theoretical model best suited to the essence of religion characterized in the second speech. The fifth speech is of decisive importance for *On Religion* because it attempts to deflect precisely this line of argumentation. It aims to clear up the misunderstanding that the theory of religion presented in the second speech amounts to the Enlightenment's natural religion—in other words, a theory incapable of coming to terms seriously with the positive religions. Schleiermacher's counter-thesis to the idea of natural religion runs as follows: "If religion is exhibited only in and through such determinate forms [i.e., in and through positive religions—N.S.], then only the person who settles down in such a form with his own religion really establishes . . . an active citizenship in the religious world . . ."[20] So this is the claim: there can be no "intuition of the universe" apart from participation in a specific form of one or another positive religion. Allow me to expand on this claim by developing Schleiermacher's argument.

---

19 See the thorough interpretation of the fifth speech by Markus Schröder, "Das 'unendliche Chaos' der Religion: Die Pluralität der Religionen in Schleiermachers 'Reden'," in *200 Jahre "Reden über die Religion": Akten des 1. Internationalen Kongresses der Schleiermacher-Gesellschaft Halle, 14.-17. März 1999*, ed. Ulrich Barth and Claus-Dieter Osthövener (Berlin: Walter de Gruyter, 2000), 585-608.

20 Friedrich Schleiermacher, *On Religion: Speeches to its Cultured Despisers*, trans. Richard Crouter (Cambridge: Cambridge University Press, 1988), 104 [261]. In citing the *Speeches*, I will quote from Crouter's translation and place the 1799 pagination found in most modern German editions in brackets.

b. Again, Why Positive Religions at All?

To begin with, it is clear from the characterization of religion in the second speech that an intuition of the universe is not possible without an individual object or item of experience eliciting it. If religion consists in accepting the individual and finite as part of the whole and as a representation (*Darstellung*) of the universe,[21] then there must be something finite and limited that is to be regarded as part and manifestation of the universe. In other words, it is in the finite that the religious subject sees infinity. Schleiermacher's conception of religion implies a connection between something individual and the whole, something limited and the universe, something finite and the infinite.

But this alone does not imply that the positive religions serve a constitutive function. Perhaps religious subjects each have their own singular intuitions of the universe, each of which is elicited in very different ways and by very different media ("seeking God in the forest"), rather than solely in and through positive religious traditions, rites, or persons. This is in a way Schleiermacher's point of view: It is not possible to determine *a priori* the means by which the "sensibility and taste for the infinite"[22] is aroused, and he does not rule out the possibility that a human being may be made an "admirer of the universe"[23] without the mediation/stimulation of one of the existing religious traditions.[24] Furthermore, he emphasizes, as he did in the second and fourth speeches, that even if a person's sense for the universe is aroused in the context of an existing religion, and therefore in the same way that thousands before and after him have or will come to experience the universe, it is nevertheless an authentic, individual religious experience free of all heteronomous features or it is nothing at all.[25] Thus, while the fifth speech engages strong polemics against natural religion,[26] its subtext is Schleiermacher's central claim that religion is an inescapably individual reality. He does raise the question of whether this individuality of religion might not rule out a constitutive role for supra-individual entities, such as the positive religions.[27] But, on the whole, Schleiermacher intends not only to show that religion is always a particular and individual experience, but also that religion necessarily occurs in the commun-

---

21 Ibid., 25 [56].
22 Ibid., 23 [53].
23 Ibid., 58 [143].
24 Ibid., 104-5 [262].
25 Ibid., 104-8 [261-72]; cf. 50 [121].
26 Ibid., 108-11 [272-79].
27 Ibid., 104-5 [262].

al forms of the positive religions with their specific ideas, convictions, rites, founders, etc. Religion *qua* "intuition of the universe" does not express itself identically in all human beings—that is his antithesis to the idea of natural religion. Conversely, religion is also not individual in the sense that each human person shapes religious rites and convictions or holy commandments of his own. The sense and taste for the infinite is elicited, formed, and shaped within the context of existing supra-individual religious traditions.

c. The Identity of Positive Religions

Schleiermacher must therefore establish a more precise connection between the intuition of the universe and positive religions, and he does so by defining more exactly what it is that makes a religion specific or concrete. This is not a matter of specifying the distinguishing features of a given religion, but of theorizing just how religions are to be distinguished from one another. In other words: How does a religion gain and sustain a distinctive identity?[28]

Schleiermacher ponders three possible answers. First, there are different symbols, doctrines, rites, and certain feelings as joy, contrition, etc., which he calls "elements of religion" or "religious material." The differences in this material or the fact that one religion has elements that another one lacks could be the basis of the specific identity. That would imply that all followers of one specific religion necessarily share the same feelings and opinions or convictions. This is a common but inadequate way to distinguish religions or to determine the identity of one given religion because, as Schleiermacher points out, these elements of religion are accidental in the sense that they can change in an individual's lifetime or in the history of a positive religion without changing the identity of the religion. Thus, an inductive method of determining the identity of a religion leads nowhere.[29]

The second possible answer to the question concerning how a religion gains a distinctive identity might refer to the different ways of symbolizing the universe or forming concepts of an ultimate reality— e.g., as a personal God, an impersonal highest principle, or a panentheistic all-inclusive substance. But by such a deduction, or through

---

28 See ibid., 100 [249-50].
29 See ibid., 100-102 [250-55].

such a *diairesis*, Schleiermacher argues, we are led to species of religions, but not to the individual positive religions themselves.[30]

Neither the given religious material nor the deduction of species or types of the intuition of the universe enables us to determine the character or the identity of a positive religion. Schleiermacher therefore suggests a third option: the identity of an individual religion is determined by an act of will, a free choice through which one specific intuition of the universe is made the organizing center to which all the religious material is related and by which relation it receives its distinctive shape:

> Let me say it briefly: An individual instance of religion such as we are seeking cannot be established other than through free choice by making a particular intuition of the universe the center of the whole of religion and relating everything therein to it. . . . thereby the whole suddenly takes on a determinate spirit; everything that was previously ambiguous and indeterminate is fixed . . . all individual elements now appear from a perspective of the same name that is turned toward that center . . .[31]

This means, e.g., that the elements the Christian tradition shares with the Muslim tradition—the conviction that God has created the world and rules it for a judgment to come—is shaped in each of these religions in a special way by virtue of its relation to one particular, individualizing intuition of the universe. Consequently, the *seemingly identical* expectation of a Final Judgment actually differs in Islam and Christianity.

"Through free choice," Schleiermacher writes, a particular intuition is made the center of a religion—but what does "free choice" mean here? In the first instance, "free choice" means that this particular way of intuiting the universe cannot be deduced from the concept of religion; it means that there is no *necessary* connection between the essence of religion and particular means of revelation, persons, or rites. In other words: It belongs to the essence of religion that it occurs by some means, but not by any particular means. Religion occurs contingently; it cannot be deduced. Put simply, religion is a historical phenomenon. This implies, secondly, that there are no privileged intuitions or privileged expressions of the intuition of the universe. In order to be a religious person, it is not necessary to become or remain a member of a *specific* religion.

But why, and above all, in which sense does an act of choice lie at the core of religion? In order to answer this question, Schleiermacher

---

30 Ibid., 102-4 [255-59].
31 Ibid., 104 [259-60].

refers to the way personal identity is constituted, implicitly adopting John Locke's description of personal identity.[32] Schleiermacher holds that a human person is constituted neither merely by a particular body, nor his life circumstances, nor by the choices he makes, nor by the influences acting upon him. All of this is indeed a part of, or material for, an individual person's identity. But this identity itself, personal identity, is consciousness of identity leading back to, and constituted by, the moment when this consciousness arose—not as an indeterminate moment, but as the consciousness that connects and organizes the given and future material of my life in a very special and particular way.

At this point, Schleiermacher draws a parallel between this concept of personal identity and the identity of an individual religion, or strictly speaking, two parallels:[33] The first is to the religious consciousness of an individual person. As just noted, a person is one and the same by virtue of the earliest consciousness connecting the various occurrences in his life. In the same way, a person's religious identity can be traced back to one decisive and underivable intuition of the universe. All the elements of his or her religious life—organized worship, participation in various rites, particular ways of symbolizing the universe through representations of God, and specific ways of dealing with this God—are related back to a definite moment of intuition in which the sense of the universe was first aroused. Something very similar holds true with respect to supra-individual religious traditions, the positive religions. All of them go back to the contingent religious experience of an individual, a founding figure (*Stifterpersönlichkeit*), who came to intuit the universe in a unique way and to symbolize and express this intuition such that it became the means for others to become "admirers of the universe."

> Every such formation of religion, where everything is seen and felt in relation to a central intuition, wherever and however it is formed, and whatever this preferred intuition may be, is a truly positive religion. In respect to the whole of religion, it is a heresy ... because something highly voluntary is the cause of its having arisen. In regard to the community of all participants and their relationship to him who first founded their religion it is its own school and discipleship, because he first saw that intuition in the center of religion.[34]

This implies that there exists not only a parallel between the religious identity of an individual person and the individual religions in the

---

32 See ibid., 106 [262-63]. Cf. chapter 27 of Book II of John Locke, *An Essay Concerning Human Understanding*, ed. Peter H. Nidditch (Oxford: Clarendon Press, 1975).
33 For the following, see Schleiermacher, *On Religion*, 106-8 [262-72].
34 Ibid., 104 [260-61].

sense of religious traditions, but that the religious traditions are based on an individual person in whose life the sense for the infinite was aroused (as it may be in many other lives). This *special* intuition and its expression thereby become the source of others' intuitions of the universe, and in this way a religious tradition comes to life, owing its existence to one individual in whose way of experiencing and symbolizing the universe others can share. One might say that the individual religions are collective religious individuals—as long as this is not taken to suggest or endorse religious heteronomy, for on this point Schleiermacher is clear:

> In religion there is, of course, a mastership and discipleship. There are individuals to whom thousands attach themselves, but this attachment is no blind imitation and they are not disciples because their master has made them into this; he is rather their master because they have chosen him as that. He who, by expressing his own religion, has aroused it in others no longer has it in his power to keep them for himself; their religion is also free as soon as it lives and goes its own way.[35]

Regarding the question concerning in which sense the individual or supra-individual religion gains its identity by an act of choice, it may be said that Schleiermacher consistently emphasizes—as in the quote above—that this bond to a master is not heteronomous. Yet it is equally true that by invoking "free choice"[36] Schleiermacher does not intend to place this identity entirely at the sovereign disposal of the individual: a person does not simply choose to be seized by a religious experience. The intuition at the beginning of a religious tradition or at the beginning of an individual religious consciousness is, rather, the result of an event of *Offenbarung* (revelation).[37] This explains Schleiermacher's contention that the universe "creates its own admirers"—namely, in an experience that is not at the disposal of the human being. The term "free choice" signifies the underivability and contingency of this event.

In summary: just as the identity of a human person is shaped by the point of origin of a consciousness connecting all the experiences in a course of life in a special way, so too one's religious identity goes back to one point of origin where the subject's capacity for religion was elicited and came into being. This holds true for the individual religious experience as well as for the supra-individual positive religions:

> Religious people are thoroughly historical.... The moment in which they themselves have been filled by the intuition that has made itself the focal

---

35   Ibid., 58 [141-42].
36   See, again, the quotation at note 31.
37   See Schleiermacher, *On Religion*, 49 [118-19].

point of their religion is always sacred to them; it appears to them as an immediate influence of the deity.... Yet this whole of religion and the religious culture of a great mass of humanity is something infinitely greater than their own religious life and the small fragments of this religion they personally exhibit. They glorify this fact, therefore, in every way ... never exhibit one of its elements, without orienting and portraying it in connection with this fact.[38]

In these sentences, the autonomy of individual religiosity is not relativized; but the individual's religion is a fragment, a limited but indispensable modification in which the supra-individual religious tradition presents and actualizes itself. The supra-individual religious traditions, for their part, are forms and shapes in which the essence of religion actualizes itself in a variety of historical positive religions. At this point, the *Speeches* are open to the history of religions—that is, to a determination of the essence of religion based on the variety of religions in the course of history.

d. Why Does Religion Need Mediation?

If one recalls how Schleiermacher emphasized the autonomy of the religious individual, the connection sketched here between positive religions and the development of the religious capacity in individuals may come as a surprise. Certainly, he never revokes the subject's autonomy. Yet he does come to emphasize the difference between master and disciple. While in the fourth speech he had strongly stressed the fact that this difference is to vanish,[39] in the fifth speech he underscores the fact that one's current religious consciousness is permanently linked to its point of origin.[40] He seems to hold that religious experience is necessarily elicited and mediated by means of a positive religion whose distinctive intuition of the universe owes its existence to a religious master, its founder. As I said, Schleiermacher revokes nothing; but the emphasis has shifted in this last speech. He now stresses the idea that, indispensably and necessarily, the formation of the individual religious capacity, the intuition of the universe, is in need of mediation.

Once again, take note that Schleiermacher does not exclude the possibility that some among us might have an intuition of the universe mediated by no particular religious tradition: "a person who does not fit into one of those that are readily available ... will surely not belong

---

38 Ibid., 112 [282-83].
39 Ibid., 7-8 [10-13], 50 [121-22], 58 [141-42].
40 Ibid., 103-4 [262-63]; 111-13 [282-84].

to any of them, but make a new one."[41] Yet Schleiermacher is obviously of the opinion that religious consciousness is usually aroused in the context of a positive religion and thus mediated by it. Given the possibility that religious consciousness may also arise outside of positive religions, how can he be so sure about this?

As far as I can see, the key to answering this question lies in the description of Christianity's essence, i.e., its core intuition, which Schleiermacher outlines in the final pages of the fifth speech.[42] The basic intuition permeating and influencing all elements and material of the Christian religion is that of the finite "straining against" the infinite, i.e., the insurmountable tendency of the finite to be something in itself and not see itself as a part of the whole. Put another way, the finite has a propensity to be non-religious, to cling to itself and not relate itself to the universe. Yet Christianity's insight into this corruption is only half of its essential intuition, for it also includes the experience of the universe overcoming this tendency and reconciling finitude's enmity:

> [The basic intuition] is none other than the intuition of the universal straining of everything finite against the unity of the whole and of the way in which the deity handles this striving, how it reconciles the enmity directed against it . . . by scattering over the whole individual points that are at once finite and infinite, at once human and divine. Corruption and redemption, enmity and mediation are two sides of this intuition that are inseparably bound to each other, and the shape of all religious material in Christianity and its whole form are determined through them.[43]

In the first instance, Christianity is the one religion at whose core lies this insight into the human tendency to be non-religious and therefore into the necessity of salvation by means of the "self-revelation" of the universe. And due to the fact that human beings cling to finite entities, this revelation must take the form of a finite entity and occur in a factual experience in which an intuition of the universe is elicited: that is the function of the positive religions as means of encountering the universe. Thus, the Christian insight into human sinfulness implies the (theoretical) insight that religion—qua intuition of the universe—needs to be elicited by means of finite entities. In other words, there is no religion that is not mediated by the positive religions. No religion without the incarnation of the Deity.

Furthermore, according to the first and second speeches, to be non-religious—to cling to the finite—is not only a characteristic of atheistic positions, but also of positions that, regarding themselves as deeply

---

41 Ibid., 104 [262].
42 For the following, see ibid., 115-22 [291-307].
43 Ibid., 115 [291].

religious or even Christian, identify religion with morals or metaphysics, i.e., doctrinal convictions, thus misunderstanding the essence of religion. Properly understood, Christianity is the positive religion that deals with this tendency to be non-religious and distinguishes pseudo-religion from true religion or, as it were, the gods from the Universe. The core of Christianity is the criticism of pseudo-religion that Schleiermacher pursues in his speeches.[44] Christianity is the self-criticism of religion.

Therefore, the general concept of religion put forth by Schleiermacher in his speeches shows itself in the fifth speech to be the very essence of Christianity: the critique of every objectification of religion or of the Universe. According to the fifth speech, it belongs to the very essence of Christianity to distinguish religion from the means by which religion is elicited and from the forms in which religion is expressed. And this is exactly what Schleiermacher does throughout the *Speeches*. The final and fifth speech, then, removes the veil from his theory of religion. The latter turns out to be a specifically Christian theory of religion—more than that, the theory is identical to the essence of Christianity.

3. Three Concluding Points

This means—and this is the first point I would like to make—that the constitutive function of positive religions as the means by which religion comes into being and thus by which the human capacity for religion is aroused is not, as Schleiermacher wants to make us believe, derived from his concept of the essence of religion. Rather, it is due to an insight that is specifically Christian. The insight is specifically Christian, *first*, in that the capacity for religion is corrupted and, *second*, in that it is therefore reliant on a medium that reinforces this capacity and brings the individual to realize that all beings are but a part of the universe. *Third*, it is a specifically Christian insight because, by realizing this, the person is reintegrated into the whole, and thus, into the universe. This implies, with respect to the fifth speech and the connection between religion and the religions, that Schleiermacher does not develop a conception of religion independently from his own devotion to Christianity. Rather, his concept of religion remains firmly tied to his Christian perspective. In a word: it is a distinctively Christian theory of religion.

---

44 Ibid., 116-19 [294-99].

With this in mind, my second point it this: it would be interesting to ask whether this is only true for this aspect of the theory. It might turn out that the entire theory of religion is fundamentally Christian and that the fifth speech's characterization of the essence of the Christian religion is the key to Schleiermacher's entire conception of religion—including the definition of the essence of religion in the famous second speech.

Finally, if we reflect upon all of this in light of the recent theologies of religion outlined in the first part of this paper, it might be the case that the distinctively Christian character of Schleiermacher's theory of religion is not a defect or fault that he could have avoided. Rather, a basic systematic or hermeneutical insight might be gleaned from the *On Religion*, especially the fifth speech. If it is true that religion can only be understood by being a religious subject or by being "seized by the universe," and that religion is not to be had except in the form of a positive religion, then it must be true that a *theory* of religion will always reflect the perspective of the theorist's specific religious tradition. Every conception of an "essence" of religion will inevitably reflect the theorist's own religious location and treat other religions from that perspective.

Schleiermacher's Contested Place in Religious Studies Today[1]

Volkhard Krech

Friedrich Schleiermacher left his mark not only on Protestant theology, but also on the study of religion generally, especially through his well-known *Speeches* on religion. And even his *Christian Faith* and other writings offer insights for Religious Studies that have hardly been fully tapped. I see his actual influence and continued potential residing (minimally) in the following four aspects of his program: 1) in an epistemologically based notion of religion; 2) in the balance struck between a general notion of religion and the concrete history of religions; 3) in the consideration given to the emergence of religion out of certain emotional and socio-psychic dispositions and, thus, his contribution to theories of social differentiation; and 4) in his considerations regarding the social forms of religion. In what follows I will briefly elaborate upon these four points.

1. An Epistemologically Based Notion of Religion

Whereas scholars like Joseph Ringmüller could still write a *Universal History of Religion* in 1772 that, despite employing phenomenological differentiations, was divided into a history of true and a history of false religion, Schleiermacher's 1799 *Reden* offered for the first time in the history of scholarship on religion an epistemological model for conceptualizing the "positive" religions. The *Speeches* develop an abstract or generic concept of religion, yet simultaneously regard the concrete historical religions as the proper subject matter for scientific reflection.[2] Because of its ability to mediate between a sufficiently universal notion of religion and the material history of religions, Schleiermacher's con-

---

1 This chapter represents a lightly revised version of the conference paper.
2 See Burkhard Gladigow, "Friedrich Schleiermacher (1768-1834)," in *Klassiker der Religionswissenschaft: Von Friedrich Schleiermacher bis Mircea Eliade*, ed. Axel Michaels (Munich: C.H. Beck, 1997), 17-28, esp. 24-25.

cept of religion exercised a significant influence on the field of comparative religion as it emerged at the end of the nineteenth century.

By defining religion as "neither thinking nor acting, but intuition and feeling"[3] and as "the feeling of absolute dependence,"[4] Schleiermacher laid the cornerstone for a concept of religion that is different from both the intellectualist theories of Victorian England[5] and the moral interpretations brought forward by Immanuel Kant, Émile Durkheim, Max Weber, and Talcott Parsons. The direction taken by Schleiermacher leads rather to Rudolf Otto, William James, Georg Simmel, Ernst Troeltsch, and beyond, to contemporary approaches within the psychology and sociology of religion. Insofar as he addresses the question of how religious certainty develops and is sustained, Schleiermacher can also be seen as a precursor of the "habits-of-the-heart" approach with a pragmatic twist.[6] For this reason his conception of religion continues to be a stimulus in the sociology of religion. I will return to this later.

Within *Religionswissenschaft*, it was first and foremost Friedrich Max Müller who adopted Schleiermacher's approach by reformulating the Romantic notion of an "intuition of the infinite within the finite." In his *Introduction to the Science of Religion*, Müller defines religion as the "faculty of faith ... a mental faculty or disposition, which ... enables man to apprehend the Infinite under different names, and under varying disguises."[7] The concept of religion as a feeling of dependence is found in British anthropology, for example, in Andrew Lang (1844–1912), who speaks of religion as "a serious mood of trust, dependence and apprehension."[8] In the German-speaking world, I could mention August Dorner, who defines religion as the consciousness of absolute dependence entailing the immediate unity of all contradictions.[9]

---

3   Religion ist "weder Denken noch Handeln, sondern Anschauung und Gefühl." Friedrich Schleiermacher, *Über die Religion: Reden an die Gebildeten unter ihren Verächtern*, ed. Rudolf Otto, 7th ed. (1899; Göttingen: Vandenhoeck & Ruprecht, 1991), 49.

4   Friedrich Schleiermacher, *Der christliche Glaube nach den Grundsätzen der evangelischen Kirche im Zusammenhange dargestellt* (1830/31), ed. Martin Redeker, vol. 1 (Berlin: Walter de Gruyter, 1960), §4. Henceforth CG (1830/31).

5   See Edward E. Evans-Pritchard, *Theories of Primitive Religion* (Oxford: Clarendon Press, 1965).

6   See Robert N. Bellah et al., *Habits of the Heart: Individualism and Commitment in American Life* (New York: Harper & Row, 1986).

7   Friedrich Max Müller, *Introduction to the Science of Religion* (London: Longmans, Green, & Co., 1882), 13.

8   Andrew Lang, *Myth, Ritual and Religion* (London: Longmans, Green, & Co., 1906), 2:1.

9   See August Dorner, "Über das Wesen der Religion," *Theologische Studien und Kritiken* 56, no. 1 (1883): 217–77, esp. 248ff; and Max Reischle, *Die Frage nach dem Wesen der*

From a more systematic point of view, however, Schleiermacher's theory of religion probably had its greatest impact on Rudolf Otto's concept of "creature-feeling" (*Kreaturgefühl*). In contrast to an understanding of religion as the feeling of utter dependence, Otto's notion of the Holy possesses, in my opinion, more potential for understanding the apparent ambivalence of religion: as the complex relationship between religion and violence shows, religion can issue in both humility and exaltation.[10]

Because of its foundation in affect or the emotions, Schleiermacher's concept of religion has found its most frequent and natural reception in the psychology of religion.[11] Yet it must be recalled that his choice of the term "feeling" was of a piece with his critical understanding of rationality as finite or limited. For Schleiermacher, reason is the subordinate product of a superior power; it does not posit or establish itself, but is always experienced as something inexplicably posited.

2. The Importance of Positive Religions and the History of Religions

The reissue of Schleiermacher's *Speeches* by Rudolf Otto one hundred years after their initial publication inspired Nathan Söderblom to devote his inaugural lecture in Uppsala to the theme "The Significance of Schleiermacher's 'Speeches on Religion': A Contribution to its Centenary."[12] In the field of the history of religions, the impact of Schleiermacher is most noticeable in Söderblom's book *The Development of the Belief in God*, in which he notes Schleiermacher's profound faith in God and gives him "a place of honor in the history of religions."[13] Yet, of all the twentieth-century historians of religion, it was William Brede Kris-

---

Religion: Grundlegung zu einer Methodologie der Religionsphilosophie (Freiburg: J. C. B. Mohr, 1889). Reischle replaces the term *Abhängigkeitsgefühl* (consciousness of dependence) with *Anbetungsgefühl* (consciousness of worship) so as to better express the activity of the religious consciousness.

10 See Rudolf Otto, *Das Heilige: Über das Irrationale in der Idee des Göttlichen und sein Verhältnis zum Rationalen* (Breslau: Trewendt and Granier, 1917).
11 See Jacob A. Belzen and Ralph W. Hood, "Methodological Issues in the Psychology of Religion: Toward Another Paradigm?" *The Journal of Psychology* 140, no. 1 (2006): 5–28.
12 Nathan Söderblom, *Betydelsen af Schleiermachers "Reden über die Religion"* (Uppsala: Schultz, 1899).
13 Nathan Söderblom, *Das Werden des Gottesglaubens: Untersuchungen über die Anfänge der Religion* (Leipzig: Hinrichs, 1916), 287.

tensen (1867–1953) who stressed Schleiermacher's importance as a resource for overcoming rationalist misconstructions of religion.[14]

Schleiermacher's conception of religion is applicable to the actual history of religions because he always kept the diversity of positive religions in mind—he calls them "Religionsindividuen" (individual religions)—and classified them into different "forms" and "sects."[15] Each form comprises a genuinely different "intuition of the universe," a phrase Schleiermacher regarded as "the most universal and highest formula of religion."[16] As a result, Schleiermacher's concept of a universal history of religions differs from its predecessors in a number of important ways. Previous definitions of the "essence" of religion presupposed an abstract notion of reason (as with, e.g., the Deists) or assumed that fear of nature and powerlessness against it had given rise to the earliest forms of religion (e.g., David Hume's). By contrast, Schleiermacher's concept of religion begins with the finitude of reason, locates the emergence of religion in the interplay between individual perception and communicative confirmation, and takes into account the real diversity in the history of religions.

Because the number of individual forms of religion is, in principle, unlimited, Schleiermacher attributes new significance to "positive" (i.e., historical) religions and contrasts real, living religions with the "dead" abstractions of Enlightenment "natural religion." His treatment of religion as "a product of time and history" implies an agenda of uncompromising historicization and—thanks to the influence of early German Romanticism—its individualization.[17]

Readers of the *Speeches* will recall that Schleiermacher's classification of different ways of "intuiting the universe" resulted in a typology in which the universe is construed, firstly, as "chaos . . . in its confusion"; secondly, as "plurality without unity"; and, thirdly, as "unity within plurality." These ideal types bear remarkable resemblance to the evolutionary scheme shaped by Herbert Spencer about seventy years later, which posits a development from an undifferentiated, incoherent and indefinite homogeneity via a differentiated, coherent and definite heterogeneity to a differentiated homogeneity.[18] Schleiermacher's con-

---

14 See, for example, William Brede Kristensen, *The Meaning of Religion: Lectures in the Phenomenology of Religion* (The Hague: M. Nijhoff, 1960).
15 For details see Klaus Eberhard Welker, *Die grundsätzliche Beurteilung der Religionsgeschichte durch Schleiermacher* (Leiden: E. J. Brill, 1965).
16 "Anschauen des Universums . . . ist die allgemeinste und höchste Formel der Religion" (Schleiermacher, *Über die Religion*, 52).
17 "Ein Ereignis der Zeit und der Geschichte" (ibid., 31).
18 See Herbert Spencer, *The Principles of Sociology*, ed. Jonathan Turner (New Brunswick, NJ: Transaction Publishers, 2002), 321, 411 passim.

ception of the history of religions is also in a sense compatible with the later typological classification of religion into fetishism, polytheism, and monotheism employed by Cornelius Peter Tiele, Max Weber, and others.[19]

Yet unlike the "evolutionism" proposed or assumed in nineteenth-century accounts of cultural history generally and the history of religions in particular, Schleiermacher did not espouse a fixed pattern of chronological development. The three basic forms of religion, understood as three ways of intuiting the universe—namely, as "chaos," as "elementary multiplicity," and as "system"—"are in fact nothing else than a customary and universally recurring division of the concept of intuition."[20] Therefore, Schleiermacher's aim is not necessarily, or at least not only, to show a chronological progression, but rather to outline a systematic differentiation whose elements can be found in individual historic religions at different times and in different constellations. Thus, it might be said that Schleiermacher's conception of the history of religions transcended classical evolutionism long before it had even been established. Nor did Schleiermacher speculate about candidates for some primordial form of religion (fetishism, animism, pre-animism, totemism, dynamism, etc.) as many other nineteenth-century scholars of religion did. This is something we can build upon today, especially in the current debate on the interactions between polytheism and monotheism.

To some extent even later phenomenology of religion, which reverted in part to Schleiermacher and turned against evolutionism, represents a regression behind Schleiermacher's position. Whereas Schleiermacher limited the fundamental characteristic of religion to the intuition of the universe and the feeling of absolute dependence and emphasized the positive religions in their individual forms, much twentieth-century phenomenology of religion has tended to essentialize or reify "religion" per se.

---

19   See Gladigow, *Schleiermacher*, 23-24.
20   "Jene drei Verschiedenheiten in der Religion sind aber in der Tat nichts andres als eine gewöhnliche und überall vorkommende Einteilung des Begriffs der Anschauung" (Schleiermacher, *Über die Religion*, 174).

3. The Emergence of Religion out of Socio-Emotional Dispositions and Theories of Social Differentiation

As mentioned above, Schleiermacher's definition of religion in terms of the "feeling of absolute dependence" usually leads directly to the psychology of religion. However, this concept also has potential for the sociology of religion, a potential that was first realized by Georg Simmel, later taken up by Peter L. Berger, and even had its impact on Thomas Luckmann's concept of "invisible religion."[21]

In defining piety as a modification of feeling, Schleiermacher did not intend to isolate religion from knowing and acting.[22] Rather, the feeling called piety "can accompany all acts of knowing alike, irrespective of their object, since it expresses especially the relation of every cognition to the whole and to the highest unity of all cognition, and thus refers to the highest and most universal order and harmony; and no one will refuse to call this a pious feeling."[23] Certain feelings that come with social relations, such as "the feeling for one's family, professional feeling, the feeling of patriotism and even universal human love," do not require piety. Yet, every action can be accompanied by "a feeling of the relation of its determinate domain to the totality of action and to its highest unity. Likewise, no one will refuse to recognize such a feeling as pious."[24] The emotions accompanying social relations can be specified as feelings of dependence. Now while self-consciousness consists in "its receptivity and its (spontaneous) activity" and is thus based on reciprocity, pious feeling in all its variations is always a pure feeling of dependence and can never designate a relationship of reciprocity.[25] The pious feeling of dependence thus has to be distinguished

---

21 See Thomas Luckmann, *The Invisible Religion: The Problem of Religion in Modern Society* (New York: Macmillan, 1967).
22 "Die Frömmigkeit an sich ist weder ein Wissen noch ein Thun, sondern eine Neigung und Bestimmtheit des Gefühls." Friedrich Schleiermacher, *Der christliche Glaube* (1821/22), ed. Hermann Peiter, vol. 1 (Berlin: Walter de Gruyter, 1984), §8. Henceforth CG (1821/22).
23 "Dagegen giebt es ein anderes Gefühl der Ueberzeugung, welches gleichmäßig jeden Wissensakt begleiten kann, ohne Unterschied des Gegenstandes, indem es vornehmlich die Beziehung jedes Erkenntnißkreises auf das Ganze und auf die höchste Einheit alles Erkennens ausdrükt, und sich also auf die höchste und allgemeinste Ordnung und Zusammenstimmung bezieht, und dies wird man sich nicht weigern, ein frommes zu nennen" (ibid.).
24 Ibid. See also Schleiermacher, *Brouillon zur Ethik* (1805/06), in *Entwürfe zu einem System der Sittenlehre*, vol. 2 of *Schleiermachers Werke*, ed. O. Braun (Aalen: Scientia Verlag, 1981), 210: "Das sittliche Bewußtsein von dem Verhältniß des Einzelnen zum Ganzen ist Pietät, wahrer Patriotismus mit religiösem Charakter."
25 See CG (1821/22) §9.

from "our relations to nature, or those that exist in human society." Nevertheless, because certain "sensuous excitations" and the feeling of absolute dependence are related, this is not a difference in principle, but only of degree.[26] On this scale, genuinely pious feelings stand closest to the feelings that are "founded on a relationship of the purest possible dependence, such as that of the child on the father and that of the citizen on his native land and its rulers."[27]

This is the point of departure for Georg Simmel's approach to the sociology of religion. Simmel cites examples of the "many human relations [that] harbor a religious element," such as "the relation of a devoted child to its parents, of an enthusiastic patriot to his country, of the fervent cosmopolitan toward humanity; the relation of the laboringman to his struggling fellows, or of the proud feudal lord to his class; the relation of the subject to the ruler under whose control he is, and of the true soldier to his army." He goes on to say that "looked at from the psychological side, all these relations, with their infinite variety of content, may have a common tone that can only be described as religious."[28] If social actions carry a religious connotation, they also express the relationship between the part and the whole. Religiosity occasions "a certain degree of emotional tension, a specific ardor and certainty of the subjective conditions, an inclusion of the subject experiencing them in a higher order—an order that is at the same time felt to be something subjective and personal."[29]

---

26 CG (1830/31) §9.
27 Feelings, "welche auf ein Verhältniß möglichst reiner Abhängigkeit gegründet sind, wie das des Kindes gegen den Vater und des Bürgers gegen das Vaterland und dessen leitende Gewalten" (CG [1821/22] §9). Also note: "Vorherrschend ist das Abhängigkeitsgefühl in dem Verhältnis der Kinder gegen die Eltern, der Bürger gegen das Vaterland" (CG [1830/31] §4).
28 "[D]ie Beziehung des pietätvollen Kindes zu seinen Eltern, des enthusiastischen Patrioten zu seinem Vaterland oder des enthusiastischen Kosmopoliten zur Menschheit; die Beziehung des Arbeiters zu seiner emporringenden Klasse oder des adelsstolzen Feudalen zu seinem Stand; die Beziehung des Unterworfenen zu seinem Beherrscher, unter dessen Suggestion er steht, und des rechten Soldaten zu seiner Armee—all diese Verhältnisse mit so unendlich mannigfaltigem Inhalt, können doch auf die Form ihrer psychischen Seite hin angesehen, einen gemeinsamen Ton haben, den man als religiös bezeichnen muß." Georg Simmel, "Zur Soziologie der Religion" (1898), in *Aufsätze und Abhandlungen 1894-1900*, ed. H.-J. Dahme and David Frisby, vol. 5 of *Georg Simmel Gesamtausgabe* (Frankfurt: Suhrkamp, 1992), 275. Also by Simmel, see *Die Religion*, in the collection *Philosophie der Mode* (1905); *Die Religion* (1906/1912); *Kant und Goethe* (1906/1916); *Schopenhauer und Nietzsche* (1907), ed. Michael Behr, Volkhard Krech, and Gerd Schmidt, vol. 10 of *Georg Simmel Gesamtausgabe* (Frankfurt: Suhrkamp, 1995), 39-118, esp. 64-65.
29 Simmel, "Zur Soziologie der Religion," 269.

Schleiermacher's concept of piety helped Simmel develop a theory of the emergence of religion: social relations of the sort named above constitute a disposition from which religion can evolve as a sphere of its own; they are, as it were, "semifinished religious products" (*religiöse Halbprodukte*). According to Simmel, all religiosity "contains a peculiar admixture of unselfish surrender and fervent desire, of humility and exaltation, of sensual concreteness and spiritual abstraction."[30] The religious quality gives the social relations mentioned above "a mark that distinguishes them from relations based upon pure egoism, or pure suggestion, or even purely moral forces."[31] In a similar way, Schleiermacher referenced states of feeling "such as penitence, contrition, confidence, and joy in God, which we pronounce pious in themselves, without regard to any knowing or doing that proceed from them."[32] Once again, *in abstracto* the feeling of absolute dependence exists independently from those states of feeling that derive from our relative dependence, and it is different from them by virtue of the fact that all empirical differences are nullified in one single whole: in "God-consciousness." Yet in order to manifest itself *in concreto*, this God-consciousness must "unite with a sensibly determined self-consciousness."[33]

This comparison suggests that the principle guiding Simmel's sociology of religion—namely, the identification of semifinished religious products as a point of origin from which to analyze the emergence and distinctive characteristics of "the religious"—seems to have been inspired by Schleiermacher's understanding of religion. From this perspective Simmel is able to pursue analogies between religious representations and social circumstances as well as the similarities between the relationship of an individual to his group and the relationship of the individual to his God. These are insights that theorization about the emergence of the religious can build upon today.

Moreover, by defining religion as having its "own province in the mind"[34] and by stressing its autonomy and resistance to appropriation by other spheres such as ethics, art, and politics, Schleiermacher laid

---

30 Ibid.
31 "eine Note, die sie von den auf Egoismus oder reine Suggestion oder rein äußerliche oder sogar rein moralische Kräfte gegründeten Beziehungen noch unterscheidet" (ibid.).
32 "[Gefühlszustände,] welche wir, wie Reue und Zerknirschung, Zuversicht, Freudigkeit zu Gott, an und für sich fromm nennen ohne Rücksicht auf ein daraus hervorgehendes Wissen und Tun" (CG [1830/31] §3).
33 God-consciousness must "[sich] mit einer sinnlichen Erregtheit des Selbstbewußtseins vereinigen" (CG [1830/31] §9).
34 "Provinz im Gemüte" (Schleiermacher, *Über die Religion*, 40).

the foundations for later theorists of social differentiation, from Georg Simmel to Niklas Luhmann. The claim that everything societal is religious put forward by sociologists like Émile Durkheim and Thomas Luckmann must be rejected by reasserting evidence for the autonomy of religion. That said, Schleiermacher himself was very sensitive to the close interactions between religion and other societal spheres, some of which amount to a kind of symbiosis. The most prominent example of this might be what he called "Kunstreligion" (aesthetic religion or religion of art), a term he coined.

4. Considerations Regarding Social Forms of Religion

Schleiermacher did not develop an elaborate sociology of religion, as Max Weber, Émile Durkheim, Ernst Troeltsch, and Georg Simmel would a century later. But Schleiermacher's differentiation between personal, organized, and public religion contains much potential yet to be exploited by the sociology of religion. I will limit my remarks to personal and organized religion.

"Personal religion" describes the case in which the individual is at once the locus (*Ort*) and the source of religion. For Schleiermacher, to be the *locus of religion* means that religion expresses itself only in the individual. In modern sociology of religion, this is referred to as the privatization of religion or "structural religious individualism"—which refers to the fact that religious content (*religiöser Inhalt*), e.g., faith, is attributed to and appropriated by the individual person. To be the *source of religion* means that individual experience (such as the contemplation of the universe or the feeling of absolute dependence) is the origin of religious content. In modern sociology of religion, especially in the wake of Thomas Luckmann's "invisible religion," this is called subjectification or "sacralization of the self."[35]

One point often overlooked by interpreters of Schleiermacher and modern sociologists of religion alike is the phenomenon Schleiermacher referred to as "oscillation," that is, the mutual dependence between individual religious experience, on the one hand, and its social stimulation and confirmation, on the other. The individual is never the sole source of religious beliefs. Schleiermacher does not see the emergence and reproduction of religion as a product of the individual alone. This becomes apparent when we examine his notion of "church."

---

35 See Hubert Knoblauch, "Die Verflüchtigung der Religion ins Religiöse," forward to *Die unsichtbare Religion*, by Thomas Luckmann (Frankfurt: Suhrkamp, 1991), 7-41.

According to Schleiermacher, "church" (i.e., religious association or community per se) is constituted primarily through a process of mutual communication based on the fact that a "consciousness of kind" (*Gattungsbewußtsein*) is inherent in every pious self-consciousness. As a consequence, the expression "immediate self-consciousness" so fundamental to Schleiermacher's theory of religion permits the construction of a universal notion of religion *only* when the explanation of this consciousness is considered as occurring within social interaction.[36] Put differently, the "feeling of absolute dependence," which the introduction of *The Christian Faith* lays down as foundational to dogmatics, appears in reconstructive analysis as something awakened by the communicative and stimulative power of bodily expression and verbal utterance.[37] Because this sort of external stimulation must be differentiated from a mere intervention from without, Schleiermacher employs the metaphor of an awakening to strike a balance between mental or subjective experience and patterns of communication. Creating religious assurance and certainty is always a process of social confirmation and therefore is not the concern of an individual alone. *Interactive* stimulation and semantic explication of the individual self-consciousness of everyone taking part in a religious interaction—and this under the implicit assumption of a *sensus communis*—is the crucial point of Schleiermacher's theory of "religious organization," which is also a theory of religious communication and should therefore not be understood as a theory limited to bureaucratic organization.

5. Conclusions

Schleiermacher stands at the *beginning* of modernity and, therefore, also at the beginning of reflection about modernity and its relationship to religion. It would thus be unfair to evaluate him according to the standards and insights of contemporary theories of religion. Yet his conceptions of religion and the history of religions in many respects form the nucleus of subsequent scholarship on religion, and they remain in some respects a resource from which we can still draw today. I see untapped potential in Schleiermacher's minimalistic definition of religion, which

---

[36] Michael Moxter has pointed this out in "Urteilskraft und Intersubjektivität: Zur Eigenart theologischer Reflexion," in *Subjektiver Geist: Reflexion und Erfahrung im Glauben*, ed. K.-M. Kodalle and A. M. Steinmeier (Würzburg: Königshausen & Neumann, 2002), 25-36.

[37] See Schleiermacher, CG (1830/31) §6; further elaboration on this matter can be found in §122.

leaves ample room for religious-historical typologies, while at the same time opening new perspectives on the emergence and reproduction of religion.

First, Romanticism should in a certain sense be understood as an early reaction to modernity. Structural individualism as the correlate of functional differentiation was later complemented by Georg Simmel's emphatically charged "qualitative individualism." This has consequences for the notion of religion: the individual is not only the locus, but is now also the source of religious experience. Schleiermacher's theory is often (and wrongly) reduced to a sort of religious individualism. Yet before rushing to this conclusion, we would do well to remember that even individualism is a social form. After all, the individual as a locus of appropriation and attribution must be socially accepted and structurally established. This view is inherent in Schleiermacher's communication theory; it was reformulated by Ernst Troeltsch, for whom even "mysticism" counts as a social form alongside of "church" and "sect."

Second, Schleiermacher's introduction of the term "sociability" (*Geselligkeit*) into reflection about religion was another way in which he took the social dimension of religion and religiosity seriously. The social form of "free sociability" (*freie Gesellkeit*) connects the private and the public by taking into account as much as possible the distinctive character of the participants in the process of social communication.

Third, Schleiermacher's church theory provides fertile ground for those subfields of Religious Studies oriented toward the social sciences. His development of a theory of religious association free from the concerns and influence of church politics marked an advance in the analysis of religious organizations.

Fourth, Schleiermacher's theory of religion has potential for understanding the relationship between religion and social theory. Despite the fact that today the anthropological foundation of religion is contested—in my opinion, rightly so, and I hold firmly to the view that sees in religion only a socially necessary element—Schleiermacher supplies a number of important insights we can continue to build upon, especially with respect to the distinctive character of the religious. In particular, if we combine and balance his theory of the constitution of religion with his social and communication theories, such mediation between subjective experience and social communication is one of the main sources for understanding the emergence and reproduction of religion as well as the problem that religion addresses. Such discussions, in my opinion, belong on today's Religious Studies agenda. Schleiermacher clearly must be considered one of the predecessors of modern Religious Studies. And while his thinking is limited by Western, Christian, or even Protestant patterns, the same remains true, *cum grano salis*, for much contemporary scholarship on religion.

The question of how to develop a universal notion of religion that can be applied to both the diachronic and synchronic dimension in the history of religions arises not only in the course of re-reading Schleiermacher, but also in view of contemporary conceptions of religion.

Last but not least, Schleiermacher's theory of religion provides fertile ground for examining the relationship between religion and other societal spheres, especially the process of sacralization in which nonreligious elements take on a religious aura.

In short, Schleiermacher's theory of religion provides—although still in a relatively undifferentiated way—the nucleus for contemporary studies in religion, research that has since developed into various fields like the history of religions, philosophy of religion, psychology of religion, anthropology of religion, and sociology of religion.

"Theologie als Universitätswissenschaft"

Recent German Debates and What They (Could) Learn from Schleiermacher

GEORG PFLEIDERER

1. Background: Recent Debates Over Theological Encyclopedia

Since the beginning of the 1990s, there have been many intense debates surrounding the meaning and function of "Theologie als Universitätswissenschaft"—theology as a university science—in German-speaking countries.[1] These debates, held in both of the major confes-

---

1 See Hans-Michael Baumgartner, "Von der Königin der Wissenschaften zu ihrem Narren? Bemerkungen zur Frage, warum Theologie zur Universität unserer Tage gehört," *Theologische Quartalschrift* 171 (1991): 278-99; Günter Meckenstock and Joachim Ringleben, eds., *Schleiermacher und die wissenchaftliche Kultur des Christentums* (Berlin: Walter de Gruyter, 1991); Johannes Wirsching, "Evangelische Theologie an der Universität: Anmerkungen," *Theologische Quartalschrift* 171 (1991): 299-315; Franz-Xaver Kaufmann, "Theologie zwischen Kirche und Universität," *Theologische Quartalschrift* 171 (1991), 265-77; Wolfgang Frühwald, "Theologie als Wissenschaft: Zum Streit der Fakultäten in der modernen Wissenschaft," in *500 Jahre herzogliches Georgianum: Jubiläumsfeier 10.-14. Dezember 1994*, ed. Reiner Kaczynski (Munich, 1995), 39-53; Hermann Timm, "Die Religion kultivieren: Wozu Theologie an den Universitäten?" *Frankfurter Allgemeine Zeitung*, June 21, 1996; Hermann Timm, "Diesseits des Himmels: Universitätstheologie im Funktionswandel: Wider das muffige Vorverständnis des Studiums," *Das Sonntagsblatt*, October 11, 1996, 20-21; Eilert Herms, "Die Theologie als Wissenschaft und die Theologischen Fakultäten an der Universität," in *Einheit und Kontext: Praktisch-theologische Theoriebildung und Lehre im gesellschaftlichen Umfeld: Festschrift für Peter C. Bloth zum 65. Geburtstag*, ed. Jürgen Henkys and Birgit Weyel (Würzburg: Stephans-Buchhandlung, 1996), 153-85; Matthias Krieg and Martin Rose, eds., *Universitas in theologia—theologia in universitate: Festschrift für Hans Heinrich Schmid zum 60. Geburtstag* (Zurich: Theologischer Verlag, 1997); Peter Neuner and Manfred Weitlauff, eds., *Theologie an der Universität: Zum 525. Stiftungsfest der Ludwig-Maximilians-Universität München* (St. Ottilien: EOS-Verlag, 1997); Ingolf U. Dalferth, ed., *Die Wissenschaften und Gott: Ringvorlesung aus Anlass des 60. Geburtstages des Rektors der Universität Zürich, Prof. Dr. Hans Heinrich Schmid* (Zurich:

Pano, 1998); Pierre Bühler, ed., *Universitäre Theologie in der Schweiz: Die theologischen Fakultäten, ihr Erbe und ihre Herausforderungen* (Neuchâtel: Université de Neuchâtel, 1999); Peter Glotz, "Der Beitrag der Theologischen Fakultäten an den Universitäten angesichts moderner/postmoderner Wissenschaftsverständnisse," in *Kirche in Staat und Gesellschaft*, ed. Bernhard Nacke (Mainz: Matthias-Grünewald-Verlag, 1998), 200-10; Christoph Türcke, "Im Würgegriff der Kirche," *Die Zeit*, January 22, 1998; Heinrich Schmidinger, "Warum gehört die Theologie als Wissenschaft an die Universität?" *Salzburger Theologischer Zeitschrift* 2 (1998): 2-6; Helga Kuhlmann, *Theologie an der Universität? Anmerkungen zu einem andauernden Problem* (Paderborn: Universität Paderborn, 2000); Gerd Lüdemann, *Im Würgegriff der Kirche: Für die Freiheit der theologischen Wissenschaft* (Lüneburg: Zu Klampen, 1998); Wolfgang Beinert, "Universitätstheologie?" *Stimmen der Zeit* 217 (1999): 75-86; Georg Kraus, ed., *Theologie in der Universität: Wissenschaft—Kirche—Gesellschaft: Festschrift zum Jubiläum: 350 Jahre Theologie in Bamberg* (Frankfurt: Peter Lang, 1998); Hans-Richard Reuter, ed., *Theologie in der Universität: Dokumentation einer Tagung im Rahmen des Konsultationsprozesses "Protestantismus und Kultur": Erfurt, 2./3. Juli 1999* (Heidelberg: Forschungsstätte der Evangelischen Studiengemeinschaft, 1999); Helga Kuhlmann, *Theologie an der Universität? Anmerkungen zu einem andauernden Problem* (Paderborn, 2000); Jürgen Werbick: "Was hat die Theologie an den Universitäten zu suchen?" Orientierung 64 (2000): 174-76; Heinrich Schmidinger, "Theologie an staatlichen Universitäten," *Bulletin* 11 (2000): 162-70; Rudolf Langthaler, ed., *Theologie als Wissenschaft: Ein Linzer Symposium* (Frankfurt: Peter Lang, 2000); Christian Albrecht, "Mit Auge und Herz: Für eine Erneuerung der Theologie als Kulturtheorie," *Evangelische Kommentare* 5 (2000): 20-23; Heiner Adamski et al., eds., *Der "Gott" der Fakultäten: Gott der Wissenschaft—Gott, der Wissen schafft?* (Münster: LIT Verlag, 2000); Ulrich Kühn, *Die Theologie im Konzert der Wissenschaften* (Leipzig: S. Hirzel, 2000); Friedrich Wilhelm Graf, "Wozu noch Theologie?" *Frankfurter Allgemeine Zeitung*, August 17, 2000; extended version in Friedrich Wilhelm Graf, *Die Wiederkehr der Götter: Religion in der modernen Kultur* (Munich: C.H. Beck, 2004), 249-78; Georg Pfleiderer, "Welchen Sinn hat es, von Gott zu reden? Vom Nutzen und Nachteil der Theologie für das Leben," *Theologische Zeitschrift* 56 (2000): 359-74; Eberhard Jüngel, "Strukturwandel der Öffentlichkeit: Herausforderung und Chance für die universitäre Theologie," in *Religiöser Pluralismus und das Christentum: Festgabe für Helmut Obst zum 60. Geburtstag*, ed. Michael Bergunder (Göttingen: Vandenhoeck und Ruprecht, 2001), 9-26; Ingolf U. Dalferth, "Theologie im Kontext der Religionswissenschaft: Selbstverständnis, Methoden und Aufgaben der Theologie und ihr Verhältnis zur Religionswissenschaft," *Theologische Literaturzeitung* 126 (2001): 3-20; Klaus Tanner, "Theologie im Kontext der Kulturwissenschaften," *Berliner Theologische Zeitschrift* 19 (2002): 83-98; Peter Neuner, ed., *Glaubenswissenschaft? Theologie im Spannungsfeld von Glaube, Rationalität und Öffentlichkeit* (Freiburg: Herder 2002); Heike Schmoll, "Der Bildungsauftrag der evangelischen Fakultäten," *Zeitschrift für Theologie und Kirche* 99 (2002): 530-44; Friedrich Wilhelm Graf, "Theologie," in *Wozu Geisteswissenschaften? Kontroverse Argumente für eine überfällige Debatte*, ed. Florian Keisinger and Steffen Seischab (Frankfurt: Campus, 2003), 109-16; Hartmut Kress, ed., *Theologische Fakultäten an staatlichen Universitäten* (Waltrop: Hartmut Spenner, 2004); Adrian Loretan, ed., *Theologische Fakultäten an europäischen Universitäten: Rechtliche Situation und theologische Perspektiven* (Münster: LIT Verlag, 2004); Wolfgang Huber, ed., *Was ist gute Theologie?* (Stuttgart: Kreuz, 2004); Petra Bahr, "Protestantische Theologie im Horizont der Kulturwissenschaften," in *Paradigmen und Disziplinen*, vol. 2 of *Handbuch der Kulturwissenschaften*, ed.

sions (Lutheran/Reformed and Catholic), focused on questions regarding the justification of the use of public funds to finance confessional theology at institutions of higher education. What exactly does theology contribute to the *universitas litterarum* today, at the beginning of the twenty-first century? Is it an advantage or rather a disadvantage for the discipline of theology to have its own faculties or departments at universities? How does theology balance its various institutional relationships: its task as a science, its relation to the church, and its relation to the political system and cultural needs of society? Can one still justify funding thirty theological faculties in Germany (in addition to a large number of other theological institutes at universities) with their relatively comfortable student-teacher ratios, compared to many other disciplines within the humanities?[2]

Friedrich Jaeger and Jürgen Straub (Stuttgart: Metzler 2004), 656-70; Ernst-Lüder Sollte, "Aktuelle Rechtsfragen der Theologenausbildung an den Universitäten des Staates," *Zeitschrift für evangelisches Kirchenrecht* 49 (2004): 351-67; Urs Baumann, ed., *Gott im Haus der Wissenschaften: Ein interdisziplinäres Gespräch* (Frankfurt: Lembeck, 2004); Christoph Markschies, "Anleitung zum Ernstnehmen: Was theologische Fakultäten für das Selbstverständnis einer Universität der Zukunft bedeuten," *Zeitzeichen* 8 (2004): 22-24; Patrick Becker and Thomas Gerold, eds., *Die Theologie an der Universität: Eine Standortbestimmung* (Münster: LIT Verlag, 2005); Friederike Nüssel, "Theologie als Kulturwissenschaft," *Theologische Literaturzeitung* 130 (2005): 1153-68; Jörg Dierken, "Restauration—Säkularisierung—Pluralismus: Theologie als Universitätswissenschaft angesichts religionskultureller Veränderungen," in *500 Jahre Theologie in Hamburg: Hamburg als Zentrum christlicher Theologie und Kultur zwischen Tradition und Zukunft*, ed. Johann Anselm Steiger (Berlin: Walter de Gruyter, 2005), 399-419; Hartmut Meesmann, "Kampf an vielen Fronten: Die theologischen Fakultäten an Deutschlands Universitäten stehen unter starkem Druck," *Zeitzeichen* 6, no. 10 (2005): 20-22; Reinhold Bernhardt, "Theologie an der Universität unter Rechtfertigungsdruck: Eine Basler Perspektive," *Informationes theologiae Europae— Internationales ökumenisches Jahrbuch für Theologie* 14 (2005): 9-27; Ulrich Schnabel and Martin Spiewak, "Götter und Gelehrte," *Die Zeit*, December 28, 2006; Ingolf U. Dalferth, ed., *Eine Wissenschaft oder viele? Die Einheit evangelischer Theologie in der Sicht ihrer Disziplinen* (Leipzig: Evangelische Verlagsanstalt, 2006); Helmut Hoping, ed., *Universität ohne Gott? Theologie im Haus der Wissenschaften* (Freiburg: Herder, 2007); Kirchenamt der Evangelischen Kirche in Deutschland, ed., *Die Bedeutung der wissenschaftlichen Theologie für Kirche, Hochschule und Gesellschaft* (Hannover: Kirchenamt der EKD, 2007); Folkart Wittekind, "Das Verhältnis von Theologie und Kirche" (lecture, Schleiermacher Forschungssymposion, Wittenberg, September, 2008); Martin Laube, "Das Wesen des Christentum als Organisationsprinzip der Theologie: Überlegungen im Anschluss an die 'Kurze Darstellung' Friedrich Schleiermachers" (lecture, Schleiermacher Forschungssymposion, Wittenberg, September, 2008).—If not noted otherwise, all translations of German quotations into English are mine.—

2 There are eighteen Protestant theological faculties at German universities: Berlin, Bochum, Bonn, Erlangen, Greifswald, Göttingen, Halle, Hamburg, Heidelberg, Jena, Kiel, Leipzig, Mainz, Marburg, München, Münster, Rostock, and Tübingen. Roman Catholic theological faculties are found at twelve public universities: Augsburg,

Such questions, emerging from the particular history and institutionalization of theology in Germany, Switzerland, and Austria, have typically been connected to theoretical discussions concerning the specific shape and purpose of theology: What kind of theology is practical for the professional needs of future pastors? What kind of theology or religious studies is suitable for addressing the contemporary religious needs of society? Is theology a particular subject within the humanities, is it a cultural science, or is it a science of the church and for the church (alone)? What are the differences between theology and religious studies, and what is the relationship between these fields of study? Moreover, how do the traditional basis and relative autonomy of theological faculties, with their curricula designed for the training of future pastors, square with the fact that the growing majority of students enrolled in theological faculties do not become pastors, but instead become either teachers of religion at public schools or pursue professions of an entirely different nature? How does and how will the ongoing decline of church membership and the diminishing public influence of the churches, on the one hand, and a resurgence of religion, on the other, affect the theological faculties? What can theology itself do to influence such developments?

It is probable—and frequently noted in the literature—that these debates and the commotion they demonstrate are, to a certain extent, reactions to the serious political and economic pressure theological faculties have experienced during the last years. The once sizeable theological faculties of Berlin, Tübingen, and Göttingen have each lost about a third of their chairs. In many German states the governments have developed and partly executed plans to reduce the number of theological faculties and theological units by closing or merging them.[3]

Bamberg, Bochum, Bonn, Freiburg, Mainz, München, Münster, Passau, Regensburg, Tübingen, and Würzburg. There are three seminaries run by the Protestant churches: (Bielefeld-)Bethel, Neuendettelsau, and Wuppertal. Roman Catholic seminaries are in Benediktbeuern, Erfurt, Frankfurt, Fulda, München, Paderborn, St. Georgen, Trier, Vallendar; and one entire university: Eichstätt. In Switzerland, Protestant theological faculties are integral parts of the public universities in Basel, Bern (shared with the Old Catholic faculty) and Zurich; in the French-speaking part of Switzerland the (former) faculties of Geneva, Lausanne, and Neuchâtel have founded a corporate network. Roman Catholic faculties are located in Freiburg, Lugano, and Lucerne, and there is a Roman Catholic seminary in Chur. In Austria, there is one Protestant theological faculty in Vienna and there are Roman Catholic faculties at the four universities of Graz, Innsbruck, Salzburg, and Vienna.

3   This occurred, for instance, in Hamburg, Schleswig-Holstein, Mecklenburg-Vorpommern, Nordrhein-Westfalen, and even in the conservative southern states of Baden-Württemberg and Bavaria. Some of the possible negative effects of combined faculty networks can be observed in the French speaking part of Switzerland. The in-

I hasten to add that most of these plans were never supported by arguments referring to the epistemological legitimacy of theology as a university science. Rather, the arguments put forward were usually statistical in nature, i.e., focused on student-professor ratios. It is a fact that between 1985 and 2005, Protestant theological faculties lost about fifty percent of their students (going from around 16,000 to around 8,000 students).[4] At the same time, theological faculties and leaders in the German Evangelical Church have on several occasions reminded politicians and presidents of universities that this decline was only a restoration of the situation of the early 1970s.[5] It is not likely that the relevant theological debates received much notice from the politicians who executed the sanctions in question. Only a small number of such debates were held in the public arena, and even these were conducted and attended almost exclusively by theologians. The majority of these debates unfolded in the rather specialized realm of theological publications. Those from other departments (usually within the humanities) who did engage in these theoretical debates were usually sympathetic with theology.[6] Those less sympathetic to theology—no doubt a large group—probably just stood aside and ignored the debates.[7]

---

ter-university theological faculty of Geneva, Neuchâtel, and Lausanne seems to have developed a tendency to threaten the future of the smaller locations (Neuchâtel, perhaps also Lausanne).

4   The numbers refer (only) to those students who study Protestant theology as a subject to qualify for the pastoral profession in the established regional churches. Currently at most theological faculties, this number of students is surpassed by those studying theology as a major or minor in masters or diploma studies to qualify for a teaching position in public schools. The systematic theologian Hermann Timm, formerly at Munich, has often argued that the traditional concepts of academic theology usually overlook this growing group among its recipients (Timm, "Die Religion kultivieren," 41).

5   In comparison to other fields in the university, theological faculties often had a rather comfortable student-professor ratio, as Friedrich Wilhelm Graf has pointed out using statistics from around 1900. See Friedrich Wilhelm Graf, "Rettung der Persönlichkeit: Protestantische Theologie als Kulturwissenschaft des Christentums," in *Kultur und Kulturwissenschaften um 1900: Krise der Moderne und Glaube an die Wissenschaft*, ed. Rüdiger vom Bruch, Friedrich Wilhelm Graf, and Gangolf Hübinger (Wiesbaden: Steiner, 1989), 103-31, esp. 104.

6   See, for example, Wolfgang Frühwald, "Theologie als Wissenschaft"; or Hermann Lübbe, "Theologie als christliche Religionskulturwissenschaft," in Krieg, *Universitas in theologia*, 43-50, esp. 48.

7   "Offers" of unfriendly takeovers of theological chairs by colleagues from other faculties are extremely rare. I personally know of only one case: a professor for media sciences in Bern suggested in a radio interview, which was printed in many Swiss newspapers, that the theological faculties (of both the Catholic and the Reformed confessions) should give sixty of their approximately ninety total chairs to media

Sophisticated internal debates in theological circles might not be a very promising reaction to the strong economic and political pressure now bearing down upon the theological faculties. Intellectual navel-gazing may also not be the best way of demonstrating the academic potential and fruitfulness of a particular university discipline for addressing and solving actual societal problems. Nevertheless, the questions raised in these debates are of vital importance to theology's self-understanding as a university discipline and its future in general. It is also clear that the problems theology is facing at present in German-speaking countries are intimately connected with various changes in political institutions that have occurred in the last few years—especially within the system of higher education, but also in religious institutions. For this reason, theology must deal with its status within the *universitas litterarum* by employing a wide range of epistemological, philosophical, historical, and sociological methods. It is the peculiar task of Protestant academic theology to weave together a coherent image of all of these strands of contemporary (Protestant) Christianity—and of itself within that frame—and to make proposals for the vital transformations to come. Precisely this understanding of the encyclopedic task of theology is the one most closely associated with the name of Friedrich Daniel Ernst Schleiermacher.

2. Phases of Encyclopedic Schleiermacherianism

It was Johann Jakob Semler's famous distinction between religion and theology that laid the groundwork for a complex, encyclopedic self-understanding of theology within an essentially modern conception of

---

studies, since such a displacement would equalize the immense difference in the student-teacher ratios between the two disciplines. Such a transfer would also be appropriate, he added, because it was not theology but media studies that was the competent interpreter of religion in its present stage—as, for example, the death of pope John Paul II had shown. If theologians were not willing to perform such an act of Christian charity, the media sciences would find other ways to keep the proposal in public discussion. See Christian Mensch, "Medienprofessoren, die neuen Theologen?" *Basler Zeitung*, April 11, 2005. Also recall the smug comment by Peter Glotz, a German intellectual and player in recent educational politics: "I do understand that some professors [of the humanities] complain about having fifty theses on their desk to revise, while the professor of theology has plenty of time to delve into Jesus." Quoted in "'Viele verschulden sich eher für ein Haus als für ihren Kopf': Interview mit Peter Glotz," *Basler Zeitung*, February 10, 2004.

Christianity.⁸ In Schleiermacher's *Brief Outline of the Study of Theology*,⁹ the challenges facing theological epistemology under the conditions of modernity receive their classic formulation, as do their proposed solutions.¹⁰ Schleiermacher's differentiated correlation of the three theological disciplines—philosophical, historical, and practical—is a result of his functional connection of academic theology to the church, specifically to the task of church governance or leadership. To perform that function adequately, an understanding of the church in its three essential dimensions is necessary.¹¹ The church must be conceived on the foundation of a general theory of man, reason, and society, one that contains the normative principles of religious association. Schleiermacher called this general fundamental theory "ethics" and defined it as the "science of the principles of history."¹² Moreover, he grounded philosophical ethics in an even more fundamental theory of "scientific construction,"¹³ which he called *Dialektik*, or "the art of conducting a conversation."¹⁴

While Schleiermacher's understanding of theology as a function of church leadership turned out to be convincing for both admirers and opponents of his theology during the nineteenth and twentieth centuries, his understanding of ethics and dialectics as foundational disciplines of (and prior to) theology was not. For many subsequent theologians, such grounding procedures shipwrecked on the rock—or rather, sunk in the quicksand—of the nineteenth century's relentless historicization of ideas and values (Schleiermacher's comparatively high awareness of the problems history causes for truth claims notwith-

---

8   See Hans-Eberhard Hess, *Theologie und Religion bei Johann Salomo Semler: Ein Beitrag zur Theologiegeschichte des 18. Jahrhunderts* (Augsburg: Blasaditsch, 1974); Botho Ahlers, *Die Unterscheidung von Theologie und Religion: Ein Beitrag zur Vorgeschichte der praktischen Theologie im 18. Jahrhundert* (Gütersloh: Gütersloher Verlagshaus, 1980).
9   Friedrich Schleiermacher, *Kurze Darstellung des theologischen Studiums zum Behuf einleitender Vorlesungen* (1811/1830), ed. Dirk Schmid (Berlin: Walter de Gruyter, 2002); *Brief Outline of Theology as a Field of Study*, trans. Terrence N. Tice (Lewiston, NY: Edwin Mellen, 1988).
10 The relationship between Schleiermacher's definition of theology as a "function of the church" and Semler's distinction between theology and religion was explicated clearly by Folkart Wittekind in a lecture entitled "Das Verhältnis von Theologie und Kirche" delivered at the Schleiermacher Forschungssymposion in Wittenberg in September, 2008.
11 See Markus Schröder, *Die kritische Identität des neuzeitlichen Christentums: Schleiermachers Wesensbestimmung der christlichen Religion* (Tübingen: Mohr-Siebeck 1996).
12 Schleiermacher, *Kurze Darstellung*, 71.
13 Friedrich Schleiermacher, *Vorlesungen über die Dialektik*, KGA II/10.1, 80.
14 Ibid., 219.

standing).¹⁵ This twofold conviction is also the hidden commonality between the antithetical theological positions of Adolf von Harnack and Karl Barth, as can be observed in their famous public correspondence of 1923.¹⁶ These documents demonstrate in exemplary fashion that neither the leading historicist theologians, such as Adolf von Harnack or Ernst Troeltsch, nor the anti-historicists, such as the dialectical theologians Karl Barth or Friedrich Gogarten, were willing to reformulate a program as idealistic as Schleiermacherian "ethics" and "dialectics"—that is to say (and as they understood it): a general, rational, all-integrative theory or meta-theory of knowledge, science, history, and society. In light of advanced historicism and the profound cultural crisis caused by the catastrophe of World War I, such theories seemed no longer possible; from now on, all such attempts suffered from an irreducible "positionality."¹⁷

In contemporary German debates about theological encyclopedia, Schleiermacher is frequently invoked; his *Brief Outline* is oft quoted. This fact illustrates a larger shift towards Schleiermacher within recent German Protestant theology. Nowadays, even Eberhard Jüngel and Wolfgang Huber,¹⁸ once well-known proponents of those early twen-

---

15 A nuanced criticism of Schleiermacher's speculative-historical approach to defining the essence of Christianity was presented by Martin Laube at the September 2008 Wittenberg Schleiermacher Forschungssymposion: "This research [developed by Schleiermacher] is connected to the presupposition of a speculative conceptual frame that is itself abstracted from historical reflection. Schleiermacher unrolls a methodology of the conceptualization of the essence of Christianity that does reflect on the historicity of its object but does not reflect on the historicity of this perspective itself. Thus he is able to abide by a stable distinction between historical genesis and normative meaning, but he reduces insight into the historical character not only of the object of theology but also of theology itself" (Laube, "Das Wesen des Christentums," 16).

16 See Johanna Jantsch, ed., *Der Briefwechsel zwischen Adolf v. Harnack und Martin Rade: Theologie auf dem öffentlichen Markt* (Berlin: Walter de Gruyter, 1996).

17 In the generation of the dialectical theologians, the great exception to this rule is, of course, Paul Tillich. In 1923, he sketched a theory of science that claimed to provide a universal, integrative system in which the scientific place and function of theology was precisely defined. See Paul Tillich, "Das System der Wissenschaften nach Gegenständen und Methoden," in *Philosophical Writings/Philosophische Schriften*, ed. Gunther Wenz, vol. 1 of *Main Works/Hauptwerke* (Berlin: Walter de Gruyter, 1989), 113-265. It is worth noting that he did not repeat this attempt in his later years.

18 Huber uses Schleiermacher's definition of theology as a function of church governance to delegitimize understandings of academic theology "that do not care for the relationship to the church but intend to decipher the phenomenon of religion in past and present." Quoted in "'Die Leute trauen sich ja in die Kirche': Ein Gespräch mit dem Ratsvorsitzenden der Evangelischen Kirche in Deutschland, Bischof Wolfgang Huber, über Tradition, Rechtstreue und Glaubensstärke," *Frankfurter Allgemeine Zei-*

tieth-century movements that initiated the turn against Schleiermacher, invoke Schleiermacherian ideas.[19] Nevertheless, the Schleiermacherianism of present Protestant efforts to formulate a viable theological encyclopedia appears to have its distinct limits, for it is difficult to name any theological book published in roughly the last thirty years that could be taken as a reformulation of Schleiermacher's attempt at a twofold grounding of theology upon foundational theories of mind and society, as outlined in the dialectics and ethics, respectively.[20]

Even if mainstream academic theology is not anti-foundationalist in a post-modern sense, it has taken on more of the skepticism of that second peak of debates over theological encyclopedias, which occurred some eighty or one hundred years ago, than might at first glance be evident. There is a broad *de facto* consensus that such a general, founda-

---

tung, February 27, 2006. For a similar criticism of contemporary neo-Protestant theologies of culture, see Dalferth, "Theologie im Kontext der Religionswissenschaft," 116. An interpretation that is rather more sympathetic to Schleiermacher is offered by Folkart Wittekind, who argues that the reference of theology to the church should be understood by virtue of the "general function of the church in the cultural life of society" (Wittekind, "Das Verhältnis von Theologie und Kirche," 11).

19 Strict and orthodox Barthian attitudes toward fundamental theology have become very rare, if not completely extinct. Although concepts of revelation are at work as theological principles in many systematic theologies, probably no German-speaking university theologian today would defend rigorously Barthian positions such as the principled rejection of any kind of apologetic theology as "natural theology." On the other hand, it is of course reasonable to question the legitimacy of many of the contemporary attempts to behave as "Schleiermacherians of a higher order." The legitimacy of claiming this legacy can be doubted at least in those cases in which systematic theology is defined narrowly as a theory of speech about the reality of God and its truth, reducing all elements of a Schleiermacherian theory of consciousness to the formal assertion that the reality his theory deals with would, of course, only be reality as it is perceived through Christian belief.

20 Saying this might do injustice to at least two of the most elaborate theological writers of the recent past, Wolfhart Pannenberg and Eilert Herms, the latter of whom explicitly intends to build on Schleiermacher's legacy. Both theologians have contributed significantly to debates about theology as a university science, and both of their programs can be understood as advanced theological systems based upon a fundamental and integral theory of science, reason, man, and society, supplied with claims to universal validity. Each, however, tries to integrate basic insights of modern anti-foundationalism by invoking the scientific fallacy: Pannenberg, via a theory of anticipation; Herms, with reference to epistemological pluralism in the tradition of William James. It must be noted that Herms can on this basis plead for a "transition to a true multiculturalism" (see Herms, "Die Theologie als Wissenschaft," 182). Nevertheless, both theories represent a theological foundationalism and attempt at theoretical integration that has become very rare in the past few decades. Relative to various kinds of mainstream theology, both systems would probably best be described as "outstanding" in the twofold sense of the word: prominent and quite lonely.

tional, and integrative theory is no longer possible, and that a theology that claims to rest on the grounds of science no longer requires such an ambitious theoretical foundation. Indeed, since the days of Pannenberg's *Wissenschaftstheorie* (1977),[21] no German-speaking Protestant theologian has attempted to reformulate a general theory of science as the foundation for theology as a "Universitätswissenschaft." And even among the few theologians who still make efforts to relate theology to a general theory of science, knowledge, and society, the prevailing insight is that theology has to deal with the empirical difference between the "Christian culture" (*christliche Gesamtkultur*) and the "public culture of an ethos of pure reason."[22] "Therefore the persistence [of public theological faculties] demonstrates the fact that Christian culture is generally accepted as a culture that up until now has neither been suppressed nor taken over or brought into line by the [public] culture of an ethos of pure reason."[23]

In sum, recent theological debates are largely marked by a pragmatic eclecticism concerning the use of philosophical theories of science. Epistemological debates such as those engaged in by Heinrich Scholz and Karl Barth in the early 1930s[24] regarding the minimal scientific standards to which theology must submit are nowadays scarcely reproduced in Protestant theology.[25] Instead, it is often argued that theology can demonstrate its scientific character simply by employing widely acknowledged methods from the humanities and thereby contribute competently to debates of general scientific interest and, in so doing, to debates of general social interest.

---

21   Wolfhart Pannenberg, *Wissenschaftstheorie und Theologie* (Frankfurt: Suhrkamp, 1977).
22   Herms, "Die Theologie als Wissenschaft," 182.
23   Ibid.
24   See Heinrich Scholz, "Wie ist eine evangelische Theologie als Wissenschaft möglich?" *Zwischen den Zeiten* 9 (1931): 8-35; reprinted in Gerhard Sauter, ed., *Theologie als Wissenschaft: Aufsätze und Thesen* (Munich: Kaiser, 1971), 212-64; Karl Barth, *Die Lehre vom Wort Gottes: Prolegomena zur Kirchlichen Dogmatik*, vol. 1/1 of *Kirchliche Dogmatik*, 10th ed. (Zurich: Theologischer Verlag, 1981); Heinrich Scholz, "Was ist unter einer theologischen Aussage zu verstehen?" in *Theologische Aufsätze: Karl Barth zum 50. Geburtstag* (Munich: Kaiser, 1936), 25-37; reprinted in Sauter, *Theologie als Wissenschaft*, 265-78.
25   Cf., however, the article by philosopher and Catholic theologian Hans Michael Baumgartner, "Von der Königin der Wissenschaften," 284-85.

3. Theology as "Orientierungswissenschaft"

To be precise, it is not Schleiermacher's fundamental philosophy as such—that is to say, it is not his claim to offer a foundational, integrative, systematic theory of the humanities—that makes him attractive for present debates. Rather, it is the fumbling and almost essayistic character of his various efforts. In contrast to his idealistic contemporaries Fichte, Hegel, and Schelling, Schleiermacher actually never published an entire and universal theoretical system of mind, science, and society. His dialectics and his ethics are works in progress, not only in the formal sense of being unpublished lectures with many changes and corrections between their various presentations.[26] They also exemplify a much more open, dialogical, and hermeneutical style of thinking than his contemporaries' stunning, yet "closed," systems. And what was then considered by many philosophical observers to be a handicap, nowadays turns out to be an advantage. Schleiermacher's fundamental philosophy of self, mind, and society is developed enough to work as a foundational theory of religion, religious communication, and religious congregations in modern societies, but it is also open enough to leave space for different theories and for the historical developments of the religious system. This is to my eyes the reason for his attractiveness in the aforementioned debates about theology's status in the university, at least for Protestant theologians. Schleiermacher is widely praised for having laid the groundwork for a truly historical understanding of religion and Christianity, one that is, at the same time, intrinsically guided by a normative understanding of the social self-realization of individual human freedom. Thus, Schleiermacher seems to provide the classical theory for the twofold needs of theology under the conditions of an advanced modernity: on the one hand, insight into the irreducible particularity of Christianity and the multitude of its social forms in both historical and contemporary perspectives; on the other hand, the reference to normative religious truth claims and to the necessity of dealing with religious pluralism in a productive way. Schleiermacher is thus an important resource for many contemporary attempts to re-conceive theology as an academic "Orientierungswissenschaft,"[27] as a science offering normative intellectual orientation, proceeding explicitly on the

---

26 This is not so different from many works of his contemporary Idealist colleagues.
27 See, for example, Peter Janich, ed., *Humane Orientierungswissenschaft: Was leisten verschiedene Wissenschaftskulturen für das Verständnis menschlicher Lebenswelt?* (Würzburg: Königshausen und Neumann, 2008); and Walter Sparn, "Theologie als kulturwissenschaftliche Disziplin an der Universität," in Reuter, *Theologie in der Universität*, 90-109, esp. 93.

grounds of the humanities after their cultural turn.[28] In a paradigmatic way, Schleiermacher developed theology as a "power of judgment in religious matters,"[29] and thereby demonstrated the particular "mandate of education"[30] pertaining to Protestant theological faculties in public universities.

The fruitfulness of Schleiermacher's theories for the present debates over theological encyclopedia can be demonstrated by examining three controversial issues:

1. the (supposedly) alternative understandings of theology as either cultural science (i.e., belonging to the humanities) or as a science in the service of church doctrine;
2. the difference between theology and religious studies and their relationship to each other; and
3. the functional differences between the tasks of academic university theology and those of the theology of church governance.

Ad 1: An extensive and controversial aspect of current debates in Protestant theology deals with the alternative self-conceptions of theology: is theology to be understood as belonging to the humanities or as a reflection of Christian church doctrine? This question is often debated very polemically. Nevertheless, even very resolute defenders of a conception of theology as a cultural science typically also acknowledge the importance of organized Christianity for the continued existence of academic theology and the formulation of some of the normative tasks of theology. If from such perspectives academic theology is defined as a description of lived (Christian) religion, usually a particular kind of "thick description" is meant that intends to offer critical (and therefore always somehow normative) reflection to the agents behind such practices. Drawing on Paul Tillich,[31] Friedrich Wilhelm Graf coined the term "theology as normative *Kulturwissenschaft*"[32] — as a normative cultural science. If Eberhard Jüngel, on the other hand, pleads for a self-conception of theology as a "foolish" science on its own terms — and of

---

28 See the following two informative studies: Bahr, "Protestantische Theologie im Horizont der Kulturwissenschaften," 656; and Nüssel, "Theologie als Kulturwissenschaft."

29 "Theologische Wissenschaft muss die Urteilsfähigkeit in Religionsdingen stärken," in Dierken, "Restauration—Säkularisierung—Pluralismus," 403.

30 Schmoll, "Der Bildungsauftrag der evangelischen Fakultäten," 535-36.

31 Tillich characterizes theology as "normative Religionswissenschaft" (religious studies in a normative perspective). Paul Tillich, "Über die Idee einer Theologie der Kultur" in *Die religiöse Substanz der Kultur*, ed. Renate Albrecht, vol. 9 of *Gesammelte Werke* (Stuttgart: Evangelisches Verlagswerk, 1967), 13-31, esp. 14.

32 See Graf, "Theologie," 115; and Graf, "Rettung der Persönlichkeit," 117-20.

theologians as the "the fools" among the scientists[33]—he doesn't thereby simply reproduce Karl Barth's total refusal to hold theology accountable to the standards of the human sciences, but rather engages in a hermeneutics that develops the essentially public character of theological debates and truth claims, thus benefitting enormously from the "great Schleiermacher."[34] Such examples may indicate that the true issue at stake in this dispute is not primarily the question of a fundamental choice between science and theology, but the question of how to conceive the relationship between them properly.[35] "Professional theologians especially must be able to look beyond the horizon of Christianity . . . , to be able to identify its essence distinctively in contrast to other religions, and to be able to distinguish religion as such from a [mere] aberration of cultural life;"[36] therefore, "the cultural meaning of theology and its reference to the church are not a contradiction."[37]

Ad 2: It is relatively easy to explain on Schleiermacherian grounds why the difference between theology and religious studies is both necessary and easily misunderstood. Simple binary distinctions between "insider" participants in religion and objective, presuppositionless "outsiders," or between theologians as "religious experts" and religious studies scholars as "experts in religion"[38] are, as recent debates have often shown, misleading for both disciplines—even if numerous scholars in our countries, especially in religious studies, still enjoy them.[39] There is, as Schleiermacher has shown in a paradigmatic way, no theology without a concept of religion and without historical and empirical

---

33 See Jüngel, "Strukturwandel der Öffentlichkeit," 22-26, esp. 24.
34 Ibid., 21.
35 Sometimes Schleiermacher is accused of having an all-too practical understanding of theology and its encyclopedic unity. Nevertheless, it is not just the "function of [pastoral] education" ("Ausbildungsfunktion"—see Baumgartner, "Von der Königin der Wissenschaften zu ihrem Narren?" 281) that constitutes the aim and unity of theology. Schleiermacher understands theology as "the program that steers the historical development of the essence of Christianity. . . . It is the aim of theology as a science to 'improve' Christianity in its respective cultural context" (Wittekind, "Das Verhältnis von Theologie und Kirche," 13).
36 Dierken, "Restauration—Säkularisierung—Pluralismus," 415-16.
37 Ibid., 417.
38 Hans-Jürgen Greschat, *Was ist Religionswissenschaft?* (Stuttgart: Kohlhammer, 1988), 129.
39 See the differentiated argumentation, for example, in Sparn, "Theologie als kulturwissenschaftliche Disziplin," 99, 103; Andreas Feldtkeller, "Religionswissenschaft innerhalb und ausserhalb der Theologie," in *Die Identität der Religionswissenschaft: Beiträge zum Verständnis einer unbekannten Disziplin*, ed. Gebhard Löhr (Frankfurt: Peter Lang, 2000), 79-96; and Dalferth, "Theologie im Kontext der Religionswissenschaft," 8-9.

studies of religion, particularly of one's own religion, and there is likewise no scientific concept of religion that is exempt from the particular historical-religious tradition in which it was coined. Representatives of religious studies and of the sociology of religion such as Joachim Matthes and Friedrich Tenbruck have convincingly rearticulated this important insight of Schleiermacher.[40] Following Schleiermacher, theology is able to interpret its obligation to specific interests of intellectual knowledge as an obligation of reflected "positionality,"[41] a condition no longer regarded as inferior to the supposedly "value-free" sciences and humanities.

Ad 3: A complex and nuanced relationship between academic and church theology is, as is well-known, at the heart of Schleiermacher's understanding of theology as presented in the *Brief Outline*. His central insight that theology is a "function of the church" presupposes a concept of the church that combines empirical and speculative, individual and collective, and functional and material aspects in a very artful manner. Theologically informed church leadership is, as Markus Schröder has clearly shown, a *praxis* guided by a complex of concepts pertaining to the historical and systematic essence of Christianity—an essence that in a certain sense always lies in the future.[42] To realize this concretely, the two constitutive forms of theology, namely, academic reflection and practical action, must cooperate.

In German-speaking countries, the gap between academic theology, on the one hand, and the theology practiced by church governments, pastors, and teachers of religion, on the other, has widened remarkably during the last decades—at least in the eyes of many representatives of the churches. Theologians who in their formative years were nourished on the thick bread of Barthian "God-talk" have difficulties understanding the benefits of a contemporary theology conceived as the critical analysis of empirical religious practice. Not infrequently do popular theologies of an older kind—or those formed as "homemade" products of regional church governments—try to bridge or reduce that gap. Such theological productions certainly provide materials upon which aca-

---

40 See Joachim Matthes, "Auf der Suche nach dem 'Religiösen': Reflexionen zu Theorie und Empirie religionssoziologischer Forschung," *Sociologica Internationalis* 30 (1992): 129-42; and Friedrich H. Tenbruck, "Die Religion im Maelstrom der Reflexion," in *Religion und Kultur*, ed. Alois Hahn, Jörg Bergmann, and Thomas Luckmann (Opladen: Westdeutscher Verlag für Sozialwissenschaften, 1993), 31-67.

41 Falk Wagner, "Funktionalität der Theologie und Positivität der Frömmigkeit," in Meckenstock and Ringleben, *Schleiermacher und die wissenschaftliche Kultur*, 291-309, esp. 294.

42 Schröder, *Die kritische Identität*, 111.

demic theology can perform its critical task.⁴³ It was once again Friedrich Schleiermacher who developed a highly differentiated theory concerning the relations between theology's "scientific" and "ecclesial" interests. Indeed, his concept of the "ideal church leader" was, as Christoph Dinkel has recently shown,⁴⁴ path-breaking, and its accurate application and further development might disclose deficiencies on both sides of the gap.

4. Remedy for a Theology under Pressure

The philosopher Hermann Lübbe, a friendly observer of the self-reflexive theological debates outlined above, has pointed out that the best argument for the presence of theology at public universities is the ongoing necessity of its task to keep the "cultural history of Christianity" present in the humanities and in society.⁴⁵ Friedrich Wilhelm Graf puts it in a similar way:

> Financial investments in theology's interpretive competence are only profitable for a European society if it has a clear interest in a constructive extrapolation of its historically Christian origins. For those who wish for the decline of Christianity and are fond of the evident crises of the churches, there is no need for academic theology. As the normative cultural study of Christianity, it's a fact that Christian theology refers to an actual interest in Christianity.⁴⁶

Thus, so long as such an interest is in fact shared by a considerable part of the society, even a secular state should be disposed to finance such an intellectual endeavor. Indeed, modern democracies should for their own sakes be interested in "good theology."⁴⁷ For "amidst a world virtually reeking with religious dispositions, the rational stabilization of religious energies that otherwise might erupt irrationally is one of the [eminent] tasks of theology and church."⁴⁸

---

43 It is nevertheless not productive to denounce those productions totally as "theology lite." Their aptness for describing the varieties, complexities, and contradictions of religion as lived today varies greatly. Not all of them are written from behind the blinders of a church-insider or from a "feel-good" religious perspective.
44 Christoph Dinkel, *Kirche gestalten — Schleiermachers Theorie des Kirchenregiments* (Berlin: Walter de Gruyter, 1996).
45 Lübbe, "Theologie als christliche Religionskulturwissenschaft," 48.
46 Graf, "Theologie," 115.
47 Huber, *Was ist gute Theologie?*
48 Frühwald, "Theologie als Wissenschaft," 50.

Schleiermacher provides an unsurpassed description of theology's multifaceted task and a classic answer to some of the problems that confront our admittedly far more complex contemporary cultural situation. The outstanding quality of Schleiermacher's theory of theology, i.e., his "encyclopedia," stems from his distinctive combination of epistemological reflection with a sociology of knowledge grounded in a flexible theory of modernity. It demonstrates its particular strength today by virtue of its ability to help us understand the motivations of Christianity's despisers as well as of those sympathetic with (Protestant) Christian religion. From Schleiermacher's perspective, both groups operate on the basis of ideas about the adequate form of the realization of individual communicative freedom in the present stage of modernity. Protestant theology must show its ability to proceed on this ground; Schleiermacher enables it to do so.

Schleiermacher and the Prospects for a Transcendental-Anthropological Theory of Religion

Feeling as a Key Notion in a Transcendental Conception of Religion

SERGIO SORRENTINO

1.

In this essay, I would like to focus my attention on Schleiermacher's interpretation of religion. In the *Speeches* Schleiermacher develops an anthropological theory of religion that aims at recognizing the transcendental constitution of religious experience. According to this theory, religion is conceived as establishing a specific region of human experience and as something human beings do. On this view, the entire person takes part in an experience that is not enclosed within the circle of subjectivity, but is rather referred to a term outside the subject, so to speak, namely, to a reality that offers itself up to be experienced. Eighteenth-century debates among deists, skeptics, and rational theists commonly presupposed on all sides that religion is a system of factual beliefs with immense moral significance. At stake in such debates were issues such as which beliefs are essential to religion, whether or not the essential beliefs are rationally defensible, and whether or not the essential beliefs really have the morally beneficial consequences attributed to them. The Christian apologist was expected to show that Christian beliefs are essential and true, or at least that they could not be rationally refuted, and that civic virtue would collapse without them. Kant's critical philosophy transformed this debate by moving the idea of God out of the domain of theoretical knowledge and giving it the status of a moral postulate. Schleiermacher, however, introduced two theoretical shifts to these traditional paradigms (the rationalistic and the supernaturalistic) for understanding religion.

The first shift contests the supernaturalistic paradigm by contending that religion is essentially an experience, more specifically, a lived experience that involves the whole of the subject in her innermost being. Religion, therefore, cannot be reduced to external or extrinsic motivations and factors, such as the transmission of information (e.g., a *notitia Dei*) or a body of doctrine, moral and social customs, or the practices of particular traditions and communities. Insofar as religious experience deals with reality (*Wirklichkeit* in Kantian terms), namely, with the one reality an individual is concerned with, its primary content is neither the conceptual ordering of our mind nor the projections of our moral striving. Rather, religious experience brings one into direct contact with a region of reality that is distinct from all other regions. Religion, then, does not exist for any purpose or serve any domain of human experience other than that which it itself brings about. Indeed, religion has an inner principle, a ground proper to it, whose unique constitution we must attempt to grasp. Such a conception of religion, moreover, includes two important features: first, the reality to which our experience refers is *one* (yet distinguishable into distinct regions); second, this one reality contains a reference to transcendence that de-centers the subject of religious experience.

The second shift introduced by Schleiermacher contests the rationalistic stance of much Enlightenment thinking about religion. Schleiermacher argues that religion is essentially distinct from other relationships to reality found in human experience. It is a specific, peculiar way to get in touch with reality, indeed, one that a person cannot generate from and by herself. It is so specific and peculiar that it comprises and establishes contact with a "totally other" reality (*das ganz Andere*). In this alternative to rationalism, one must seek religion within an original connection set up by our existence, that is, within a fundamental, existential relation, in which two existing subjects or terms relate to each other asymmetrically. Here again, religion is conceived as an experience that de-centers the human subject engaged in it. This original, existential relationship brings about a peculiar experience of reality constituted by an irreducible intentionality proper to it.

Schleiermacher draws the conclusion that what the "cultured despisers" despise is not religion, but dogmas and customary practices—only the husks and not the kernel, a mere echo and not the original sound of lived religious experience. However, what many defenders of religion are defending is not genuine religion either, since they make of it a mere prop for morals and social institutions. Rather, religion has a sphere of its own that it can maintain only if it renounces all claims to anything that belongs either to knowledge or to morality. To make the idea of God the apex of science, for instance, is not the religious way of having God. Similarly, to make religion a matter of good behavior is to miss its true, passive nature; religion is not human activity, but a being acted upon by God. If human nature is not to be truncated, religion must be allowed to take its place as an indispensable third alongside knowing and doing.

2.

To better understand this conception of religion, which matured gradually over the course of Schleiermacher's career, we must attend to its central category, "feeling." Indeed, Schleiermacher developed the notion of "feeling" precisely in order to explain religious experience. "Feeling" emphasizes the fact that religion (i.e., human religious experience) is not constituted by a "self positing itself," but has to be referred to a "self being posited." This, however, does not imply that religion belongs to a field of experience inaccessible to concepts. Instead, we might say that concepts (associated with the *intellectus*) that intrude upon religious fields of experience make up one of the levers Schleiermacher used to carry out his hermeneutical effort in the field of religious experience. Actually, feeling, taken as a transcendental structure constitutive of religious experience, is a mode of human existence; it is not a specific faculty, but is at the root of the play among faculties. Religious experience, as Douglas Hedley puts it, is "affective rather than cognitive, an ecstatic mood of apprehending eternal deity."[1]

When we approach the basic concepts of Schleiermacher's thought, there are two reasons to be very cautious. First, these basic terms must be analyzed in light of semantic variations, which sometimes occur even within the same text. Second, they should not be interpreted according to a philosophical meaning alien to Schleiermacher's writings, but rather according to their genealogy and explicit systematic purport. This approach is valid for concepts that are at the core of Schleiermacher's philosophy, such as "intuition" (*Anschauung*), "feeling" (*Gefühl*), "transcendent" and "transcendental," "self-consciousness" and "immediate self-consciousness," and "world consciousness."

Let's consider two cases that seem to be representative of Schleiermacher's thinking. The first one relates to the notion of "feeling" (*Gefühl*), the second to the notion of "intuition" (*Anschauung*). When we attempt to reconstruct the genesis of the concept of *Gefühl* in Schleiermacher's conceptual universe, we find that this term, far from being merely ambiguous, is polysemous: "feeling" occurs with a very different meaning in different contexts. For instance, "the constitutive value of feeling within knowing," as found in the essay "On What Gives Value to Life,"[2] bears no direct relation to the feeling referred to in the so-called letter "To Cecilie,"[3] and even less to the feeling that occurs in the

---

1 Douglas Hedley, *Living Forms of the Imagination* (London: T&T Clark, 2008), 115.
2 Friedrich Schleiermacher, "Über den Wert des Lebens," in KGA I/1, 419.
3 Friedrich Schleiermacher, "An Cecilie," in KGA I/1, 205-212.

argument of a letter to Wilhelm Dohna.[4] Indeed, the "feeling" of a fanatic, which arises in opposition to reason, is one thing; feeling as self-consciousness, which underlies both theoretical and practical reason, is quite another. In the former case, "feeling" must submit to reason in the interest of truth. In the latter, the feeling associated with self-consciousness—and here I have in mind Schleiermacher's mature philosophy of the *Dialectic* and the *Christian Faith*—constitutes the interest of truth.

A second instance—one in which the young Schleiermacher is concerned with the diagnosis of present society and with the "feeling of equality"—is altogether inconsistent with the genealogy of the notion of "feeling" that is the focus of my present argument. In this case as well, two contexts that are quite different must be compared. In "On the Highest Good," Schleiermacher explicitly refers to Rousseau's concept of alienation,[5] but this reference is made in order to highlight the paradox inherent in the ideal of going back to nature. In "On What Gives Value to Life," we surely misunderstand the essay's argument if we infer that withdrawing into the interiority of feeling stands in tension with the egalitarian implication Schleiermacher draws from the "feeling of equality." In making this mistake we no longer understand what is meant by "the interiority of feeling"; it can mean simply the place that the wise man (the philosopher) takes refuge when he is critically distancing himself from an alienated reality. But the guiding thread of "On What Gives Value to Life" does not convey the message of an opposition between the wise person and the rest of humanity, nor is its basic attitude one of resignation.

Our second case, the concept of "intuition" (*Anschauung*), proves as well to be a term that displays strong semantic variations, sometimes even within the same context. This fact can lead to serious misunderstandings of Schleiermacher's argumentation, especially with regard to the central definition of religion in the *Speeches*. A typical example of this occurs in the opening lectures on ethics in the *Brouillon*.[6] This piece is actually theoretically quite complex. Its definition of freedom, for example, does not so much refer the psyche (soul) of a human being as it denotes the function of a "ruling impulse" played by the "capacity for ideas." More to the point, its usage of the term "Anschauung" suggests a range of quite disparate meanings. To begin with, Schleier-

---

4   Letter #326, in KGA V/1, 424-28.
5   Friedrich Schleiermacher, "Über das höchste Gut," in KGA I/1, 113.
6   Friedrich Schleiermacher, *Brouillon zur Ethik* (1805/06), in *Entwürfe zu einem System der Sittenlehre*, vol. 2 of *Werke: Auswahl in vier Bänden*, ed. Otto Braun (Aalen: Scientia Verlag, 1981), 80-83.

macher is not arguing about the "intuition of life," an expression that occurs in a later context.⁷ Moreover, the intuition from which concepts and principles for ethics might be deduced (as occurs in the later lectures on philosophical ethics and in the *Dialectic*) is not at issue. Rather, what we might call an anticipating intuition is in play, one that is to be thematically unfolded in the presentation—the "narration," as he puts it in the second lecture of *Brouillon*—of "ethical life." Secondly, the whole argument in the context cited turns on three different conceptual meanings of *Anschauung*: (a) The first conceptual meaning essentially designates the empirical perception of a single thing—i.e., of an object determined within space and time; it is, then, a discrete moment within the *continuum* of history. So, it is the empirical perception of a single event that is ethically framed. From this standpoint, ethical theory cannot break free from the historical and empirical element; it does not relate to an *a priori* element, and therefore it is not capable of being organized in a strictly deductive pattern. If one does not grasp this perspective and see it as operative throughout his entire philosophical effort, one cannot help but conclude that the empirical, historical element does not give substance to speculation in his philosophy. This conclusion, however, clashes severely with the entire framework of Schleiermacher's philosophy. (b) The second conceptual meaning of *Anschauung* connotes a "philosophical view" achieved by the right balance between empirical and conceptual elements. In this sense, *Anschauung* qua "vision" is distinguished from its opposite, i.e., "the mode of thinking and feeling" (*Gesinnung*) from which an *ethos* (a type of ethical behavior) originates. In fact, *Gesinnung* is located at the source of the behaviors and values that frame a culture, and it governs the patterns that constitute a "moral habit;" *Anschauung*, on the other hand, theorizes these patterns scientifically. Thus, the relationship between *Gesinnung* and the scientific impulse is by no means unilateral, but rather varies and gives rise to a range of historically verifiable correlations. (c) The third conceptual meaning refers to an "anticipating intuition," i.e., to an "original intuition" that contains the entire material that is later to be thematically developed. "The whole [ethical world] is intuitively given in this act of a pure knowing."⁸ This original intuition is not to be conceived as something merely *a priori*, but rather as a knowing anticipation of the whole symbolic order that frames the human *ethos* (i.e. the human world and culture). Thus, it denotes the priority of living to a secondary, subsequent reflection or a conceptual mediation, even

---

7   Ibid., 88.
8   Ibid., 82.

though such living is already shaped (i.e., symbolically framed and organically instituted). That is why the original substance of this kind of intuition, which has to do with the prerequisites of understanding, cannot be concentrated into a formula, a *noema* (concept), or a proposition (principle), unless we want to divorce ourselves from the "continuity of [perceptual] intuition" of history (and of empirical reality in general).[9]

This, then, is the complex pattern of argument developed in the single context I chose for illustration. The issue concerns how to get moral theory (*Sittenlehre*) off the ground: should one proceed deductively from principles, or from a *continuum* of historical and empirical contents (*Anschauung*)? Schleiermacher chose the second alternative. This is why he begins with (moral) intuition, within which a human being is grasped as both body and soul, i.e., as nature and freedom. The entire historical, perceptual content, insofar as it is an act of pure cognition (*Erkennen*), is present in this sort of "moral intuition."

3.

When Schleiermacher worked out his theory of religious experience, he blended together a specific meaning of the notion of feeling with the *noema* of "immediate self-consciousness." In so doing, he mediated Kant's critique of reason with Spinoza's thought, and thereby brought about a new and original form of transcendental philosophy, one that dispensed with all the older "aesthetico-logical" approaches of pre-Kantian Enlightenment philosophy. It is here worth emphasizing that the young Schleiermacher's critical grappling with Kant's and Spinoza's ideas led him to the discovery of the transcendental character of "immediate self-consciousness" or "feeling."[10] For the *paradigm of inherence*, which emerged from that early encounter, amounts to a new philosophical approach based upon a consciousness that takes hold of a real being, so that thinking and being inhere in each other. In this way the transcendental constitution of real being comes to the fore. This is precisely the point Schleiermacher strives after in working out this new approach: a self that is always acting (i.e., self-consciousness)—which, however, is not so much a representing consciousness (i.e., is immediate) as substantively existing (i.e., feeling)—is conceived as a condi-

---

9   Ibid.
10 See Schleiermacher, "Spinozismus," "Kurze Darstellung des Spinozistischen Systems," and "Über dasjenige in Jacobis Briefen und Realismus, was den Spinoza nicht betrifft, und besonders über seine eigene Philosophie," in KGA I/1.

tion of the possibility for the constitution of actual acts of consciousness and of realities that bring about consciousness. Moreover, that this immediate "existing" accounts for and guarantees the parallelism, so to speak, between thinking and being, and at the same time grounds the objective validity of cognitive and volitional acts, is to be understood not so much in the sense of pre-Kantian philosophy as in the sense of the arguments developed later in Schleiermacher's *Dialectic*.

It is therefore nonsense to speak of an immediate consciousness of the self and the world, for within the paradigm of inherence there can be no question of an "immediate consciousness of the self" or of an "immediate consciousness of the world." These notions are quite alien to Schleiermacher's philosophical view. On the other hand, to place the ground of consciousness "in a being that transcends consciousness" is indeed a typical feature of theories occurring in the pre-Kantian philosophical tradition, but it by no means matches the genuine intention of Schleiermacher's theory.

As for the theoretical value of "feeling," this notion has mostly been the victim of thoroughgoing distortions in the history of Schleiermacher interpretation. These distortions, moreover, are all the more troubling since *Gefühl* is the very hinge of his conception of religion, a *noema* that allows us to think of *religious experience* and to give an account of its transcendental constitution. In order more fully to understand this notion, it is worth outlining the history of its insertion into Schleiermacher's intellectual universe. "Feeling" first makes its appearance in the essay "On the Highest Good," where Schleiermacher radically revises Kant's concept of the highest good. So as to avoid resorting to God as a postulate of morality, Schleiermacher excludes happiness and sensibility from the "highest good" and defines this concept not as an empirical state of affairs to be realized in endless time, but rather as the "the unity of moral laws of reason."[11] However, the crucial issue motivating the criticism of Kant in this essay is Schleiermacher's belief that no obligation for the practical behavior of empirical subjects follows from the universality and necessity of moral law, since finite wills are only indirectly determined by motives that are subjectively drawn from the moral law. This is where the notion of *moral feeling* comes into play. In fact, the genealogy of this notion is to be carried out by focusing on the notion of *immediacy*, for immediacy has to do with the inherence of distinct moments. Thus *moral feeling*, which mediates between reason's requirement and empirical affairs, makes the motives of moral law effective for our will. This is the main thesis of the essay "On Freedom"

---

11   Schleiermacher, "Über das höchste Gut," 90-91.

as well. Consequently, one cannot interpret feeling as some "third faculty" beside theoretical and practical reason. More precisely, we must search for the origin of such a notion not along the lines of the *moral sense*, but rather by following Schleiermacher's inquiry into an instance of immediacy and into the paradigm of inherence. Of course, Schleiermacher never refers to feeling as a faculty, but rather speaks of it only as the "ground of all theoretical and practical faculties."[12]

4.

Finally, as far as the *Speeches* are concerned, religion is conceived as a distinct region of experience, and experience as a whole is constituted by knowing, doing, and feeling. Each of these instances is constitutive of a particular area of experience, inasmuch as each of them is to be traced back to its own condition of possibility, which occurs precisely in connection with a remarkable extension of the transcendental concept of experience. At the same time, within such a division of experience into regions, corresponding "ethical communities," i.e., collective history-making subjects, come to light. Moreover, the *Speeches* assert the irreducible distinctiveness of religious experience and probably for the first time in the field of philosophical inquiry highlight the original and autonomous principle (or source) of its constitution.

Nonetheless, it is to be stressed that according to the *Speeches* there are two features that exclude an object from the intentionality of feeling (i.e., "feeling" taken as a constitutive condition of the possibility of religious experience). First, religion, which is precisely traced back to the genus of feeling, does not at all have the same object as knowing. Religion refers properly to the universe (*Universum*), the infinite, or in other words, the divine. In contrast, "knowing" refers to finite things in the world. Thus, properly speaking, religion has no "object"; rather, it is shaped as a set of lived experiences that cannot be characterized by its referring to an object. On the contrary, it should be referred to a subject that is shaped as a term of an "absolute passivity," i.e., of a receptivity that denotes two subjects in a peculiar, indeed, asymmetric relationship. This relationship is expressed conceptually in the *Speeches* by the hendiadys "intuition and feeling." These do not denote two distinct intentional acts; they are, rather, expressions of one and the same intentional act. Consequently, they do not refer to an "original unity" within

---

12 Andreas Arndt, "Kommentar," in Friedrich Schleiermacher, *Friedrich Schleiermacher Schriften*, ed. Andreas Arndt (Frankfurt: Deutscher Klassiker Verlag, 1996), 1050.

which the unity of self-consciousness and world-consciousness might be given. The intentional term meant by that hendiadys is anything but an original unity. Instead, "intuition and feeling" refers to a *totality* in relation to which the only possible (but at the same time necessary) relationship is the one of an *existing* (i.e., inherent in one's existence) *passivity*, of a receptivity that is lived within an act of unitary concentration of the whole of finitude. Here, it is a question of the originated (not originating) unity of the whole of finitude. Schleiermacher's focus on intuition and feeling refers us to the originating totality of the universe (or the infinite); here, where the self is concentrated in its utmost intensity, religious experience has its origin.

As I suggested above, the originality of Schleiermacher's approach to the philosophy of religion owes itself to his notion of feeling. Already in the *Soliloquies* there is a distinction between the feeling of freedom, which generally arises in the context of moral action, and the feeling that occurs in merely subjective states. One might suppose, however, that here feeling gets another distinct meaning that must be adequately grasped. In fact, in the former case, feeling is connected with intuition (*Anschauung*); it thus has an objective bond. In the latter case, religious and moral feeling respectively are tied to a subject. As for the religious feeling, it refers to an "objective" (so to speak) term only thanks to the intuition (*Anschauung*) of the universe; on the other hand, the moral feeling gets its objective term thanks to the intuition (*Anschauung*) of the ethical world. Consequently, there is a conceptual distinction between religion and morality, for we are referred to different states of feeling. These distinct domains are characterized by different kinds of unity: morality has to do with the human world, while religion is concerned with the absolute unity of the universe. Schleiermacher's philosophy of religion attempts, via its autonomy as a discipline, to keep both "unitary forms" of experience—namely, religion and morality—conceptually distinct.

5.

Two important results stem from the paradigm proposed by Schleiermacher. First, it allows one to overcome the critical judgment that feeds the suspicion with which rationalists (or the despisers of religion) approach religion and its manifestations. For the rationalists trace the reality of religion to what does not actually constitute it. Schleiermacher, by contrast, sets to work and enhances, as it were, a "heuristic reason," an exercise of reason that establishes the genetic origin (the constitution) of religious experience and thus accounts for its peculiar reality. Schleiermacher understands religion as an actual experience of human beings and thus explains why religion is a decisive, indefeasible component of the human, historical world. Secondly, this new paradigm takes into account "positive," i.e., individual, historical religions with a *principium individuationis* of their own. It distinguishes them from each other and regards them as ethical realities that belong to the lived experience of individuals. This treatment of particular religions includes two peculiar features. On the one hand, it attempts to account for the historicity and individuality of religions. In other words, it asks how and why the historical plurality of religions and the complex phenomenology of the individual religions result from the framework of religious experience. According to Schleiermacher, all religions are entitled to equal dignity insofar as they all instantiate the original structure of religious experience and shape it into a specific, historical province of the human ethos. On the other hand, Schleiermacher's treatment of the religions engages a critical reason that is able to discriminate what is *authentic* from what is *inauthentic* within the complex phenomenology of individual religions. In other words, it can distinguish which elements are mixed in as substitutes or surrogates for more authentic contents and expressions. Four moments or steps in this paradigm for understanding religion will now be identified.

The first moment issues in a comprehension of the historical-positive elements that are found at the heart of any religious experience and includes the exercise of both *critical reason* and *heuristic reason*. The former aims at discriminating the authentic from the inauthentic elements. It is a necessary moment in every investigative approach to the religions. The latter aims at an insight into the individuality and essential features of a given historical form of religious experience. If one does not grasp the proper core, the essence, of an individual historical religion, one will lack the criteria necessary for testing whether its actual features are authentic or not as well as for understanding and assessing its historical development. The fifth speech argues that such a criterion is decisive for determining the nature and content of a given religion, and specifically of Christianity as a historical religion.

The second step consists of a comparative theory of religions. Given the historical-positive individuality of religions as well as the transcendental structure of religious experience, a comparative approach becomes necessary for understanding religion. Such an approach intends neither to level, nor to set into competition the various religions. Its purpose, rather, is to set out the values (of course, these values are specified in relation not only to doctrines but also to the modes of worship, morals, and experiences of salvation) embodied in the religions compared. It indeed makes use of analogies between religious phenomena, but it does not establish a ranking or primacy among religions. Instead, it has a *critical* and an *evaluative* function. The former allows one to recognize the specific differences that make up the individuality of each historical-religious formation and clarify the historical reasons for its being. The latter accounts for the historical trajectory or evolution of a particular religion, since the history of a religion is precisely connected to the circumstances of its actual evaluation. In the third speech, such a comparative approach is based upon the effort to tackle the main factors influencing the historical life of a religion, namely the creativity and free communication of one's own religious life. This results in a threefold typology of religions, which anticipates the propositions (§§7-10) borrowed from the "philosophy of religion" and elaborated in the introduction to *The Christian Faith*.

The third step provides a thematic treatment of the essence of religion. This is perhaps the most explicitly philosophical feature of this paradigm for understanding religion, and it comprises two moments. The first points out the constitutive structure that accounts for religious experience. The second moment focuses on the reasons why such a structure unfolds in a plurality of individual formations, for they are all constituted by that transcendental structure, yet as true individuals they remain irreducibly different. Only in this framework does religion, insofar as it is a condition of possibility that warrants an actual relationship with the *Universum* (i.e., with the divine), show itself to be really meaningful for human beings and their history. This, in fact, is the main point of the second speech, which argues that the transcendental core of religion (insofar as it is the "function" that brings about and determines the "systems" of religious experience and belief) involves a relationship with a term (*das Universum*) that withdraws from a human being's finite experience—and accordingly calls into question what people do, are, and experience—even though it is to be apprehended as what makes sense of the ultimate human condition, as what fulfills the whole of human existence.

The final step of Schleiermacher's approach develops a theory of religious communication. Within the context of human experience, religion is linguistically involved in the system of communication. This brings about a community that is shaped by both symbolizing and organizing activities, though with the prevalence of the former. Communication is not a secondary feature of religious experience; it belongs instead to religion's innermost nature. This is the reason why the particular formation of religious experience takes the form of a community. Community accounts for both the individuality of a religious formation and its historicity. It also accounts for the free, responsible, and creative participation of single individuals who within a community are joined together by bonds of reciprocal communication. In fact, community and communication are the main theme of the fourth speech.

6.

Schleiermacher's first book offered much more than a shrewd *ad hominem* defense of Christianity; it inaugurated a fresh stage in the critical analysis of religion. Indeed, the importance of Schleiermacher's search for distinctive religious categories is even acknowledged by those who reject his conclusions. He not only exposed the urgent need to reconceive the task of theology, he also opened the way to more profound and sympathetic treatments of the psychology and history of religion than either traditional theology or the critiques of "free-thinkers" had been able to achieve. Christian theologians and freethinkers agreed in treating the study of world religions as the anatomy of a sickness (the difference being that the freethinkers were not inclined to make Christianity an exception). Schleiermacher looked at religions as manifestations of human wholeness. He did not really mean to move religion out of the domains of knowledge and morals and to confine it instead to the domain of emotions. He expressly denied that he intended any such separation. By "intuition and feeling" he meant the immediate, pre-reflective self-consciousness that cannot be confined to any single aspect of human selfhood, but underlies the whole of it. Nor did Schleiermacher fall into a psychologism that would enclose the religious subject in the sphere of its own subjectivity. For all his interest in the imagination, Schleiermacher's theory of religion is marked by a strong sense of the reality of the transcendent, even though he thought it impossible to have the transcendent as an object.

Symbolism in Schleiermacher's Theory of Religion

PETER GROVE

In a discussion of Schleiermacher and the question of a transcendental theory of religion it may seem most natural to focus on his later work, above all on *The Christian Faith*. This paper, however, will instead take up Schleiermacher's *On Religion: Speeches to its Cultured Despisers* from 1799. Presupposing a broad definition of "transcendental" as referring to a theory that tries to account for a phenomenon, e.g., religion, by assuming the activity of the human subject, I'm going to interpret the early version of Schleiermacher's theory of religion in terms of symbolism. Kant will be present as the founder not only of transcendental philosophy, but also of the modern theory of symbolism.[1] I'll begin with a preliminary interpretation of the notion of religion in the *Speeches* and then aim to deepen that interpretation by relating it to Kant's *Critique of the Power of Judgment* and to early German Romanticism. In conclusion, I'll draw a line to more recent theology and theory of religion.

1.

First, we must ask if the *Speeches* offer something that might count as a transcendental theory of religion. In fact they do offer at least some elements of such a theory. This becomes clear from the remarks the first speech makes about the formation of concepts and about theory in religion,[2] among other things that "[e]very expression, every product of the human spirit can be viewed and apprehended from a dual standpoint." Only the first of these standpoints is relevant here. It refers to non-empirical constituents of religion in the form of certain activities of the human spirit: "If one considers religion from its center according to

---

1 See Scholz, "Symbol. II," 723-24. A list of full references can be found at the end of this chapter.
2 Schleiermacher, *On Religion*, 11, 12, 15; *Über die Religion*, 22, 24, 31.

its inner essence, it is a product of human nature, rooted in one of its necessary modes of action or drives."[3]

A detailed and comprehensive elaboration of this theory is not given in the *Speeches*. The closest they come is, of course, the second speech, which in line with its title contains a consideration of religion "according to its inner essence." The outlines of the theory are presented in the central section of this text,[4] a section upon which Schleiermacher places special emphasis and that stands out in the second speech by virtue of its relatively stronger theoretical character. These are the famous passages that contain the definition of religious consciousness as intuition and feeling—intuition of the universe being the most important notion for the purpose of this paper.

But is there really any connection between the preliminary remarks of the first speech with their emphasis on a special activity of mind and the determination of religious consciousness as intuition in the second? A widespread interpretation claims that our text primarily understands religion as a kind of passivity.[5] The following aims to show that this interpretation misses a very central point.

To begin with, it should be noted that the section mentioned above in fact explicitly asserts the fundamental role of spontaneous activity in religious consciousness. This agrees not only with the quotation from the first speech, but also with a broader idea, stressed frequently in the *Speeches*, about the importance of the activity of the person in religion.[6] Our text from the second speech expresses the point in general terms in its last subsection, which is about the problem of an adequate treatment of the unity of intuition and feeling, a section often favoured in the passivity-interpretations. Here Schleiermacher refers to "the innermost creation of the religious sense"—what is creative here, it should be noted, is religious sense—and to "the higher and divine religious activity of the mind."[7] This is applied to religious feeling[8] as well as to religious intuition. Application to the latter is seen in the recurring phrase that refers to intuition as "the original and first deed" or "act" of the mind.[9] Yet more important than such phrases is the question of just

---

3   Schleiermacher, *On Religion*, 11-12; *Über die Religion*, 22.
4   Schleiermacher, *On Religion*, 24-33; *Über die Religion*, 55-78.
5   See, for example, Albrecht, *Schleiermachers Theorie der Frömmigkeit*, ch. 2. For further references see Ellsiepen, *Anschauung des Universums*, 274.
6   See, for example, Schleiermacher, *On Religion*, 22, 57; *Über die Religion*, 48, 138.
7   Schleiermacher, *On Religion*, 31, 32; *Über die Religion*, 72, 73.
8   Schleiermacher, *On Religion*, 31; *Über die Religion*, 68.
9   Schleiermacher, *On Religion*, 26, 31; *Über die Religion*, 58, 73.

how the spontaneous activity under consideration constitutes religious intuition.

To answer this question we must keep in mind the way Schleiermacher builds up his theory of religion in the *Speeches*. The argumentation almost consistently proceeds in this way: first, an argument is presented that belongs to theory of consciousness in general; this argument is then applied to religious consciousness. Such a procedure doesn't exclude differences between consciousness in general and religious consciousness. On the contrary, as we shall see, the latter differs in an important way from the former.

The first in this series of double steps is the crucial one. In the following I modify the Crouter translation, using "presentation" for the German "Darstellung" and reserving "representation" for "Vorstellung."

> All intuition proceeds from an influence of the intuited on the one who intuits, from an original and independent action of the former, which is then grasped, apprehended, and conceived by the latter according to one's own nature. . . . what you thus intuit and perceive is not the nature of things, but their action upon you. What you know or believe about the nature of things lies far beyond the realm of intuition.
> The same is true of religion. The universe exists in uninterrupted activity and reveals itself to us every moment. Every form that it brings forth, every being to which it gives separate existence according to the fullness of life, every occurrence that spills forth from its rich, ever-fruitful womb, is an action of the same upon us. Thus to accept everything individual as a part of the whole and everything limited as a presentation of the infinite is religion. But whatever would go beyond that and penetrate deeper into the nature and substance of the whole is no longer religion, and will, if it still wants to be regarded as such, inevitably sink back into empty mythology.[10]

Schleiermacher speaks synonymously of "accepting something as," "regarding as," and "representing something as."[11]

At first glance the line of interpretation I have sketched may appear out of place here. But it appears so only when the two-step construction and the analogies and differences between sensible and religious intuition are overlooked. Three points are important.

First: the epistemic structure of religious intuition as such. Religious intuition is not just intuition of something, but intuition of something as something, or, in other words, not just "intuition of the universe," but "intuition of the individual as a presentation of the universe." This complex structure differentiates religious intuition from

---

10 Schleiermacher, *On Religion*, 24-25; *Über die Religion*, 55-56.
11 Schleiermacher, *On Religion*, 25; *Über die Religion*, 56-57.

sensible intuition and gives it the character of an interpretation.[12] As interpretation, religious intuition can only be generated through the spontaneous activity of the intuiting subject. So, here we have "the higher and divine religious activity of the mind" in intuition.

Second, there is the relation between higher, religious intuition and empirical intuition. Schleiermacher does not give a straightforward explanation of this. It is, however, possible for us to provide one from his philosophical premises. Given Schleiermacher's Kantian epistemology, sensible intuition is a condition without which a particular thing cannot be present to a human subject.[13] Therefore, religious intuition cannot be independent of empirical intuition, but instead must necessarily be related to it.[14] Through this relation to sensible intuition, religious consciousness contains a receptive element as well as an active one, and, as a whole, is comprised of a polarity of receptivity and spontaneity.

The third point is as fundamental to religious intuition as the second: when something is seen as something, something(1) is interpreted by means of something(2), and, thus, an idea of the latter is presupposed—in the case of religious intuition, an idea of the universe. Thanks to his eagerness to distinguish religion from metaphysics, Schleiermacher explains this proposition even less than he explains the relation of religious intuition to sensible intuition. Thus, the epistemic status of the concept *Universum* never becomes clear in the *Speeches*. Once again, an answer can be provided from Schleiermacher's philosophical presuppositions: the idea of the universe must have the status of an "idea of reason" in the Kantian sense of the term, namely, a concept without a sensibly given correlate.[15]

---

12 See Grove, *Deutungen des Subjekts*, 293-95. Ulrich Barth has provided important leads for this analysis; see, for example, Barth, "Was ist Religion?" In the early literature the element of interpretation was emphasized in 1917 by Rudolf Otto, who also relates it to Kant's third critique. See Otto, *The Idea of the Holy*, 150-53; *Das Heilige*, 175-78. In American scholarship it was noted in Richard B. Brandt's 1941 *The Philosophy of Schleiermacher*: "So religion is interpretation, the seeing of an event as a part or manifestation of the whole, the perception of its meaning or significance or unique purpose in the plan and order of the whole" (98).
13 See, for example, Schleiermacher, *On Religion*, 26; *Über die Religion*, 58.
14 Grove, *Deutungen des Subjekts*, 299-300; Ellsiepen, *Anschauung des Universums*, 373-76.
15 Kant, *Critique of Pure Reason*, 401-2, 409; KrV B, 383-84, 396-97.

2.

I shall now go on to relate Schleiermacher's theory to the *Critique of the Power of Judgment*. As already indicated, Schleiermacher alludes to Kantian theories, and that may very well include Kant's aesthetics. We know that Schleiermacher was familiar with the third critique, although not as intimately as he was with the first two.[16] However, I am not claiming that he is arguing on the basis of the former. My point is that there are important structural correspondences between the *Speeches* and *Critique of the Power of Judgment*.

It would be fruitful to examine all of the main theories of the Kantian aesthetics in this perspective, but I'll concentrate on the theory of symbolism, presented in section 59.[17] This theory is linked to Kant's theory of aesthetic ideas, but its relevance within his philosophy goes far beyond aesthetics. Among other things it affects the theory of religion and theology, as Kant's notion of a legitimate "symbolic anthropomorphism" shows;[18] this latter clearly influenced Schleiermacher's treatment of the idea of God in *The Christian Faith* and in the *Dialectics*.[19]

Concerning the *Speeches*, three points in Kant's theory of the production and use of symbols seem important. First is the fact that symbolism makes up a specific achievement of reflective judgement not explained earlier in the third critique.[20] In the introduction, Kant defines reflective judgement as the faculty of thinking a particular that is given as contained under a universal that is not given, but has to be

---

16 See Grove, *Deutungen des Subjekts*, 91 n. 315, 126-27 n. 477, 284 n. 157, 361 n. 115.
17 Kant, *Critique of the Power of Judgment*, 225-28; KU, 254-60. On this, see above all Pieper, "Kant und die Methode der Analogie"; and Kubik, *Die Symboltheorie bei Novalis*, 51-80. The symbol belongs to Kant's anthropology and so it is treated in section 38 of his 1798 *Anthropology from a Pragmatic Point of View*, 84-85; AA VII, 191-92.
18 Kant, *Prolegomena to Any Future Metaphysics*, 97; AA IV, 357. This notion is here explained by aid of the idea of analogy, which is fundamental for Kant's notion of a symbol in general (Kant, *Prolegomena to Any Future Metaphysics*, 97-102; AA IV, 357-62). The subject is treated by Kant in different contexts, for instance, *Critique of Pure Reason*, 609; KrV B, 705-6; *Religion within the Boundaries of Mere Reason*, 83n; AA VI, 64-65n.
19 See Schleiermacher, KGA I/13.1, 40 (§4.4); *The Christian Faith*, 18: "The transference of the idea of God to any perceptible object, unless one is all the time conscious that it is a piece of purely arbitrary symbolism, is always a corruption, whether it be a temporary transference, *i.e.* a theophany, or a constitutive transference, in which God is represented as permanently a particular perceptible existence." This critical remark about the religious representation of God is supplemented by an explanation of legitimate anthropomorphism in the postscript to *Glaubenslehre* §5 (KGA I/13.1, 51-53; *The Christian Faith*, 25-26). Cf. Schleiermacher, *Vorlesungen über die Dialektik*, 271.
20 Recki, "Die Dialektik der ästhetischen Urteilskraft," 189.

found.²¹ This means that the particular is here considered in a way different than in determining judgement, where the particular is subsumed under a pre-given universal. An act of reflective judgement is aimed at the particular as such and not just as an instance of a rule. And since the universal—in the form of a concept of understanding—is not given, the particular is not determined and, thus, not really cognised in such a judgement. In recent scholarship the achievement of reflective judgement has sometimes been described as an interpretation.²²

Second is Kant's distinction of symbols from what he calls marks.²³ The latter are merely "designations of the concepts by means of accompanying sensible signs, which contain nothing at all belonging to the intuition of the object"²⁴ and "which in themselves signify nothing."²⁵ By contrast, a symbol is a sign that has an intrinsic connection to what is signified. Something in the symbol determines that the symbol refers to something. Kant conceives this relation between the symbol and the symbolized as an analogy. As is usual in his later thinking, the analogy is understood as a proportional analogy, and it is one founded on an inference of reflective judgement: based upon the three known parts of the two relations, reflective judgement seeks the fourth part, which in this case lies beyond all experience.²⁶

Finally, there is the distinction between schema and symbol as kinds of "presentation" (*Darstellung*). In Kant's philosophy, "to present" means to provide a concept with a corresponding intuition and thereby ensure its objective reality.²⁷ This distinction corresponds to the distinction between determining and reflective judgement. In the one case, the presentation is carried out by a schema that mediates between category and intuition. But a real presentation of ideas of reason, Kant states, is impossible. Nevertheless, we must present them and we do so through symbols, figuratively and metaphorically applying categories to objects of ideas, yet without claiming any cognition of them. Thus Kant arrives at the following definition: a symbol is an "indirect" presentation, a presentation "by means of an analogy (for which empirical intuitions are also employed), in which the power of judgment per-

---

21 Kant, *Critique of the Power of Judgment*, 66-67; KU, xxv-xxvi.
22 See, for example, Barth, "Religion und ästhetische Erfahrung," 244.
23 See Kubik, *Die Symboltheorie bei Novalis*, 53-55.
24 Kant, *Critique of the Power of Judgment*, 226; KU, 255.
25 Kant, *Anthropology from a Pragmatic Point of View*, 84; AA VII, 191.
26 Kubik, *Die Symboltheorie bei Novalis*, 67-68. Kubik (69-70) also tries to spell out the analogy presented in the quotation below.
27 See, for example, Kant, *Critique of the Power of Judgment*, 78; KU, xlix. See also Ellsiepen's overview in *Anschauung des Universums*, 301-5.

forms a double task, first applying the concept to the object of a sensible intuition, and then, second, applying the mere rule of reflection on that intuition to an entirely different object, of which the first is only the symbol."[28] Under Kantian epistemological presuppositions, a symbol in this pointed sense is—to use a phrase that so far as I know was coined by the early Romantics—a "presentation of the unpresentable."[29]

The *Critique of the Power of Judgment* gives several examples of symbols. One of them, which in Kant's critical philosophy is much more than a mere example, is the cognition of God. Regarding Kant's thesis that "all of our cognition of God is merely symbolic,"[30] it can be said that Kant's corresponding explanation of symbolic anthropomorphism in his *Prolegomena* somehow shows a similarity with the analysis of religious consciousness as intuition in the *Speeches*: it operates with an as-structure, that is, a "considering something as if" (*ansehen als ob*).[31]

Apart from this, if we compare Schleiermacher's notion of religion with Kant's theory of symbolism, it can be noted that a Kant-inspired notion of presentation also has a central place in the *Speeches*.[32] Continuing with our interpretation, we can accordingly identify in Schleiermacher's understanding of religious intuition the taking of the object of an empirical intuition as a presentation of an object of an idea of reason, and this in such a way that no real cognition of the latter is claimed. Thus there is a fundamental structural correspondence with Kant's notion of symbolic cognition,[33] and from this it seems quite natural to understand the notion of religion in the *Speeches* in terms of religious interpretation qua symbolic interpretation.

In his recent book on the Spinozistic basis of Schleiermacher's early theory of religion, Christof Ellsiepen compares Kant and Schleier-

---

28 Kant, *Critique of the Power of Judgment*, 226; KU, 256.
29 On the prehistory in A.G. Baumgarten und Kant, see Bahr, *Darstellung des Undarstellbaren*.
30 Kant, *Critique of the Power of Judgment*, 227; KU, 257.
31 Kant, *Prolegomena to Any Future Metaphysics*, 97; AA IV, 357. Cf. Kant, *Critique of Pure Reason*, 609; KrV B, 706. See also Barth, "Die religiöse Selbstdeutung der praktischen Vernunft," 303-6.
32 On Schleiermacher's appropriation of this notion from Kantian philosophy before the third critique, see his early essay "Über das höchste Gut" from 1789. In this critique of the doctrine of the postulates Schleiermacher endorses Kant's restriction of the presentation of ideas of reason (99-100).
33 Ellsiepen, *Anschauung des Universums*, 378: "In its mental function Schleiermacher's religious intuition, like Kant's symbolic presentation, is an indirect realization of an idea, this being a representation that is only thought and defies direct intuition" (translation mine). I wish to thank Christof Ellsiepen for comments on the discussion to follow.

macher in an illuminating way, but he reaches a conclusion that seems, with respect to the *Speeches*, to exclude the notion of analogy and symbol: "For Kant the analogy does not at all lie at the level of objects of representations, but in the way of mentally handling these objects." On the other hand, the indirectness in Schleiermacher's case is one that, according to Ellsiepen, "without analogical refraction refers to the substance of the representations as such."[34] As far as I can see, this conclusion follows from problematic presuppositions: To begin with, Kant's theory of symbolism is understood from his theory of judgement of taste, but the latter does not form the basis of the former or of the theory of aesthetic ideas.[35] At the same time, Ellsiepen's conclusion does not do justice to the notion of analogy as originated from logic.[36] Concerning Schleiermacher, Ellsiepen in my view underestimates the element of figurative representation, the importance of which, as in Kant, is implied by the *Speeches*. This should become clearer in the last short step in my analysis, a step that will show that an interpretation of Schleiermacher's version of the "presentation of the unpresentable" in terms of symbolism can be defended in another, simpler way.

Until now my analysis has neglected the fact that "presentation" has equivalents in the *Speeches*. These include especially "picture" or "image" (*Bild*)[37] and "mirror" (*Spiegel*),[38] as well as "symbol," "analogy," and "allegory."[39] The important thing is not only the explicit use of the notions of symbol and analogy, but also what all these equivalents to presentation tell us about the element of figurative representation in question. They show that in the *Speeches*, as in the third critique, there is an intrinsic connection between the presentation and the presented: the former shows a correspondence to the latter, through which the presentation refers to the presented.

All of this connects Schleiermacher not so much to Kant as to the philosophy of early German Romanticism, especially that of Friedrich Schlegel, although, through that philosophy, there is still a link to Kant's theory of symbolism.[40] I confine myself to a quote from Schlegel's lectures on transcendental philosophy in Jena in 1800-01.

---

34 Ibid., 378-79 (translation mine).
35 See Kulenkampff, *Kants Logik des ästhetischen Urteils*, 160-65.
36 See Kubik, *Die Symboltheorie bei Novalis*, 67.
37 Schleiermacher, *On Religion*, 28, 37, 92; *Über die Religion*, 65, 87, 229-30.
38 Schleiermacher, *On Religion*, 24, 38; *Über die Religion*, 55, 89.
39 Schleiermacher, *On Religion*, 24, 65, 24; *Über die Religion*, 53, 159, 54.
40 See Scholz, "Symbol. II," 723-28. On Novalis' theory of symbolism, see Kubik, *Die Symboltheorie bei Novalis*, according to which Novalis belongs in the legacy of understanding symbolism inaugurated by Kant (78).

Here it is claimed that we must insert a certain concept between the individual and the infinite to explain the relation between them, namely, "the concept of a *picture* or *presentation, allegory* (εἰκών). Thus, the individual is *a picture of an infinite substance.*"[41] Schlegel could here have used the concept of a symbol as well. So despite the different theoretical contexts of his lectures and the *Speeches*, all these concepts are completely in line with those of Schleiermacher, indicating the close affinity between the views of both thinkers.

3.

This analysis should, of course, be continued into an examination, first of all, of the explicit theory of symbolism in Schleiermacher's later philosophical ethics. However, if my interpretation of the *Speeches* is tenable, Schleiermacher's theory of religion turns out to be one of the very first after Kant[42] to give symbolism the central place in religion. It also proves to be a remarkable predecessor to more famous theories of symbolism in religion that were developed in theology and philosophy more than a hundred years later. Schleiermacher's understanding of religious cognition and language as symbolic lends itself most naturally to comparison with the views of Paul Tillich. Of course, Schleiermacher's sketch in many respects is inferior to a theory like Tillich's. But this does not prevent Schleiermacher, thanks to the transcendental design of his theory, from having important things to say to his distant successor. Take, for instance, Tillich's famous idea that a symbol participates in the reality symbolized. Schleiermacher agrees that there is an intrinsic link between the symbol and the symbolized and tries to account for it in terms of a theory of consciousness and cognition. Yet it also follows from my analysis that Schleiermacher at the same time presupposes a distinction between symbol and symbolized. This presupposition he shares with Kant and his Romantic companions, and insofar, he differs in principle from Goethe and Schelling, whom Tillich, I presume, at this point joins. One might ask whether this distinction between symbol and symbolized and thereby also the indirectness of symbolism are not threatened by Tillich's notion of symbolic participation. There appears, at least, to be a deficit of interpretative activity

---

41 Schlegel, *Philosophische Vorlesungen*, 39 (translation mine).
42 Kubik, *Die Symboltheorie bei Novalis*, 77: "Not only is Kant's notion of a symbol from the very outset motivated by theory of religion, Kant is also the real creator of theory of symbolism in religion" (translation mine).

here and elsewhere in Tillich's theory of symbolism. Compared with such a theoretical "lapse of the hermeneutic dimension" of religious consciousness,[43] Schleiermacher's version of a transcendentally oriented theory of religion shows its continued relevance.

References

Albrecht, Christian. *Schleiermachers Theorie der Frömmigkeit: Ihr wissenschaftlicher Ort und ihr systematischer Gehalt in den Reden, in der Glaubenslehre und in der Dialektik*. Berlin and New York: Walter de Gruyter, 1994.
Bahr, Petra. *Darstellung des Undarstellbaren: Religionstheoretische Studien zum Darstellungsbegriff bei A. G. Baumgarten und I. Kant*. Tübingen: Mohr Siebeck, 2004.
Barth, Ulrich. "Religion und ästhetische Erfahrung: Interdependenzen symbolischer Erlebniskultur." In *Religion in der Moderne*, 235-62. Tübingen: Mohr Siebeck, 2003.
—. "Religion und Sinn." In *Religion—Kultur—Gesellschaft: Der frühe Tillich im Spiegel neuer Texte (1919-1920)*, edited by Christian Danz and Werner Schüßler, 197-213. Münster: LIT Verlag, 2008.
—. "Die Religionstheorie der 'Reden': Schleiermachers theologisches Modernisierungsprogramm." In *Aufgeklärter Protestantismus*, 259-89. Tübingen: Mohr Siebeck, 2004.
—. "Die religiöse Selbstdeutung der praktischen Vernunft: Kants Grundlegung der Ethikotheologie." In *Gott als Projekt der Vernunft*, 263-307. Tübingen: Mohr Siebeck, 2005.
—. "Was ist Religion? Sinndeutung zwischen Erfahrung und Letztbegründung." In *Religion in der Moderne*, 3-27. Tübingen: Mohr Siebeck, 2003.
Behler, Ernst. "Symbol und Allegorie in der frühromantischen Theorie." In *Studien zur Romantik und zur idealistischen Philosophie*, 2:249-63. Paderborn, Munich, Vienna, and Zurich: Verlag Ferdinand Schöningh, 1993.
Brandt, Richard. *The Philosophy of Schleiermacher: The Development of His Theory of Scientific and Religious Knowledge*. Westport: Greenwood Press, 1971.
Ellsiepen, Christof. *Anschauung des Universums und Scientia Intuitiva: Die spinozistischen Grundlagen von Schleiermachers früher Religionstheorie*. Berlin and New York: Walter de Gruyter, 2006.
Fricke, Christel. *Kants Theorie des reinen Geschmacksurteils*. Berlin and New York: Walter de Gruyter, 1990.

---

43 Barth, "Religion und Sinn," 212 (translation mine). Granted, Barth is not discussing the underdeveloped role of interpretation in Tillich's theory of symbolism, but rather in his early theory of meaning.

Gasché, Rudolphe. "Überlegungen zum Begriff der Hypotypose bei Kant." In *Was heißt "Darstellen"?* edited by Christiaan L. Hart Nibbrig, 152-74. Frankfurt: Suhrkamp Verlag, 1994.

Götze, Martin. *Ironie und absolute Darstellung: Philosophie und Poetik in der Frühromantik.* Paderborn, Munich, Vienna, and Zurich: Ferdinand Schöningh, 2001.

Grove, Peter. *Deutungen des Subjekts: Schleiermachers Philosophie der Religion.* Berlin and New York: Walter de Gruyter, 2004.

Kant, Immanuel. *Anthropologie in pragmatischer Hinsicht.* In *Gesammelte Schriften* (abbr. AA) VII, edited by the Königlich Preußische Akademie der Wissenschaften, 117-333. Berlin: Georg Reimer, 1902–.

—. *Anthropology from a Pragmatic Point of View.* Translated and edited by Robert B. Louden. Cambridge: Cambridge University Press, 2006.

—. *Critique of the Power of Judgment.* Edited by Paul Guyer. Translated by Paul Guyer and Eric Matthews. Cambridge: Cambridge University Press, 2000.

—. *Critique of Pure Reason.* Translated and edited by Paul Guyer and Allen W. Wood. Cambridge: Cambridge University Press, 1998.

—. *Kritik der reinen Vernunft: Zweiter Auflage 1787* (abbr. KrV B). AA III.

—. *Kritik der Urtheilskraft* (abbr. KU). In AA V, 165-485.

—. *Prolegomena to Any Future Metaphysics That Will Be Able to Come Forward as Science.* Translated by Paul Carus and James W. Ellington. Indianapolis: Hackett Publishing Company, 1977.

—. *Prolegomena zu einer jeden künftigen Metaphysik, die als Wissenschaft wird auftreten können.* In AA IV, 253-383.

—. *Die Religion innerhalb der Grenzen der bloßen Vernunft.* In AA VI, 1-202.

—. *Religion within the Boundaries of Mere Reason.* In *Religion within the Boundaries of Mere Reason and Other Writings.* Translated and edited by Allen Wood and George di Giovanni, 31-191. Cambridge: Cambridge University Press, 1998.

Kong, Byung-Hye. *Die ästhetische Idee in der Philosophie Kants: Ihre systematische Stellung und Herkunft.* Frankfurt: Peter Lang, 1995.

Kubik, Andreas. *Die Symboltheorie bei Novalis: Eine Ideengeschichtliche Studie in ästhetischer und theologischer Absicht.* Tübingen: Mohr Siebeck, 2006.

Kulenkampff, Jens. *Kants Logik des ästhetischen Urteils.* 2nd ed. Frankfurt: Vittorio Klostermann, 1994.

Otto, Rudolf. *Das Heilige: Über das Irrationale in der Idee des Göttlichen und sein Verhältnis zum Rationalen.* Munich: Beck, 1987.

—. *The Idea of the Holy: An Inquiry into the Non-Rational Factor in the Idea of the Divine and its Relation to the Rational.* Translated by John W. Harvey. 3rd ed. London: Oxford University Press, 1925.

Pieper, Annemarie. "Kant und die Methode der Analogie." In *Kant in der Diskussion der Moderne*, edited by Gerhard Schönrich and Yasushi Kato, 92-112. Frankfurt: Suhrkamp Verlag, 1996.

Recki, Birgit. "Die Dialektik der ästhetischen Urteilskraft und die Methodenlehre des Geschmacks (§§55-60)." In *Kritik der Urteilskraft*, edited by Otfried Höffe, 189-210. Berlin: Akademie Verlag, 2008.

Schlegel, Friedrich. *Philosophische Vorlesungen (1800-1807)*. Edited by Jean-Jacques Anstett. Vol. 12 of *Kritische Friedrich-Schlegel-Ausgabe*, edited by Ernst Behler et al. Munich, Paderborn, Vienna, and Zurich: Verlag Ferdinand Schöningh and Thomas-Verlag, 1964.

Schleiermacher, Friedrich Daniel Ernst. *The Christian Faith*. Edited by H. R. Mackintosh and J. S. Stewart. Edinburgh: T&T Clark, 1999.

—. *Der christliche Glaube nach den Grundsätzen der evangelischen Kirche im Zusammenhange dargestellt: Zweiter Auflage (1830/31)*. In KGA I/13.1.

—. *On Religion: Speeches to its Cultured Despisers*. Translated and edited by Richard Crouter. 2nd ed. Cambridge: Cambridge University Press, 1996.

—. "Über das höchste Gut." In KGA I/2, 81-125.

—. *Über die Religion: Reden an die Gebildeten unter ihren Verächtern*. Berlin: Johann Friedrich Unger, 1799.

—. *Vorlesungen über die Dialektik*. In KGA II/10.1.

Scholz, Oliver R. "Symbol. II." In *Historisches Wörterbuch der Philosophie*, 10:723-38. Basel: Schwabe & CO AG Verlag, 1998.

Stolzenberg, Jürgen. "Das freie Spiel der Erkenntniskräfte: Zu Kants Theorie des Geschmacksurteils." In *Kants Schlüssel zur Kritik des Geschmacks: Ästhetische Erfahrung heute—Studien zur Aktualität von Kants "Kritik der Urteilskraft,"* edited by Ursula Franke, 1-28. Hamburg: Felix Meiner Verlag, 2000.

—. "Weltinterpretationen um 1800." In *200 Jahre "Reden über die Religion": Akten des 1. Internationalen Kongresses der Schleiermacher-Gesellschaft Halle 14.-17. März 1999*, edited by Ulrich Barth and Claus-Dieter Osthövener, 58–78. Berlin and New York: Walter de Gruyter, 2000.

Sørensen, Bengt Algot. *Symbol und Symbolismus in den ästhetischen Theorien des 18. Jahrhunderts und der deutschen Romantik*. Copenhagen: Munksgaard, 1963.

Tillich, Paul. "Das religiöse Symbol." In *Writings in the Philosophy of Religion/Religionsphilosophische Schriften*, 213-28. Vol. 4 of *Main Works/Hauptwerke*. Berlin and New York: Walter de Gruyter and Evangelisches Verlagswerk, 1987.

Todorov, Tzvetan. *Symboltheorien*. Translated by Beat Gyger. Tübingen: Max Niemeyer Verlag, 1995.

Schleiermacher, Realism, and Epistemic Modesty

A Reply to My Critics[1]

JACQUELINE MARIÑA

In this paper I hope to answer some objections raised in response to the claims I put forward in my presentation "Metaphysical Realism and Epistemological Modesty in Schleiermacher's Method" at the Schleiermacher conference in Chicago last fall. I will begin by briefly restating what I mean by 1) Schleiermacher's realism and 2) his epistemological modesty. I will then flesh out these terms by attending to some of the objections to my thesis put forward by my colleagues during the question and answer period.

In order to avoid confusion, it is important to understand what it is I mean when I call Schleiermacher a *realist*. By this I do not mean that he is any kind of naïve realist, or that he adheres to a correspondence theory of truth. Schleiermacher's realism is, as he calls it a "higher realism." Part of my project here is getting straight on what this higher realism amounts to. It is no doubt true that a key feature of Schleiermacher's project involves careful attention to the role of human *experience* in the apprehension of the transcendent ground. Yet Schleiermacher's focus on human experience does not ignore the fact that religious experience is, for him, always experience *of* the Absolute, and that it is *to* the Absolute that religious symbols point. From the standpoint of Schleiermacher's metaphysics, the Absolute is that which establishes and preserves everything that is; it is that which ultimately works in and through history to transform human beings into God-like persons. Schleiermacher's theory of religion does not reduce religion to

---

[1] Another version of this paper will appear as "Metaphysical Realism and Epistemological Modesty in Schleiermacher's Method," in *Rethinking the Enlightenment: Philosophy, Theology, and Secularization in Modern Thought*, ed. N. Jacobs and Chris Firestone (South Bend: Notre Dame University Press, 2010). The original version of this paper was presented at the Schleiermacher conference at the University of Chicago under this title.

mere anthropology; to claim that it does is to misunderstand him on a grand scale.

Nevertheless, Schleiermacher is quite attentive to the *conditions* of human knowing and experiencing. Concern with these conditions was not new to theology; Thomas Aquinas had already noted: "the thing known is in the knower according to the mode of the knower."[2] What was new to theology was the comprehensive character of Schleiermacher's account of human subjectivity, an account that both recognized and stressed the finite and conditioned character of all human apprehensions. This account, heavily influence by Kant's metaphysics and epistemology, went beyond even Kant in recognizing not only the contribution of the human subject to all knowing and experiencing, but the contribution of human communities—themselves historically conditioned—to human knowing as well. These insights were especially applied to religious experience. Because Schleiermacher's theory begins with a comprehensive account of human subjectivity, it is theoretically equipped to recognize the validity of different religious experiences without degenerating into relativism. This I will call its *perspectivalism*. This paper will be a discussion of these two themes—Schleiermacher's realism and his perspectivalism—and their significance for a theory of religion.

1. A Higher Realism

Schleiermacher called his own brand of realism a "higher realism." The later Schleiermacher contrasted his own position with the idealism of Fichte, in which the I knows only itself. Fichte, famously, eliminated Kant's thing in itself and all of Kant's dualisms: for him there is nothing distinct and "outside" the self with which the self interacts. There is nothing that exists *in itself*, that is, apart from its relation to the subject and unknowable by the subject. In order for knowledge to be possible, Fichte argued, there must be a subject-object identity, and hence, in any act of knowledge, the self only really knows itself. For the mature Schleiermacher, on the other hand, the Absolute really does transcend consciousness: it is distinct from the self, while at the same time remaining the ground of the self.[3] Moreover, other finite individuals are

---

2   Thomas Aquinas, *Summa Theologica*, II/II, Q. 1, Art. 2, in *Basic Writings of Saint Thomas Aquinas*, ed. Anton Pegis (New York: Random House, 1945), 2:1057.
3   Schleiermacher differs significantly from Fichte on this point. Günter Zöller has correctly noted that Fichte "insists on the presence of the absolute in the I. It is the absolute itself that manifests itself under the form of the thinking and willing I."

also genuinely distinct from the I. Hence, for Schleiermacher, there are *real* relations between the self and others, and between the self and the Absolute. Even in the earliest edition of the *Speeches* (1799) Schleiermacher recognizes these real relations.[4] While there is no doubt that there are Spinozistic tendencies in his earlier works, the mature Schleiermacher leaves these behind, becoming more consistent in thinking through the necessary conditions for real relations between individual substances.[5]

Famously, in *The Christian Faith* Schleiermacher grounds genuine religion in "the feeling of absolute dependence" or what he also calls the "God-consciousness." This "feeling" is not one feeling among others that can be made an object *of* consciousness, but is given at the very ground of consciousness itself, in what Schleiermacher calls the immediate self-consciousness. In self-consciousness, the self makes itself its own object, and can thereby distinguish between itself and the world. However, the relation between self and world, between the spontaneity and receptivity of the self, presupposes an original unity of consciousness, a moment given in pure immediacy, wherein the two are one. It is this original unity of consciousness that makes possible the transition between the moments of spontaneity and receptivity. The consciousness of absolute dependence is given in this moment of pure immediacy; it is "the self-consciousness accompanying the whole of our spontaneity, and because this is never zero, accompanying the whole of our existence, and negating absolute freedom."[6] God is the "Whence of our active and receptive existence" (CF §4.4). However, while the Absolute must accompany all moments of consciousness (since it grounds the self), consciousness of God is not directly given in the immediate self-consciousness.[7] What is given, rather, is a consciousness of the self as

---

Zöller, "German Realism: The Self-limitation of Idealist Thinking in Fichte, Schelling, and Schopenhauer," in *The Cambridge Companion to German Idealism*, ed. Karl Ameriks (Cambridge: Cambridge University Press, 2000), 206.

4 In *On Religion* he notes, "All intuition proceeds from an influence of the intuited on the one who intuits . . ." *On Religion: Speeches to its Cultured Despisers*, ed. and trans. Richard Crouter (Cambridge: Cambridge University Press, 1996), 24. I discuss this passage at length below.

5 I discuss this issue at length in my book *Transformation of the Self in the Thought of Friedrich Schleiermacher* (Oxford: Oxford University Press, 2008), especially in chapters 3, 4, and 6.

6 Friedrich Schleiermacher, *The Christian Faith*, ed. H.R. Mackintosh and J.S. Stewart (Edinburgh: T&T Clark, 1999), §4.3. Henceforth cited in text as CF.

7 This has been argued by both Manfred Frank and Robert Adams in their contributions to *The Cambridge Companion to Friedrich Schleiermacher*, ed. Jacqueline Mariña (Cambridge: Cambridge University Press, 2005). See Robert Merrihew Adams,

absolutely dependent, in particular in regard to its own spontaneous action in relation to the world. The consciousness of absolute dependence is the consciousness that "the whole of our spontaneous activity comes from a source outside us" (CF §4.3). Consciousness of the self as dependent arises from the consciousness of a "missing unity" in the river of the soul's life as it flickers from spontaneity to receptivity. One of the most insightful analyses of Schleiermacher's understanding of the feeling of absolute dependence is that of Manfred Frank, which is worth quoting at length here:

> Consciousness feels itself to be *absolutely* dependent on Being, and this dependence is indirectly represented as the dependence on the Absolute. When immediate self-consciousness (or feeling) flickers from one to the other pole of the reflexive rift, this does not shed light on the positive fullness of a supra-reflexive identity, but rather on its lack. Schleiermacher notes that in the moment of "transition" ([C] 286) from object to subject of reflection, self-consciousness always traverses the space of a "missing unity" (C 290, §LI). Since the self cannot attribute this lack to its own activity, it must recognize this lack as the effect of a "determining power transcending it, that is, one that lies outside its own power" (C 290). The self can only ascribe to itself the ground of *knowledge* of this dependence. Schleiermacher can thereby say that the cause of this feeling of dependence is not "effected by the subject, but only arises *in* the subject" (CF §3.3). However, in feeling, the activity of the self is "never zero," for "without any feeling of freedom a feeling of absolute dependence would not be possible" (CF §4.3).[8]

We can think of this "missing unity" as the horizon or backdrop of consciousness. This horizon comprehends both self and world and is the condition of the possibility of both their difference from one another *and* their relation. It is traversed by consciousness itself insofar as consciousness must move between itself as the subject of reflection and the world that is given to it to know. Consciousness comes to an *explicit* awareness of this missing unity only in reflecting upon the transcendental conditions of the possibility of the moments of self-consciousness, in which there is an antithesis between self and world. Both the immediate self-consciousness and the feeling of absolute dependence are only given along *with* the sensuous self-consciousness; that is, only insofar as the self distinguishes between itself and its world can it arrive at an awareness of the underlying unity conditioning the possibility of its making this distinction. There is an important sense, of

---

"Faith and Religious Knowledge" (35-51) and Manfred Frank, "Metaphysical Foundations: A Look at Schleiermacher's *Dialectic*" (15-34).

[8] Frank, "Metaphysical Foundations," 31. In-text citations of "C" refer to what Jonas believed to be handwritten notes to the lectures of 1822. These are reproduced in Schleiermacher, *Dialektik*, ed. Manfred Frank (Frankfurt: Suhrkamp, 2001).

course, in which this underlying unity is given in the immediate self-consciousness. However, while the *traversal* of this missing unity occurs at the level of the immediate self-consciousness, one only becomes aware of its implications (namely, absolute dependence on the Whence of our active and receptive existence) through reflection. This distinction should help answer the question put forward by both Robert Adams and Wayne Proudfoot, namely, that of how the consciousness of absolute dependence can be both immediate and have intentional content.[9] The basis for the feeling of absolute dependence is given in the immediate consciousness, but its implications, and hence its intentional content, are only given as one reflects on this experience as a condition of the possibility of self-consciousness.

In the *Dialektik* Schleiermacher asks, "How does it [the immediate self-consciousness] relate to the transcendental ground?" And he answers, "We consider the latter to be the ground of the thinking being in regards to the identity of willing and thinking. The transcendental ground precedes and succeeds all actual thinking, but does not come to an appearance at any time. This transcendental ground of thought accompanies the actual thinking in an atemporal manner, but never itself becomes thought."[10] The Absolute transcends consciousness so thoroughly that it "does not come to an appearance at any time." For Schleiermacher, consciousness of God is not given directly in the immediate self-consciousness. As noted above, what is directly given is a consciousness of the self *as* absolutely dependent. Co-posited along with this consciousness is the Absolute itself.

Some Schleiermacher scholars have insisted that Schleiermacher is self-consciously aware that all he has arrived at is a *consciousness* of the Absolute, leaving the skeptical question of whether there actually *is* an Absolute completely untouched.[11] On such a reading, one never moves past consciousness and its objects: on the one hand, there is the *feeling* of absolute dependence given in the immediate self-consciousness; on the other hand, there is its correlate, the consciousness of God or the Absolute, which must be co-posited along with it. But both the feeling and its correlate are, so to speak, mere elements of consciousness carrying no metaphysical implications beyond themselves.[12]

---

9   This problem was the subject of Wayne Proudfoot's presentation at this conference and is discussed by Robert Adams in "Faith and Religious Knowledge."
10 KGA II/10.2, 568.
11 This anti-realist reading was expressed by several of the Schleiermacher scholars participating in the Chicago conference.
12 Robert Adams recognizes a related problem when he notes, "Can we say then that according to the *Christian Faith* God is not the intentional object of the essential reli-

There are several reasons to be highly suspicious of such an anti-metaphysical reading. First is the fact that Schleiermacher clearly posits a transcendental ground and its effects throughout his theological and philosophical works; for instance, in the passage just quoted, Schleiermacher clearly tells us that the "transcendental ground precedes and succeeds all actual thinking." Second, the anti-metaphysical reading ignores much of the work that Schleiermacher is doing in positing both the immediate self-consciousness and the feeling of absolute dependence. And third, the whole of Schleiermacher's theology cannot be made sense of without assuming his metaphysical realism. It is to the second and third of these reasons that I now turn.

Can Schleiermacher legitimately move past mere reports concerning states of human consciousness? The answer lies in the nature of his analysis of "the consciousness of absolute dependence." Is this a mere phenomenological report, analogous to, let us say the phenomenological report of the person in a fever who is conscious of feeling cold? If so, then of course Schleiermacher cannot move beyond a report on consciousness and its objects, since in both cases there is no guarantee that the mind actually reflects the real. However, Schleiermacher does not arrive at his description of the immediate self-consciousness and the feeling of absolute dependence through any kind of phenomenological introspection. He arrives at them through an *analysis of the conditions of the possibility of consciousness itself*. And this means that both his analysis of the immediate self-consciousness and of the consciousness of absolute dependence have significant metaphysical implications. As I have argued above, Schleiermacher's analysis of the consciousness of absolute dependence is grounded in the immediate awareness of the rift that consciousness must cross as it transitions from the subject to the object of reflection. If we can grant Schleiermacher that this rift is a real one, that is, that there *is* a genuine distinction between self and world, then we can also grant him the dependent character of both self and world: both presuppose a horizon conditioning the consciousness of

---

gious consciousness, the feeling of absolute dependence, but only of thoughts that reflect that feeling?" His answer to this particular problem differs from the one I offer below in that it does not rely on the "thick" description of the feeling of absolute dependence that I analyze. However, Adams is certainly correct in insisting that "Schleiermacher is plainly committed to the *correctness* of his interpretative description of piety as a feeling *of* absolute dependence. He gives us no reason to think that this feeling can be specified or identified except in terms of religious concepts expressing such intentionality, as Proudfoot rightly points out. And Schleiermacher seems equally committed to the correctness of the inference from absolute dependence to a whence that can be called 'God'" (Adams, "Faith and Religious Knowledge," 38).

both. But this means the self is conscious of its absolute dependence because it *is* absolutely dependent. And once we posit the self as absolutely dependent, it follows that we can also posit *that* upon which the radically conditioned self depends. We arrive not *merely* at a *consciousness* of the Absolute, but on the Absolute as the condition of the possibility of consciousness itself. And the latter, as the ground of consciousness, must be real. To summarize: if it can be shown that *a condition of the possibility of self-consciousness* is a consciousness of absolute dependence (which is itself based the reality of the absolute dependence of consciousness), then the Absolute is a condition of the possibility of consciousness itself. And this is a metaphysical claim.

It seems to me that this reading of Schleiermacher is fundamentally sound, and that Schleiermacher can legitimately move from his "thick" description of the feeling of absolute dependence to the positing of a metaphysical Absolute. What of course still remains problematic—certainly at this stage—is the identification of this Absolute with God. A much less robust understanding of this Absolute—for instance, an identification of it with Being—would still do the required work. Nevertheless, it is important to point out that Schleiermacher understands the "God-consciousness" he describes at the beginning of *Christian Faith* as an abstraction from the Christian God-consciousness that he is presupposing as the primary datum for his theology.

I now briefly turn to my third point: Schleiermacher's theology makes no sense if we do not attribute to him the conviction that God, and not just the consciousness of God, is real and genuinely effective. Schleiermacher's theology, like that of Albert Magnus and Aquinas before him, is based on the "way of causality." He claims in the *Christian Faith* that "all the divine attributes to be dealt with in the *Glaubenslehre* must go back in some way to the divine causality since they are only to elucidate the feeling of absolute dependence" (CF, §50.3). This of course means that Schleiermacher does not claim to have any knowledge of God as God is *in se*. Nevertheless, we do have knowledge of God in relation to us. Of particular importance for this knowledge is the redemption that God effects in us through Christ. This redemption is powerful and transformative not only of persons, but of whole communities as well. What is the source of this redemption? Schleiermacher is clear that it is not something we effect in ourselves; it has its basis in a source outside ourselves, namely in the communicated perfection and blessedness of Christ. And as I have argued elsewhere, Schleiermacher conceived of all the moments of Jesus' sensuous self-consciousness as utterly conditioned by the divine influence.[13] This influence is the source of Jesus' transformative power on human consciousness. While Schleiermacher is careful not to make any claims concerning God's nature as God is *in se*, he clearly posits God as the ultimate author of our salvation in Christ. Once again, this transformation is the result of a very real power whose source lies beyond what we are ourselves capable as radically conditioned and finite subjects.

Insofar as Schleiermacher affirms the existence of the Absolute, and acknowledges that what is real is independent of our conceptions of it, he is a metaphysical *realist*. His realism can be contrasted with contemporary anti-realism in religion, which affirms that all existence claims concerning God should simply be re-understood as commitments to a certain way of life.[14] For Schleiermacher, on the other hand, all religious expressions point past themselves to the "Whence of our active and receptive existence (CF §4.4)." While for Schleiermacher religious expressions are reflective of human experience, they do not merely refer to human ways of being in the world or to human experience, but also point to the transcendent Ground of all human experience. Hence while the disciplines of psychology, sociology, and anthropology might shed light on religion, religion can in no way be reduced to a study of the objects of those disciplines. Moreover, crucial to Schleiermacher's enterprise is the claim that God not only exists, but that God is also continuously *active* in the providential direction and care of humanity. This is a key point to keep in mind, especially given the high premium that Schleiermacher places on human transformation, which is effected in us by the loving source of all existence.

2. Perspectivalism

It is, of course, important to keep in mind that this "Whence" is apprehended *through* human experience. What is revealed is never a proposi-

---

13 See "Transformation of the Self through Christ," chapter 7 of my book *Transformation of the Self*.

14 One example of such anti-realism is the position put forward by Don Cuppit, who emphasizes the human world "bounded by language, time and narrativity and radically outsideless." For Cupitt there just is nothing outside our linguistic practices that constrains them in any way, and as such we must return "science into its own theories, religion into its own stories and rituals—and history into its own varied narratives." Don Cuppit, *After All* (London: SMC Press, 1994), 17. For a discussion of realism and anti-realism in religion, see Roger Trigg, "Theological Realism and Anti-realism," in *A Companion to Philosophy of Religion*, ed. Philip L. Quinn and Charles Taliaferro, (Cambridge: Blackwell, 1999), 213-22.

tion mirroring the structure of what is known, but an experience *of* the transcendent ground. Schleiermacher tells us that revelation does not "operate upon [one] as a cognitive being," for that "would make the revelation to be originally and essentially *doctrine*" (CF §10.3). Furthermore, this experience is completely different in kind from the experience we have of finite objects in the world. It occurs at the level of the immediate self-consciousness grounding our awareness of both self and world. As such, the original religious experience is never of anything *in* the world but is, rather given in pure immediacy, at that fleeting moment prior to reflection of the self as distinct from the world. Religious doctrines, beliefs, and practices arise from a culturally conditioned reflection upon this experience, which is always one of finite subjects. Hence the religious experience of other persons may be different from one's own, and yet just as valid. As Schleiermacher notes: "Each person must be conscious that his religion is only part of the whole, that regarding the same objects that affect him religiously there are views just as pious and, nevertheless, completely different from his own, and that from other elements of religion intuitions and feelings flow, the sense for which he may be completely lacking."[15] Hence while Schleiermacher is a *metaphysical realist*, epistemologically he is a *perspectivalist*. God is real, but our cognitive access to God is always finite and conditioned. Not only does our state influence how we perceive and how we can be affected, but our historical and cultural standpoint influences the range of how religious experience can be *interpreted* and its significance expressed.

This range of how religious experience is interpreted can nonetheless be quite broad, since key to the task of interpretation is the imagination. In Kant's system, which clearly influenced Schleiermacher, the imagination mediates between sense and understanding, synthesizing the data of perception and readying it for the application of concepts. But experience can be imagined and re-imagined in different ways. This is especially true for the broader implications of an experience, which can then be connected with other aspects of human experience in myriad ways. The religious experience, occurring as it does at the level of the immediate self-consciousness, is not the experience of an object existing over against a subject. As such, what is experienced transcends all of our cognitive capacities, and our concepts are never adequate to it. Occurring, as it does, at the level of the immediate self-consciousness, the genuine religious experience is one with global implications. It affects every aspect of the subject's life, particularly how

---

15 Schleiermacher, *On Religion*, 27.

the subject understands herself and her relation to the world. Here, in particular, the role of the imagination is paramount. In *On Religion*, Schleiermacher makes the bold statement that "belief in God depends on the direction of the imagination." He continues:

> You will know that imagination is the highest and most original element in us, and that everything besides it is merely reflection upon it; you will know that it is our imagination that creates the world for you, and that you can have no God without the world. Moreover, God will not thereby become less certain to anyone, nor will individuals be better able to emancipate themselves from the nearly immutable necessity of accepting a deity because of knowing whence this necessity comes. In religion, therefore, the idea of God does not rank as high as you think. Among truly religious persons there have never been zealots, enthusiasts, or fanatics for the existence of God; with great equanimity they were always aware of what one calls atheism alongside themselves, for there has always been something that seemed to them more irreligious than this.[16]

A person who has a genuine religious experience must continually strive to understand its significance for his or her life. Interpretation of such experience, as well as a grasp of its implications for life as a whole, involves both the imagination and the use of concepts. If the religious experience is revelatory of that which is of ultimate concern, then it must also be capable of transforming priorities in what is worth valuing. Genuine religion thereby implies a comprehensive integration of one's view of oneself and of the world with the understanding of this religious experience itself; in both, imagination and concepts are involved.

Nevertheless, Schleiermacher stresses that in religion "the idea of God does not rank as high as you think." So while Schleiermacher praises the importance of the imagination in integrating and understanding religious experience, at the same time he claims that the concepts used to make sense of that experience *are not* of the highest importance. Why is this? Important here is Schleiermacher's observation that among the truly religious there have never been zealots and enthusiasts. In fact, one of the principal points of the second speech in *On Religion* is that the persecution and spitefulness that "wrecks society and makes blood flow like water" often associated with religion does not arise from genuine or true religion. It only arises when religious experience is systematized in such a way that it is fettered. Those who "inundate religion with philosophy and fetter it to a system" are the corrupters of religion, and it is they, Schleiermacher claims, who are

---

16 Ibid., 53.

responsible for the perversion of the religious drive.[17] It is, of course, true that some degree of "systematization" is involved in any attempt to take the religious experience seriously and to thereby understand it. Schleiermacher himself wrote *The Christian Faith*, a fine piece of systematic theology. There are, however, two important dangers associated with systems: first, a system can become so comprehensive that it ceases to allow the religious experience to break *through* it. Elements of the system can encompass so many aspects and can be so tightly interwoven so as not to allow any room for anything foreign to these ideas (such as a transformative experience) to break in. Second, closely related with this first danger is the mistaking of this system for ultimate reality itself. Here something finite and conditioned, something human, is taken as absolute. But this is nothing less than idolatry, and from it springs the zealotry and enthusiasm that lies at the bottom of the religious intolerance that can so easily degenerate into religious warfare.

Persons that are truly religious have faith in *God*, that is, in the love and wisdom of ultimate reality. They recognize that God remains God regardless of what ideas one—or others—may have of God. God does not need to be defended, for the Absolute cannot be assailed. It is only all too human ideas that can be threatened and need defense. This is what Schleiermacher means when he says, "God will not thereby become less certain to anyone, nor will individuals be better able to emancipate themselves from the nearly immutable necessity of accepting a deity because of knowing whence this necessity comes." Accepting a deity, that is, standing in relation to the Absolute, is an immutable necessity. Yet, the religious experience is one that each person must have for him or herself in the inner sanctuary of the soul; the Absolute is always experienced *from* a particular perspective. Religious systems, and the enthusiasm and zealotry of the system builders who take themselves to have a privileged access to the Absolute, can only get in the way of this genuine experience. A truly transformative religious experience thereby carries with it *epistemological modesty*. This epistemological modesty goes hand in hand with Schleiermacher's *metaphysical realism*. What is real is independent of our conceptions of it, which are always limited and partial. The object of true religion is "the great, ever-continuous redemptive work of eternal love," not *our* ideas of the real.[18]

---

17 Ibid., 28.
18 Ibid., 43.

3. An Objection to Epistemological Modesty, and a Rejoinder

A significant concern with this proposal is that epistemological modesty can too easily turn into what might be called "epistemological nihilism."[19] Does this position not leave us in a quandary, since according to it, we can never really know God, but only our ideas of God, which are radically historically conditioned? How does Schleiermacher's position avoid the radical implications expressed by John Hick in his *Interpretation of Religion*?

> [W]e cannot apply to the Real *an sich* the characteristics encountered in its *personae* and *impersonae*. Thus it cannot be said to be one or many, person or thing, substance or process, good or evil, purposive or non-purposive. None of the concrete descriptions that apply within the realm of human experience can apply literally to the unexperiencable ground of that realm. For whereas the phenomenal world is structured by our own conceptual frameworks, its noumenal ground is not. We cannot even speak of this as a thing or an entity.[20]

This position leaves us simply adrift, without any real sense of direction. If we cannot even legitimately say that the object of religion is good or evil, purposive or non-purposive, then religion looses its point. This is an important objection that is not easy to overcome. Nevertheless, a correct understanding of Schleiermacher's position shows that he has the resources to answer it.

It is important to keep in mind that Schleieramacher's perspectivalism is a consequence of his realism. In *On Religion* he tells us:

> All intuition proceeds from the influence of the intuited on the one who intuits, from an original and independent action of the former, which is then grasped, apprehended, and conceived by the latter according to one's own nature. If the emanations of light—which happen completely without your efforts—did not affect your sense, if the smallest parts of the body, the tips of your fingers, were not mechanically or chemically affected, if the pressure of weight did not reveal to you an opposition and a limit to your power, you would intuit nothing and perceive nothing, and what you thus intuit and perceive is not the nature of things, but their action upon you.[21]

That is, Schleiermacher posits real relations between ourselves and others, and between ourselves and the Absolute. This means that our access to others and to the Absolute arises from their influence upon us.

---

19   The phrase was used by John Crossley at the conference.
20   John Hick, *An Interpretation of Religion* (New York: Palgrave, 2004), 246.
21   Schleiermacher, *On Religion*, 24-25.

But what this influence is depends on two things: first, the powers of that which influences us, and second, our *capacities* to be affected in certain ways (our own "nature"). It is only because we are capable of being affected in certain ways that we can perceive, but these very capacities play an important role in shaping the content of perception. As such, this very realism and the positing of real relations implies that we do not have access to things as they are *an sich,* but only to how they affect us. Furthermore, how we are affected by things is then interpreted by us through our own culturally conditioned categories.

At this point it important to keep in mind a key feature of realism, allowing us to distinguish it from idealism and anti-realism. In a short paper on realism and anti-realism in religion, Roger Trigg defines realism in the following way: "What we have beliefs about is not meant to be *logically* related to them."[22] That is, *what* we have beliefs about is distinct from our ideas about it, and we cannot make inferences from our ideas about something to the actuality of the thing. We can only make inferences from one idea to another. But if beliefs are not logically related to what they are about, then what is our relation to things? Such a relation is a *real* relation, that is, a relation of *influence* where one thing affects another.

How might such realism allay the qualms mentioned above? In *The Christian Faith,* Schleiermacher affirms that piety is "the consciousness of being absolutely dependent, or, which is the same thing, of being in relation with God" (CF §4). God is the "Whence of our active and receptive existence" (CF §4.4); faith then, is the consciousness of being absolutely dependent upon God. It cannot be stressed enough, however, that for Schleiermacher the object of faith is not the consciousness of being absolutely dependent (for then the object of faith would be something human) but rather, this real relation of absolute dependence itself. As creatures, we stand in absolute dependence on God. Moreover, as Schleiermacher would develop in later sections of *The Christian Faith,* God's absolute causality is qualitatively different from finite causality. In finite causality, one thing influences another, and the influence of one thing upon another is always conditioned by the capacities of that thing to be affected by the other. In God's absolute causality, on the other hand, God establishes the very existence of that which receives the divine influence. Hence nothing is left outside of God's power with respect to how the divine influence is to be received. For Schleiermacher, the process of the complete divinization of the cosmos is only a matter of time, and is assured in virtue of God's absolute causality.

---

22 Trigg, "Theological Realism and Antirealism," 217.

Given this stress on real relations, Schleiermacher's emphasis is ultimately not on what *we* can know about God, but on God's relation to us, which has real effects on us, namely our transformation and divinization. This transformation is not dependent upon our ideas of God, but rather on God's direct influence upon us.

Schleiermacher and Transcendental Philosophy

FRANKLIN I. GAMWELL

What is the relation, if any, between Schleiermacher's achievement and transcendental philosophy?[1] Address to this question requires at the outset a relevant definition of "transcendental." In contrast to its principal use in scholastic thought, the term now readily evokes reference to Kant's critical philosophy, where transcendental conditions are those necessary to human reason as such, theoretical and practical, and thus equivalent to what Kant calls metaphysical principles. Mindful of this reference, I will use "transcendental" in a broad sense to mean the following: Transcendental conditions constitute subjectivity, that is, existence with understanding, as such, so that every possible act of understanding presupposes them. Transcendental philosophy seeks to explicate these conditions.

It follows that true transcendental statements are pragmatically necessary; every subject who denies what any such statement asserts engages in a pragmatic self-contradiction, implying in the act of denial what is denied. For instance, if subjects as such are, with Kant, bound by the moral law, then "something bound by the moral law exists" is pragmatically necessary, and every subject who denies this statement implies in doing so the existence of something bound by the moral law—as Kant sought to show. I have formulated the statement as one about existence, but it might also be presented as a statement about subjectivity, for instance, "some subject is bound by the moral law." Again assuming that subjects as such are so bound, we can see that this statement, too, is pragmatically necessary. Every subject who denies it implies in doing so that some subject is bound by the moral law. Arguably, moreover, the statement is also logically self-contradictory: being bound by the moral law is a property entailed by being a subject.

---

1   I mean by "relation" a positive relation. Some might take separation to be, in its own way, a relation, but I use the term such that independence is the absence of a relation and thus ask what relation there is, *if any*, between Schleiermacher's achievement and transcendental philosophy.

Still, the formulation of transcendental statements as existential statements has the following advantage: it allows a clear distinction between two kinds of transcendental statements, namely, those whose necessity is only pragmatic and those whose necessity is also logical. Thus, "something bound by the moral law exists" is, while perhaps pragmatically necessary, not logically necessary, at least if we allow that only existence with understanding is moral or immoral. But "something temporal exists" is, on some understandings of existence, both pragmatically and logically necessary, because this statement asserts a condition presupposed not only by every act of subjectivity but also by strictly every possibility. Confining oneself to statements about existence, in other words, clarifies how transcendental conditions might be present in a strict as well as a broad sense. In the broad sense, true statements about such conditions include all pragmatically necessary existential statements, and in the strict sense, true statements about such conditions are existential statements that are also logically necessary. One might use "metaphysical" in the same systematically ambiguous way, but I will here reserve that term for transcendental conditions in the strict sense, that is, conditions of existence as such.

1. Philosophy and Dogmatics: A Reading of Schleiermacher

In stipulating these designations of "transcendental," I am not asserting that subjectivity or existence as such does have necessary conditions. Here at the outset, I mean only to provide some precision for the question: What is the relation, if any, between Schleiermacher's achievement and transcendental philosophy? The answer depends on how his introduction to *The Christian Faith*, with its propositions borrowed from philosophical reflection, should be understood.

This understanding can be approached through the arresting statement found toward the end of the introduction's definition of dogmatics: "Our dogmatic theology will not . . . stand on its proper ground and soil with the same assurance with which philosophy has so long stood on its own, until the separation of the two types of proposition is so complete that, *e.g.*, so extraordinary a question as to whether the same proposition can be true in philosophy and false in Christian theology, and *vice versa*, will no longer be asked" (§16, Postscript).[2] I will not seek to sort out all this statement might mean but, rather, will

---

2   All parenthetical references are to Friedrich Schleiermacher, *The Christian Faith*, ed. H.R. Mackintosh and J.S. Stewart (Edinburgh: T&T Clark, 1989).

focus on why, for Schleiermacher, dogmatic and philosophical truth are so separated that asking whether true dogmatic statements are true in philosophy is an improper or pointless question. This focus will suffice to clarify the relevant function of Schleiermacher's introduction and, further, the respect in which his achievement is related to transcendental philosophy. Also, I will not seek to detail the definition or definitions Schleiermacher gives to "philosophy." It will suffice if this term, in its relevant meaning, designates the science of self-conscious life in general.

That Schleiermacher begins with propositions from philosophy confirms what he says in §1, namely, that his introduction is not itself a part of dogmatics. It then follows that his statement separating truth in dogmatics and truth in philosophy, appearing in the final part of the introduction, is not itself a dogmatic but is, rather, a philosophical statement. Logic also commends this conclusion. Were the separation itself dogmatic, philosophers would, against Schleiermacher's statement, still have good reason to ask "the extraordinary question." Moreover, his account would be problematic in a way characteristic of any attempt to circumscribe the meaning and truth of Christian faith entirely within the Christian experience of Jesus and thus with complete independence from philosophy. So to assert is to imply that self-conscious existence includes no common human experience on the basis of which the difference between dogmatics and philosophy can be explicated. But that implication, however negative in form, is itself a statement about self-conscious existence in general and thus is philosophical in character, and thereby the supposed independence of Christian faith from all philosophical implications becomes self-refuting.

Indeed, a similar problem invades every assertion that meaning and truth are in all respects circumscribed by tradition or lifeworld or epoch in the history of Being and, therefore, by some specific location in the human adventure—however generously that location might be marked. The supposed meaning and truth of *this* assertion are about all locations of understanding, and thus any subject who so asserts engages in a pragmatic self-contradiction. Karl-Otto Apel, I believe, has it right: "Whoever seriously speaks of the conceptual meaning of 'meaning' and 'truth' as being in the last instance dependent on events or fate—that is [asserts] that the *logos* of our discursive claim to meaning and truth is in principle subordinate to time—thereby cancels the claim to the meaning and truth of their discourse."[3] In any event, Schleier-

---

3   Karl-Otto Apel, *Selected Essays, Volume Two: Ethics and the Theory of Rationality* (New Jersey: Humanities Press, 1996), 178.

macher's account is not vulnerable to this problem because, for him, the separation of dogmatic from philosophical truth is a philosophical conclusion, so that this difference is not itself a dogmatic truth or, to say the same, the introduction is not itself a part of dogmatics.

Whether the introduction's philosophical discussion is intentionally transcendental is, however, another question. Against that reading, one might argue, Schleiermacher's apparently persistent appeal to introspection (see, e.g, §4.1) at least suggests that he presents a kind of empirical inquiry, summarizing the general facts of self-consciousness as they appear. Still, the generic description seems to explicate features of self-conscious existence as such, those present wherever it could conceivably occur, and invites a reading of them as transcendental conditions, especially when Schleiermacher uses such phrases as "essential element of human nature" (§6.1) and "absolutely general nature of man" (§33.1). For instance, his assertion that every moment of self-consciousness includes both a feeling of partial dependence and a feeling of partial freedom and, thereby, of "our coexistence with the world" of others seems to preclude the possibility that self-conscious existence could ever occur otherwise—and, if this is so, then every denial that these feelings exist would be pragmatically self-contradictory, the act of denial implying what it denies.

Indeed, I am persuaded that transcendental arguments for something like these two feelings can be successfully formulated—because a moment of self-consciousness can never be consciousness only of self (and, therefore, is partially dependent on some other or others) and can never be entirely determined by others (and, therefore, is partially free). But I will not further pursue those arguments. Clarity about the logic of Schleiermacher's philosophical introduction to his Christian dogmatics is served, I will argue, by taking his general conclusions, whether so intended or not, to explicate transcendental conditions.

The relation to Christian dogmatics is approached when general self-consciousness is said to include a feeling of God, a relation unlike any relation to the world because the co-determinant is not given and, in that sense, not an object. "As regards the feeling of absolute dependence. . . , this feeling cannot in any wise arise from the influence of an object which has in some way to be *given* to us" (§4.3). If one takes Schleiermacher's account to allow transcendental arguments for feelings of partial dependence and partial freedom, one can see in his discussion of absolute dependence the potential for similar reasoning. Always partially dependent, we can have no feeling of absolute freedom—or, to say the same, self-conscious existence is finite or within the world. But our very existence as finite, "the whole of our spontaneous activity" (§4.3), cannot be its own source. Moreover, no finite thing in relation to which we are partially dependent and partially free and thus exist in reciprocity—nor, for that matter, all finite things together (see §32.2)—can be the source of finite existence as such. Hence, immediate consciousness of our existence as finite includes a feeling of the infinite source of all and, in that sense, of a nonobjective or non-given "Whence."

For the moment, at least, I am not concerned to assess this argument. Whether or not it is sound, the importance of a transcendental formulation here becomes apparent. To be a self *is* to be finite, and thus one cannot be *self*-conscious without an awareness of one's finitude. If we thereby feel our absolute dependence, then self-conscious existence without this feeling cannot be so much as possible. Anticipating discussion to be pursued shortly, we may repeat the point as follows: If subjective existence without this feeling were so much as possible, then the feeling when it is present would depend on some conditions particular or specific to certain self-conscious individuals. The feeling would then become indistinguishable from what Schleiermacher calls a particular or specific religious affection, for instance, specifically Christian faith, and dogmatics could not have a philosophical introduction. Whether a transcendental account is read out of or into Schleiermacher's discussion, the general human relation to God could not be what he asserts it to be except as so understood, and my assumption that his analysis has this transcendental character is, in truth, essential to his conclusion.

As is well-known, Schleiermacher's description of this feeling has been widely criticized as nonsensical because it asserts a consciousness that is independent of any intentional object, that is, an object experience of which is inseparable from thought and thus from conceptual content.[4] On this reading, if I understand correctly, Schleiermacher describes the feeling in a manner analogous to Kant's description of "intuitions without concepts," even while the feeling is, Schleiermacher says, a conscious relation to God. For Kant, there is no human experience without concepts; "intuitions without concepts are blind."[5] Similarly, the criticism argues, there can be no human experience of God independently of thought. But whether or not Schleiermacher's account is finally convincing, this criticism is, I am persuaded, misplaced or, at least, misleading. He never denies that one's immediate relation to God

---

4   In speaking of an intentional object as inseparable from thought, I do not imply that it is necessarily dependent on language, such that the subject in question must have a linguistic representation of the object.

5   Immanuel Kant, *Critique of Pure Reason*, trans. Norman Kemp Smith (New York: St. Martin's Press, 1929), 93 (A51/B75).

is intentional and, to the contrary, persistently speaks of its object or its "co-determinant." What we require, on my reading, is attention to his differing meanings of "object" as something to which a subject does or might relate.

In one sense, all feeling, whether of God or of something in the world, is nonobjective. Having said that every self-consciousness involves "another factor besides the Ego," Schleiermacher continues: "But this Other is not objectively presented in the immediate self-consciousness" (§4.1). If, for the moment, we limit attention to things in the world, the "Other" is, on my reading, objectively presented only when consciousness reflects on and thereby represents (re-presents) what is immediately presented—or, as we may say, when consciousness is explicitly focused on something that is or has been immediately given. In the sense that having objects involves such reflection, immediate consciousness has no objects, and for this reason feeling is to be distinguished from knowing and doing, both of the latter two being, on Schleiermacher's use of terms, aspects or activities of reflective consciousness. But this accounting implies that feeling also relates the subject to objects in another sense, that is, to objects as immediately given—or, we may also say, as objects of implicit consciousness. Although nothing is reflectively represented in these feelings, they nonetheless have intentional objects. Were this not the case, one could not be immediately conscious of being partially dependent and partially free, since consciousness of oneself as so being necessarily distinguishes the self from what is given and thus distinguishes the given as an object.

With respect to being absolutely dependent, immediate consciousness distinguishes the self from God, and thus an intentional object is also present. But this object is unique because it is not *given*—or, as Schleiermacher also says, "we do not set ourselves over against any other individual being, but, on the contrary, all antithesis between one individual and another is in this case done away" (§5.1). What, then, is this difference between an object that is given and one that is not? On my understanding, Schleiermacher here differentiates objects that reflection or objective consciousness can designate literally in positive terms, on the one hand, from, on the other, the object that reflection can designate literally only by negation. Speaking of our immediate relation to God can designate the object literally only with such terms as "*not* another individual being" or "*not* an object of reciprocity" or "the absolute *un*divided unity" (§32.2) or "*in*finite" (§56.1)—and only in this sense is the co-determinant, unlike those in our feelings of the world, "nonobjective." Thus, Schleiermacher speaks of God in a way relevantly similar to Kant's conception of noumena. For Kant, to be sure, we can have no intuition of noumena and, therefore, no intuition of God, even while we can think of God as completely unconditioned and can affirm God's existence as a postulate of practical reason. For Schleiermacher, unlike Kant, the God whom we literally represent solely by negation is also the object of an immediate or implicit consciousness, which is presupposed by both theoretical and practical reflection.

It then follows that our feeling of absolute dependence has no content that reflection might call metaphysical or moral—at least if metaphysics represents existence as such, and moral thinking represents purposes or ends of action, in literal and positive terms. Both require immediate objects that are given, and the intentional object in our immediate relation to God is not given, that is, can be literally designated only by negation. In this sense, the feeling of absolute dependence is the "indispensable third" to metaphysical and moral content in our immediate self-consciousness.[6]

Precisely because its co-determinant is not given, this feeling in itself "is not the consciousness of ourselves as individuals of a particular description, but simply of ourselves as individual finite existence in general" (§5.1). Still, we live only as particular individuals, and thus the constitutive consciousness of God is never present except as "conjoined with" or in "reciprocal relation" with (§5.3) the sensible self-consciousness, the feelings of given or worldly objects that partially determine us as particular individuals, and "these sensible stimuli must be regarded as infinitely various" (§9.1). In this reciprocal relation, the feeling of absolute dependence becomes "a particular religious emotion" (§5.4) or a particular religious piety, that is, a feeling that varies depending on the sensible consciousness with which it is conjoined. Actual moments of human life integrate "the higher consciousness" and "the lower consciousness," whose "co-existence" may also vary depending on whether the one or the other is more or less dominant in "the unity of the moment" (§5.3). "The more the subject, in each moment of sensible self-consciousness, with his partial freedom and partial dependence, takes at the same time the attitude of absolute dependence, the more religious is he" (§5.3).

We can also make the point this way: Against theologians for whom the meaning and truth of Christian faith are circumscribed entirely within the Christian experience of Jesus, Schleiermacher asserts a common human experience of God. But God as thereby presented can be designated literally only by negation, and thus there is no common

---

6   Friedrich Schleiermacher, *On Religion: Speeches to its Cultured Despisers*, trans. John Oman (New York: Harper and Row, 1958), 38.

human experience of *God in relation to the world*.⁷ How the higher consciousness integrates with the lower consciousness cannot, therefore, be given philosophical or transcendental formulation. *That* such integration occurs is transcendental, but *what* integration occurs is entirely a particular religious piety. In this respect, so far as I can see, Schleiermacher repeats with reference to immediate self-consciousness what Aquinas says of theistic demonstration: "Through affirmations . . . we know *what* a thing is . . . ; but through negations . . . we know *that* it is distinct from other things, yet what it is remains unknown. Now such is the proper knowledge we have of God through demonstration."⁸

In this sense, Schleiermacher's conclusion denies anything that might be called "religion in general." If that expression is used, "nothing can fitly be understood by it but the tendency of the human mind in general to give rise to religious emotions, always considered, however, along with their expression, and thus with the striving for fellowship, *i.e.* the possibility of particular religions" (§6, Postscript). That conclusion, then, warrants Schleiermacher's arresting statement about dogmatic and philosophical truth, at least insofar as asking whether true dogmatic statements are true in philosophy is a pointless question. Because positive awareness of God is not transcendental but always specific to some or other religious emotions, the science of dogmatics can only be the precise and systematic description of the "common distinctive quality of the religious emotions" (§10, Postscript)—or, we may also say, the faith—specific to the Christian community (or a particular Christian community). Statements that are true within that description can never be philosophically true or false precisely because there is no common human experience of God in relation to the world.

To be sure, certain dogmatic statements about God and the world may indeed sound like general statements of a philosophical kind, in part because the dogmatic theologian not only may but also must borrow language from philosophy to formulate her or his systematic description. But this dependence on philosophy is "only in form" (§19, Postscript); that is, the language is used to describe feelings of God in relation to the world, religious emotions, to which philosophy has no access. Even then, there are certain philosophical views "unfit for use in dogmatic language," namely, "those which make no separation between the conceptions of God and the World, admit no contrast be-

---

7   Again, I mean by "relation" a positive relation. One might say that experience of God as solely "not the world" is an experience of God in relation to the world, but I so use "relation" that relation is absent in this description of God. See note 1 above.

8   St. Thomas Aquinas, *Summa Contra Gentiles*, bk. 3, pt. 1, trans. Vernon J. Bourke (Notre Dame, Indiana: University of Notre Dame Press, 1975), 127-28 (39.1).

tween good and evil, and thus make no definite distinction in man between the spiritual and the sensible" (§28.1). Borrowing language used to articulate such views will misrepresent the Christian experience. When needed, if I understand correctly, "the business of [theological] Apologetics" (§28.3) is then to confirm by philosophical argument, perhaps through the general analysis of self-consciousness, that these views are unconvincing. One is again reminded of Aquinas, for whom natural reason cannot know the essence of God but can show that proofs for the nonexistence of God do not succeed.

Because it describes the specific religious affections of the Christian church (or a Christian church), dogmatics systematically redescribes feelings of God in relation to the world whose initial expression or communication is symbolic because their positive content is inseparable from a specific or particular determination of the sensible self-consciousness. Dogmatics, we can say, interprets Christian symbolic expressions and, making no philosophical claim to truth, is, in its own way, inescapably symbolic. Insofar, at least, there is common ground between Schleiermacher and Paul Tillich, for whom theology can speak positively of God only in symbolic terms.

2. Dogmatics and Philosophy: An Alternative to Schleiermacher

The foregoing is, at best, a terse reading of how transcendental philosophy might be read out of or into Schleiermacher's achievement and thus be seen to warrant his separation of dogmatic and philosophical truth. Summarily stated, meaning and truth in dogmatics imply transcendental philosophy because the former systematically interprets a particular religious faith or piety and thus depends on a logically prior explication of religion as a common human possibility. At the same time, dogmatic and philosophical truth are separated because the common human experience on which religion is based has no positive character a particular religious faith might in its specific way actualize.

If that summary will suffice, we may turn to the question: Is Schleiermacher's account convincing? We can approach this assessment by returning to the final note in my reading, namely, that all positive language about God is symbolic. At least to first appearances, that view seems to be self-defeating. If positive designation of God can never be literal, the possibility of speaking symbolically about God seems to be destroyed, since we then can explicate a symbol's meaning only in terms of other symbols and thus cannot distinguish speaking *about God* from merely expressing our private subjectivity or merely misusing language whose literal use designates something within the world. For Schleiermacher, however, dogmatic explication of specific religious affections does designate positively or in relation to the world the God of whom subjects as such are conscious in the feeling of absolute dependence, even if the co-determinant of that common human experience can be literally represented only by negation. Schleiermacher's solution, then, turns on whether an object of immediate consciousness can be designated by complete negation.

To the best of my reasoning, we here reach a thoroughly fundamental issue in philosophy and theology, and I wish to argue that designation by complete negation is meaningless, not a genuine thought. In sum, the reason is this: A supposed thought whose content is completely negative cannot be distinguished from another that is merely putative because it has no content at all. Consider, for instance, the supposed thought of a colorless yellow rose. Although one may utter the words, one cannot in fact have the thought because its supposed object has no content. One may think of something colorless, and one may think of something yellow, but one cannot think of something simultaneously colorless and yellow. Moreover, this supposed thought is completely negative. Purporting to think of something colorless, one designates something as not yellow; purporting to think of something yellow, one designates the same thing as nothing other than something yellow—and "something not yellow and nothing other than something yellow" is a complete negation. Hence, if some other complete negation—for instance, the "co-determinant" in our feeling of absolute dependence, as Schleiermacher intends this term—is to make sense, it must somehow be relevantly different from merely putative thoughts that have no content at all. In truth, however, there can be no such difference because the supposed content of each is completely negative, and a difference must be positive. A supposed difference in content that is in no way positive is no different than no difference at all. Hence, a supposed thought whose supposed content is completely negative is no different from a merely putative thought that is, in truth, no thought at all.

We might repeat the point as follows: Every supposed designation by complete negation is or implies an existential statement, "x exists" (or, if one prefers, "x is real") that is said to be logically possible, where the grammatical subject, x, has no positive content. At least insofar, then, every such statement is equivalent to statements of the form "x exists" (or "x is real") that are logically impossible because the grammatical subject is meaningless—for instance, "a colorless yellow rose exists (or is real)." If statements such as "an absolute undivided unity is real" or "a God infinite in all respects exists" are to be so much as logically possible, their grammatical subjects must somehow be distinguished from those that are nonsense. But no such distinction is possible if the former, as the latter, are completely negative.

This argument, I recognize, begs for sustained development in relation to objections. But if, as I am persuaded, it can be sustained, we should conclude that every assertion purporting to designate something by complete negation is meaningless. It then follows that Schleiermacher's project is profoundly problematic. If the common human experience of God has a co-determinant that cannot be literally represented in positive terms, there can be no such experience to co-exist with every sensible consciousness as a religious emotion. The immediate consciousness of absolute dependence, as Schleiermacher understands it, is a feeling no subject could have on land or sea. Because his account of that feeling is what warrants his separation of dogmatic and philosophical truth, we should also conclude that something is fundamentally problematic in Schleiermacher's conception of the dogmatic theological task.

Nothing in this critique says that we are not immediately aware of God. But if we are, the meaning of "God" cannot be what Schleiermacher takes it to be. If a philosophical analysis of self-consciousness shows that subjectivity as such relates to a unity beyond the world, the intentional object of this feeling must be one that reflection can designate literally in positive terms. An implicit consciousness of God does indeed, I am inclined to think, constitute existence with understanding. But I will here assume rather than argue for that conclusion—in order, first, to pursue what must be the case if Schleiermacher's philosophical introduction to dogmatics is so transformed as to be convincing, and then, second, to comment on what is implied for the Christian theological task.

As a reality reflection can designate literally in positive terms, God as an intentional object in common human experience must be, in its own way, *given*. Because God could not be so designated except in distinction from ourselves and all others in the given world, what is immediately present must be God in relation to the world. Hence, this immediate consciousness is the kind of feeling Schleiermacher finds only in religious emotions to which philosophical analysis has no access. Because this consciousness constitutes subjectivity as such, moreover, it must be a transcendental condition, a necessary condition of being a subject, so that every subject who denies an implicit awareness of God in relation to the world engages in a pragmatic self-contradiction.

Indeed, this awareness, we may conclude, involves transcendental conditions in both the broad and strict senses defined at the outset. The conditions are transcendental in the broad sense precisely because the awareness constitutes subjectivity as such. If aware of God in relation to the world, moreover, self-consciousness also involves transcendental conditions in the strict sense, that is, conditions of existence as such. This is because God is a reality other than anything within the world and, therefore, can be literally and positively distinguished from all worldly individuals only in terms that designate conditions of existence as such—worldly existence as such, on the one hand, and divine existence, on the other. To be sure, many have held that no existential affirmation can be *logically* necessary, that is, true transcendental statements in the strict sense are impossible, because, to cite Hume's dismissal of all a priori reasoning to God's existence: "Whatever we conceive as existent, we can also conceive as non-existent, there is no being, therefore, whose non-existence implies a contradiction."[9] But this objection has already been turned aside if, as previously argued, designation by complete negation is nonsensical. The conclusion there reached implies that "nothing exists," the sheer absence of all existents, is meaningless, so that "something exists," that is, sheer something or other, is a logically necessary statement, its denial being logically impossible. Moreover, anything implied by "something exists," any condition of existence as such, is also logically necessary and thus transcendental in the strict sense.

Contrary to Schleiermacher, then, constitutive awareness of God includes metaphysical content, that is, content whose representation by reflective consciousness designates existence as such in literal and positive terms. If we assume, with Schleiermacher, that every moment of human life is marked by a feeling of partial freedom, our immediate consciousness also includes moral content. Awareness of self in relation to God and the world implies awareness of one's subjectivity as a specification of the metaphysical conditions. Unless those conditions define the good one should decide to pursue, conscious freedom could not be such a specification of them. More than some others, I recognize, this last implication may elicit a call for further argument in relation to objections. But here, perhaps, it is sufficient that such objections are not likely to come from theists, for whom an understanding of God's cha-

---

9 David Hume, *Dialogues Concerning Natural Religion* (New York: Hafner Publishing Company, 1943), 58.

racter typically implies and is implied by a comprehensive good to which human purposes ought to be directed.

In sum, the transformation of Schleiermacher I propose understands our common human experience to be an implicit understanding of self in relation to God and the world that defines the self in terms of a divine purpose. As a condition of subjectivity as such, this self-understanding is a transcendental condition in the broad sense, and it includes the transcendental character, in the strict sense, of God and the world. At the same time, however, subjects consciously decide in some measure what to become, and thus we humans live by way of implicit decision for a self-understanding, that is, an understanding of ourselves in relation to God and the world. Because this decision may be, in the deepest sense, immoral as well as moral, we thereby either embrace the immediate consciousness constitutive of every subjective moment or become what we are by way of a false self-understanding. But the latter is never merely a mistake, because we are always also aware of the alternative we ought to elect. A self-understanding at fault is always duplicitous because one is inescapably aware of the alternative that defines integrity.

I will simply assert that this transcendental understanding of human life finds its most adequate resource in the neoclassical metaphysics first comprehensively presented by Alfred North Whitehead and subsequently refined for philosophical theology by Charles Hartshorne. Naturally, that assertion will not approach critical acceptance without a thoroughly extended discussion. Still, their basic contribution, I believe, is a systematic formulation that does not, in Whitehead's terms, "pay compliments" to God by making the divine reality an exception to the most general categories applicable to all other things. Literal designation of God solely by negation pays such a compliment. In this respect, Schleiermacher speaks of God in the manner found throughout so-called classical theism. I have especially in mind the putative conception of God as eternal or unchangeable in all respects and thus the reality to which none of the general categories applicable to things in the world literally applies.

Literally speaking of God only by negation is what led Kant to deny possible knowledge of God and to call such supposed knowledge "transcendental illusion," and Schleiermacher's inheritance of classical theism is, or so I have argued, the basic reason why he does not successfully discover a relation to God in our immediate self-consciousness. In contrast, neoclassical theism allows literal and positive designation of the divine character because God is conceived as the eminently temporal individual. For this reason, God is not a co-determinant with whom we have no reciprocity or an object not given. To the contrary, the eminently temporal individual is the universal individual, the only one who affects and is affected by strictly all others and thus the one on whom the exercise of our freedom has everlasting influence.

Still, we need not argue for neoclassical metaphysics in order to see what the previous discussion implies for Christian theology. If the transcendental transformation of Schleiermacher I have outlined is convincing, the dogmatic task cannot be adequately defined in the way he does. It is, on my accounting, perfectly proper to understand dogmatics as the precise and systematic description of Christian faith—or, we might say, disciplined or critical reflection on the meaning of Christian faith. Moreover, we may quite agree that "religion in general" is an expression fitly understood to designate only the possibility of particular religions, whereby systematic description of the faith characterizing a religion is not itself philosophy. Given the transformation, however, the designation of "religion" and "religious" is also altered. Schleiermacher takes any feeling of God in relation to the world to be a religious emotion and thus particular to some individual or, through communication, specific to some community of faith. But if subjects are necessarily conscious of God in relation to the world, then all humans, we may say, live by taking an implicit decision of faith, whose authenticity and thus inauthenticity can be defined philosophically. Thereby, our common human experience has a positive character that a particular religious piety may in its specific way actualize. Hence, a particular religion can only consist of expressions that claim to represent decisively our constitutive awareness of God and the world, and the function of religion is to mediate or cultivate implicit decisions that are authentic.

The implication for Christian theology is this: Asking whether a true dogmatic statement is true in philosophy is no longer improper—at least insofar as dogmatic statements are about ourselves in relation to God and the world. For Schleiermacher, the question is pointless precisely because feelings of God in relation to the world are all particular religious affections to which philosophy has no access. But if subjectivity as such is a decision of faith, then a true dogmatic statement, one that correctly describes the meaning of Christian faith, may be false in philosophy because Christian faith does not, at least in the respect explicated by the statement, include a true representation of subjectivity as such. Similarly, a true dogmatic statement may be true in philosophy precisely because Christianity is a true religion. This does not deny that dogmatics does not itself pursue whether a Christian understanding of God in relation to the world is philosophically true. But neither can truth in dogmatics be separated from truth in philosophy. Instead, the dogmatic task implies not only a logically prior transcendental analysis of religion as a common human possibility but also a logically subsequent transcendental assessment of its conclusions. In both respects, then, Christian systematic theology includes philosophy even while remaining a distinctive form of reflection because constituted by its distinctive question about the meaning and truth of Christian faith. Whether true dogmatic statements are true in philosophy is, moreover, finally the all-important theological question, because finally the task of theology is to assess whether Christian faith is a true representation of our common human experience and, thereby, a servant of our authentic humanity.

Transcendental Theories of Religion

Then and Now

Jörg Dierken

My concern here is the impact of transcendental philosophy on modern theories of religion. I shall proceed in three steps: First, I will comment on the roots of modern transcendental theories in the thought of Kant, focusing on "subjectivity." Second, I will reconstruct Schleiermacher's conception of "intersubjectivity." Finally, I will outline some consequences for contemporary theories of religion.

1. Kant: Transcendental Philosophy and Subjectivity

Transcendental theories originate in the critical thought of Kant.[1] Religion assumes a secondary role here,[2] for Kant's primary interests were epistemology and moral theory, both of which take the fundamental performances (*Vollzüge*) of human subjectivity as their point of departure. The "synthetic unity of apperception"—that is, the *spontaneous activity* of the Ego in the processing of the manifold of given contents (*Gehalte*), which are brought into categorially structured connections through this process in such a way that they are experienced as the

---

1 See "Transzendental; Transzendentalphilosophie," in vol. 10 of *Historisches Wörterbuch der Philosophie* (Basel: Schwabe, 1998), cols. 1358-1438, esp. 1379ff.
2 The explicit combination of the concepts "transcendental" and "theory of religion" occurs rather seldom, despite the fact that such theories belong implicitly to the tradition of Kantian thought. Arising chiefly in Protestant rather than in Catholic contexts, this type of theory focuses on religion understood as a component of the *conditio humana*, that is, as it is practiced by human beings. By contrast, "transcendental theology," a term primarily used in Catholic contexts, emphasizes forms of thought that regard God as the condition for the possibility of the knowledge of the world and the self. The following reflections concentrate on my own systematic outline of transcendental theories of religion as found in Kant and Schleiermacher. Some comments on the—still to be written—conceptual history of the term can be found in ibid., cols. 1426ff.

thoughts *of the Ego*—is "the highest point to which one must affix all use of understanding, even the whole of logic and, beyond that, transcendental philosophy."³ For Kant, "transcendental" refers to cognition "that is occupied not so much with objects but rather with our mode of cognition of objects insofar as this is to be possible *a priori.*"⁴ (The receptivity of sensibility, the other "root" of cognition, is explained from this perspective). Kant's transcendental investigation of pure will is based on principles that are given a priori⁵ and rooted in the will's general form. From the transcendental freedom of the rationally spontaneous will there emerges the idea of universal validity as the normative rule for all empirical willing and acting.⁶ Thus, in its practical mode, human subjectivity distances itself from everything external, be it the "pathological" disposition of human beings arising from their sensible nature, a given order, or religious tradition. For Kant this means that the principle of morality is *autonomy*.

Proceeding from basic performances of subjectivity has several consequences for a theory of religion. The locus and origin of religion cannot lie in that which is utterly beyond subjectivity. This also holds for the concept of God: by means of the critique of theistic schemata, religion is joined to the performances of subjectivity. These can become the basic point of reference for religion to the extent that the structural unconditionality (*strukturelle Unbedingtheit*) of subjectivity enters into a dialectical relationship with human finitude. From a theoretical point of view, this dialectic arises in the twofold root of cognition, which encompasses the spontaneity of the understanding and the receptivity of sensibility. From a practical point of view, the subject of the pure good will is at the same time also a natural being shaped by interests and dispositions, and it is for this reason that its autonomy is asserted in the form of the prescription of the moral law. Moreover, from both points

---

3   Immanuel Kant, *Critique of Pure Reason*, trans. and ed. Paul Guyer and Allen W. Wood (Cambridge: Cambridge University Press, 1998); *Kritik der reinen Vernunft*, vol. 3 of *Werkausgabe*, ed. Wilhelm Weischedel (Frankfurt: Suhrkamp, 1977), B 134 n. All Kant quotations are from the Cambridge Edition of the Works of Immanuel Kant. Page references follow the convention of citing the Akademie-Textausgabe pagination of Kant's works, which lines the margins of the Cambridge and Suhrkamp editions.
4   Kant, *Critique of Pure Reason*, B 25. Kant here distinguishes his use of "transcendental" from the ontological doctrines of traditional metaphysics concerning the transcendentals. The latter designate the trans-categorial grounds or goals of the mind.
5   See Immanuel Kant, *Groundwork of the Metaphysics of Morals*, in *Practical Philosophy*, trans. and ed. Mary J. Gregor (Cambridge: Cambridge University Press, 1996); *Kritik der praktischen Vernunft—Grundlegung zur Metaphysik der Sitten*, vol. 7 of *Werkausgabe*, ed. Wilhelm Weischedel (Frankfurt: Suhrkamp, 1978).
6   See Kant, *Critique of Pure Reason*, B 560ff.; *Groundwork*, BA 108, 123.

of view, all of the performances of subjectivity take place within natural and social—and thus historically *contingent*—circumstances. For Kant's thought, it is essential that the dialectic connected to the refraction of finitude by subjectivity cannot or should not be simply overcome. His thought thus remains within what may be described as the *perspective of the finite,* and it is from this perspective that strategies for a critical engagement with the intellectual and social consequences of this dialectic are conceptualized.[7] With this there emerges at the same time a "rational need" for reflectively visible symbolizations of—as it were—the other side of the dialectic of the finite.[8] It is here that religion and its contents come into play, doing so in such a way that the symbols are communicated inter-subjectively through the reception of historical linguistic images. Religion thus stands at the intersection between the rationally explicable dialectic of reason and historical social existence. This reveals three striking nodal points in Kant's theory.

First, religion and its mode of belief are clearly distinguished from theoretical knowledge. It is true that the notion of the "unconditioned" imposes itself on reason when, in the contemplation of the multiply determined, reason is confronted with "the totality of conditions."[9] As a consequence of this, the concept of God is made into ideal of reason that encompasses the *totality* of all predicates and is directed towards the universal determination of all things. Importantly, however, this concept of God is only a regulative one for the application of the understanding: it does not correspond to any tangible reality: even if it did, it would at any rate be a merely finite entity. In the same way that its content relates to the performances of the understanding with their tendency towards unity, the idea demands a totality grounded in the unconditioned, to which—as the true locus of the idea of God—practical reason advances.[10] This is because it conceptualizes a comprehensive order, but does so in terms of purposive, rather than causal concepts. For this reason, only the concept of *freedom* can unite the ideas of God

---

7 In this sense the "transcendental dialectic" leads to the notion of the ideas of reason as being ultimately regulative in character. It does so in the course of its critical examination of inappropriately reifying modes of understanding of these ideas, whereby the latter are placed on the same footing as empirical objects. This regulative status is also accorded to the relation of the practical idea of the highest good to the practice of morality under conditions of finitude.
8 Of greatest relevance here is the idea of God, from which lines can be drawn to a moral world, and to a final determination of subjectivity.
9 Kant, *Critique of Pure Reason,* B 379.
10 This is the central point of Kant's critique of the proofs of the existence of God in the *Critique of Pure Reason.*

and immortality[11] in a way that is accessible to man, that is to say, in the form of religion.[12] In this rational religion, man is integrated into a moral practice whose conditions and goals he can actually believe.

Second, it is central to the theory of religion that religion, though it is intimately connected with practical reason, can under no circumstances provide the foundation of morality. Morality is based on the principle of autonomy, and as such does not serve as an instrument for the motivation of moral action. This fact limits the reach of the political and social functionalization of religion. Instead, religion has the task of integrating those dichotomies that inevitably come to the fore in a grounding of morality in autonomy that takes place under conditions of finitude. Thus, if morality is not to be destroyed, there needs to be a prospect of a final—and certainly also counterfactual—proportioning of virtue and happiness. This is the concept of the highest good, which states that the moral law must be compatible with the processes of life in the sensible realm. Ultimately, that is, there must be a unification *of reason and nature* that nonetheless always remains tied to the *practice* of moral life. Without God and moral-religious faith, however, this task of integration remains unresolved.

This transcendental access to religion, however, is still far removed from real processes of life in the sensible realm, however much religion is given the function of comprehending the fundamental and limiting concepts of reason in this context. It is for this reason that religion is assigned, thirdly, the task of contending with the metaphysical-theological limit-problems of reason within the sphere of the historically contingent. And it is here that the central claim of Kant's transcendental theory of religion is made. The systematic apex of his writings on religion[13] does not consist in his using religion as an instrument for the implementation of morality. Nor does religion's primary task lie in clearing up problems left over from the critical theory of reason, such as the phenomenon of radical evil. Rather, what is involved here is tracing the development of rational faith in the historical and symbolic forms of communication of the "faith of the church." Through a dramatic dialectic, the normativity of rational faith takes the form of a

---

11 The idea of immortality is the vanishing point of a moral determination of man that is not restricted by finitude.
12 See Immanuel Kant, *Critique of the Power of Judgement*, trans. and ed. Paul Guyer and Eric Matthews (Cambridge: Cambridge University Press, 2000); *Kritik der Urteilskraft*, vol. 10 of *Werkausgabe*, ed. Wilhelm Weischedel (Frankfurt: Suhrkamp, 1979), B 468.
13 See Immanuel Kant, *Religion within the Boundaries of Mere Reason*, in *Religion and Rational Theology*, trans. and ed. Allen W. Wood and George di Giovanni (Cambridge: Cambridge University Press, 1996); *Die Religion innerhalb der Grenzen der bloßen Vernunft*, vol. 8 of *Werkausgabe*, ed. Wilhelm Weischedel (Frankfurt: Suhrkamp, 1978).

permanent unrest that brings "ecclesiastical faith" and its social forms into a creative interplay of correction and reconstruction. Religion is thus concerned with ground- and limit-problems of reason under the historically contingent conditions of finitude.

For transcendental theories of religion that take Kant as their point of departure, religion conceptualizes the unconditioned in the conditioned through the latter's own inner dialectic. As much as it lies between the two, it remains tied to the perspective of the conditioned. That is to say, religion marks the point of transition from the transcendentality of reason to the empirical realm of the historical. This conception of religion may be overlain by tendencies towards the restriction of the "faith of the church" to a vehicle of morality, as in the work of Kant himself. And Hegel's theory of religion is not free of tendencies towards the reflective assimilation of the religious dialectic in the contemplative self-satisfaction of Absolute Spirit. The later Fichte, distancing himself from the idea of the merely historical as the source of blessedness, focuses on the thought of the "self-annihilation" of the finite Self in the Absolute, although he does conceive of the freedom of the self-realization of the finite Ego as an appearance of the Absolute. In the face of such tendencies, the approach of transcendental theories of religion invites correction and modification—as can be seen in an exemplary manner in Schleiermacher.

2. Schleiermacher, or the Theory of Religion Between Subjectivity and Intersubjectivity

Schleiermacher's theory of religion is unimaginable without its Kantian background. Nevertheless, it remains embedded in a theory of social life. The *Glaubenslehre* enters the picture here as a critical theory of historical forms, employing "borrowed principles" from ethics.[14] Dogmatics is related to the church as a community "that only arises through free human actions."[15] For Schleiermacher, dogmatics focuses on processes of *intersubjective communication*. That is to say: all instances of individual piety ultimately involve a striving towards communication with other human beings. As such, piety in fact corresponds to processes of community formation. Philosophical ethics, according to

---

14 See Friedrich Schleiermacher, *Der christliche Glaube nach den Grundsätzen der evangelischen Kirche im Zusammenhange dargestellt* (1830-31), ed. Martin Redeker (Berlin: Walter de Gruyter, 1960); *The Christian Faith*, ed. H. R. Mackintosh and J. S. Stewart (London: T&T Clark, 2003), §2. Henceforth CG.
15 CG §2.2.

Schleiermacher, conceives of religion as an activity of "individual symbolization."[16] By this is meant a presentation (*Darstellung*) of reason (which, for Schleiermacher, is always fundamentally tied to nature) articulated by means of the individual employment of sensible signs, which are received by others and thereby come to form an "organic union."[17] So conceived, religion exhibits a range of connections to other social forms, such as the state, the family, and friendship. Yet, despite these relations of reciprocity, religion ultimately retains its independence. Indeed, already in the *Speeches*, religion is contrasted sharply with metaphysics and morality: its "essence is neither thinking nor acting, but rather intuition and feeling";[18] it aims at finding the "infinite" expressed in the "individual and the finite."[19] Corresponding to passivity as the basic feature of intuition and feeling is an activity of communication by means of which the "religious world [appears] as an indivisible whole."[20] The "One and All"[21] of the universe expresses itself through intuition and feeling in the individual person, and the individuals for their part form a whole through free communication.

Schleiermacher's concept of religion also has a basis in a theory of subjectivity. This is demonstrated clearly by the introduction to *The Christian Faith*. Here the concept of intuition is discarded. Feeling or, as it is now also referred to, "immediate self-consciousness" describes subjective lived states in which the differences between the self and objective contents are blurred. That is to say: in feeling, the self and its contents are one. Immediate self-consciousness thus also constitutes the interface between the receptive dimension of knowledge and the emergent dimension of action. As such, it forms the transition between both opposing tendencies and is thus implicitly present in each of their processes. Its inner unity thus corresponds to the totality of the reciprocal relations of activity and passivity of the self and its contents in its knowing and acting. Because of this totality of reciprocal effects, the

---

16 Friedrich Schleiermacher, *Ethik (1812/13)*, ed. Hans-Joachim Birkner (Hamburg: Meiner, 1981); *Lectures on Philosophical Ethics*, ed. Robert B. Louden (Cambridge: Cambridge University Press, 2002), §§196ff (Highest Good, Part III, On the Church).
17 Ibid., §209 (Highest Good, Part III, On the Church).
18 Friedrich Schleiermacher, *Über die Religion: Reden an die Gebildeten unter ihren Verächtern* (1799), ed. Hans Joachim Rothert (Hamburg: Meiner, 1970), 50 (original pagination); *On Religion: Speeches to its Cultured Despisers*, trans. and ed. Richard Crouter (Cambridge: Cambridge University Press, 1996), 22. "Feeling" (*Gefühl*) in Schleiermacher has a holistic meaning; its early Romantic connotations differ from the overly empirical concept of "emotion" as well as the physical concept of "sensation."
19 Schleiermacher, *Über die Religion*, 51; *On Religion*, 23.
20 Schleiermacher, *Über die Religion*, 187; *On Religion*, 76.
21 Schleiermacher, *Über die Religion*, 51; *On Religion*, 23.

unity of the subject joins itself, in feeling, "with the co-posited other."[22] The conjunction of both is the "world." "World" is the unity of the many in the continuity of self-consciousness, which at the same time becomes the "consciousness of our being in the world."[23] In this transcendental line of reasoning, the Spinozan "HEN KAI PAN" shines through the elementary processes of subjectivity.

This becomes clear in Schleiermacher's explanation of how immediate self-consciousness becomes aware of its own peculiarity in the nexus of the subjective faculties. It is always already given to itself — even in its highest peak of intensity — and already finds itself in its own states. It is finite in its very infinity or, as Schleiermacher puts it, it knows itself "from somewhere else."[24] This elementary *passivity* of its makeup constitutes the "absolute dependence" of the subject. However, without any feeling of *freedom* this would be impossible. For utter dependence can only be inferred through an indirect reflection which, given the reciprocal relativity of freedom and dependency, indicates that absolute freedom is impossible. The indirectness of this reflection is an expression of the fact that the feeling of dependency is only articulated in a mediated way, that is, through symbols. "God" describes its "whence" (*Woher*) and the "world" stands for the locus of its existence in multiple interrelations. This means that for the self, God and the world form the basic framework of its articulation.[25] Expressed in terms Schleiermacher's *Dialektik*, the correlative ideas of God and world represent unity without multiplicity and unity that encompasses the multiplicity of the individual.[26]

---

22 CG §4.2.
23 Ibid.
24 CG §4.3.
25 This is the source in Schleiermacher's theory of subjectivity for his theorem concerning the threefold form of dogmatic propositions, according to which propositions about God and propositions about the world are derived from propositions about the self. See CG §30.
26 Friedrich Schleiermacher, *Dialektik (1814/15)*, ed. Andreas Arndt (Hamburg: Meiner, 1988), §219. The nexus of both ideas permits the explication of the "transcendental ground" that is inferred from a line of reflection on the conditions of the possibility of certainty in knowing and willing, the subjective locus of which is feeling. As the unity of being and thought, real and ideal, it assumes the role of the idea of God in traditional ontotheology. To be sure, the transcendence of this ground comes into view in a transcendental line of reasoning, which, via reflection upon the correlative interaction of thought and willing, knowing and acting, discovers their unity as an implicit condition. For this reason, the ground as such cannot be positively explicated, even though its content is partially contained in all acts of thinking and willing, and thus constitutes the condition of their possibility. That it is present in the immediacy of self-consciousness or feeling clearly distinguishes Schleiermacher's

To be sure, the activity (*Vollzug*) of immediate self-consciousness is not wholly tied to its religious symbolization. Nonetheless, it is only through the latter that it becomes transparent to itself, and this also makes its communication possible. Through an internal dialectic of the two, religion makes its appearance in life. The "consciousness of God within this is always in another" and "it is only in an individual that one is conscious of totality, only in an antithesis . . . is one conscious of unity."[27] The consciousness of God becomes manifest in subjective states of piety through its modification of "sensible self-consciousness," that is, the consciousness that is caught up in world-relations. The forms and degree of piety become evident in the ease with which the countervailing forces of worldly self-consciousness (pleasure and pain) are integrated, allowing the consciousness of dependency to come to the fore through the ensuing "life-enhancing" changes. Suffering and assurance, sin and redemption can thus be connected to specific forms of action and interpretations of the world that range from pessimistic fatalism to ethical optimism. As a result, the given states of the subjects are transformed, as can be seen in the Christian idea of redemption as a transition from an "old" to a "new man" in the one and the same person.

Subjective piety develops in and through intersubjective communication, and the symbolic presentation of piety takes place in the context of communication with others. For Schleiermacher's transcendental concept of religion, then, *subjectivity* is inseparable from relations of *intersubjectivity*. The universal structural core of subjectivity, namely, immediate self-consciousness, belongs to everyone, but because each subject has its own proper self-relationship, it belongs to each in its own individual way. Feeling is always the subject's own feeling; piety is only lived and represented by its respective subject. The contingent corporeality of the individual enters into both, but so too does the biographical formation of the religious self-consciousness, which always takes place in communicative exchange with others. Religion is directed toward unity and totality, but it is also concerned with the singularity of individuals in their free spontaneity. In a permanent dialectic of the two, the theme of finitude emerges as the opposing pole to the holistic thrust of the theory. Thus, one individual is not also the other; individuals in their particularity do not represent copies. In the face of singularity of this kind, a dimension of the infinite also becomes apparent. For others are also contained virtually in the specific character of

---

transcendentalism from approaches taken in the ontotheological tradition of transcendentals.

27 Schleiermacher, *Dialektik*, §215.2.

individuals, insofar as an individual in his or her peculiarity differs from them and thereby is related to them. Individuality does not owe itself entirely to one's particular spatiotemporal placement or given natural characteristics. Rather, it consists in an ethical process of the formation of personal character. And this requires communication with others—for enrichment just as much as for delimitation. Dissent and divergence belong to this communication just as much as the shared elements of language and signs, without which the given matter of controversy could not even be identified. Through the religious and ethical process of the *cultivation of individuality*, subjectivity and intersubjectivity are thus joined to one another. Both are, in logical terms, equally primordial.

These elements always appear, however, within the asymmetries of historical and contingent life circumstances. For this reason, Schleiermacher's transcendental theory enters into empirical matters of historical social relations; the theory of religion passes over into a description of historically conditioned cultures. This, however, does not simply involve the recounting of historical facts and events in an unreflective way: empirical content also needs to be processed conceptually. Specifically, a combination of the ethical "formulae" for historical social relations enables the "picture book" of history to be critically appraised, and specific types—for example, the essential determinations of various religions and their communicative formation of community—to emerge and be categorized. From such a taming of the contingency of historical multiplicity there arises an optimism about progress. Thus, for example, Christianity is regarded as the "religion of the religions."[28] It represents the summit of all stages of religious development, and is the most complex form of religion.[29] The employment of conceptual criteria is essential to the judgment of religions for the purpose of comprehending the universal in the particular in degrees of more and less, better and worse. Because it is conceptually warranted in this way, Schleiermacher's move into the historical-sociological sphere is made without completely surrendering to the unavoidable contingency of this realm. This, however, is achieved at the cost of sacrificing the historical validation of certain key ideas of the history of religion—not least the idea of the optimism of progress.

With this we have sketched out the terrain upon which the controversial debates on transcendental theories of religion have taken place. The history of religions and religious studies emphasized the historical

---

28   Schleiermacher, *Über die Religion*, 293; *On Religion*, 116.
29   CG §§7-10.

and cultural relativity of religious phenomena, while on the other side of the debate, existentialism and radical theories of revelation accentuated the difference between religion and culture. The various critiques of religion, moreover, also called into question the validity of a connection between reason and historical religion. While they operated with criteria that were as external to religion as possible, they were also able to restrict the rationality of the description of religion to the analytics of the internal understanding of religious language and symbolism—in so far as the latter have not been rejected by positivistic or naturalistic positions as entirely meaningless. The legacy of transcendental theories of religion is to be found in the context of these controversial debates, which were in part provoked by these theories themselves.

3. Between Reason and History: On the Legacy of Transcendental Theories of Religion

The major transcendental approaches to the question of religion focus on the transition from reason to the empirical realm. In doing so they share the conviction that the very core of religion is the discovery of the *universality of reason* in the *particularity of the empirical content* of historical and cultural life. With this a practical interest is joined to the critical cultivation of religious forms so that religious consciousness may attain reflective insight within itself. Although reason is itself contained in the empirical life of religion, clear differences between the two are necessary in order that transition and critique can be possible. Both enable the balanced structure of a theory of subjectivity and a critical metaphysics of the finite, on the one hand, and, as its counterparts, history, culture, and symbolic communication, on the other. These differences—which, speaking formulaically, amount to the distinction between faith and knowledge—must not, however, be abstractly fixed. This is because theories of subjectivity and metaphysics of finitude are themselves part of a cultural history of ideas; indeed, their discursive treatment occurs within the latter's sociality. The consciousness of the difference between knowledge and faith connects its reflexivity with normative positioning and the critical correctives of other cultural strata. At the same time, this consciousness preserves the insight that even pure reason cannot be explicated simplistically in terms of a single form and, therefore, transitions from reason to religion are rational. This twofold dialectic lies at the heart of the legacy of transcendental theories of religion. In most cases under a different name and with different accents,[30] it is present as a challenge in all those theories of religion that in some way or other are concerned with the rationality or *validity* of religion as it *occurs historically*.[31]

The legacy and challenge of transcendental theories of religion is the demand for a rational appraisal of historical forms of practiced religion. If its central claim is that an appraisal of this kind can be effective within the sphere of religion itself, and should not merely be imposed from without, then it can be expected that such theories of religion will gravitate towards an investigation of concrete religious practice. As a result of this shift, theories of religions will be increasingly challenged to open themselves to, and acknowledge the wealth and plurality of, empirical religious forms.[32] The rise of globalization in the twentieth and twenty-first centuries has dissolved the classic borders of the geography of religions and cultures and created a dizzying array of phenomena existing side-by-side: the toleration of difference, the marginalization and even violent exclusion of those of other faiths, and the syncretistic adaptations of extremely diverse fragments of meaning. The spread of secularization has led to the erosion of those milieus that once sustained religious identities, a phenomenon which stands in stark contrast to the "return of religion" in most regions of the world. In order to be able to take these developments into account, theories of religion that draw upon the legacy of transcendental thought will have to significantly revise their concept of religion as a historical entity. In addition to integrating the approaches of sociology, the cultural sciences, and the philosophy of language with their various "turns,"

---

30 The artificial title "transcendental" is used especially in Catholic traditions to designate ways of thinking that apply the phenomenological notion of the intentionality of consciousness to God and his transcendence. It is bound up with a turn from religion to theology, which surely marginalizes many important points within the Kantian tradition of the critique of reason.

31 Ernst Troeltsch in particular connected this issue to the tradition of "critical transcendentalism." It was arguably the abiding theme of his life's work—one he was able to describe incisively, but never able to resolve—and his attempts contain numerous terminological echoes of the transcendental tradition. The number of imitators has, of course, remained low. Ernst Troeltsch, *Zur religiösen Lage, Religionsphilosophie und Ethik*, vol. 2 of *Gesammelte Schriften* (Tübingen: J.C.B. Mohr, 1922 [reprint Aalen: Scientia, 1982]), vii.

32 This involves appropriating the insights of historicism and religious studies (*Religionswissenschaft*). The historicism of the nineteenth century, for instance, disenchanted the ideas of progress and development in the history of religion and went so far as to undermine the whole idea of a historically provable "absoluteness" of one religion, the Christian. And religious studies, understood as the neutral, historical, and sociological examination of religion, has made us sensitive to the fact that in matters of religion, categories concerned with questions of validity are connected to specific positions on the spectrum of religious forms.

the transcendental approach must take the contingency of religion into account in such a way that the multifarious accumulations of forms that arise through the reshuffling, over-layering, and shifting of themes are properly attended to. That said, an increased openness to concept-resistant empirical data must not be permitted to suspend or annul a categorially founded, praxis-oriented right to the *exercise of judgment in questions of validity*.

An opening of this kind is possible on the basis of the internal dialectic provided by transcendental theories of religion. The initial positions of the logic of subjectivity and the transcendental guiding ideas of totality and freedom remain, as it were, shifting weights in the balance of the theories, even if the transition to the contingency of the empirical realm must be developed differently by us than it was by its seminal thinkers. Out of the nexus of basic figures in the transcendental theory of religion and the accent they place on the perspective of the finite, a tilting of the theory in the direction of *praxis* could result. This does not exclude other conceptual configurations of the guiding ideas,[33] and with the insight gained into the relativity of the historical constellations, a *will* to find one's own place within the sphere of religion can be released. Through its own dialectic it can press for a strengthening of religious enlightenment by means of a reflexive recognition of its own blind spot. All "positing of the 'I'" has a quasi-fundamentalist character; it can, however, be reined in through the cultivation of a sensitivity to alterity. Religious enlightenment assumes that even in the most diverse forms of religion, basic and comprehensible questions of human life are dealt with—albeit in different, even contradictory ways. A philosophy of religion that developed an empirically-substantiated typology of religious phenomena could, for example, trace the lines from the transcendental idea of unity to far Eastern forms of religion, whereas the idea of freedom seems to open perspectives on Judaism as rooted in the spirit of the counterfactual. Each of these, in turn, corresponds to a distinct approach to the conduct of life. And to this one could add the reciprocal relations to their respective social forms. For a typology of this kind, it is important to describe how basic motives that are not directly in view nonetheless continue to operate below the surface. For this reason, issues such as the manner in which inclusion takes place through exclusion, or the nature of the dynamic developed by the integration of forms of belief resistant to assimilation, become central ques-

---

33 So, for instance, following Kant and Hegel against Schleiermacher, the idea of God itself can be conceptualized in terms of difference and freedom. At the same time, following Schleiermacher, the intersubjectivity of religious communication and the finitude of human reason (Kant) is to be accentuated.

tions of a critical theory of religion that locates the transcendentality of reason within the dialectic of actual religious life. The insight that it itself has its contingent place in the history of ideas and the history of religion of Western modernity allows the transcendental theory of religion to position itself reflexively in the context of its own judgments. This is already the case when it assumes a relationship between religion and reason and views both as a matter of conscious life that comes to terms with itself through internal communication.[34]

Translated by Martin Rodden

---

34 For this formulation, see Dieter Henrich, *Bewußtes Leben* (Stuttgart: Reclam, 1999).

Mediating Schleiermacher

The Prospects for a Transcendental-Anthropological Theory of Religion[1]

David E. Klemm

What are the prospects for Schleiermacher's transcendental-anthropological theory of religion? Let me be blunt in making a claim: the prospects are *dire*, but the need has never been *higher*. The prospects are dire for several reasons. First, we live in an increasingly apocalyptic climate in which humans confront both cultural devastation and endangerment to natural life. Within the crisis situation, a split is widening between rising religious groups who boldly commit themselves to tribal gods and the cohort of humanists and new atheists who issue ever more strident attacks on religion and theology. Mediating positions are disappearing, and that means trouble for Schleiermacher, who epitomizes the mediating stance.

Second, the humanistic disciplines have developed an allergic reaction to "theory" as such and are deeply suspicious of normative, constructive thinking. Many studies of religion either restrict themselves to examining historical minutiae or they interpret religion as a social construction that conceals ideological goals.

Both of these developments are arguably responses to the prevailing condition of *nihilism*—the progressive self-devaluing of highest values. Nihilism is no longer the uncanny guest standing at the door; nihilism is normalized in our time.[2] The successors of Nietzsche make the very idea of a systematic, normative theory of religion an untimely meditation.

---

1 My thanks go out to Gary Bailey, with whom I have had fruitful conversations about Schleiermacher for many years. His understanding of the texts and the questions arising from them never ceases to amaze me. I am also grateful to William Schweiker for his helpful comments on this paper and for years of friendship.

2 See James C. Edwards, *The Plain Sense of Things: The Fate of Religion in an Age of Normal Nihilism* (University Park: Pennsylvania State University Press, 1997).

Given this situation, this paper asks whether or not Schleiermacher's theory of religion *falls* to the critiques of Nietzsche and his successors? If so, our interest in Schleiermacher is only historical. If not, then what constructive contributions can Schleiermacher make to current projects in thinking? The dual thesis of this paper is that Schleiermacher does not fall to these critiques, and that his theory of religion contributes directly to the supreme task within the time of nihilism, namely, the constructive re-valuing of highest values. My argument, however, is that the Schleiermacher we most need is *not*, at least initially, Schleiermacher the father of modern Protestant theology, but rather Schleiermacher the systematic philosopher, who locates confessional theology as a particular task within an integrative, non-absolutistic, inter-relational dynamics of thinking. Schleiermacher's theory of religion arises most fundamentally within dialectic, the highest form of philosophy, not within his dogmatics where its appearance is borrowed.

To make this case, my paper first summarizes Nietzsche's threefold assault on 1) theory, 2) the subject of theorizing, and 3) the idea of God, in order to present Schleiermacher's anticipations of these critiques on all three fronts. In its conclusion, the paper offers a prospectus for pursuing Schleiermacher's unique contribution to current thinking.

1. Nietzsche and the Demise of Theory, Subject, and God

Minimally, a *theory* is a rationally constructed representation, model, or critically determined thought about *what is*, about *being* that presents itself to the mind and senses.[3] A theory aims at truth and is animated by a desire to know. With just that much in hand, we hear the ghost of Nietzsche howling from above. In "On Truth and Lying in a Non-Moral Sense," among other places, Nietzsche hammers away on the notion of a "true" representation, the possibility of which requires some access to things as they are in themselves. Nietzsche argued that a theory, as a complex representation of what is, has nothing but other representations against which to test its claim for truth. Sensory images of empirically given reality, no less than concepts, are representations. All representations come to expression in language, and language is figurative through and through. Therefore, all we have are figurative

---

3 For a much more complete account of a theory in terms of scientific modeling, see David E. Klemm and William Klink, "Constructing and Testing Theological Models," *Zygon: Journal of Religion & Science* 38 (2003): 495-528.

expressions of figurative expressions, *ad infinitum*, which implies that no *true* representations exist, just "a mobile army of metaphors, metonymies, (and) anthropomorphisms."[4] The lofty goals of theory reduce to life's will to enhance and to preserve itself.[5] Theories have the instrumental value of providing security, certainty, and stability in a brutal world. The broad legacy of Nietzsche and his followers has put all forms of theorizing under suspicion today.[6]

Nietzsche's apparent undercutting of theory is logically linked to his unraveling of the Cartesian *cogito*, the indubitable first principle and foundation of much modern theorizing.[7] In Nietzsche's view, if true representations cannot be distinguished from dissimulations, then even the "I" of "I think" is merely one more trope, a fiction that purports to unify a "bristling multiplicity of instincts" under a flimsy law of causation.[8] Nietzsche's followers have been busy ever since deconstructing the so-called autonomous subject.

Finally, the crowning blow in the self-devaluing of highest values is the death of both the God of metaphysics and the biblical God in their identity and difference. In the Christian West, God is the eternal Truth. Under conditions of nihilism, however, theology is unmasked as an illusory supra-sensory justification for earthly life, a life which lacks intrinsic value of its own.[9] Love of God is really contempt for worldly life.

---

4   Friedrich Nietzsche, "On Truth and Lying in a Non-Moral Sense," in *The Birth of Tragedy And Other Writings*, ed. Raymond Geuss and Ronald Speirs, trans. Ronald Speirs (Cambridge: Cambridge University Press, 1999), 146.
5   Friedrich Nietzsche, *The Will to Power*, ed. Walter Kaufmann, trans. Walter Kaufmann and R. J. Hollingdale (New York: Vintage, 1968), 380. Nietzsche also writes, "It is our needs that interpret the world; our drives and their For and Against. Every drive is a kind of lust to rule; and each one has its perspective that it would like to compel all the other drives to accept as a norm" (ibid., 267).
6   Twentieth-century Derridian deconstruction further unmasks the will concealed in theorizing activities as a will to provide security, certainty, and stability in a chaotic and dangerous world. See Mark C. Taylor, *After God* (Chicago: University of Chicago Press, 2008), 10-11.
7   Friedrich Schleiermacher, *Friedrich Schleiermachers Dialektik* (1822), ed. Rudolf Odebrecht (Darmstadt: Wissenschaftliche Buchgesellschaft, 1988), 66-67.
8   Friedrich Nietzsche, *Will to Power*, 267-72. I am quoting Paul Ricœur in his study of Nietzsche as adversary of Descartes in *Oneself as Another* (Chicago: University of Chicago Press, 1992), 15.
9   See Erich Heller, "The Importance of Nietzsche," in *The Artist's Journey into the Interior and other Essays* (New York: Harcourt Brace Jovanovich, 1965), 181.

2. Schleiermacher's Anticipations of Nihilism

How does Schleiermacher stand in relation to this threefold attack? Schleiermacher anticipates these issues most clearly in the *Dialektik*, which is for him the highest philosophical discipline. Dialectic is systematic thinking about the essence, structure, and limits of any and all thinking that intends to become knowing. As such, dialectic is theorizing about the conditions of the possibility of theory. The project culminates in an investigation into the first principle of knowing.[10] Schleiermacher calls this first principle the "transcendent-transcendental ground." It is the highest idea, the meta-theological "God" of the system of dialectic.

The formal system of concepts and rules that emerge in the *Dialektik* do not, however, merely hover in the thin air of reflexive deductions. Schleiermacher's *Dialektik* has an existential starting point, namely, the lived experience of dispute (*Streit*) among different thinkers, such as one finds in his beloved dialogues of Plato. Schleiermacher's reflections in the *Dialektik* never lose their focus on the commonplace experience of conversational disagreement.

According to Schleiermacher, genuine dispute requires at least two different thoughts concerning one and the same thing. Dispute in the nature of the case seeks its resolution in agreement, which to be successful must be completed in knowledge rather than opinion. Dialectic is the art of leading a dispute to successful agreement in knowing, and as such dialectic revalues "Truth" as regulative ideal and norm, intrinsic to thinking itself, the realization of which is approached incrementally even as Truth withdraws behind all efforts to attain it. The question is: does Nietzsche have a genuine dispute with Schleiermacher? I think not. For Nietzsche to be in dispute with Schleiermacher, the two thinkers must have different thoughts about the same thing. However, on all three points of contention, Schleiermacher anticipates and agrees with the core elements of Nietzsche's critiques. Let us examine this claim.

3. Schleiermacher on Theory

Consider first the Nietzschean challenge to theory. In Schleiermacher's thought, theoretical reason determines the *essence* of some empirically or historically given reality. The aim of essence-determination is to

---

10 Schleiermacher, *Dialektik*, 66-67.

produce knowledge both of what the thing *is* and what it *is not*. Surprisingly, however, Schleiermacher agrees with Nietzsche that all we have are representations. However, Schleiermacher adds that representations are of systematically different kinds, which permits critical mediation between them.

The fundamental, ontological distinction that grounds the different kinds of representation discloses itself in the reflexive activity of thinking about thinking, which necessarily divides into the *activity of thinking* and objective *being* as that about which thinking thinks. In other words, Schleiermacher accepts the central claim of idealism that being is being only as determined by thinking. Thinking and being are codependent and inter-related concepts. There is no thinking without the positing of being as the "about which" of thinking, and there is no being that is not posited by thinking. Nietzsche cannot deny this claim.

From the dual ontological structure of thinking and being, Schleiermacher derives the epistemological distinction between the *organic function* and the *intellectual function* as two poles of thinking.[11]

The organic function signifies bodily receptivity to sense impressions. Its activity is *perception* and the representation it produces is the *image*. Do we have independent access to reality outside of representation? In bodily sensation our sense organs are affected, and the resulting stimulations constitute the occasion for thought; they give us something to think about. Reason establishes their systematic independence from the thinking activity as such. But sensation is a form of subjective consciousness; in it, activity and object are in undivided unity. As soon as we think about sensation, the stimulus weakens somewhat and the division between thinking and being opens. The immediacy of sensation is mediated into a perceptual image—a representation—which in turn is categorially determined by formal thinking. We receive sensations as if from external reality independent of thinking, but thinking cannot know the origin of sensation.

The intellectual function donates intelligible forms of thought by which to unite and divide the manifold of sense material. Its activity is *thinking in the narrow sense*, and its product is the *concept*. As Schleiermacher explains the twofold art of concept-formation, at the empirical level, identities and differences among the empirical appearances are sorted out in order to produce an aggregate *image* of the object. At the reflective level, revisions and expansions are made among known concepts so as to apply them to that objective image. Concepts and images mutually condition one another in the inter-relational process of critical

---

11   Schleiermacher, *Dialektik*, 138-44.

mediation: one adjusts concepts in light of the image, and one refigures images according to revisions in concepts. In forming a theoretical judgment that articulates the essence of an object, one joins a subject-concept with a predicate-concept into a well-formed *Satz* or proposition that reflects the individuality of the essence and then tests it with independent reference to the given object. Intuition (*Anschauung*) is the "seeing" or understanding of the convergence between perceptual images and concepts.[12] Thinking is thus always a connecting of organic and intellectual elements.

For Schleiermacher, the sought-for "essence" as determined by theory is precisely the intuited connection that emerges in the time of critical mediation between the relatively universal concept and the relatively particular image or percept. The essence of a thing has the ontological status of an *individual* that can neither be derived from the universal concept nor abstracted from the particular image, but is intuited *between* them in what Heidegger will later call the "as" structure of understanding.[13] Theory emerges through the activity of mediating among representations.

It should be clear that all thinking involves both the organic and intellectual functions. Pure form with no material content, as well as pure matter with no formal arrangement, are unrealizable limit concepts at which point thinking ceases. Actual thinking always contains some material content, minimally that of the linguistic sign; and actual perceiving always includes some formal element, minimally the concept of a "chaos of sensations." Thinking is therefore always the back-and-forth activity of combining and distinguishing between formal and material elements, refining a leading intuition through the intellectual and organic functions. Theoretical thinking aims at a fully determined intuition of essence in which there is perfect agreement between image and concept.[14]

The entire process of essence-determination, according to Schleiermacher, is "critical" in an unrestricted way. Finite human thinking can infinitely bend back on itself to correct and re-imagine new determinations of essence. For Schleiermacher, theory is always tentative, revisable, subject to critique, and open to its own refutation. Moreover,

---

12 For further elaboration, see David E. Klemm, "The Desire to Know God in Schleiermacher's *Dialektik*," *New Athenaeum/Neues Athenaeum* 5 (Lewiston, NY: Edwin Mellen Press, 1998): 129-46, esp. 135.

13 Martin Heidegger, *Being and Time*, trans. John Macquarrie and Edward Robinson (New York: Harper & Row, 1962), 188-90; *Sein und Zeit* (Tübingen: Max Niemeyer, 1972), 148-50.

14 Schleiermacher, *Dialektik*, 157-62.

Schleiermacher systematically recognizes that language is the concrete communicative medium of all thinking.¹⁵ Hence, speakers of different languages can only approximate identity in thinking, for an irreducible particularity adheres to every language. Nonetheless, difference in language cannot cancel the aim of resolving dispute in agreement based on knowledge, otherwise individuals could not rise above the particularity of their respective languages to grasp universal thoughts. Consequently, dialectic determines hermeneutics and rhetoric as two systematically derived "arts of thinking" (*Kunstlehre*) subordinate to dialectic.¹⁶

4. Schleiermacher on the Subject

The main target of Nietzsche's critique of the subject as *cogito* is Descartes.¹⁷ Descartes purported to demonstrate the *existence* of the "I" on the ground that the "I" necessarily appears in the methodical act of doubting itself.¹⁸ "But what then am I?" Descartes answers "a thing that thinks," that is, a mind, soul, intellect, or reason construed as a substance without extension or other singular determinations, but only a point-like, ahistorical, universal identity in the diversity of its operations.¹⁹ As a result, the mind-body problem arises, because the Cartesian "I" has no essential relation with an actual person. Nietzsche rejoins in *The Will to Power*: "'There is thinking: therefore there is something that thinks': this is the upshot of all Descartes' argumentation. But that means positing as 'true *a priori*' our belief in the concept of substance—that when there is thought there has to be something 'that

---

15 For further elaboration of "die Sprachgebundenheit des Denkens" in Schleiermacher, see David E. Klemm, "Dispute, Dialogue, and Individuality in Schleiermacher's *Dialektik*," *New Athenaeum/Neues Athenaeum* 4 (Lewiston, NY: Edwin Mellen Press, 1995): 81-104.

16 Friedrich Schleiermacher, *Hermeneutics and Criticism and Other Writings*, ed. and trans. Andrew Bowie (Cambridge: Cambridge University Press, 1998), 7-8.

17 See the aphorisms (#481-92) under "Belief in the 'Ego': The Subject," in Friedrich Nietzsche, *Will to Power*, 267-72. See also Friedrich Nietzsche, *Beyond Good and Evil* (New York: Vintage, 1966), 66.

18 "I must finally conclude that this proposition, I am, I exist, is necessarily true whenever it is put forward by me or conceived in my mind." *Meditations on First Philosophy*, in vol. 2 of *The Philosophical Writings of Descartes*, trans. John Cottingham, Robert Stoothoff, and Dugald Murdoch (Cambridge: Cambridge University Press, 1984), 17.

19 The description comes from Paul Ricœur, *Oneself as Another*, 7.

thinks' is simply a formulation of our grammatical custom that adds a doer to every deed."[20]

Schleiermacher's theory of the self anticipates and agrees with Nietzsche's critique. For Schleiermacher, subjectivity is one element in the dynamic structure of selfhood, which cannot be defined as a substance as bearer of properties. His focus in the dialectic is on the subject as *temporal activity* of relating itself to what is other than itself as this organic person here, recognizing itself concretely in otherness, and relating itself back to itself, as a unique individual who is changed in the process. The two-in-one structure of the self has three elements. *Subjectivity* is the universal element of the thinking activity, which posits itself both as thinking and being, while retaining its unity in the difference that is itself. It bears no resemblance to substance as a bearer of properties. The second element is the particular, organic, existing *person* here, in whom the "I" posits itself. The third element is the *individuality of the self* which emerges in time through the subject's activity of connecting its thinking with personal organic being in immediate self-consciousness.

The *systematic principle* of the structure of the self is formulated in terms of the "life process" as the dynamic activity of the subject's "abiding in itself" or taking what is given into itself in *receptivity*, and "passing beyond itself" or expressing its own projects onto the world in *activity*. The life process determines three fundamental forms of objective consciousness: the form of *feeling*, the form of *doing*, and the form of *knowing* as the mixed case.[21] These three basic forms are codependent and interrelated in actual life.

In addition to being one of three forms of objective consciousness, however, feeling is also the name of the subject's immediate self-consciousness that "I am," of "how it goes with me," and that "this act is mine."[22] The subject is immediately conscious both of its *self-positing* through the intellectual function and of its *not having posited itself in this way* through the organic function. The former "expresses the subject for

---

20   Nietzsche, *Will to Power*, 268.
21   The English translation of *The Christian Faith* reads: "an alternation between abiding-in-self (*Insichbleiben*) and a passing-beyond-self (*Aussichheraustreten*) on the part of the subject." Friedrich Schleiermacher, *The Christian Faith*, ed. H. R. Mackintosh and J. S. Stewart (Edinburgh: T. & T. Clark, 1976), §3.3. Henceforth CF.
22   See David E. Klemm, "Schleiermacher on the Self: Immediate Self-Consciousness as Feeling and as Thinking," in *Figuring the Self: Subject, Absolute, and Others in Classical German Philosophy*, ed. David E. Klemm and Günter Zöller (Albany: State University of New York Press, 1997), 169-92.

itself"; the latter expresses "its co-existence with an Other."[23] Taken together, they determine the totality of self-consciousness as one of reciprocity between the subject and its corresponding Other, that is, reciprocity between feelings of freedom and dependence.[24] Feeling as immediate self-consciousness *accompanies* all acts of objective consciousness in the forms of knowing, doing, and feeling. Feeling as immediate self-consciousness is the "essence of the subject" as the unity "which manifests itself in those severally distinct forms."[25] The essence of the subject is the undefinable, uniquely individual, self-differentiating unity of the self's engagement with otherness in the difference of temporal, empirical acts of knowing, doing, and feeling. The Nietzsche-inspired critiques of the autonomous subject do not apply to Schleiermacher's theory, which revalues the integrity of human selfhood beyond both Cartesian dualism and Nietzsche's hypothesis: "The subject as multiplicity."[26]

5. The Idea of God in Schleiermacher's Theory of Religion

Let us turn now specifically to Schleiermacher's theory of religion, famously defined as the feeling of absolute dependence. This theory is *transcendental*, because it determines religion as a moment in the self-positing activity of the subject, that is, a moment in the mediating or synthesizing activity that connects and distinguishes sensations into images in the organic function and links them with concepts from the intellectual function. This synthesizing activity is, in Kant's words, "an art concealed in the depths of the human soul" and is the work of the transcendental imagination. No empirical or introspective evidence allows us to apprehend this activity; we know of it only as the condition of the possibility of any act of knowing. This theory is also *anthropological*, because it appeals to nothing outside of the dynamics of human consciousness as a unifying unity of differences between thinking and being.[27]

Schleiermacher offers both transcendental and phenomenological arguments concerning the relation between human being and divine being. The transcendental argument is that an original absolute identity

---

23 CF §4.1.
24 CF §§4.1-4.2.
25 CF §3. See also Schleiermacher, *Dialektik*, 288n.
26 Nietzsche, *Will to Power*, 270.
27 Kant, *Critique of Pure Reason*, ed. and trans. Paul Guyer and Allen Wood (Cambridge: Cambridge University Press, 1998), A141/B180.

of thinking and being (*Urwissen*) is the ultimate condition of the possibility for actual dispute to arise at all. He defines *the idea of God* as the principle of the wholly undifferentiated origin point of thinking that relates to being. God is the idea of an undetermined origin point of any thinking activity. It is the primary presupposition of the desire to know. Similarly, for successful resolution of dispute, we must postulate a systematically completed totality of thought as the condition of relating different and competing thoughts to their common "about which" in being. He defines the *idea of the world* as the principle of the wholly differentiated totality of thinking about being. The world is the idea of being as perfectly determined in its totality. It is the final presupposition or goal of the desire to know.[28] Together the idea of God and the idea of the world constitute the limits of all finite thinking about being. The ideas of God and world are necessary conditions for the possibility of actual dispute, and hence are "transcendental" in status. But because God and world are indisputable trans-empirical principles of actual disputes, their referents must necessarily fall outside actual thinking about being. In this sense Schleiermacher assigns these ideas a "transcendent" status as well. Together the ideas of God and world constitute the "transcendent-transcendental ground" of knowing. The absolutely *first principle of knowing* is the necessary correlation (the identity of the identity and difference) between the ideas of God and world. This correlation cannot be further determined by finite human knowing.[29]

The phenomenological argument analyzes the self-evident givenness of feeling as immediate self-consciousness. Schleiermacher reasons that in the temporal shifts in consciousness between thinking and willing, the transition point or "Übergang" between them, the "Nullpunkt" of their co-activity, is filled only with "feeling as immediate self-consciousness." The moment of transition between forms of objective consciousness discloses the essence of the subject as phenomenon, and, at the same time, it ineluctably discloses the religious relation of the subject to the first principle or absolute ground.[30] Feeling, as immediate self-consciousness, is the reflection (*die Abspiegelung*), analogy (*die Analogie*), or indirect representation (*die Repräsentation*) of the transcendent-

---

28 Schleiermacher, *Dialektik*, 218-22.
29 In the *Dialektik*, Schleiermacher defines the idea of "God" in correlation to the idea of the "world." This creates a potential ambiguity, because the highest concept, the absolutely first principle of knowing, which typically is identified with the concept of "God," is, therefore, the necessary *correlation* between the ideas of God and world.
30 Ibid., 288. See also CF §3.4.

transcendental ground of knowing within the life process.³¹ It is so, because in this moment "We bear in ourselves the identity of being and thinking; we ourselves *are* being and thinking, thinking being and existing thinking."³² Immediate self-consciousness is itself the finite appearance of the absolute unity of opposites. In immediate self-consciousness, we are aware that the entire structure of the self is finite and is utterly dependent on its absolute ground.

How, then, does Schleiermacher's idea of God stand relative to the "death of God"? I want to argue that Schleiermacher's dialectical idea of God is beyond the death of God construed as an *object* of either religious imagination or reflective thought. Schleiermacher revalues the idea of God as the absolute principle and original knowing that manifests itself in the immediate self-consciousness accompanying all finite activities of relating thinking to being. Schleiermacher's God cannot be made an object of thought without destroying the divinity of God.³³ Schleiermacher's God, as the absolute activity of self-positing, is the life process itself in the integrity of its self-transcending structure.

6. Conclusion: Mediating Schleiermacher

If Schleiermacher's dialectically conceived theory of religion does survive radical critique, where and how does it contribute to current thinking? Schleiermacher's theory contributes to the crucial task today of articulating and embodying a post-critical, second immediacy in religion. This task is crucial in both individual and social terms. Individuals continue to feel torn between the first immediacy of religious feeling and the demands of critical reflection. Given this split, most educated adults abandon religious communities. At the social level, the split produces the conflict between competing religious groups and attack-minded secularists. This problem has existed at least since the time of Schleiermacher's *Speeches*, and it grows in magnitude on the global stage today, in spite of the efforts of Schleiermacher's successors to heal the rift, most especially Heidegger, Tillich, and Ricœur.³⁴ What can

---

31 Schleiermacher, *Dialektik*, 289n.
32 Ibid., 270.
33 CF §4.4.
34 I have elsewhere argued that already in the *Speeches* Schleiermacher occupies and commends a standpoint that is both "above religion" (*Über die Religion*) and above critical reflection. See David E. Klemm, "Culture, Arts, and Religion" in *The Cambridge Companion to Friedrich Schleiermacher*, ed. Jacqueline Mariña (Cambridge: Cambridge University Press, 2005), 251-68.

Schleiermacher donate today that is not already found in these thinkers?

The answer is that Schleiermacher's theory of religion is uniquely embedded in a dialectical system which includes hermeneutics as well. What does this give us? First, from the standpoint of dialectic, significant distinction among four levels of consciousness come clear: a) the *initial immediacy of consciousness* in which subjective feeling and objective perception are identical, b) *sensible or objective consciousness* in which subjective feeling and perception are clearly distinct, c) *critical reflection* or essence-determination, which questions the claims of objective consciousness, and d) *dialectical (or theological) consciousness*, which grounds the possibility of critical reflection and systematically orders all activities of thinking.

Dialectic makes it clear that objective consciousness can coexist with religious feelings and beliefs held in the first immediacy, but that critical reflection necessarily negates naïve religious beliefs and dispels the religious feelings that accompany them. Most importantly, Schleiermacher's dialectic also revalues religious consciousness in a second immediacy where the feeling-perception antithesis again collapses in the subject's feeling of finitude—the subject's awareness that the totality of finite existence is determined by an unknowable "Whence." In this second immediacy, religious consciousness can accompany both objective consciousness and critical reflection. At this level, the theory of religion reveals both the *poverty* and the *wealth* of the second immediacy. It is *rich* in appearing in the reciprocity of freedom and dependence, joy and sorrow, and their identity and difference in holy sadness. But it is *poor* in not knowing and not having the absolute, and in losing the vibrancy of its own life when critically reflected.

Second, Schleiermacher's hermeneutics provides a guide for actually performing or embodying religion in a second immediacy. If so, the system invites a teleological suspension of dialectic insofar as the desire to know motivating dialectic drives thinking *beyond* dialectic into a vital world where we might freely experience the self-manifestation of the unknowable absolute within the cultural domains of ethics, science, art—and positive forms of religion. In this sense, religion, lived in a second immediacy, is the intrinsic non-dialectical goal of dialectic. Let me explain this point briefly.

Schleiermacher knew that any approach to a second immediacy depends on hermeneutics as the strategy of mediating between meanings that are felt and intuited in primary languages and their conceptual explication. Hermeneutics for Schleiermacher is theoretically grounded in the recognition that all meaning, indeed all being, is mediated. As a practice, however, hermeneutics points beyond dialectic to the lived experience of and attunement to what Heidegger called "the meaning that dwells in all that is."[35]

The link between hermeneutics and the theory of religion is that, for Schleiermacher, language is the light of feeling.[36] All actual religious consciousness depends on a pre-given, contingent, historical appearance of religious language—symbols, stories, and rituals that evoke and actualize individualized religious feelings, giving them genuine and real content beyond what dialectic can describe. Schleiermacher's strategy of textual interpretation—involving critical mediations among comparative, divinatory, grammatical, and technical/psychological methods—leads to meanings that enable the critical thinker to let go of dialectic, to suspend critical thinking, and to respond freely in religious feeling to the power of living language with the added feeling of conviction that he or she can justify, if required, the felt response. Only through hermeneutics can the critical thinker be *free for* the positive religious communities, yet also be *free from* the limitations of the first, pre-critical immediacy.

Third, dialectic importantly provides to Schleiermacher's hermeneutics a *norm* or *standard* for testing whether or not a primary expression or structural configuration in language actually manifests, and thereby enables, the feeling of absolute dependence. That norm is whether or not the linguistic expression or structural feature makes the unknowable transcendent-transcendental ground present in its absence. Once hermeneutics is comprehended together with dialectic, it is not possible to say, as Hegel did, that for Schleiermacher religious feeling is merely subjective. Religious feeling, dialectically justified and tested, is a critically mediated felt response to the objective appearance of the absolute in language.

Clearly, we cannot simply return to and adopt Schleiermacher's thought any more than we can return to the early nineteenth century. Schleiermacher's system must be mediated through our consciousness of the history of its reception and effects, and in cognizance of real historical changes. But given the life-affirming quality of Schleiermacher's thought, the task of mediating Schleiermacher, and of comprehending his enormous contributions to revaluing the highest values, remains very much a task that should beckon all of us.

---

35 Martin Heidegger, *Gelassenheit* (Pfullingen: Verlag Günther Neske, 1979), 13.
36 CF §15.1.

Schleiermacher and the Future of Historical-Empirical Dogmatics

Dogmatics of Redemption

The Nature and Status of Christian Doctrine within the *Glaubenslehre*

Dietrich Korsch

My contribution to this volume is to clarify §15 of the *Glaubenslehre*: *"Christian doctrines are accounts of the Christian religious affections set forth in speech."*[1] But since this proposition alone seems too formal, I shall connect it to §14: *"There is no other way of obtaining participation in the Christian communion than through faith in Jesus as the Redeemer."*[2] What I propose to discuss, then, is the relationship between *doctrine as speech* (*Glaubenssatz als Rede*) and human *affect* (*Gemütszustand*), and this in light of the meaning of Christian *redemption* (*Erlösung*). To do this, I will devote the first section of my paper to a characterization of the place of the *The Christian Faith* in the history of Christian doctrine. We will see that the *position* of the *Glaubenslehre* in this historical framework (which I understand to indicate the *nature* of Christian doctrine) will require us to seek out the *function* of the *Glaubenslehre* within religious communication (which I understand as indicative of the *status* of Christian doctrine). My thesis will be that Schleiermacher's *Glaubenslehre* represents a modern type of dogmatics that is able to serve as a hermeneutical instrument for interpreting human life as well as a means for the kerygmatic deepening of Christian faith.

---

1 "Christliche Glaubenssätze sind Auffassungen der christlich frommen Gemütszustände in der Rede dargestellt." Friedrich Schleiermacher, *Der christliche Glaube nach den Grundsätzen der evangelischen Kirche im Zusammenhange dargestellt* (1830/31), in KGA I/13.1, §15. Henceforth CG, followed by the proposition.

2 "Es gibt keine andere Art, an der christlichen Gemeinschaft Anteil zu erhalten, als durch den Glauben an Jesum als den Erlöser" (ibid., §14).

1. The *Glaubenslehre* within the History of Christian Doctrine: Or, the Nature of Christian Doctrine in Schleiermacher

It is obvious that the source and role of Christian doctrine has changed in history. However, we must assume at the very beginnings of Christianity a religious communication issuing from a Jewish context and closely related to the Old Testament, yet concentrated on the person and the fate of Jesus in a such a manner that a transition (*Übergang*) was provoked and a new religious movement came into existence. The New Testament contains evidence of many tensions and divergent accents involved in its formation, a wealth of understandings kept in check only by the local preferences of diverse early traditions bearing witness to Jesus. As soon as Christianity became a religious institution, the need to unify its core message had to be emphasized. The birth of doctrine, then, occurred with this binding together of various modes of preaching and religious self-understanding in early Christianity. It is admirable that the ancient church was able to concentrate so intensely on the essentials of Christianity, namely, on the conceptions of the triune God and of Jesus as God-man. And it is clear that these two insights belong closely together; one cannot exist without the other. But it is also clear that the concentration on these fundamentals had immense strategic relevance for religious proclamation within early Christianity: by identifying the distinguishing characteristics of what counts as essentially Christian, such core doctrines served as touchstones for Christian preaching during the time of transition to a new religion. We can characterize this kind of doctrine as a type of *prescriptive dogmatics*.

Matters change when the Christian faith becomes "universal." The catholic period of Christianity still has its transitions (*Übergänge*) to faith, conversions that happen more or less voluntarily. But now the character of doctrine begins to change. It no longer tends to prescribe a particular standard of preaching and basic structures of faith for the purpose of reaching certainty, but aspires to describe the givenness of this world and the character of eternity beyond. The religious function recedes and doctrine begins to take on the function of articulating a worldview. This movement is completely concurrent with the transformation of the church into a worldly institution that bears increasing responsibility for the secular lives of believers. Meanwhile, the moment of transition in one's religious life has shifted from conversion as an act of joining the church to a gradual religious progress throughout one's life under the rule of the gospel as the guide to behavior and belief.

This medieval type of *descriptive dogmatics* underwent a severe critique by early Protestantism. The Reformation movement more or less brought the initial emphasis on making a transition to real faith, on constituting an authentic and immediate relation to God, back into the framework of the now widespread Christianity of the time. For this reason, Luther insisted on penance as an outstanding model of Christian renewal. And as we can see in Melanchthon's *Loci*, all of the traditional material of dogmatics was shaped in a new way, namely, concentrated on the overcoming of the law by the gospel, on the forgiveness of sin, and on the justification of the sinner. The emphasis was so strongly laid upon this transition from the person qua sinner to person qua justified in Christ that all questions concerning whether such a change of life must not presuppose some continuities between the Old Adam and the New were ignored or silenced. Dogmatics, however, regained its early function of informing the preaching and guiding the application of the gospel to Christian lives.

If we now place Schleiermacher's *Glaubenslehre* against this background, we can observe the following: Schleiermacher followed in the tradition of the Reformation by concentrating the whole of Christian doctrine on the process of transition, namely *redemption*. But he attempted to address the unresolved issue concerning the continuity between the old and the new man in a way that was completely different from the medieval Catholic position. He saw that what can and must be respected as the enduring structure with regard to which *redemption* is communicated is not the nexus of man and world, but rather the specifically religious dimension of human existence as lived under the challenge of an non-worldly based freedom. Schleiermacher thereby opened up a new field for the reconstruction of Christian doctrine, namely, religion as an anthropological structure of self-understanding. Correspondingly, he defined a new approach to Christian doctrine—a hermeneutical one that serves to understand the givenness of life and the various attempts to conduct one's life in the spotlight of religious renewal or *redemption*. Religion concerns us in every moment of our lives—this is what is permanent and consistent. But to live life in an individual manner we need to concentrate on the sharp difference between sin and redemption as a means of effecting a singular transition into a heretofore unknown domain of our own lives—this is the moment of transition. Religion establishes independence from the world (*Weltunabhängigkeit*): this is the transformation of the notion of transition under the conditions of an abiding temporal situation. For this reason I propose to call Schleiermacher's *Glaubenslehre* a *hermeneutical dogmatics*.

Through this characterization, the *Glaubenslehre* finds its place within a typology of Christian doctrine, and such a characterization enables us to see two crucial traits of the *Glaubenslehre*. The first, the anthropological one, has long-term and wide-ranging consequences. As soon as religion is defined as an autonomous dimension of human existence, it can be explored for its own sake. It is not to be submitted to the normal way of understanding human behavior and to the reigning scientific ways of perceiving the world. This, from the perspective of theology, marks the birth of an autonomous Religious Studies. If religion is an anthropological phenomenon, then there must be several methods of dealing with it in a scholarly way. Opening the field of religion means exploring the field for religious competition. That is to say, religious phenomena are compared with each other as such, even though it is true that they always stand in historical contexts related, of course, to concrete surroundings such as culture, climate, technological development, etc. To be sure, the theological approach within the academic study of religion depends upon the study of history—an insofar, it has its necessary historical side. But it is remarkable the extent to which Schleiermacher's conception of dogmatics is able to support and advocate Religious Studies according to their methodological requirements. That means that with respect to Schleiermacher's legacy, a serious conflict between theology and Religious Studies is not necessary.

The second crucial trait I want to highlight is a dogmatic one. Schleiermacher begins his considerations not only from an anthropological point of view—namely, that religion has already touched the interior life of man—but also from the Reformation conviction that belief is the deepest possible determination of the human heart and that this determination has actually occurred. This is the reason for speaking of Christian doctrines as "accounts of the Christian religious affections set forth in speech." If we bear in mind that these affections (*Gemütszustände*) are shaped by the difference that marks the movement of transition (between sin and redemption), then we can see that all statements—or better: communications, so as to include language games—that are formulated to re-present Christian faith are intended to precipitate and accompany this transition. This means, evidently, that they all have a pragmatic use, irrespective of their semantic content. The "setting forth in speech" (*die Darstellung in Rede*) is, strictly speaking, not simply a reflection of religious affections (*innere Gemütszustände*), but rather a severe critique of the ways in which religious communication is often used in Christianity. Hence, it follows that even the affections lack any suggested immediacy; as born out of a communicative interaction among persons, they are themselves induced by these communications. Thus, the task of dogmatics in the *Glaubenslehre* is not merely descriptive with regard to inner states of consciousness, but also deliberate and critical towards the claimed immediacy of affections. The work of deliberation taking place in every moment feelings are uttered paves the way for a critical testing of the ostensible immediacy of states of feeling.

Now to summarize the first part of my paper: Schleiermacher's *Glaubenslehre* represents a type of dogmatics that operates simultaneously in a hermeneutical and a critical-kerygmatic manner. Its hermeneutical aspect invites a relation to Religious Studies and enables the comparison among religions without negating their claims to truth and authenticity. The kerygmatic aspect underscores the critical nature of dogmatics, which is to sharpen by way of reflection and deliberation the way religious experience is modeled in religious communication. A remaining point requires further treatment, namely, the question of how the hermeneutic and the kerygmatic aspects are interwoven. This leads us to the second part of this paper, the *status* of the *Glaubenslehre*.

2. The Function of Christian Doctrine: Or, the Status of the *Glaubenslehre*

What is remarkable is the fact that the function of the *Glaubenslehre* flows directly from its nature. To see this, we need only look more closely at the coherence of the two distinguished aspects. By doing so, we will reach a conclusion that may seem rather surprising.

There can be no doubt that the constructions and distinctions Schleiermacher deals with in the famous third and fourth propositions of the *Glaubenslehre* are among the most important and well-known of his theorems. Nevertheless, they still present a challenge to the understanding. I will here take up just one element of the theory. We all remember well the distinction between "immediate" (*unmittelbares*) and "sensible self-consciousness" (*sinnliches Selbstbewußtsein*). The normal condition is one in which our *self-consciousness* is bound up with the consciousness of states in the world, and that this situation gives us the impression of freedom as well as of dependence. Indeed, if we seek to analyze this situation of the self further, we find that it can neither be derived from a total dependence (which would leave us unable to account for the existence of freedom) nor from an original kind of self-made freedom (which would scarcely be able to explain the occurrence of restrictions in the world—unless, of course, we wished to become Fichteans). In other words: immediate self-consciousness cannot be derived from innerworldly conditions; nor can it immediately posit itself. For this reason we must inquire about an origin of this immediate consciousness that does not itself originate in the world. The important consequence of these well-known reflections is that our innerworldly freedom has a transcendental basis, and, furthermore, that religion is the way we communicate about this structure of our existence. What I wish to stress with regard to this reconstruction of Schleiermacher's theory is the need to hold two kinds of communication together: the religious communication about the foundation of freedom and the everyday communication about the partial realization of freedom in the world. As soon as the specific religious function is distinguished as such (and understood as the absolute basis of finite freedom), there comes into existence a constant tendency that demands realizing freedom in our empirical life. Schleiermacher's identification of this distinction is the beginning of a realization of self-understanding and, consequently, of responsible actions of self-conscious subjects. To put it another way, religions as such bear within themselves an inexorable trend to deal with freedom and to promote freedom, at least once the precise distinction between religious and sensible self-consciousness has been made. In other words, the identification of religion as such as the consciousness of the ground of our finite freedom—the moment when Religious Studies as a field of its own comes into existence—is a landmark on the map of freedom.

If we take this result to be a structural moment within any religion, it is easy to see that the theme of transition becomes crucial for a Christian dogmatics built upon this theoretical basis. We must realize that the distinction in question has been made in time; there was a time before, and now we live in the time after. This performative aspect will be reflected in the structure of any given religion. This means that any religion has to configure the transition from a state of predominant dependence to one of predominant freedom. And the quality of religion can be gauged by its ability to describe the process of transition realistically and accurately. From this perspective, we can appreciate the *Glaubenslehre* as an outstanding example of a dogmatics organized to represent and help realize this transition. Moreover, we can understand—and I am pleased here to be in agreement with Julia Lamm—why Schleiermacher's "treatise on grace" really is the core of his dogmatics.[3] There is not time to discuss this extensively, but allow me at

---

3 Julia A. Lamm, "Schleiermacher's Treatise on Grace," *Harvard Theological Review* 101, no. 2 (2008): 133–68.

least to give you a brief glimpse into the movement of transition that Schleiermacher has in mind.

"Regeneration" (*Wiedergeburt*, CG §107) is the comprehensive term for this movement as a whole, the transition to a new or redirected life. The metaphor is striking. It refers to a fundamental change of life that can be effected only through the impact of something outstanding. Such a total renewal of life occurs only when the basis of freedom has appeared in a manner we can grasp. This means that we can speak about regeneration only as a consequence of the appearance of Christ as the personal representative of a divinely grounded freedom. Through contact with Christ in the words of the gospel we come under the influence of a new form of life, which we are to adopt in undergoing the transition as a redirection or redetermination of life— "conversion" (*Bekehrung*, CG §108). The moments in this transition unfold as follows: confronted by Christ with the new way of living in the spirit of freedom, we regret being dependent upon any other thing, and we look back to our old determination with a feeling of "repentence" (*Buße*). But we can do this only if we simultaneously look forward and are ready to accept the pure determination by and towards freedom. This is the point of "faith" (*Glaube*), which is the necessary positive counterpart to the negative feeling of repentance. We can say that in this double awareness of repentance and faith we experience a change of determination in our life.

But the change of determination requires accomplishing and fulfilling this new way of life as well. This is the true meaning of "justification" (*Rechtfertigung*, CG §109). We must not forget that we once really acted under the old determination, that is, we performed many wrongful deeds. The vestiges of old life must be erased—and this happens in the "forgiveness of the sins" (*Sündenvergebung*). When we accept this forgiveness—which is clearly a matter of faith—we become "children of God" (*Kinder Gottes*). This "*Gotteskindschaft*" means that we belong totally to God after the transition to a new life. It remains to the doctrine of "sanctification" (*Heiligung*, CG §110), which comes next in Schleiermacher's account, to describe the new form of life (*Lebensform*) as dominating one's life praxis and to inform our thinking so that we do not confound the absolute basis of our freedom with the relatively free actions that are born out of that freedom and represent it.

To summarize this point briefly: In his "treatise on grace," Schleiermacher fully meets the demand to describe the process of transition that is implicitly involved in religion. And he does so by arguing that the transition is absolutely fundamental insofar as it involves a total redirection or redetermination of human existence—just as the metaphor of "regeneration" vividly suggests. In this way dogmatics fulfils the role of describing a change in one's form of life and thereby functions as a hermeneutics of life. Without the precision of dogmatic description, life would be poorer and less transparent to itself. With it, dogmatics contributes to the advancement of freedom.

This insight, however, brings us to our next consideration. We hold that dogmatics contributes to the clarification of self-understanding by virtue of its religious symbolization of freedom. But how can we assert that dogmatic description is really capable of producing such a radical transition? Are we to suppose that the conceptual presentation alone is what changes lives?

To answer these questions we must return to the introduction of the *Glaubenslehre*. What is communicated in the hearing of the gospel—the reality of freedom based in God—is not strange to human ears. We want to find a solid foundation for the freedom we feel. But it comes to us powerfully only by the words of Christ in which his inner life finds verbal expression. We must therefore admit that the anthropologically grounded elementary striving for freedom only becomes satisfied by a historical event, a human person. But if there really existed a person such as we suppose Jesus was, then all the words that come to us in the media of historical communication possess an inexhaustible content. Each time that the gospel is preached, freedom is realized in Jesus. What dogmatics, in turn, articulates is nothing other than a structural description of the infinite movement of life as this movement is communicated in and as gospel in historical reality. The process of religious communication in Christianity lives by the reality of Christ present in it. The description of "religious affections" shows itself to be part of a religious movement in which the reality of freedom is symbolized as well as transmitted. If we do not forget the initial insight that the conceptual distinction between religious and sensible self-consciousness implies an act of freedom in itself, we now find that this distinction plays a fundamental role within the universal development of freedom in history. Theological reflection must itself be understood as a matter of realizing freedom, and this holds for the discovery of religion as such.

* * *

Allow me to conclude: I set out to explain two fundamental traits of Schleiermacher's *Glaubenslehre*. I wanted to emphasize the fact that his dogmatics was proposed at the crossroads of Christian doctrine. It looks back upon history and takes up the original duty of dogmatics to structure the Christian gospel. Yet it does so by expanding the basis for understanding the gospel to that of the religious field. The religious task of symbolizing "transitions" now becomes the task of actualizing freedom, and this latter task is the distinguishing mark of Christianity among the religions. This leads to the second point I wanted to make: the characterization of a religious transition as the grounding of a new life (regeneration or *Wiedergeburt*) is the most dramatic case of transition that we can imagine. Such a life lives from the reality of liberation that has appeared in Christ. Hence the dogmatic construction also serves this aim—more conceptually, to be sure, but nevertheless with a kerygmatic impact. Thus, as my final thesis concerning the nature and status of Schleiermacher's *Glaubenslehre*, I would reiterate that it has a kerygmatic as well as a hermeneutical character, and submit that these are the two most crucial attributes for a Church dogmatics in general. For this reason, I would not hesitate to call the *Glaubenslehre* a Church dogmatics of its own kind.

Now given that an overarching theme of this conference is the relationship between theology and the study of religion, permit me one final remark, namely, that the nature and status of the *Glaubenslehre* should be of consequence for theorization in Religious Studies as well. This can be seen in two ways. First, we must not forget that the academic study of religion arose from a specific period in modern intellectual history. In contrast to ancient and early modern philosophies of religion, Religious Studies/*Religionswissenschaft* appears to acknowledge the intrinsic worth of the religions. Overlooked is the fact that Schleiermacher's theory of *immediate self-consciousness* actually offers a theoretically satisfying scheme for articulating the presupposition of Religious Studies. If this were more widely recognized, however, a second consequence not at all at home in Religious Studies circles would follow. Religious Studies practitioners typically respect the particularity of religions by dealing with them historically. The claims for the superiority of one religion over others are ignored, and value judgments are generally suppressed. Yet Schleiermacher's theory of the independent status of religion suggests that such restrictions lack plausibility. According to my reconstruction of his account, anyone who treats religion—to whatever extent and with whatever intensity—and anyone who wishes to examine the specifics of a religion, takes part in the history of realizing freedom. Thus even the most "scholarly" and arid investigation breathes the air of freedom. Likewise, even the most recent politically correct debates regarding the living religions are impregnated by the idea of freedom originating in the religions themselves. Religious Studies, therefore, contributes in one way or another to the realization of freedom. Those who advocate Religious Studies understand the program's significance and may, therefore, confidently promote the discipline.

The Cognitive Status of the Religious Consciousness

The Nature and Status of Dogmatic Propositions in Schleiermacher's *Glaubenslehre*

WALTER E. WYMAN, JR.

Christian theology has faced an ongoing epistemological crisis since the rise of the modern world. In academic circles today, theology is widely suspected of being a discipline without a subject matter whose putative claims to truth need not be taken seriously. If the crisis had its origins in the Enlightenment, it has only been exacerbated with the emergence of the hermeneutics of suspicion and postmodern philosophies.

Friedrich Schleiermacher, the first major post-Enlightenment Protestant theologian, faced the epistemological crisis within theology that had been engendered by Kant's critical philosophy. In the *Critique of Pure Reason* and *Prolegomena to Any Future Metaphysics*, Kant had specified the conditions of the possibility of knowing that ruled out in principle knowledge of transcendent realities: the soul, the world, and God. To be sure, the concept of God could reenter human thought as a regulative idea of pure reason and as a postulate of practical reason, and Kant allowed some breathing space for a rational religion. But the prospects for an intellectually viable Christian dogmatics were, after Kant, hardly promising.

Although Schleiermacher does not explicitly state that he is seeking a path forward for Protestant dogmatics after Kant, it is plausible to interpret his theological method as a response to the limits of knowing articulated by the critical philosophy. *The Christian Faith*, his dogmatics (or, as he called it for important reasons, *Glaubenslehre*[1]), revolutionized theological method. Schleiermacher himself characterized his method

---

1   Literally "doctrine of faith." All quotations from the *Glaubenslehre* will refer to Friedrich Schleiermacher, *The Christian Faith*, ed. H. R. Mackintosh and J. S. Stewart (Edinburgh: T. & T. Clark, 1928). Henceforth CF, followed by the proposition and, where appropriate, section number.

as "empirical"; later scholars, uncovering affinities to more contemporary currents of thought, have characterized it as phenomenological.[2] Dogmatics proceeds by analyzing and describing the Christian self-consciousness: "Christian doctrines (*Glaubenssätze*) are accounts of the Christian religious affections set forth in speech" (CF §15). Rather than claiming to have access to supernaturally revealed truths or to metaphysical knowledge of transcendent realities, Schleiermacher began with the phenomenon of Christian piety. The Christian theologian can get on with the business of dogmatics by analyzing the Christian consciousness.

Schleiermacher's revisionist theological method itself, however, gives rise to new doubts about the epistemological status of dogmatic propositions. If dogmatics analyzes and describes a subjective state of mind, does it make any truth claims about reality? For those with a robust confidence in the reality of revelation and certainty about the knowledge of God, Schleiermacher was clearly guilty of subjectivism or psychologism. Schleiermacher, it was alleged, so far from rescuing theology after Kant, had given up the ship and failed to make any cognitive theological claims at all. Commenting on proposition 15, just cited, Hugh Ross Mackintosh boldly asserts: "If words mean anything, doctrine is for [Schleiermacher] a statement about our feeling, not about God."[3] Although he has a very different constructive agenda than Mackintosh, George Lindbeck advances a similar interpretation. For the experiential-expressivist position, represented archetypically by Schleiermacher, doctrines are "non-informative and non-discursive symbols of inner feelings, attitudes, or existential orientations."[4] A nonrealist or reductionist reading of Schleiermacher has not, however, completely won the day. Andrew Dole, seeking to do justice to the subtlety and complexity of Schleiermacher's position, claims in an article titled "Schleiermacher's Theological Anti-Realism" that despite the anti-realist motifs in his thought "a form of realism about theological claims . . . would seem to occupy the core of Schleiermacher's theological method." Schleiermacher's theological realism is, according to Dole,

---

2   Friedrich Schleiermacher, *On the Glaubenslehre*, ed. and trans. James Duke and Francis Fiorenza (Chicago: Scholars Press, 1981), 45; B. A. Gerrish, *Continuing the Reformation* (Chicago: University of Chicago Press, 1992), 153, 174-75; R. R. Williams, *Schleiermacher the Theologian* (Philadelphia: Fortress Press, 1978).
3   H. R. Mackintosh, *Types of Modern Theology* (New York: Charles Scribner's Sons, 1939), 66.
4   George Lindbeck, *The Nature of Doctrine* (Philadelphia: Westminster, 1984), 16.

a chastened realism, for he sought to "advance as few claims as possible about mind-independent reality."[5]

This essay addresses the problem of the epistemological status of dogmatic propositions in Schleiermacher's *Glaubenslehre*. Is Schleiermacher best understood as some kind of epistemological realist, either bold or chastened, who intends to make assertions about mind-independent realities? Or is he best understood as a reductive anti-realist?

Schleiermacher's epistemological position is quite subtle. To formulate the epistemological problem of his dogmatics as a disjunction–he must be either a realist or a nonrealist–fails to do justice to his distinctive solution to theology's epistemological problem. The reason for this is Schleiermacher's distinction between the objective and subjective consciousness and his location of religion or piety in the latter. Feeling (or the subjective consciousness) is not a cognitive faculty like empirical knowing or philosophical speculation. It is a category mistake to see expositions of piety (of religious states of consciousness) as cognitive assertions about transcendent realities; piety is a way of believing, not of knowing. While this appears to open the door to the psychologism to which Mackintosh objects, it is confidence in the veridicality of the religious consciousness that allows Schleiermacher to escape the potentially reductionistic implications of a phenomenological method. B. A. Gerrish's formulation nicely articulates the nuances of Schleiermacher's epistemological position: "The truth of dogmatic assertions is the correctness with which they describe the Christian way of believing; they do not strictly *assert* the Christian way of believing or claim what Christians believe is true, even if the dogmatician, as a Christian, *thinks* it is true."[6] Christian dogmatics does not make metaphysical assertions, for the system of doctrine does not deal with the objective consciousness (CF §33, Postscript). The "conceptions of divine attributes and modes of action" and "utterances regarding the constitution of the world" that dogmatics derives from the "descriptions of human states" (CF §34) are held by the believer to be true on the basis of confidence in the veridicality of the religious consciousness, but they are not strictly speaking

---

5   Andrew Dole, "Schleiermacher's Theological Anti-Realism," forthcoming in *Analytic Theology*, ed. Oliver Crisp and Michael Rea (Oxford: Oxford University Press, 2009). I am grateful to Prof. Dole for sending me the proofs of his article. By "realism" Dole means making "claims to truth about mind independent realities." By contrast, "reductive theological anti-realism" is "the position that theological statements can be translated into statements of another kind without residue."

6   Gerrish, *Continuing the Reformation*, 265.

assertions about transcendent realities. Thus Schleiermacher holds a version of realism, but he adheres to the limitations of Kantian epistemology.

To make a case for this thesis concerning the epistemological status of dogmatic propositions, I will begin by taking a closer look at Schleiermacher's understanding of the nature of dogmatics. Then I will consider the cognitive status of the religious consciousness. I will conclude by taking into account Schleiermacher's differentiation of dogmatic propositions into three types.

1. The Nature of Dogmatics

Schleiermacher carefully chose the epigraphs for *The Christian Faith*, and they put us on the track of his understanding of the nature of dogmatics: "Nor do I seek to understand in order that I may believe, but I believe in order that I may understand. For he who does not believe does not experience, and he who does not experience, does not understand."[7] The standpoint of the one engaging in dogmatics is belief. "A genuinely dogmatic treatment" presupposes faith, Schleiermacher informs us (CF §19.4). To be sure, a non-believer may be able to provide a "report" of Christian doctrines, but "a dogmatic treatment of doctrine is not possible without personal conviction."[8] Moreover, "Dogmatics is only for Christians," and so far from seeking to prove "the truth or necessity of Christianity," the *Glaubenslehre* presupposes "that every Christian, before he enters at all upon enquiries of this kind, has already the inward certainty that his religion cannot take any other form than this" (CF §11.5; see also §19.1). When he asserts that dogmatics "has nothing whatever to do with those who do not admit the fundamental fact" (CF §28.3), Schleiermacher seems to have in mind something akin to Paul Tillich's notion of the "theological circle."[9] The

---

7 Anselm, Proslogion 1, De fide trinitatis 2. These epigraphs for *The Christian Faith* were unaccountably omitted from the Mackintosh and Stewart translation. See KGA I/13.1, 1.

8 Friedrich Schleiermacher, *Brief Outline on the Study of Theology*, trans. Terrence Tice (Richmond: John Knox, 1970), §196. Henceforth BO, followed by proposition number.

9 "Theology is necessarily existential and no theology can escape the theological circle," Tillich writes; "the theologian is determined by his faith" and "every theology presupposes that the theologian is in the theological circle." Paul Tillich, *Systematic Theology*, vol. 1 (Chicago: University of Chicago Press, 1951), 23.

epistemological relevance of this first point is that anyone engaged in dogmatics is already convinced of the veridicality of the Christian consciousness.

There is another sense in which Christian faith, or the Christian way of believing, is the presupposition of the *Glaubenslehre*. Not only is the faith of the theologian presupposed; the *Glaubenslehre* presupposes its data or object: the Christian consciousness or Christian faith itself. "Dogmatics has simply the fundamental inner fact of Christian piety, which it presupposes" (CF §28.2). It is not the task of dogmatics to establish or "ground" this consciousness.[10] Christian piety is a fact of consciousness and of history; it is the task of dogmatics to expound it. This is the import of the very definition of dogmatics: "Dogmatic theology is the science which systematizes the doctrine prevalent (*geltend*) in a Christian Church at a given time" (CF §19; cf. BO §195).[11] It is also the meaning of the "ecclesiastical value" of dogmatic propositions, which resides in their "reference to the religious emotions (*fromme Gemütserregungen*) themselves" (CF §17.1).

These considerations point in the direction of an essentially descriptive understanding of the dogmatic task. The descriptive character of dogmatics is the import of the location of dogmatic theology in the system of the sciences as well. Dogmatic theology is located within historical theology, which is itself a branch of historical science (*Geschichtskunde*).[12] This placement means that dogmatics is an empirical science: *Geschichtskunde* belongs to the empirical side of the humanistic disciplines rather than to the speculative side, which Schleiermacher calls Ethics.[13] Thus we may say that dogmatics is descriptive or phenomenological in so far as it expounds what is factually there: the Christian consciousness or Christian piety.

---

10   Schleiermacher explicitly discusses the issue of the "grounding" of dogmatics in the *Sendschreiben*, and denies that in the introduction to the *Glaubenslehre* he intends to do any such thing (Schleiermacher, *On the Glaubenslehre*, 56-58, 76-80).

11   Translators have problems with the term *geltend*: Mackintosh and Stewart render it as "prevalent"; Tice renders it as "current," while correctly observing that *geltend* "bears the meaning of valid more than prevalent" (BO, 72 n. 2). Schleiermacher explains what he means by "valid" in *The Christian Faith*: "dogmatic expressions of that which, in the public proceedings of the Church . . . can be put forward as a presentation of its common piety without provoking dissension and schism" (CF §19.3).

12   BO §69: Historical theology is part of the "modern science of history," as Tice renders *Geschichtskunde*.

13   See Friedrich Schleiermacher, *Lectures on Philosophical Ethics*, ed. Robert Louden (Cambridge: Cambridge University Press, 2002); and my analysis of the system in Walter E. Wyman, Jr., "Schleiermacher's Theology," *Encyclopedia of Christianity* (Grand Rapids and Leiden: Eerdmans and Brill, 2005), 4:852-63.

We may take a further step in exploring the epistemological question by reflecting on the question, "What is dogmatics *for*?" Although dogmatics has both an ecclesiastical and a scientific dimension, as a component of the positive science of theology it exists to serve the leadership of the church, not the interests of science (BO §198). "Dogmatic procedure has reference to preaching (*Verkündigung*), and only exists in the interests of preaching" (CF §19.1). One of its tasks is to give to "practical activity the norms for popular communication" (BO §198). The "didactic form of expression . . . arises mainly out of the problem of settling the apparent conflict between individual metaphors and figures" and "for freeing the expression from . . . ambiguity and uncertainty" (CF §18.2). Although I have characterized dogmatics as descriptive, these considerations show that Schleiermacher conceived of dogmatics as normative as well. It exercises control over the poetic and rhetorical language of the Church. Moreover, it plays a role in the development of the doctrine of the Church from the present into the future.[14] In the "critical process" that dogmatics undertakes, the adequacy of church doctrines, including that of the Protestant confessions, is tested against Christian experience (CF §95.2).

One could conclude that the normative function of dogmatics does not necessarily imply an epistemologically realist stance. One could conclude that it amounts to no more than the giving of rules for the appropriate employment of Christian language, along the lines of Lindbeck's proposal for a cultural-linguistic conception of doctrine. After all, the criteria of theological adequacy announced in CF §19.1, internal coherence and derivation from the Christian consciousness, are compatible with a non-realist epistemology.

B. A. Gerrish has persuasively argued that doctrinal rules cannot regulate religious language "without implying, and thus implicitly making, truth claims."[15] The normative function of dogmatics entails a more robust epistemological stance than a non-realistic cultural-linguistic approach. An obscure paragraph in the *Brief Outline* suggests that Schleiermacher held a more epistemologically robust stance, even if not a full blown epistemological realism. "A dogmatic proposition is more complete as it possess a divinatory as well as an assertory character" (BO 202). This proposition contains two difficult technical terms: *divinitorisch* and *assertorisch*. The divinatory character, Schleiermacher tells us, is "the degree of clarity with which one apprehends the whole

---

[14] See Schleiermacher's discussion of the Christian "principle" and its development in BO §198, §200, and CF §19.3.

[15] B.A. Gerrish, "The Nature of Doctrine," *Journal of Religion* 68, no. 1 (January 1988): 91.

existing state of doctrine," a view compatible with a descriptive, non-realist position. "In the assertory character . . . is shown the degree of surety in one's own view," he explains. The very term "assertory" suggests a more robust epistemological status. In Kant's first critique "assertory" refers to the modality of judgments. There Kant explains a three-way distinction between assertory, problematic, and apodeictic judgments: "Problematic judgments are those in which affirmation or negation is taken as merely possible (optional). In assertoric judgments affirmation or negation is viewed as real (true), and in apodeictic judgments as necessary" (B100).[16] This evidence is suggestive, although by no means decisive. Schleiermacher's own explanation in the *Brief Outline* is somewhat cryptic, and I am not aware that he elaborates on the term "assertoric" elsewhere. Perhaps all he means is that the dogmatician expounds an interpretation of doctrine in the assurance that it is the right one. But the term may imply a certainty about the truth of the belief so expounded.

Dogmatic propositions arise "out of logically ordered reflection upon the immediate utterances of the religious self-consciousness" (CF §16, Postscrtipt). It was Schleiermacher's consistent insistence, from the *Speeches* onward, that doctrines are secondary, the product of reflection upon piety. Contradicting the rationalist view that "the ultimate foundation of faith always rests on insight into the necessary interrelation among comprehended ideas," Schleiermacher insisted that "pious feeling is not derived from a representation, but is the original expression of an immediate existential relationship."[17] Theology is the "daughter of religion," not vice versa, and one's piety can be better than one's religious ideas.[18] But if this is so, where do doctrines come from? And what is their epistemological status?

We may begin by asking what Schleiermacher means by "reflection on the immediate utterances of the religious self-consciousness." What does Schleiermacher mean by "immediate utterances" (*unmittelbare Aussagen*)? I think that what he must mean are the *Glaubenssätze* of proposition 15: "Christian doctrines (*Glaubenssätze*) are accounts of the Christian religious affections set forth in speech." The choice of "doctrines" to translate *Glaubenssätze* is perhaps infelicitous.[19] A close read-

---

16   Immanuel Kant, *Critique of Pure Reason*, trans. Norman Kemp Smith (New York: St. Martin's Press, 1965), 109-10.
17   Schleiermacher, *On the Glaubenslehre*, 40.
18   Ibid., 41, 39.
19   In the Mackintosh and Stewart translation of *The Christian Faith*, the word "doctrine" is used to translate *Glaubenssatz, Lehre,* and *Lehrstück,* obscuring any differences of meaning among the three terms.

ing of the argument in CF §15 shows that a *Glaubenssatz* appears when an internal mental state is expressed verbally. A *Glaubenssatz* can take very different forms: poetic speech (a psalm or a hymn), rhetorical speech (a sermon or proclamation), or finally descriptively didactic speech (the language of dogmatic theology). All of these contain, if I have understood him correctly, *Glaubenssätze*. "Doctrine," implying as it does a formal conceptual statement of a theological claim, may not be the right translation for *Glaubenssatz*, though it is hard to think of a better alternative.[20]

Now if dogmatic propositions elevate the more direct verbal expressions of a subjective state of consciousness (*Glaubenssätze*) to proper dogmatic form, that is, to dialectically formed "descriptively didactic" language, the question returns: what is the cognitive status of such propositions? Do dogmatic propositions yield cognitive assertions about mind-independent realities? Insofar as Schleiermacher's *Glaubenslehre* observes the epistemological limits defined by Kant, dogmatic propositions, as descriptive accounts of Christian beliefs, cannot claim the status of epistemological realism. But Christian dogmatics proceeds on the basis of confidence in the veridicality of the Christian consciousness. We must turn to the question of the cognitive status of the religious consciousness.

2. The Cognitive Status of the Religious Consciousness

As early is 1799, Schleiermacher was insisting that "[R]eligion's essence is neither thinking nor acting, but intuition and feeling."[21] His terminology shifted, and later editions of the *Speeches* show a preference for *Gefühl* over *Anschauung* as the place to locate religion. But what persists is the denial that religion or piety is *knowing*. The classic formulation of the second edition of the *Glaubenslehre* is that piety in itself "is neither a knowing nor a doing, but a modification of feeling or of immediate self-consciousness" (CF §3). To understand properly what is being said, at least some grasp of Schleiermacher's intricate theory of consciousness is necessary.

"Sensible life" (*sinnliches Menschenleben*) consists of feeling and perception. The "accumulation of perception" (*Wahrnehmung*) constitutes

---

20 "Faith-proposition" is clunky and arguably a good deal worse. "Verbal expression of faith" is a possibility.
21 Friedrich Schleiermacher, *On Religion: Speeches to its Cultured Despisers*, trans. Richard Crouter (Cambridge: Cambridge University Press, 1996), 22.

the objective consciousness. The realm of feeling or the self-consciousness is the realm of social, moral, and self-regarding feelings. This is the subjective or sensible self-consciousness (CF §5.1). But in addition to the sensible self-consciousness Schleiermacher posits the existence of a "higher self-consciousness," which is constituted by the feeling of absolute dependence. The feeling of absolute dependence is, of course, "the self-identical essence of piety" (CF §4).

What Schleiermacher has done is to locate piety within the economy of human consciousness: it belongs to feeling (*Gefühl*), to the subjective, not the objective consciousness, and to the higher, not the sensible self-consciousness. At this point interpreters are most in danger of committing the fallacy of misplaced concreteness. The feeling of absolute dependence is not Christian (or indeed, any other kind of) piety. It is a radical abstraction that does not, by itself, occupy a moment of consciousness, but always exists only in connection with the sensible self-consciousness. The feeling of absolute dependence becomes real only, so to speak, with a qualifier: as Christian, Jewish, or Muslim piety, etc. The content of any of these pieties, including the Christian, includes more than the bare feeling of absolute dependence. Thus, Christian piety is always a consciousness of alienation from God and fellowship with God resting on a communication from the Redeemer (CF §63).

What is the epistemological payoff of these observations? It is Schleiermacher's consistent intention to assert that piety, or the religious consciousness, is not knowledge. The degree of one's knowledge is not the degree of one's piety (CF §3.4).[22] Schleiermacher has put forward an alternative to rational religion and to orthodoxy, both of which locate religiousness in assent to the truth of propositions. Christian faith is not an objective consciousness of the world; it belongs to the realm of feeling or immediate self-consciousness. But does this mean that it is devoid of cognitive significance? Our problem can be formulated as the question: what is the epistemological status of the subjective consciousness?

"It is not in any wise meant," Schleiermacher asserts, "that piety is excluded from all connexion with knowing." What is the relation between "Christian piety in itself and . . . Christian belief (*Glaube*), in so far as it can be brought into the form of knowledge"? Piety, Schleiermacher states, is "the object" of dogmatic knowledge, "the knowledge that can only be explicated in virtue of a certainty that inheres in the determinations of self-consciousness" (CF §3.4).

---

22 See also Schleiermacher, *On the Glaubenslehre*, 38-43.

The conclusion to this train of thought is that Schleiermacher is affirming a kind of realism, but it is a highly qualified realism. Piety, by virtue of its location in the human consciousness, is not knowing; it is not objective consciousness of the world. But it would be a mistake to conclude from this that Schleiermacher is a non-realist and that non-religious (that is, reductionistic or psychologistic) accounts of religious language have equal epistemic rights with religious accounts. The reason for this state of affairs is the status of the religious consciousness itself. "It is possible to give a non-religious explanation of this sense of absolute dependence," Schleiermacher concedes in CF §32.2. But he immediately goes on to argue that "we can only regard this explanation as a misunderstanding." Without going into the details of his argument, which turns on the distinction between reciprocal interaction and absolute dependence, we need only consider his conclusion: "The feeling of absolute dependence . . . is not to be explained as an awareness (*mitgesetztsein*) of the world's existence, but only as an awareness (*mitgesetztsein*) of the existence of God, as the absolute undivided unity" (CF §32.2). Schleiermacher's argument here is a defense of the veridicality of the God-consciousness. God is, as Schleiermacher says, co-posited (*mitgesetzt*) with the feeling of absolute dependence itself. While a metaphysical argument for the reality of God has no place in Christian dogmatics, and while actual metaphysical assertions cannot be deduced from the subjective consciousness, the Christian is within her or his epistemic rights to trust that the religious consciousness is about something besides him or herself. Certainty, as Schleiermacher asserts, "inheres in the determination of consciousness" (CF §3.4).

As far as the specifically Christian consciousness is concerned, it is not produced by the individual's subjectivity but is formed by the common spirit (*Gemeingeist*) of the Christian community. Through this common spirit the individual enters into living fellowship (*Lebensgemeinschaft*) with the Redeemer and is both redeemed (strengthened in his or her consciousness of God) and reconciled (experiences blessedness rather than suffers from evil). No one can present evidence and argument to show that God created the world, or that God is love, or that Jesus had both a perfect God-consciousness and experienced perfect blessedness. These are utterances whose *referent* transcends the self: that is, the intention is realist, to make true statements about realities outside of the self's subjective feelings. The propositions intend to tell the truth, but they can only be believed (on the basis of trust in the veridicality of pious experience), not known to be true.

3. Three Types of Dogmatic Propositions

As is well known, Schleiermacher distinguishes between three forms of dogmatic propositions: "descriptions (*Beschreibungen*) of human states," "conceptions (*Begriffe*) of divine attributes and modes of action," and "utterances (*Aussagen*) regarding the constitution of the world" (CF §30). How are these propositions possible? And what is their cognitive status–what do they provide knowledge of?

The propositions of the first form follow immediately from Schleiermacher's premises. The feeling of absolute dependence is the essence of piety, but it "only puts in an appearance" in concrete form "as a real self-consciousness in time." Therefore, "all propositions of dogmatics must be capable of being set up as formulae" for "a definite state of mind" (CF §30.1).

What are the states of mind that are articulated by propositions of the first form? Schleiermacher analyzes the Christian consciousness into that which is presupposed by the Christian consciousness (Part One), the consciousness of sin (Part Two, First Aspect), and the consciousness of grace (Part Two, Second Aspect). Given this three-fold organization, there are three basic states of mind (expressed in three propositions) under which all of the details later fall. First, "the world exists only in absolute dependence on God" (CF §36). Second, "We have consciousness of sin wherever the God-consciousness . . . determines our self-consciousness as pain . . ." (CF §66). Third, "We have fellowship with God only in a living fellowship with the Redeemer. . . " (CF §91). The doctrines of Creation and Preservation, of Sin and Grace (including both Christology and Regeneration-Sanctification), are derived from these states of mind.

It would take more space than is available to explore thoroughly the question of the cognitive status of propositions of the first form. A single example will have to suffice. What *knowledge* does the doctrine of Creation assert? "The religious consciousness which is here our basis contradicts every representation of the origin of the world which excludes anything whatever from origination by God, or which places God under those conditions and antitheses which have arisen in and through the world" (CF §40). The doctrine of Creation does not tell us *how* the world came into being, a matter that the religious consciousness has no interest in, but rather articulates the notion presupposed by Christian piety that "the world exists only in absolute dependence on God" (CF §36). The cash value of "God created the world" is that nothing whatever is excluded from origination by God. The doctrine of Creation is not asserting scientific claims that could be verified or refuted by scientific procedures.²³ It is making a claim about divine causality: the world is dependent upon a transcendent yet immanent ground.²⁴

Propositions of the first form are the "fundamental dogmatic form." Propositions concerning God and the world must be developed out of the first form. Schleiermacher knows he is in problematic territory: utterances regarding the constitution of the world could belong to the natural sciences (that is, to the objective consciousness, not to inner experience), and propositions regarding divine attributes and modes of action could be properly metaphysical. Both kinds of assertions would transgress the epistemological limits of the critical philosophy; in neither case would such propositions be properly dogmatic (CF §30.2). How, then, are dogmatic propositions regarding God and the world possible?

There is space to consider only propositions regarding God. "All attributes which we ascribe to God are to be taken as denoting not something special in God, but only something special in the manner in which the feeling of absolute dependence is to be related to him" (CF §50). Dogmatics must proceed by asking what divine attributes "correspond" to "the different moments of the religious self-consciousness" (CF §50.3). In contrast to Descartes, who rationally deduced the attributes of God from the concept of a perfect being,²⁵ Schleiermacher derives the doctrines of divine holiness and justice as well as divine wisdom and love from the Christian experiences of sin and grace. The knowledge of God that is conveyed in dogmatic propositions is the concept of God and modes of divine action that are entailed by Christian experience.

4. Conclusion

In his dogmatics, Schleiermacher observes the limits of knowing that had been articulated by Kant's critical philosophy.²⁶ Theologically,

---

23 Recall the famous "eternal covenant" passage of the *Sendschreiben an Lücke*, where Schleiermacher explains his determination to avoid such conflicts. He is "firmly convinced" that "every dogma that truly represents an element of our Christian consciousness can be so formulated that it remains free from entanglements with science" (Schleiermacher, *On the Glaubenslehre*, 64).
24 See CF §46 and §51.
25 See *Discourse on Method*, Part Four.
26 Whether and what knowledge might be possible philosophically are questions beyond the scope of this investigation. An answer to these questions would require,

what is known is the Christian consciousness, the contents and implications of which are spelled out in dogmatic propositions in three forms. H. R. Mackintosh's suspicion that Schleiermacher's position is reductionistic is unwarranted. His mistake is in his negation ("not about God"), for it ignores both the referent of dogmatic language and the presupposed confidence in the veridicality of the Christian consciousness. Andrew Dole is correct in perceiving that Schleiermacher has realist intentions. The referent of (some) dogmatic language is realities that transcend the subjective consciousness. Yet the cognitive status of that language is modest. Dogmatic propositions provide, not knowledge of transcendent realities, but an analysis of the Christian way of believing. Their claim to truth rests on the conviction of the veridicality of the Christian consciousness.

Ernst Troeltsch once coined the term "agnostic epistemology" to characterize Schleiermacher's position (as well that of the Ritschlians who came after him).[27] Although Troeltsch overemphasized the purely practical character of religious language and erroneously assigned dogmatics to practical theology, he was surely correct to see in Schleiermacher a conception of religious knowledge that "renounces any theoretical-scientific knowledge that adequately and actually grasps the transcendent world." Religious knowledge, for Schleiermacher, is "independent over against rational knowledge" and is "traced back to its own sources." It follows that the term "knowledge" in dogmatics can be used only "in an improper, atheoretical sense."[28]

Schleiermacher wrestled with the intellectual problems of his own distinctive, post-Kantian, situation. Can he provide any guidance in our much different age, as theologians contend with the suspicion that their discipline lacks a subject matter? Schleiermacher's position that the object of dogmatics is the Christian faith, a distinctive way of believing, does provide one kind of answer to the suspicion that theology lacks a subject matter. Given that premise, dogmatics can get on with its descriptive and normative tasks and the liberal arts study of religious ideas can proceed. But such a phenomenological approach clearly has its limitations with respect to the question of the truth of the Christian way of believing. The question, "What is it reasonable to believe?" be-

---

of course, an investigation of Schleiermacher's *Vorlesungen über die Dialektik* (KGA II/10).

27 Ernst Troeltsch, "Rückblick auf ein halbes Jahrhundert theologischer Wissenschaft," in Ernst Troeltsch, *Zur religiösen Lage, Religionsphilosophie und* Ethik, vol. 2 of *Gesammelte Schriften* (Tübingen: J.C. B. Mohr, 1913), 200-209, esp. 200-201, 207-8.

28 Ibid., 201, 200.

comes even more pressing once confidence in the veridicality of the Christian consciousness erodes and an analysis of religion that turns on the feeling of absolute dependence loses its credibility. If *Glaubenslehre* as a descriptive, phenomenological dogmatics is to be successful in meeting the demands of theological adequacy of the present, it will require resources beyond what Schleiermacher has to offer.

"Non-binding Talk"[1]

The Fate of Friedrich Schleiermacher's Concept of Historical-Empirical Dogmatics

To Han Adriaanse on the occasion of his seventieth birthday

ARIE L. MOLENDIJK

Allard Pierson (1831-1896) is doubtless a remarkable figure in Dutch intellectual history. Born in 1831 into a wealthy, Pietist family, he resigned as a Protestant minister at the age of 34 (unable to reconcile his own views with those of the church), taught afterwards (from 1870-74) at the Heidelberg Theological Faculty,[2] and went on to occupy the first Dutch chair of Aesthetics, Art History, and Modern Languages (established at the University of Amsterdam).[3] In 1876, Pierson published a nearly 150-page discussion of two works in dogmatics in what was then the leading Dutch intellectual journal. The review, entitled "A Funeral," is one of the most devastating critiques in the history of Dutch theology. In the same spirit as the Dutch once fought Catholicism, Pierson declared that we now have to uncover the sophisms and the utter inaptitude of traditional Protestant dogmatics in any possible form.[4] The year 1876, in which the most important reorganization of modern Dutch Higher Education took place, including the Faculties of Theology, was not (as Pierson probably had hoped) the end of theological dogmatics as an academic discipline. Notwithstanding several ups and downs, the field did, however, became more and more marginalized

---

1 The title is a translation of Karl Barth's phrase "unverbindliches Gerede," in *Kirchliche Dogmatik,* vol. 4, pt. 1 (Zürich: Evangelischer Verlag, 1953), 427; *Church Dogmatics,* vol. 4, pt. 1 (Edinburgh: T&T Clark, 1956), 387.
2 Pierson, "Heidelberg" (1888), in *Uit de verspreide geschriften van Allard Pierson: Feuilletons verschenen in 1858-1889* ('s-Gravenhage: Martinus Nijhoff, 1906), 85-91.
3 Arie L. Molendijk, "Abschied vom Christentum: Der Fall Allard Pierson," in *Post-Theism: Reframing the Judeo-Christian Tradition,* ed. Henri Krop, Arie L. Molendijk, and Hent de Vries (Leuven: Peeters, 2000), 141-57.
4 Allard Pierson, "Ter Uitvaart," *De Gids* 40, no. 3 (1876): 185-249, 434-500, esp. 496.

over the course of the twentieth century.⁵ In 2008, the recently appointed dogmatician of the Amsterdam Free University organized a colloquium on the occasion of his inaugural address that challenged the negative image of the field.⁶ Even within theological departments, it seems, the relevance of dogmatic theology is doubted.

One might be inclined to attribute these developments in the Netherlands to a deficient reception of German theology in general and the writings of Friedrich Schleiermacher in particular. And indeed, the poor—not to mention hostile—reception of his work in Dutch theology in the first half of the nineteenth century cannot be denied. As the first translations appeared in the mid-1830s, one of the leading theological journals commented that it is below the dignity of a Protestant minister (and it was a Protestant minister who did the job) to translate Schleiermacher's work without severely criticizing it.⁷ At the beginning of the nineteenth century, most Dutch systematic theologians were convinced that they were beyond of the "speculative fantasies" and "leaps into the air" of their German colleagues. Intriguing as this piece of reception history may be, I will not delve further into it. Rather I want to (1) take a closer look at Schleiermacher's concept of a historical-empirical dogmatics, then (2) turn to a theologian who claimed to be heavily influenced by Schleiermacher in the way he envisioned the field, Ernst Troeltsch. My focus will be on those elements in their conceptions of dogmatics that may help explain the problems that its practitioners are presently facing.

1. Schleiermacher's Concept of *Glaubenslehre*

Schleiermacher's treatment of dogmatics as part of the historical division of the encyclopedia of theology is often hailed as a major innovation. Schleiermacher himself was conscious of the fact that he differed in this respect from previous theologians and claimed that the justifica-

---

5   Arie L. Molendijk, *The Emergence of Science of Religion in the Netherlands* (Leiden: Brill, 2005), chap. 3, sec. 4.
6   "Pleidooi voor herwaardering dogmatiek," *Reformatorisch Dagblad*, July 4, 2008, http://www.refdag.nl/artikel/1350409/Pleidooi+voor+herwaardering+dogmatiek.html/.
7   See K.H. Roessingh, *Verzamelde Werken*, vol. 1 (Arnhem: Van Loghum Slaterus, 1926), 26; J. Herderscheê, *De modern-godsdienstige richting in Nederland* (Amsterdam: Van Holkema & Warendorf, 1904), 36-37. On the reception of Schleiermacher, see P.J. van Leeuwen, *De betekenis van Fr.E.D. Schleiermacher voor de theologie in Nederland* (Haarlem: Bohn, 1948).

tion for this relocation of the field can only be found in its exposition.[8] Both church statistics and dogmatics are discussed in Schleiermacher's *Brief Outline of the Study of Theology* under the heading of "The Historical Knowledge of the Present Condition of Christianity." Dogmatic theology is defined in the *Glaubenslehre* as the science of the coherence of the teachings of a specific church at a specific stage of history.[9] The term "systematic theology," which is also used there, has, according to Schleiermacher, the advantage that it points to the (necessity of a) coherent exposition of a body of teachings, but the term obscures both the historical character of the discipline and its orientation toward the leadership of the church.[10] Schleiermacher's view that dogmatics must be beneficial for the guidance of the church fits well with his overall conception of theology as a positive science, which implies above all that it is necessarily related to a specific way of belief, practice, and (ecclesial) community.

Two elements in this concept of dogmatics are of special importance for our discussion. First, dogmatics is not a mere description of, or report on, the current teachings of a church community; individual conviction on the part of the theologian is a prerequisite. Second, it is not necessary that different dogmatics pertaining to the same church and time period be equivalent or in agreement (*unter sich übereinstimmen*).[11] As far as the first issue is concerned, Schleiermacher did not deny the possibility of a description of the teachings that were (presumed to be) valid in a certain period. He argued, however, that the coherence or systematic connection of the teachings current in a church can only be demonstrated by someone who is convinced of their value and truth. Neither an idiosyncratic exposition (of heterodox teachings), nor a purely irenic collection of those convictions that no one disputes will suffice. Rather, the dogmatician must take a stance in the struggle of diverging views in order to come to a precise, trustworthy, and convincing exposition. He must show how the dominant "principle" of the current age has developed so as to be able to, in turn, outline the possibilities for improvement that are consonant with that principle. What

---

8   My discussion is based on the second edition of Schleiermacher's theological encyclopedia, *Kurze Darstellung des theologischen Studiums* (1830), in KGA I/6; and the second edition of his *Glaubenslehre*, *Der christliche Glaube nach den Grundsätzen der evangelischen Kirche im Zusammenhange dargestellt* (1830/31), in KGA I/13. Henceforth KD and CG, respectively. Here see KD §195.
9   "Dogmatische Theologie ist die Wissenschaft von dem Zusammenhang der in einer christlichen Kirchengesellschaft zu einer gegeben Zeit geltenden Lehre" (CG §19).
10 KD §97.
11 KD §196; cf. KD §97.

comes from a previous period is likely to be ecclesiastically fixed, whereas the future course of doctrinal development will have to be "presaged" by the individual.[12]

This means that the dogmatician not only needs a clear overview of the current dogma, but must be sure about his own point of view as well.[13] This observation has an important consequence: Schleiermacher's stress on the individual *Ansicht* and judgment of the dogmatician implies that there can be a variety of dogmatics. This variety is reinforced by his claim that even if one agrees about the dominant principle, it can be conceived in different ways. Varying dogmatics may all have an equal claim to churchliness (*Kirchlichkeit*).[14] In Protestant churches there is no need for complete conformity and agreement. Different views can be current and to some degree accepted, as long as they are not officially (*amtlich*) contested by the church leadership.[15] So Schleiermacher accepted in principle a plurality of dogmatics, even within one particular church. Two basic presuppositions, however, hold this pluralism in check. First, on this view, dogmatics is oriented toward a particular church, acknowledges this church's authority, and seeks mutual understanding within its community. Second, the church teachings are considered to evolve in an organic way, which makes it possible for the dogmatician to detect a guiding principle. But the gate to pluralism was opened further yet by another basic feature of the *Glaubenslehre*: its discussion of dogmatic statements and principles of faith (*Glaubenssätze*) as articulations of pious states of mind (*fromme Gemütszustände*).[16] This could be and has been interpreted as a move down the road toward a highly individualized expression of the faith of religious communities.

Schleiermacher characterized dogmatics as the learned and didactic exposition (*darstellend belehrend*) of the Christian faith. Next to the other two main forms of transmission—the poetic and the rhetorical (*der dichterische und rednerische Ausdruck*)—the didactic (sometimes called the logical or dialectical) way of exposition is especially helpful for clarifying the structure and coherence of the Christian faith. Dogmatics aims at the highest degree of precision and seeks to overcome disagreement and seeming contradictions among utterances expressed in the other forms of communication. Schleiermacher also recognized that there are religious communities that do not develop a dogmatics at all. The

---

12 KD §199; cf. KD §202.
13 KD §202.
14 KD §200.
15 KD §196.
16 CG §15.

dogmatic approach presupposes, he argued, both a culture in which scholarship has gained an independent status (separate from the arts and commerce) *and* a religious community in which scholarship is valued and accepted as an aid for guiding the expression of the pious self-consciousness.[17] The implicit corollary of this observation is, of course, that the significance of dogmatics can also dwindle in Christian communities. At present, there are doubtless many Christians all over the globe who have a rather low opinion of dogmatics (or theology in general) and regard it as a threat to their belief.

2. Historicizing Dogmatics

Schleiermacher's view was clearly important for Ernst Troeltsch's understanding of dogmatics. Although it has been claimed that Troeltsch overstated the similarities between their conceptions,[18] it is evident that, like Schleiermacher, he considered dogmatics to be a *Glaubenslehre,* that is, an exposition of the Christian faith at a certain moment of history. Troeltsch's own concept and execution of dogmatics is somewhat unclear, and Walter Wyman is probably right when he points to the tension between Troeltsch's view of dogmatics as historical theology and his actual practice, which must ultimately be characterized as philosophical theology.[19] Troeltsch's own *Glaubenslehre* was not historical to the end, but turned speculative and even metaphysical at the very moment that he introduced the dichotomy between historical-religious and actual-religious elements of faith.[20]

What interests me most here, however, is not the way Troeltsch developed his own theology and dogmatics (and the possible inconsistencies accompanying this venture), but his view of dogmatics as a theological discipline. It comes as no surprise that his view on this matter is also thoroughly historical. The entries pertaining to dogmatic themes that he wrote for the first edition of the encyclopedia *Die Religion in Ge-*

---

17 CG §16.
18 Hans-Joachim Birkner, "Glaubenslehre und Modernitätserfahrung: Ernst Troeltsch als Dogmatiker," in *Umstrittene Moderne: Die Zukunft der Neuzeit im Urteil der Epoche Ernst Troeltschs*, ed. Horst Renz and Friedrich Wilhelm Graf (Gütersloh: Gerd Mohn, 1987), 336-37.
19 Walter E. Wyman, Jr., *The Concept of Glaubenslehre: Ernst Troeltsch and the Theological Heritage of Schleiermacher* (Chico, CA: Scholars Press, 1983), 161-67, 193; cf. Arie L. Molendijk, *Zwischen Theologie und Soziologie: Ernst Troeltschs Typen der christlichen Gemeinschaftsbildung: Kirche, Sekte, Mystik* (Gütersloh: Gerd Mohn, 1996), 158ff.
20 Ernst Troeltsch, *Glaubenslehre* (Munich: Duncker & Humblot, 1925), 72.

schichte und Gegenwart are all structured along a historical trajectory. The entry on dogmatics itself, for instance, starts with a general discussion of the phenomenon among various religions, and then treats in chronological order the Catholic, Old-Protestant, and New-Protestant conceptions of dogmatics. Such an approach makes the reader aware of the transformations of dogma and the discipline itself during the course of the history of (Western) Christianity.

Troeltsch nicely summarized the general tendency to historicize dogmatics in the following observation taken from his 1908 survey of the preceding half-century of theology: "Dogmatics has everywhere abandoned the demonstration of scientifically valid general truths in favor of personal, subjective convictions of a confessional sort, and seeks to harmonise these with the church's dominant tradition and forms of expression."[21] It loses its authoritative character and becomes a confessional expression of the individual appropriations of the Christian substance of life.[22] Of course, one may try to stick to a fixed confessional creed and a traditional dogmatics, but it is more sensible to admit that religious life just does not conform to any official, prescribed standards.[23] This transformation of the task of dogmatics follows, according to Troeltsch, from a renewed understanding of the church. This new understanding again leads not only to tolerance, but also to relativism and subjectivism in the churches themselves. To convey this view, Troeltsch pointed to examples of an extreme variety of opinions even within the leadership of one particular Protestant congregation.[24] Troeltsch admitted that within a particular church community, a specific traditional form of the Christian spirit (*überlieferte Formung des christlichen Geistes*) can be fundamental and authoritative (*verbindlich*), but for Protestants generally this binding tie (*Bindung*) has become very loose.[25] Karl Barth's verdict on Troeltsch's *Glaubenslehre* as "nonbinding talk" is not completely beside the point, since this type of dogmatics seems to have hardly any authoritative character at all.

Troeltsch's view of the field, of course, has been severely criticized as individualistic, relativistic, and even anarchistic, and a large part of the twentieth century has indeed been dominated by a countermovement that allegedly preferred stable dogmas to individualized faith. However, if we take a closer look at what is actually happening at

---

21 Troeltsch, "Half a Century of Theology: A Review" (1908), in *Writings on Theology and Religion*, ed. Robert Morgan and Michael Pye (London: Duckworth, 1977), 58.
22 Troeltsch, *Glaubenslehre*, 4.
23 Ibid., 16-17.
24 Ibid., 16.
25 Ibid., 4.

the moment in many of the Western, mainline churches—and to some extent also in evangelical and charismatic churches—can we then simply dismiss Troeltsch's view? Must we not admit that, to a large extent, he was correct in his analysis of church life and in his diagnosis of the loss of (ecclesiastical) authority? Recall how Troeltsch himself reacted to critiques of the individualized, less binding, and less authoritative modes of religiosity and forms of Protestant community. In his important article, "The Dogmatics of the 'Religionsgeschichtliche Schule'"— written, incidentally, for the University of Chicago Divinity School's *American Journal of Theology*—Troeltsch not only proposed his own view, but also addressed possible objections:

> It may be said that such a dogmatics is individualistic and anarchistic, and that it is not suited for a social religious life and for preaching in the church. The first assertion is certainly not true. A dogmatics of this kind, rather, strives constantly to make the closest possible connection with the living power of historical Christianity . . . But, on the other hand, it presupposes an individual diversity among different dogmatic theologies in a church, and to that extent renounces the unyielding power of a dogma to which all alike must be subject [*entbehrt der festen Kraft eines gleichen, alle bindenden Dogmas*]. . . . [I]t is the duty of the churches, if they are to meet the needs of life itself, to guarantee individual freedom. Hence a dogmatics such as we have indicated can meet the needs of many believers, while the needs of different groups will be met by a different sort of dogmatics. If the churches are not able or willing to exercise this broad-mindedness, they will inevitably fall more and more into the background. They must understand that a new epoch in the spiritual development of humanity must be able to find expression in the churches or else it will pass the churches by [*oder die Kirchen beiseite schieben*]. If they cannot actually do justice to the movement, they are essentially defeated [*innerlich überwunden*] and must content themselves with dominion over a narrow circle of reactionary [*rückständig*] believers.[26]

Such an outcome, of course, has to be avoided in Troeltsch's view, and the churches must therefore be transformed into flexible institutions offering a large degree of freedom to their members.

In this citation, there are many crucial words, two of them being "needs" and "freedom." Troeltsch's view of what dogmatics can and ought to be is to a great extent determined by his view of what is going on in the intellectual and spiritual world of his time. He is not only looking back at what once was, but is looking ahead as well. Even for interpreters who are sympathetic to him, this can be hard to swallow. In a very nice essay, Hans-Joachim Birkner, for example, discusses

---

26 Troeltsch, "The Dogmatics of the History-of-Religions School" (1913), in *Religion in History* (Minneapolis: Fortress, 1991), 101-2.

Troeltsch's view of dogmatics in terms of a loss of meaning and complete privatization of the field,[27] which goes explicitly against Troeltsch's intention to strengthen community as far as possible. One may fear, of course, that dogmatics will go down the road to complete subjectivization and thus become obsolete because of its sheer lack of relevance for a broader church community, but that is not what Troeltsch meant. He did not mourn losses, but called for a transformation of dogmatics, so that it could help ministers preach and serve the needs of their congregations in the tradition of the Christian faith, thereby making "it possible for the community as a whole to retain a sense of historic continuity and to come to an understanding with conservative dogmatic treatises."[28] Troeltsch's adversaries have claimed that this is the end of dogmatics, but the pluralization of points of view and the fact that the Protestant churches have lost the authority to prescribe their views to the believers are developments that must be taken into account—at least by liberal theologians. What this transformation actually implies depends to a great extent on how one sees the field, but for proponents of dogmatics as *Glaubenslehre* such as Troeltsch, it was evidently not the end of dogmatics.

3. Postscript

In this last section I want to extend my discussion to the contemporary theological landscape and make some remarks concerning the present state of the art of dogmatics. This is a hazardous undertaking, given that the situation seems to be somewhat unclear. Since the posthumous appearance of Troeltsch's *Glaubenslehre*, there has doubtless been a vast production of dogmatic work, and the massive volumes of Karl Barth's *Church Dogmatics* made an especially lasting impression on generations of theologians until the 1970s and 1980s. Presently, though, it is much harder to survey and judge the situation. Dogmatic treatises do still appear, and vacancies for dogmaticians are still filled, but most observers would be hesitant to say that the discipline is flourishing at the moment.

It seems very hard nowadays to produce a full-fledged dogmatics, and those scholars who nevertheless try their hand at it scale down their claims in at least two respects. First, it is seldom claimed that the whole traditional ground of the field is covered. Even an older and in-

---

27 Birkner, "Glaubenslehre und Modernitätserfahrung," 331, 337.
28 Troeltsch, "The Dogmatics of the History-of-Religions School," 100.

fluential *Glaubenslehre* as the one first published in 1973 by the Leiden dogmatician Hendrikus Berkhof explicitly leaves out elements that were treated in older works, because these are deemed to be no longer relevant to present-day believers.[29] Second, the claim to present a normative overview that binds one's own church community is either significantly weakened or altogether dropped. The most influential Dutch dogmatician of the last quarter of the twentieth century, Harry Kuitert, published a book about the Christian faith under the title "The Generally Doubted Christian Belief: A Revision," in which he explained his own beliefs.[30] Most of his readers will have missed the allusion in the title to the "general and undoubted Christian belief" of the Apostolic Creed, but the book was a best seller, and in later publications Kuitert went even further, stripping down the Christian faith to an utter minimum. Finally, he arrived at what could be nicely summarized as an "atheistic shade of religion," an expression already used in the nineteenth century, denoting a form of "Christian belief" that made Allard Pierson feel sad and melancholic.

The example of Kuitert shows very clearly that there is a market for theological and spiritual literature, at least in the Netherlands, but that the dogmatic approach—which Schleiermacher had characterized as the learned and didactic mode of expression—seems not to be the most popular one. Other modes of Christian communication, such as the inspirational, poetical, witnessing, and biographical, seem to resonate much more easily and are increasingly practiced by learned theologians. Even if we acknowledge the existence of mixed forms of presentation,[31] the systematic exposition of Christian teachings seems to hold little attraction (to writers no more than readers) and the heyday of dogmatics or, for that matter, *Glaubenslehre* seems to lie behind us. In general, our age does not seem to be the age of full-fledged systematics in any form and traditional dogmatics, of course, aims at a systematic and comprehensive coverage of the Christian faith. Establishing a special chair for specific loci such as Sin or Justification to make things easier for the Ordinarius in dogmatics does not seem to be a great help, since the point of the discipline is to provide a full and integrated picture, not an amalgam of fragments.

---

29   H. Berkhof, *Christelijk Geloof: Een inleiding tot de geloofsleer* (Nijkerk: Callenbach 1973), xviii-xix.
30   "[O]ns algemeen, onbetwijfeld christelijk geloof." H.M. Kuitert, *Het algemeen betwijfeld christelijk geloof: Een herziening* (Baarn: Ten Have, 1992).
31   An example of what I have in mind here is Friedrich Wilhelm Graf, *Moses Vermächtnis: Über göttliche und menschliche Gesetze* (Munich: C.H. Beck, 2006).

A more fundamental reason for the decline of dogmatics (already mentioned by Troeltsch) is that the (Protestant) churches have changed from authoritative and even compulsory institutions to associations with a high degree of freedom. Ordinary believers no longer accept traditional beliefs in the way they were authoritatively handed down by the church leaders, but decide for themselves to a much greater degree than in past centuries. This explains how thirty percent of the members of the main Dutch Protestant Church presently believe, if statistics can be trusted, in reincarnation. Especially since the 1960s, the old structures of authority have been significantly challenged, and this has had repercussions for the churches and the religious field as such.

To summarize the trend as I see it, one could say that the transformation of dogmatics into a *Glaubenslehre* is a token of a changing religious climate, in which lived religion in its many varieties becomes the basis for theologies that can no longer be defined and prescribed merely by a small elite cadre of church leaders. Doubtless, Schleiermacher had the life of the church and the reigning beliefs in mind when he wrote his dogmatics, but as the variety of church life grew in the course of history and the factual religious freedom and pluralism were acknowledged and even accepted, it became ever more difficult to maintain "the unity of the heterogeneous" (Troeltsch). Thus, dogmatics was transformed into an exposition of the Christian faith (or parts of it) according to the personal belief of a professional theologian with a view of what would be convincing to the broader church community. As the diversity grew still more and the autonomy and authenticity of personal belief were valued more deeply, it became harder and harder to present a normative view, let alone "force" this view upon church members or theology students.

One might object that I exaggerate and that the loss of authority is perhaps not so obvious as I suggest. Perhaps, but as the dialectic between professionals and lay people and between authority and autonomy—especially in the religious domain—have changed, it will hardly be possible to restore or enforce an authoritative view of Christian faith that is somehow binding. A modern *Glaubenslehre* may invite people to rethink their belief, but it is no longer an offer that cannot be refused. It can take into account the existing religious and dogmatic variety within a church community by becoming even more historical-empirical, but—as both Schleiermacher and Troeltsch rightly stressed—dogmatics cannot be reduced to simply taking stock of what is going on. It must offer a view of its own and present at least a guiding principle to invite its readers to follow this particular track—being aware of other possible tracks, wherever they may lead, and, even without really knowing where we are heading on this particular track, simply trusting that in the end things will be alright. This may be a far cry from the authoritative exposition of the Christian faith that dogmatics was supposed to supply in the old days, but it may be the final consequence of the historical turn of a field that is becoming modest about what it can achieve in the radically pluralized worlds of late-modern Christian faith(s).

Attunement and Explicitation

A Pragmatist Reading of Schleiermacher's "Theology of Feeling"

KEVIN W. HECTOR

1. Introduction

a. One of Kant's fundamental insights is that it is a mistake to think that what one *ought* to infer, judge, believe, do, and so on, can be read directly off the face of some "given," that is, some fact of the matter conceived as strictly external to any norms we apply to it. His paradigmatic argument to this effect is the Transcendental Deduction, where Kant claims that sense-experience is meaningless apart from the application of concepts (which, for Kant, are a kind of rule), yet that sense-experience itself does not determine which concepts should be applied. The appropriate concepts, that is to say, "are not borrowed from experience; on the contrary, they have to confer upon appearances their conformity to law, and so...make experience possible." Kant thus draws the remarkable conclusion that "the understanding itself is something more than a power of formulating rules through comparison of appearances; it is itself the lawgiver of nature."[1] Kant takes the point to be suitably general: it is a mistake, he insists, to think that any datum (including sense-experience, Scripture, the contents of one's own mind, "the moral law," etc.) can dictate what one ought to do or think apart from one's application of norms to that datum. As is well known, this argument leads Kant to draw several important conclusions about "objects": if (a) concept-application is necessary to one's perception of objects, such that (b) one cannot perceive objects apart from the concepts one applies to them, it apparently follows (c) that one has no access to objects as they are in themselves, that is, apart from one's conceptualization of them, (d) that concepts therefore mediate the world to one,

---

1 Immanuel Kant, *Critique of Pure Reason*, trans. Norman Kemp Smith (New York: Palgrave Macmillan, 1929), A126.

and (e) that, for all one knows, the world itself could be entirely otherwise than one perceives it. Kant thus claims, for instance,

> that all our intuition is nothing but the representation of appearance; that the things which we intuit are not in themselves what we intuit them as being, nor their relations so constituted in themselves as they appear to us, and that if the subject, or even only the subjective constitution of the senses in general, be removed, the whole constitution and all the relations of objects in space and time, nay space and time themselves, would vanish. As appearances, they cannot exist in themselves, but only in us. What objects may be in themselves, and apart from all this receptivity of our sensibility, remains completely unknown to us.[2]

The effect of these claims, as Kant himself realizes, is that the realm of noumena (which includes human subjects, along with the concepts they bring to bear on experience) seems to be cut off entirely from the realm of phenomena (that is, everything one experiences): he remarks that

> an immense gulf is fixed between the domain of the concept of nature, the sensible, and the domain of the concept of freedom, the supersensible, so that no transition from the sensible to the supersensible (and hence by means of the theoretical use of reason) is possible, just as if they were two different worlds, the first of which cannot have any influence on the second; and yet the second *is* to have an influence on the first, i.e., the concept of freedom is to actualize in the world of sense the purpose enjoined by its laws.[3]

Kant is aware of the fact that, in view of his own theoretical constraints, he cannot claim to *know* how these realms might be bridged, but he claims that such a bridge must be at least reasonably thinkable: "it must be possible," he argues,

---

2   Ibid., A42=B59; cf. Bxx, A30=B45, A43=B60, and A44=B62. I am aware that it is controversial to ascribe these views to Kant. Terry Pinkard, for instance, claims that the "gulf" is theoretically indispensable for Kant as a way of exempting human freedom from the realm of causation (*German Philosophy 1760-1860* [Cambridge: Cambridge University Press, 2002], 19-65), whereas John McDowell claims that Kant does not in fact end up with such a "gulf" (see his Woodbridge Lectures, "Having the World in View," *Journal of Philosophy* 95 [1998]: 431-91). For the purpose of framing Schleiermacher's notion of *Gefühl*, it suffices to note that it was precisely this view that was widely ascribed to Kant in the generation immediately following him. On this point, see the works cited in note 5 below.

3   To understand Schleiermacher's response to Kant, it is important to note that this "gulf" between nature and freedom corresponds with the "gulfs" between noumena and phenomena, subject and object, duty and feeling, etc. For a helpful treatment of the relationships among them, see Paul Guyer, "Feeling and Freedom: Kant on Aesthetics and Morality," *The Journal of Aesthetics and Art Criticism* 48 (1990): 137-46.

to think of nature as being such that the lawfulness of its form will harmonize with at least the possibility of [achieving] the purposes that we are to achieve in nature according to laws of freedom. So there must after all be a basis *uniting* the supersensible that underlies nature and the supersensible that the concept of freedom contains practically, even though the concept of this basis does not reach cognition of it either theoretically or practically . . .[4]

As is well known, Kant proposes two kinds of judgment—aesthetic and teleological—as the means by which the connection between these two realms might be rendered thinkable; as is also well known, many of Kant's successors were unpersuaded by this solution, in consequence of which a generation of philosophers and theologians worked to find some alternative means either of bridging Kant's "gulf" or avoiding it altogether.[5]

Schleiermacher's project can be read as a helpful response to this problem—or so I shall argue—but before turning to him, it should be noted that this "gulf" is still very much with us. Sallie McFague speaks for many when she asserts that "language always stands between us and reality," and is, accordingly, "the medium through which we are aware of both our relationship to 'what is' and our distance from it," such that "distance is forever between us and what we know."[6] The picture according to which there is a "gulf" between objects-as-conceptually-mediated and objects-in-themselves is still with us, in other words, and, indeed, it has achieved in some quarters the status of dogma (i.e., an unquestioned, and so apparently self-evident, belief).

Schleiermacher's notion of *Gefühl* renders this picture optional—thereby exhibiting it *as* a picture—by setting another picture alongside

---

4   Kant, *Critique of Judgment*, trans. Werner S. Pluhar (Indianapolis: Hackett, 1987), 5:175-76.
5   Dissatisfaction with the Kantian "gulf" became particularly evident in the so-called "Nihilism Controversy" (it would be more precise to describe it as a "solipsism controversy") that arose in the late 1780s through the early 1800s, for which see J.H. Obereit's *Die verzweifelte Metaphysik zwischen Kant und Wizenmann* and *Die wiederkommende Lebensgeist der verzweifelten Metaphysik* (both 1787), Jacobi's "Letter to Fichte" (1799), and the anonymous *Nachtwachen von Bonaventura* (1804). In addition to that of Schleiermacher, responses to this problem include Fichte's *Wissenschaftslehre* (1794), Schelling's *System des transcendentalen Idealismus* (1800), and Hegel's *Phänomenologie des Geistes* (1807).
6   Sallie McFague, *Metaphorical Theology: Models of God in Religious Language* (Philadelphia: Fortress, 1982), 34, 54, cf. 64. See also John Caputo, *The Prayers and Tears of Jacques Derrida* (Bloomington: Indiana University Press, 1997), 21-25; and Jean-Luc Marion, *The Idol and Distance* (New York: Fordham University Press, 2001).

it.[7] His strategy, as I understand it, is to avoid Kant's "gulf"—without violating Kant's scruples about reading norms off the face of some "given"—by reversing Kant's explanatory order: whereas Kant begins with a picture according to which a person, standing on one side, as it were, applies concepts to a manifold of sense-data, which stands on the other, and then appeals to a transcendental sense of harmony and purposiveness to bridge the gap between the two, Schleiermacher manages to avoid the gap altogether by taking a relatively non-transcendental notion of the "sense of harmony" as his explanatory primitive.[8] In what follows, I will elaborate and defend this strategy, which I am inclined to describe as "pragmatic," in three steps: I will argue, first, that we can understand that which Schleiermacher takes as basic, namely, *Gefühl*, as a person's non-inferential "attunement"; second, that we can explain this attunement as one's internalization of that which circulates through custom; and third, that theology is the paradigmatic means by which this attunement is rendered explicit (and so judgeable). The sum of these arguments, if successful, is a picture that (a) renders at least some varieties of Kant's "gulf" optional, without (b) violating Kant's scruples about "givenness."

b. Before proceeding to my argument, three clarifications are in order. First, to understand the sort of reading on offer, it is important to distinguish between what one might call *de dicto* and *de re* interpretation.[9]

---

[7] There is considerable evidence that key aspects of Schleiermacher's thought—particularly the theoretical role of *Gefühl*—develop in response to precisely this problem. See, among several other examples, his "Notizen zu Kant: Kritik der praktischen Vernunft" (in KGA I/1), where Schleiermacher explicitly criticizes Kant's inability to connect freedom with phenomena and his failure to account for one's motivation to act morally (129), and his review of Kant's *Anthropology from a Pragmatic Point of View* (in KGA I/2), which Schleiermacher characterizes as proof that Kant's separation of the noumenal and phenomenal selves renders a coherent anthropology impossible (365-69). On Schleiermacher's development along these lines (with attention to several other texts), see Julia A. Lamm, "The Early Philosophical Roots of Schleiermacher's Notion of *Gefühl*, 1788-1794," *Harvard Theological Review* 87, no. 1 (1994): 67-105.

[8] This is not to suggest that Schleiermacher conceived his project in precisely these terms, since it is not clear the extent to which he was influenced by the third *Critique*.

[9] Here I am following Robert Brandom's version of the distinction, for which see chapter seven of his *Making It Explicit: Reasoning, Representing, and Discursive Commitment* (Cambridge: Harvard University Press, 1994); and "Pretexts," in *Tales of the Mighty Dead: Historical Essays on the Metaphysics of Intentionality* (Cambridge: Harvard University Press, 2002). It is worth considering in this connection Keith Donnellan's famous example of "the man in the corner drinking champagne," for which see his "Reference and Definite Descriptions," *The Philosophical Review* 75, no. 3 (1966): 281-304.

If one is willing to accept some version of semantic holism, to the effect that one can interpret another's doxastic commitments only in terms of their relationship to a whole network of other commitments, it follows that there are at least two ways of specifying the content of those commitments, depending upon the set of collateral commitments one brings to bear.[10] In any interpretive transaction, there are available at least two sets of collateral commitments: on the one hand, those to which the one interpreted him- or herself is committed (or, at the very least, to which he or she *could* have been committed, given his or her historical and intellectual circumstances), and on the other, those to which the interpreter him- or herself is committed (or which are at least available to him or her). This is a rather drastic simplification, but it should suffice to establish the distinction I have in view: the former mode of interpretation, according to which one tries to understand another's commitments, as far as possible, in terms of his or her own possible and actual commitments, is what I am calling a *de dicto* content-ascription, whereas the latter, according to which one understands those same commitments in terms of the interpreter's as well as the one interpreted's own actual and possible commitments, could be termed a *de re* content-ascription.[11] The interpretation to be defended here is of the *de re* variety: the collateral commitments I bring to bear are not all available to Schleiermacher, and at some points may appear to run against the grain of Schleiermacher's own commitments (or at least his way of understanding those commitments). It seems to me that this sort of approach is warranted as long as one is clear about what one is up to, and in any event, its propriety will be defended indirectly as part of the argument that follows.[12]

---

10   The paradigmatic argument in favor of such a claim is advanced by W.V.O. Quine, "Two Dogmas of Empiricism," in *From a Logical Point of View* (Cambridge: Harvard University Press, 1953). I defend an argument along these lines in chapter four of my forthcoming book, *Theology Without Metaphysics: God, Language, and the Spirit of Recognition*.

11   Needless to say, there is no such thing as pure *de dicto* or *de re* interpretation, since each depends to some extent upon the other, but competent judges will nevertheless be able to distinguish clear cases of each, and that is all the present point requires.

12   This clarification is related to another: I am aware that some of my interpretations have been defended—and contested—elsewhere. I cannot enter into these debates in the confines of this paper, but I should at least mention the following: on the propriety of understanding Schleiermacher's notion of *Gefühl* as "attunement"—and drawing some correlation with Heidegger's use of *Befindlichkeit*—see R. Stalder, *Grundlinien der Theologie Schleiermachers I: Zur Fundamentaltheologie* (Wiesbaden: F. Steiner, 1969), esp. the much discussed claim on p. 334; as well as Emilio Brito, *Heidegger et L'Hymne du Sacré* (Leuven: Leuven University Press, 1999), 622-27. For pragmatist-friendly readings of Schleiermacher, see Andrew Bowie's recent writings

Second, a brief word is in order about what I mean by "pragmatism": pragmatism, at least in its most recent iterations, could be described as a recurrent rebellion against "metaphysics," dualisms, the pathos of distance, the Myth of the Given, and so on; a rebellion which is carried out, on its negative side, by (i) resisting unlimited explanatory demands as well as (ii) the urge to reify explanatory posits that either lie outside of ordinary experience or that leave us out of the picture; and, on its positive side, by trying to explain phenomena, as far as possible, in terms of what we do—our practices, our answerability to one another, and so on.[13]

Finally, given that I am claiming only that Schleiermacher's proposal renders Kant's "gulf" optional, one might wonder why one would want to exercise this option. Indeed, some recent theorists have claimed that this gulf—and one's awareness of it—is precisely what protects objects (including other persons) from being completely subjected to, and so enclosed within, one's conceptualization of them.[14] So why would one want to do without it? In response, it is important to note, first, that the very idea of concepts either mediating one's relationship to objects or "enclosing" that to which they are applied is itself dependent upon a rather inflated notion of concepts. In view of the extensive criticism to which this notion has been subjected over the past thirty years, as well as the deflationary alternatives available, it should be apparent that one's avoidance of Kant's "gulf" does not by itself collaterally commit one to the totalization of objects.[15] Second, there is rea-

---

on Schleiermacher, including his introduction to *Hermeneutics and Criticism* (Cambridge: Cambridge University Press, 1998). For readings of Schleiermacher on sociality, see vol. 4 of the *New Athenaeum/Neues Athenaeum* (1994) dedicated to the subject and Bernd Oberdorfer's *Geselligkeit und Realisierung von Sittlichkeit* (Berlin: Walter de Gruyter, 1995).

13 For some representative examples of contemporary pragmatism, see Wilfrid Sellars, *Empiricism and the Philosophy of Mind* (Cambridge: Harvard University Press, 1997); Bas van Fraassen, *The Empirical Stance* (New Haven: Yale University Press, 2001); Robert Brandom, *Making It Explicit*; Donald Davidson, *Subjective, Intersubjective, Objective* (New York: Oxford University Press, 2001); and Richard Rorty, *Objectivity, Relativism, and Truth* (Cambridge: Cambridge University Press, 1991). Note that pragmatism, as I am using the term, is not strictly identical with "instrumentalism"; the latter, in my view, should be seen as one of the tools pragmatists have used to achieve their goals, rather than as pragmatism itself.

14 For examples of this claim, see the works listed in note 6 above.

15 On this point, see, for instance, Donald Davidson's "A Nice Derangement of Epitaphs," in *Truth, Language, and History* (Oxford: Oxford University Press, 2005). The claim, simply stated, is that once we are disabused of the picture according to which language is a *tertium* over and above interpretive transactions, we will no longer think of language as standing between us and something outside of us, since lan-

son to think that as long as we remain in the grip of the "gulf"-picture, we will be tempted either to see ourselves as answerable to certain experts (such as scientists) whom we take to have an inside track on "things in themselves," or—far more common in contemporary theology—to pay ourselves metaphysical compliments in order to bridge that "gulf." Consider a recent example of the latter: Catherine Pickstock and John Milbank, leaders of the influential "Radical Orthodoxy" movement, argue (a) that the apparent "gulf" between subject and object *must* be bridged, and (b) that it *can* be bridged only on the basis of their version of Christian neo-Platonism. Their proposal, briefly stated, is to bridge the "gulf" by appeal to both subject and object's participation in the divine: an object is "true," they claim, only when it is "copying God in its own manner, and tending to existence as knowledge in the divine mind," and one has knowledge of an object only insofar as one "participates in the divine knowing" by "catching [the object] on its way back to God."[16] Pickstock and Milbank readily admit that this sort of knowledge "cannot be observed or empirically confirmed," such that "to advance to this source [of knowledge] is of course to advance in unknowing," yet they maintain that "it is only in terms of this unknowing increased through faith, that we confirm even our ordinary knowing of finite things."[17] Note well what has happened: the idea that there is a gulf between subject and object is supposed to be solved by appeal to neo-platonic metaphysics, and this metaphysics (and, presumably, the claims it has been called upon to underwrite) is then insulated from criticism. Unfortunately, this sort of approach is as influential as it is

---

guage is no different from other aspects of the environing circumstances with which one must skillfully cope. As Davidson concludes, "linguistic ability is the ability to converge on a passing theory from time to time—this is what I have suggested, and I have no better proposal. But if we do say this, then we should realize that we have abandoned not only the ordinary notion of a language, but we have erased the boundary between knowing a language and knowing our way around the world generally" (107). One can find several of Davidson's key premises, interestingly enough, in Schleiermacher's own corpus—as witness, for instance, his claim that "there never are two expressions meaning exactly the same thing, and . . . every proposition acquires a somewhat different meaning when it is placed in a different context," such that one's ability to express and interpret meaningful sentences depends upon a kind of know-how. Schleiermacher, *Der christliche Glaube nach den Grundsätzen der Evangelischen Kirche im Zusammenhange dargestellt*, ed. Martin Redeker (Berlin: Walter de Gruyter, 1960), §25.1, henceforth CG. Cf. Schleiermacher's *Kurze Darstellung des theologischen Studiums zum Behuf einleitender Vorlesungen* (1811/1830), ed. Dirk Schmid (Berlin: Walter de Gruyter, 2002), §265, henceforth KD.

16 John Milbank and Catherine Pickstock, *Truth in Aquinas* (London: Routledge, 2001), 9-10, 12 (emphasis subtracted).
17 Ibid., 17-18.

troubling, but in what follows, I will argue that Schleiermacher provides a helpful means by which to question the presuppositions that have lent it an air of plausibility.

2. The Circulation of Attunement

a. Turning to the first section of my argument, then, we begin with the endlessly contested notion of *Gefühl*, which plays the role of explanatory primitive in Schleiermacher's theology. As is well known, this notion is contested with respect both to its meaning and to its defensibility, though one's verdict on the latter is obviously dependent upon one's take on the former. This much, at least, seems clear: for Schleiermacher, *Gefühl* refers to "the immediate presence of whole, undivided existence (sensible as well as spiritual), the unity of a person and his or her sensible or spiritual world," an immediate presence where "the subject-object opposition is entirely excluded as inapplicable."[18] *Gefühl* refers, that is, to a pre-reflective harmony or at-one-ness between oneself and one's environing circumstances, though it is important to note that this harmony includes a kind of comportment or disposition toward those circumstances—important, because Schleiermacher understands *Gefühl* as prior to knowing and doing, yet providing direction to each.[19] It is

---

18   The first quotation is from Henrich Steffens, *Von der falschen Theologie und dem wahren Glauben* (Breslau: Josef Max, 1823), 99, which Schleiermacher cites approvingly at §3.2 of the *Glaubenslehre* (the full text of which is supplied in Martin Redeker's editorial notes—see CG, 17n). The second is from Schleiermacher, *Friedrich Schleiermachers Dialektik*, ed. Rudolf Odebrecht (Leipzig: J.C. Hinrichs, 1942), 287. Translations mine.

19   In the *Sendschreiben*, Schleiermacher describes *Gefühl* as a disposition (*Gesinnung*)—see *Schleiermachers Sendschreiben über seine Glaubenslehre an Lücke*, ed. Hermann Mulert (Gießen: Töpelmann, 1908), 14-15; cf. the *Ästhetik*, where he asserts that *Gefühl* is a "becoming-affected (*Affiziertwerden*)," which is the basis for creative movements as well as one's organic relationship to objects and is thus one's "tuning (*Stimmung*)" — see *Friedrich Schleiermachers Ästhetik*, ed. Rudolf Odebrecht (Berlin: Walter de Gruyter, 1931), 46-51, 71. For the claim that *Gefühl* provides direction (*Richtung*) to knowing and doing, see CG §4.1; cf. the first edition of *Der christliche Glaube*, where he asserts that *Gefühl* is "a determined-ness (*Bestimmtheit*) of the self-consciousness" which "is the ground of each impulse" (KGA I/7.1, 28). In the *Brouillon zur Ethik*, he describes *Gefühl* as that which enables one to distinguish that which is "fitting" from that which is "strange." He describes the mark of such "strangeness" as *Unlust* (and, by parity of reasoning, the mark of "fittingness" as *Lust*), which is precisely parallel to Kant's use of *Lust* and *Unlust* to describe *sittliches Gefühl* in the *Metaphysics of Morals* (6:399); he then explains this *Gefühl* as "astuteness" (*Scharfsinn*) with respect to knowing, "conscience" (*Gewissen*) with respect to practical reason, and "tact" (*Takt*) with respect to one's manners. Friedrich Schleiermacher, *Brouillon zur Ethik*

also important to note that this at-one-ness, because pre- (or non-) reflective, does not involve conscious deliberation; it is, rather, simply "how one finds oneself" in one's circumstances.[20] *Gefühl* thus has to do with the innumerable ways in which one is affected by, and copes with, various circumstances prior to and apart from conscious reflection and judgment—the ways, in other words, that one is always already disposed toward or "in tune with" oneself and one's environment. For example: one hears a Christmas carol and is overcome with nostalgia (or revulsion); a teacher says "3 x 4" and the number "12" springs automatically to mind; one spies a misspelled word and it just looks wrong; a child runs in front of one's car and one hits the brakes before one has even realized what is happening. Innumerable examples could be adduced, but the pattern should be familiar enough: one has an immediate, non-inferential "feel" for oneself and one's environment, and it is by means of this "feel" that one is always already attuned to one's circumstances.

For Schleiermacher, then, *Gefühl* refers to one's pre-reflective attunement to one's circumstances.[21] To elaborate this notion further, it will help if we consider a much-remarked problem facing Schleiermacher's proposal.[22] The problem can be stated in the form of a dilemma: on the one hand, in order to avoid Kant's "gulf," it is crucial that *Gefühl* be construed as an *immediate* (i.e., non-reflective, non-deliberative, non-conceptual) consciousness of and attunement to one-

---

(1805/06), ed. Hans-Joachim Birkner (Hamburg: Meiner, 1981), eighty-sixth instructional hour, 147. Finally, it is worth noting that Schleiermacher himself translates *Gefühl* into English as "common sense" and "sympathy" (Schleiermacher, *Brouillon*, sixtieth instructional hour, 103).

20   Schleiermacher describes (CG §32, Leitsatz) the feeling of absolute dependence, for instance, as an "immediate self-consciousness of finding-oneself-absolutely-dependent" (*unmittelbare Selbstbewußtsein Sich-schlechthin-abhängig-Finden*); at §32.2, Schleiermacher again uses the phrase *Sich-schlechthin-abhängig-Finden*. Schleiermacher thus claims (CG §3.3) that *Gefühl* is distinguished from *Wissen* by virtue of the fact that *Gefühl* is not brought about by a person but rather "comes about" (*zustande kommen*) within him or her and thus belongs wholly and completely to the realm of receptivity (*Empfänglichkeit*); cf. his discussion of *Gefühl* as "*Affiziertwerden*" in *Ästhetik*, 46ff.

21   It would be more precise to say that *Gefühl* means *at least* this for Schleiermacher, since I have not attempted to demonstrate that this is the term's only relevant sense. It suffices for present purposes that this is among the term's central senses for Schleiermacher.

22   A version of this problem is central to the interpretation of Schleiermacher on offer in what are arguably still the two most influential treatments of him in the English-speaking world, namely, Wayne Proudfoot's *Religious Experience* (Berkeley: University of California Press, 1985) and George Lindbeck's *The Nature of Doctrine* (Louisville: Westminster John Knox, 1984).

self and one's circumstances; yet in order to avoid Kant's critique of "givenness," on the other hand—his critique, that is, of the idea that some datum could exert normative constraint upon one's beliefs, judgments, and so forth, prior to and apart from any norms one might apply to it—it would appear that one's attunement to circumstances must be "mediated" by the application of concepts.[23] Schleiermacher solves this problem by arguing that attunement is simultaneously non-inferential *and* norm-laden, and he lends plausibility to this claim by explaining attunement in terms of the circulation and internalization of custom.[24] On Schleiermacher's account, a person expresses his or her attunement through a variety of gestures, while at the same time his or her attunement is an imitation (and internalization) of others' expressions. His model can be summarized in the following steps: (1) A person responds non-inferentially to some (internal or external) circumstance and his or her gestures simultaneously express this response to others with whom he or she identifies; Schleiermacher thus claims that

> attunement, as a self-contained determination of the disposition ... will also, simply in virtue of the kind-consciousness [*Gattungsbewußtseins*], not be exclusively for itself, but rather primordially and without determinate aim or connection become something outward through countenance, gesture, tone, and indirectly through words, and thus become to others a revelation of the inner. (CG §6.2)

(2) Insofar as others identify with this person—and identify his or her expression as "how one responds" to certain circumstances—they may imitate that response in similar circumstances. As Schleiermacher claims,

> this bare expression of feeling ... arouses in others to begin with only a representation of the expressed disposition-state; simply by virtue of kind-consciousness, however, this passes over into lively imitation [*lebendige Nachbildung*], and the more the perceiver is able to pass over into this state (due in part to greater livingness of expression and because of nearer affin-

---

[23] Schleiermacher himself acknowledges the premise underlying each horn of the dilemma, though he questions a particular construal of the latter. With respect to the former, he writes, for instance, that "thought can only embrace what is sundered," such that "the incoming of existence to us, by this immediate union, at once stops as soon as it reaches consciousness." Friedrich Schleiermacher, *On Religion*, trans. John Oman, 3rd ed. (New York: Harper & Row, 1958), 41-42, 43-44. With respect to the latter, he claims that "the construction of a fact [*Tatsache*], the connection of the outer and inner into a historical view, is to be seen as a free activity of the mind [*eine freie geistige Thätigkeit*]" (KD [1830] §152).

[24] This is not to suggest that Schleiermacher's move was entirely unprecedented; we see something similar in Hegel, Schelling, and in Kant's further consideration of the conditions of autonomy.

ity), the easier will this state be brought forth by means of imitation. (CG §6.2)

(3) Once the latter has become reliably disposed to respond non-inferentially in this way, the response has become his or her own attunement to these circumstances; still others may then identify his or her response as how "we" respond and imitate it, and so on; "a multifarious community of attunement" thus emerges in which each person is "both expresser and perceiver," both imitator and imitated (CG §6.2).[25] (4) By means of this process, the kind-consciousness definitively shapes one's self-consciousness (and vice-versa, as we shall see). Schleiermacher claims that, as a result of this process of circulation, an individual's attunement is modeled after that of others to such an extent that the kind-consciousness is included within (*Mitenthaltensein*) his or her self-consciousness (CG §60.2).[26] This explains why a person's gestures can be perceived by others as an expression of that person's attunement (as in (2) above), and provides the background in terms of which Schleiermacher will explain how the Redeemer's God-consciousness is mediated through the community he founded.[27] (5) The kind-consciousness is not only the condition of *Gefühl*'s circulation, it is also continually produced by that which circulates. As Schleiermacher claims, it is "the inner union of kind-consciousness with the personal self-consciousness which procures all recognition [*Anerkennung*] of others as of similar essence" (CG §60.2), or again, that it is precisely by virtue of this "ever-renewing circulation of self-consciousness

---

25 Schleiermacher elsewhere writes of "the individual's participation in the circulation [*Umlauf*] and dissemination [*Fortpflanzung*] of excitations [*Erregungen*]" through "his or her excitableness [*Erregbarkeit*] through and effectiveness on that community" (CG §6, Zusatz). It is important to note that not every expression is either imitated or offered for imitation, such that some expressions have no connection with the kind-consciousness (cf. CG §60.2).

26 Schleiermacher thus claims that "just as no act of feeling is complete and customary [*sittlich*] if it does not become a suggestion for anyone in search of intimation, while at the same time being the intimation of what others would like to suggest, so none can arise except in connection with the collectivity [*Zusammenhang mit der Gesamtheit*] of suggestion and intimation which we must presuppose for each individual act." Schleiermacher, *Ethik (1812/13)*, ed. Hans-Joachim Birkner (Hamburg: Meiner, 1990), 267-68; *Lectures on Philosophical Ethics*, ed. Robert B. Louden (Cambridge: Cambridge University Press, 2002), 198 (translation revised).

27 With respect to the former, Schleiermacher claims that the "inner union of kind-consciousness with the personal self-consciousness . . . is alone the precondition of the fact that the inner is known and perceived along with and by means of expressions" (CG §60.2); with respect to the latter, Schleiermacher insists that this is a necessary condition for the Redeemer's God-consciousness to be communicated to and through the redeemed (CG §60.3).

[*immer erneuernden Umlauf des Selbstbewußtseins*]" that one can come to "some determinate recognition [*bestimmter Anerkennung*] of which individuals belong to a community and which do not" (CG §6.4).[28] It is only because one recognizes another's expressions as similar to one's own that one can recognize him or her as "one of us," in other words, or "of the same kind" — and because such regularity of expression is a product of this process of circulation and internalization, it follows that the kind-consciousness is likewise to be explained in terms of it.[29] On Schleiermacher's account, then, a person's outward expression manifests his or her disposition toward some circumstance; this expression is perceived by someone else as how "we" respond to these circumstances; the latter thus imitates that expression in similar circumstances until he or she has become reliably disposed to respond in this way, at which point the response is an expression of his or her own disposition; others may then perceive his or her outward expression as how "we" respond, and so on. Particular ways of being attuned to circumstances thus circulate through a community and are internalized as one's own attunement, in consequence of which one finds oneself with an immediate, non-inferential "feel" for oneself and one's environment.

b. Such attunement provides one with a kind of primordial directedness, inclination toward, or immediate "take" on oneself and one's circumstances, and it is in terms of this inclination that Schleiermacher is able to avoid Kant's "gulf" without falling prey to his critique of "givenness." Kant's critique, recall, applies to the supposition that what one *ought* to infer, judge, believe, do, and so on, can be read directly off the face of some fact of the matter conceived as strictly external to any norms one applies to it. Schleiermacher accepts this critique, yet he responds to it — on the present reconstruction — by saying that it is a mis-

---

28 Schleiermacher is here describing what he refers to as a "Kirche," but given that his notion of "Gemeinschaft des Gefühls" is advanced precisely for the sake of explaining the church in abstract terms, it seems warranted to take the latter as exemplifying the former. For evidence that this is Schleiermacher's intention, see his letters to Lücke, where he claims that the "general" claims of the *Glaubenslehre's* introduction "are no more than outlines that would be filled in with their true content from the ensuing discussion" (*Schleiermachers Sendschreiben*, 57).

29 Schleiermacher's point about the condition of the possibility of "kind-consciousness" is intriguingly similar to Donald Davidson's famous claim that "[i]f we cannot find a way to interpret the utterances and other behavior of a creature as revealing a set of beliefs largely consistent and true by our own standards, we have no reason to count that creature as rational, as having beliefs, or as saying anything." Davidson, "Radical Interpretation," in *Inquiries into Truth and Interpretation*, 2nd ed. (Cambridge: Cambridge University Press, 2001), 137.

take to construe all norm-application on the model of an explicit judgment, particularly since this assumption encourages one to think of the realm of the normative as standing on one side (as that which a subject brings to experience) and the realm of experience on the other (as that to which norms are applied). We can understand Schleiermacher as responding in the following terms: because he has described one's non-inferential response to circumstances as already including a normative or "directive" dimension (as a product of one's socialization in certain norm-laden practices), Schleiermacher is able to avoid this mistake, since, on his account, the relevant norm is supplied without one's having to think about it; simply being in the presence of certain objects suffices to bring about a norm-laden response in one, from which it follows that there need be no epistemic intermediaries standing between objects and oneself.[30] One can thus do without the picture according to which there seems to be a "gulf" between oneself and objects, particularly since it would appear that one's immediate, norm-laden attunement to circumstances must be prior to those circumstances' appearance as putatively un-normed raw material to which norms are then applied.[31] To see why this is the case, consider a simple example: one hears someone say, "Would you mind holding the door for me?" One understands the person's noises as a series of words only if one breaks them up into distinct, word-like units, but assuming that the noise itself does not supply these breaks, it follows that they must be supplied by the listener. Yet, in the vast majority of cases, a competent speaker of English will not have to decide where the breaks belong; without thinking about it, he or she simply hears the noise *as* words. One's response is thus norm-laden, but nevertheless non-inferential.[32] If one then de-

---

30 For an extended argument to this effect, see Davidson, *Inquiries into Truth*, esp. "On the Very Idea of a Conceptual Scheme"; Davidson, *Subjective, Intersubjective, Objective*, esp. "A Coherence Theory of Truth and Knowledge"; and Brandom's description of reliable differential response dispositions in chapter four of *Making It Explicit*.

31 There is a fairly wide convergence of philosophers on this point; see, for instance, John McDowell's "Having the World in View"; Davidson's "A Nice Derangement of Epitaphs"; and the three chapters from Davidson and Brandom mentioned in the preceding note.

32 As this example should make clear, this model accommodates—but by no means requires—the possibility that one may initially become attuned to certain circumstances through explicit instruction and judgment, though these ways of being attuned count as such, in the present sense, only after they become part of one's immediate "take" on oneself and one's circumstances. So, for instance, as a child, one might learn to read by trying to imitate the sounds that others associate with certain letters, but once one has become a competent reader, one no longer has to think about how to do so; in the vast majority of instances, one can read line after line of text without having to reflect explicitly upon what one is doing. To do the work

cides to reflect upon the means by which one understood these noises as words, one may do so in terms of one's application of particular norms to particular objects, but this step must be an explanatory latecomer relative to the normativity implicit in one's non-inferential responsive disposition, for otherwise, a regress would follow: if (a) all norm-application were construed in terms of explicit judgments about how to apply a particular norm to particular circumstances, and (b) these judgments are themselves susceptible to normative assessment, then (c) the norm-application by which the latter judgment was judged would itself be susceptible to judgment, and so on, from which it follows (d) that if all norm-application is construed in terms of explicit judgments, an infinite regress of judgments would be required in order to apply any norm. The moral of this story, to paraphrase Wilfrid Sellars, is that the game of explicit norm-application, unlike that of implicit normative responsive dispositions, is not a game that one could play though one played no other, which entails that the former cannot be explanatorily prior to the latter.

It is with good reason, then, that Schleiermacher insists that *Gefühl* is prior to deliberate acts of knowing and doing and provides them with "direction" (*Richtung*), since it is only against a background of non-inferential normative dispositions that explicit acts of knowing or doing can take place. That is to say, it is only because there are all sorts of things that one does not have to think about that one can think explicitly about any one of them (or, by parity of reasoning, that one can undertake to enact an intention): one can multiply large numbers, for

---

Schleiermacher requires of it, at any rate, this model had better accommodate such explicit-cum-implicit attunement, for otherwise, it is exceedingly difficult to explain how the Redeemer's God-consciousness could have been communicated to the disciples in a "non-magical" way. This fact provides the resources, in turn, by which to distinguish the non-discursiveness of any particular responsive disposition from the supposition that such dispositions must be "radically independent" of discursive practice. Such a distinction might suffice to acquit Schleiermacher of most of Professor Proudfoot's charges in *Religious Experience*, just as it might illustrate Proudfoot's point about descriptive vs. explanatory adequacy. That is to say, whereas one's responsive disposition may appear independent of discourse from a *descriptive* point of view, an adequate *explanation* of that disposition may have to appeal to one's prior internalization of discursive practice. Again, though, this should not be taken to suggest that one's internalization of custom *always* depends upon explicit training or instruction, since, on the one hand, evolution seems to have played a role in attuning us in certain ways, and on the other, one finds oneself imitating all sorts of attunements without even realizing it—as witness, for example, the disconcerting experience of growing up and discovering that one acts like one's parents, or the research which shows that parents "gender" their children without realizing that they are doing so. We will return to these issues in a moment.

instance, only if one does not continually have to make explicit judgments about what numbers correlate with certain marks on a page, about whether the conditions are such that one is a reliable perceiver of such marks, about the product of each simple multiplication, about how one inscribes a mark which corresponds to that product, and so on. Indeed, if every act of knowing or doing were itself to be explained in terms of explicit reflection and judgment, one would never be able to know or do anything, since that reflection, as itself a kind of knowing and doing, would have to be explained in terms of further reflection, and so on, in yet another regress. Because one's acts of knowing and doing are always set against the background of norms implicit in one's attunement, on the other hand, no regress is implied. Schleiermacher's claim that *Gefühl* is logically prior to knowing and doing thus seems eminently sensible.

c. Thus far, a pragmatist reconstruction of Schleiermacher's notion of *Gefühl*. At this point, page limits force a choice: I can either spell out how this notion would explain absolute dependence, sin, redemption, and the like, or say more about the notion of attunement itself. In what follows, I have decided to focus on the latter, but in order to do so, a bit more needs to be said about the former.[33] So then: Schleiermacher explains "sin" in terms of the difficulty of bringing one's sensible self-consciousness into tune with God, and explains this difficulty, in turn, as due at least partly to the fact that one is attuned by (and attunes) a community whose customs are not themselves in tune with God[34]; he explains the redeemed state of "blessedness," on the other hand, as the ability to bring one's entire sensible self-consciousness effortlessly into tune with one's God-consciousness[35]; and, accordingly, he claims that

---

33 I have defended these views at greater length in Kevin Hector, "Actualism and Incarnation: The High Christology of Friedrich Schleiermacher," *International Journal of Systematic Theology* 8, no. 3 (July 2006): 307-22; and Hector, "The Mediation of Christ's Normative Spirit: A Constructive Reading of Schleiermacher's Pneumatology," *Modern Theology* 24, no. 1 (2008): 1-22.

34 Schleiermacher describes sin, generally speaking, as a kind of "bondage" (*Gebundensein*), and this bondage, in turn, as "lack of facility [*nicht vorhandene Leichtigkeit*] for introducing the God-consciousness into connection with actual moments of life [*wirkliche Lebensmomente*] and keeping it there" (CG §11.2). He then claims that this bondage is intersubjectively mediated, as when he writes that "the actual sin of the earlier (generation) is that which brings forth the sin of the later," while the later generation, in turn, brings forth sin in still later generations (CG §72.6).

35 Schleiermacher thus describes (CG §5.4) blessedness (*Seligkeit*) as a "persistent state" (*beharrlicher Zustand*) in which one expresses the higher self-consciousness in every moment of sensible self-consciousness with "ease" or "facility" (*Leichtigkeit*).

Christ redeems one by living a life completely in tune with God and by founding a community in and through whose customs this attunement circulates.[36] On Schleiermacher's account, then, one is redeemed just insofar as Christ's attunement has become one's own, and his attunement becomes one's own as one internalizes the customs that mediate that attunement. "The supernatural becomes natural," in other words, precisely in that the Spirit of Christ's attunement is circulated through ordinary mechanisms of customariness.

* * *

We can thus understand Schleiermacher as defending an account according to which (a) *Gefühl* is one's non-inferential attunement to one's circumstances, and (b) explicit acts of knowing and doing are to be explained in terms of this attunement, such that (c) Kant's "gulf" loses some of its grip on us. There is much to recommend this account, but it also faces several problems related to the fact that *Gefühl* operates pre-reflectively. First, not everything that circulates in a community is conducive to the flourishing of its members, nor does everything that is customary within the church actually bring one into tune with Christ's God-consciousness.[37] Second, precisely because these customs circulate pre-reflectively, they come to seem "natural," and can accordingly serve to reinforce certain social arrangements without anyone noticing that they are doing so—and without anyone having to engage in explicitly coercive acts in order to enforce these arrangements. And finally, if one's attunement is mediated to one largely apart from one's conscious decision, it might appear to be "unfree," in the sense of being a way of life that has merely been *given* to one, rather than recognizably *due* to one. In order to address these problems, we need to explain the means by which prevailing custom might be judged.

---

36 Schleiermacher claims that Christians "take the institution of Christ to be an approximation to the above-described state of absolute facility and constancy [*Leichtigkeit und Stetigkeit*] of pious stimulation," that is, the state of blessedness, and they see the communion founded by him "as a communication and propagation [*Mitteilung und Verbreitung*] of that redeeming activity" (CG §14.1, §11.4; with respect to the latter, cf. CG §14.1, §60.3).

37 Schleiermacher refers to these as "diseased conditions" (CG §21.1; KD [1830] §40).

3. Explicitation and Normativity

If redemption is a matter of being brought into tune with God by partaking of Christ's own attunement, if the latter is mediated through customs that circulate in the community he founded, and if there may be a discrepancy between that which in fact mediates Christ's attunement and that which merely circulates as such, it follows that Schleiermacher needs to provide some means of arriving at a criterion by which to judge that which has currency. In this section I will outline Schleiermacher's claims about the derivation and application of such a criterion, claims that in turn shed further light on the way in which attunement circulates.

a. How is it, then, that such a criterion should be derived, applied, and so forth? Schleiermacher insists that a criterion cannot be derived on the basis of "mere description," since, taken by itself, such description "has neither measure nor formula by which to distinguish the essential and invariant from the changeable and coincidental."[38] A putatively "merely descriptive" approach would face the following dilemma: if it had no means by which to make judgments about its data, it could not distinguish which patterns in the data ought to count as normative, whereas if it did have some means by which to make such judgments, it would by its own lights beg the question.[39] We must bring some criterion with us when we consider current practice, accordingly, but Schleiermacher insists that such a criterion must be understood as emerging within contingent, historical conditions, since "all so-called *a priori* constructions in the realm of history have always failed in the task of showing that what has thus been derived from above is actually identical with that which is historically given."[40] Suppose one were to claim, for instance, on the basis of putatively *a priori* deduction, that the essence of every historical religion is spirit's realization in spirit. Would adherents of these religions grant that this is the essence of their reli-

---

38 CG §2.2.
39 So, for instance, "what is diseased in the Church can only be recognized by reference to some definite representation of the distinctive nature of Christianity, and . . . in the investigations upon which this representation is founded the diseased phenomena must also be taken up, provisionally, as part of the basic data to which the critical method is to be applied" (KD [1830] §63). A similar problem faces the supposition that one could discern the essence of a religion simply by contrasting it with other religions—in order to arrive at a norm on this basis, one would need some means by which to distinguish salient differences from unimportant ones, which means that one needs a norm in order to arrive at one.
40 CG §2.2.

gion? If not, by what right would one claim that these persons are in fact wrong about their religion? Apart from some basis in the religion itself, it is hard to see how such a claim could avoid begging the question. It would thus appear that although one cannot derive the relevant norm by mere description—that is, apart from the application of some norm—neither can this norm be supplied strictly "from above." To do the work required of it, the criterion by which to judge prevailing attunement must be recognizable on the basis of that attunement—as in some respect internal to it—yet able to judge that attunement, and so, strictly speaking, irreducible to it.

How might one fulfill these conditions? Schleiermacher arrives at an answer by following the career of a particular candidate for circulation, namely, the claims of theology. Theology's task, according to Schleiermacher, is to make the prevailing attunement (or, in this case, piety) explicit, but since theological claims are likewise candidates for circulation, and yet circulate more explicitly than other expressions, they afford us a means by which to gain insight into the general nature of an expression's circulation and judgment. On this basis, Schleiermacher arrives at the following claims: he argues, first, that one can make the prevailing piety explicit (and so render its content judgeable) only by understanding it in its circulation; second, that one can understand it in its circulation only by grasping it along with the normative, historical trajectory which it aims to carry on; and third, that this trajectory provides one with the means by which to judge particular expressions of piety.[41]

To see how Schleiermacher arrives at these claims, consider the fact that he understands theology as "the discipline which systematizes the doctrine prevalent [*geltende Lehre*] in a Christian Church at a given time," and he understands such doctrines, in turn, as "accounts of the Christian pious disposition-states portrayed in speech"—as accounts, that is, of "that which, in the public proceedings of the Church . . . can be heard as a portrayal of its common piety . . ."[42] Doctrines are thus offered both as an expression of current piety and as themselves candidates for currency, as is evident in the authority conferred upon the

---

41 Two notes: first, it may be worth noting that I am using the terms "prevailing," "current," and "customary" more or less interchangeably, and that the content of each term should be understood along the lines specified in what follows. Second, something should be said about the extent to which feeling changes when rendered explicit. It seems to me that if feeling is rendered explicit in its circulation, then it is changed with respect to its form (viz., its immediacy), but not with respect to its content.

42 CG §19, Leitsatz; §15, Leitsatz; §19.3.

community's acceptance of these expressions. At its most basic, the acceptance in view involves the community's recognition of a particular expression *as* an expression of its piety, which entails that, to gain currency, the expression must be recognizable as such. Schleiermacher's explanation of the nature of "currency" can be seen as an elaboration on the conditions of meeting this requirement. Two conditions are particularly relevant. First, for a theological claim to circulate as an expression of the community's piety, it must be recognizable as going on in the same way as precedents that have circulated as such. It is for this reason that Schleiermacher claims that "we could not at all grant the name of Dogmatics to a presentation composed of nothing but idiosyncratic doctrines," and that, indeed, "even the earliest presentations of the evangelical faith could bear that name only insofar as they linked up with what went before and had most of their system in common with what was ecclesially given."[43] In order to be recognizable as an expression of the community's piety, an expression must be recognizable as going on in the same way as previous expressions which the community recognizes as such. Being recogniz*able* as an expression of the community's piety is obviously distinct from being recogniz*ed* as such, however, which leads to a second condition, namely, that a community treat this expression as normative for subsequent expressions. To recognize a candidate expression is to treat it as going on in the same way as precedent expressions of the community's piety, which means that subsequent expressions can then be recognizable as such if they go on in the same way as a series of precedents, which now includes the expression in question.[44] As Schleiermacher puts it, a doctrine counts as an expression of Christian piety only if a community "finds its norm" in that doctrine—only if, that is, it takes that expression as normative for future expressions of piety. Taken together, these conditions indicate that, in order to make an expression explicit in its circulation, one must exhibit it as carrying on the normative trajectory implicit in a series of recognized precedents and as exerting normative

---

43   CG §25.1.
44   As Schleiermacher comments, "an edifice [of doctrine], even if entirely coherent, of nothing but wholly peculiar opinions and views, which, even if really Christian, did not link themselves at all to the expressions used in the churchly communication of piety [*Mitteilungen der Frömmigkeit*], would always be taken only as a private confession and not as a dogmatic presentation, until there came to be attached to it a likeminded society [*gleichgesinnte Gesellschaft*], and there thus emerged a public preaching and communication [*öffentliche Verkündigung und Mitteilung*] that found in that doctrine its norm" (CG §19.3).

constraint on future candidates for currency.[45] On this model, accordingly, an expression's currency can be made explicit in terms roughly similar to those one might use to explain a judge's decision in the common law tradition, namely, its relation to prior decisions which exert precedential constraint over the present one and to subsequent decisions which it in turn constrains. In the common-law tradition, a judge decides a novel case by looking to prior decisions that he or she recognizes as relevant; the judge thus justifies his or her decision in terms of its going on in the same way as certain authoritative precedents. If the judge's decision is recognized as going on in the same way as these precedents, however, his or her decision will exert normative authority over still other decisions. On this account, then, the norm according to which a novel expression is assessed is provided by prior expressions that have been recognized as expressions of "our" attunement—and if the novel expression is recognized as going on in the same way, it contributes to the norm according to which still other expressions might be recognized.[46]

Two important consequences follow from this account. It follows, first, that the normative criterion (or "essence") by which candidate expressions are to be judged is itself the product of a trajectory implicit in expressions recognized as precedential: one judges a candidate expression of the prevailing piety by determining whether it goes on in the same way as other expressions one recognizes as such. The normative criterion by which to judge Christian consciousness is, accordingly, a product of the history of that consciousness—a product, that is, of Christians' own recognitive attitudes—rather than something supposedly prior or external to those attitudes. The essence of Christian consciousness, in other words, is a product of the ongoing negotiation of what circulates as precedential. (Schleiermacher thus provides a way of freeing us from the assumption—common to Richard Rorty as well as Radical Orthodoxy—that answerability to God is necessarily incompatible with answerability to one's peers.) It likewise follows that the normative criterion or "essence" changes, if only slightly, each time a new expression is recognized as going on in the same way as precedent expressions, since, on the one hand, the essence is itself a product of the normative trajectory implicit in a series of precedents, and on the other,

---

45 Or, as Schleiermacher puts it (KD [1811] Introduction, §33), one must understand it as "a product of the past and a kernel of the future" (*als Produkt der Vergangenheit und als Keim der Zukunft*).

46 Brandom elaborates an analogy along these lines in "Some Pragmatist Themes in Hegel's Idealism." I spell this out in relation to Schleiermacher in my "Christ's Normative Spirit" and in chapter three of my forthcoming *Theology Without Metaphysics*.

the recognition of a further precedent contributes to the shape of that trajectory. It is thus not surprising that, on Schleiermacher's account, some expressions that initially appear to be heterodox—on the basis of what one might predict, prospectively, from the point of view of the normative trajectory as it has unfolded up until the novel expression— are retrospectively recognizable as carrying on that trajectory and thus acknowledged to be orthodox, such that the meaning of "orthodoxy" changes over time.[47]

This explicitation of circulation thus sheds light on the way in which attunement circulates through custom: individual expressions of attunement are treated as carrying on the normative trajectory of "our" attunement, and so as precedential for further expressions, inasmuch as others conform their own expressions to them; the latter expressions are treated as precedential for still further expressions, and so on; in this way, the community continually attunes each member, and each member continually contributes to the community's attunement.

b. By making theology's circulation explicit, accordingly, Schleiermacher provides us with an explanation of how attunement circulates, how it can be made explicit, and how it can be judged. This account could be elaborated in several directions, but for now, it seems best to conclude this section by using its resources to respond to one of the longest-standing objections to Schleiermacher's notion of *Gefühl*, namely, that it fails to do justice to human freedom.[48] As Hegel famously maintained,

---

47 Thus Schleiermacher: "Consider . . . how much there is which was originally decried as heterodox in our Church, which afterwards came to count as orthodox [*als orthodox gelten ließ*] but always through an earlier orthodoxy becoming obsolete"; again: "if heterodox matter comes to be counted as being better attuned to the spirit of the Evangelical Church than is the letter of the Confessions, then the latter become antiquated and the former becomes orthodox" (CG §25, Zusatz). This prospective/retrospective distinction is crucial to understanding how "changes [*Veränderungen*] nevertheless do not compromise the unity of [the Church's] essence," since it explains how novel expressions can be seen as both carrying on and contributing to that essence (KD [1830] §47). The distinction likewise explains why church leaders need know-how, since that which counts as carrying on Christianity's essence is only retrospectively recognizable as such—it is not, in other words, something that one could simply predict on the basis of Christianity's career up to that point (see KD [1830] §265).

48 There are two further objections to which I cannot here do justice, the first of which has to do with the normative status of "primitive Christianity." Schleiermacher sometimes seems to encourage us to think that the norm by which to judge Christianity is unproblematically to be sought in Christianity's original expression, as when he claims, for instance, that "the more any given historical career is occupied in the process of expansion, so that increasingly the inner unity of its life appears on-

one of the problems with *Gefühl* is precisely its *immediacy*: for Hegel, to be free with respect to one's beliefs or actions is to legislate them to oneself, and to legislate them to oneself is precisely to mediate them to oneself on the basis of reasons (and so *reclaim* them as one's own). Hegel thinks that apart from such mediation-to-self, one has no means by which to see one's beliefs and actions as one's own, as due to one, rather than simply given to one, such that Schleiermacher's theology of *Gefühl* necessarily fails to account for human freedom.

In view of the preceding account, it is not hard to see how Schleiermacher might respond to this charge. On Schleiermacher's account, one's attunement counts as "one's own" in at least two crucial respects. First, his model of circulation funds a fairly robust version of "expressive freedom," according to which considerable space is made for one's own novel, "self-expressive" expressions. In this connection, it is important to recall Schleiermacher's distinction between that which

---

ly in encounter with other forces, all the more do these forces, in turn, enter into the various individual situations that make it up. As a result of this state of affairs, the purest perspective on its distinctive nature can only come in relation to its earliest expression" (KD [1830] §83). There is a sense in which Schleiermacher does indeed think that "primitive Christianity" is normative for subsequent Christian expression, but it is important to note that, for Schleiermacher, the normative conclusions to be drawn from primitive Christianity are themselves candidates for circulation, since "the concept of normative standing is also one which cannot be reduced to fixed, immutable formulas . . ." (KD [1830] §108). Cf. KD [1830] §103, where Schleiermacher writes that "The Christian writings that come to us from the age of primitive Christianity are not all the proper subject matter of exegetical theology simply on that account, but only insofar as they are held capable of contributing to the original, and therefore for all times normative, presentation of Christianity." What we need, then, is an understanding of the normative Spirit of Christ keeping these norms in circulation, which Schleiermacher supplies in his discussion of Scripture in CG—and which he characterizes as a fairly "Catholic" understanding of Scripture (cf. his *Sendschreiben*, 43).

Second: if the only available criterion by which to judge prevailing custom is itself a product of custom, it seems reasonable to wonder whether this account could possibly fund of radical critique of the status quo. I cannot do justice to this criticism here, but in order to intimate how a proper response might be formulated, it should be noted that theology is not the only way in which one's internalization of custom can become explicit. As Axel Honneth has argued, for instance, experiences of disrespect can likewise make explicit the norms implicit in that which circulates as customary, and these experiences play an indispensable role in resisting oppressive social patterns. Axel Honneth, *Disrespect: The Normative Foundations of Critical Theory* (Cambridge: Polity, 2007); *The Struggle for Recognition: The Moral Grammar of Social Conflicts* (Cambridge: Polity, 1995); *The Fragmented World of the Social: Essays in Social and Political Philosophy* (Albany: State University of New York Press, 1995); and, with Nancy Fraser, *Redistribution or Recognition? A Political-Philosophical Exchange* (New York: Verso, 2003).

is retrospectively recognizable as carrying on a normative trajectory and that which could be prospectively foreseen as doing so—as that which appears, from one point of view, as "the emergence of something novel, without precedent," yet from the other as "built up from something already available."[49] To see how this funds expressive freedom, consider a simple example: suppose someone suggests "5" as a candidate for carrying on the series "1, 2, 3, 4 . . ." From a retrospective point of view—looking back, that is, over the series "1, 2, 3, 4, 5"—it may look as if it were self-evident and predictable that this is the way the series would go on, but from a prospective point of view, things look different, since the series itself does not decide which way it should be carried on; it could just as well have been carried on with "1" or "3" or any number of other candidates, which means that, prospectively speaking, the series' continuation is unpredictable. This means, in turn, that when a candidate is recognized *as* carrying on the trajectory, this affects what it *means* to do so. And since the recognition of future candidates further determines what it means to "go on in the same way," it follows that this "same way" cannot be determined in advance. An expression counts as carrying on a normative trajectory, therefore, not because it was prospectively predictable, but because it is retrospectively recognizable as such. This entails, on the one hand, that one's constraint by norms does not amount to determination by them (in the sense of strict "determinism"), since the norm implicit in a series of precedents leaves open the possibility that the series will be carried on in novel and unpredictable ways. On the other hand, the fact that these novel expressions are retrospectively recognizable as carrying on such a trajectory explains how they can be meaningful for others, too, since it enables others to see one's expression as the conclusion of a series of precedent expressions. Thus one's constraint by precedent not only does not foreclose the possibility of novel expressions, it also supplies the condition of the possibility that others will be able to understand (and imitate) them.[50] In this way, novel expressions "preserve the mobility" of attunement and "make room for other ways of framing

---

49   KD (1830) §78.
50   Consider here the example of language: linguists have demonstrated that the vast majority of sentences that are uttered or written have never been uttered or written before. Novelty is thus the rule in language use. Yet, for the most part, we have no trouble either producing or understanding these novel utterances, precisely because we can recognize them as going on in the same way as a certain set of precedents. Likewise with novel metaphors, malapropisms, and the like: for such novelty to be understandable, it is necessary that it be constrained by norms, but for it to be genuinely novel, those norms cannot render one's performances predictable.

it"[51]: because the normative trajectory implicit in a series of precedent expressions changes every time a new expression is recognized as carrying it on, it follows that novelty begets novelty. The introduction of a metaphor, for example, may lead to new ways of thinking about some subject, ways that were in some respect unthinkable before the metaphor was introduced; these new ways of thinking may in turn open up still further possibilities, and so on. As a result of being constrained by precedent, accordingly, one can produce novel expressions, and as a result of such novelties, a whole range of further possibilities is introduced. In sum, because the norms by which one's performances are constrained are the product of an ongoing process of recognition, it follows, first, that novel expressions are retrospectively recognizable (and so intelligible) as carrying on, but not determined in advance by, a normative trajectory, and second, that the trajectory itself is affected by such expressions, such that a novel expression renders possible still further novelty. Schleiermacher thus provides a helpful account of one dimension of expressive freedom—and given the extent to which (a) the circulation of expressions opens up new possibilities, and (b) one's attunement is shaped by such expressions, it follows (c) that one's own possibilities are expanded (rather than foreclosed) on this model.

This brings us to a second respect in which one's attunement counts as "one's own." On the model defended here, one intends one's expression of *Gefühl* to be recognizable as such by those with whom one identifies, and one intends this by trying to go on in the same way as precedent expressions which one recognizes as "ours." One's recognition of certain persons and expressions thus confers authority upon them, such that one's answerability to them depends upon one's acknowledgment of them. A norm's authority over one is therefore precisely the authority one has conferred upon it. On Schleiermacher's account, moreover, the norm to which one answers is not only *authorized* by one's recognition of it, it is also *constituted* by that recognition, since the norm in question is nothing other than the trajectory implicit in certain expressions which one recognizes as "ours." And finally, insofar as one's own expression is recognizable as carrying on that trajectory, it contributes to the norm according to which still other expressions might be recognized. In expressing one's *Gefühl*, in other words, one not only confers authority upon expressions which one recognizes as precedential, one seeks this same authority for one's own expression. On this model, accordingly, one's expression is indeed constrained by "our" norms, yet these norms in turn are authorized, constituted, car-

---

51 KD (1830) §203.

ried on, and shaped by one's own recognitions and expressions, in such a way that "the communal impulse is satisfied in each person through all and in all through each person . . ."[52] One can thus see oneself as determining these norms' authority over one, as constructing them, administering them, directing them, and so on, from which it follows that one can see these norms (and the expressions they constrain) as self-legislated.

Schleiermacher thus appears entitled to claim that one's attunement can be seen as due to one and in that sense as free, yet there is an important respect in which Schleiermacher's account still differs from Hegel. Hegel's argument, briefly stated, is that one's beliefs and actions count as self-legislated just in case one mediates them to oneself on the basis of "objectively" or "universally valid" reasons, and it is not hard to see why: Hegel's central concern is with "positivism," that is, the holding of some doxastic or practical commitment simply because it has been given to one (by one's family, faith tradition, etc.), in consequence of which he insists that the reasons by which one reclaims one's commitments must meet a very high standard, namely, that of "objective principle."[53] This explains why Hegel goes to such lengths to demonstrate that Christianity alone—as philosophically elaborated—corresponds to the essence of religion and is, for that reason, "absolute." For his part, Schleiermacher seems occasionally inclined to strive to meet such a standard—as when he tries in the *Dialektik*, for instance, to demonstrate that the coherence of one's life (as a series of knowings and doings) must be explained in terms of a prior absolute dependence—but he opposes in principle the assertion that one's entitlement to one's commitments (and thus one's freedom with respect to them) necessarily depends upon one's ability to provide reasons for them,

---

52 KD (1830) §166. Cf. "Toward a Theory of Sociable Conduct," where Schleiermacher describes freedom in terms of "a reciprocal action that is interwoven among all the participants but one that is also fully determined and made complete by them." Schleiermacher, "Versuch einer Theorie des geselligen Betragens," in KGA I/2, 169; *Friedrich Schleiermacher's "Toward a Theory of Sociable Conduct" and Essays on Its Intellectual-Cultural Context*, ed. Ruth Drucilla Richardson, trans. Jeffrey Hoover (Lewiston, NY: Edwin Mellen Press, 1995), 24. On this point, at least, Hegel and Schleiermacher are quite close, as witness Hegel's famous description of *"Geist"* as "the unity of the different independent self-consciousnesses which, in their opposition, enjoy perfect freedom and independence: 'I' that is 'We' and 'We' that is 'I.'" G.W.F. Hegel, *Phenomenology of Spirit*, trans. A.V. Miller (Oxford: Oxford University Press, 1977), §177.

53 Hegel thus objects to Schleiermacher on the grounds that the latter fails to justify his commitments in terms of "laws" and "objectivity." See Hegel, *Faith and Knowledge*, trans. Walter Cerf and H.S. Harris (Albany: State University of New York Press, 1977), 152.

"absolute" or otherwise. Two points should be registered in defense of this position: first, one of the reasons that Schleiermacher rejects the idea that only those who provide "absolutely valid" justification count as justified in holding (and so free with respect to) their commitments is that it seems to entail that elite theorists alone count as free, rational, and so on.[54] This leads to a second point, namely, that it is eminently plausible that one's justification in holding (and so freedom with respect to) some commitment outruns one's ability to give reasons for it. Consider chicken-sexers, who, I am told, are reliably able to distinguish male from female chickens, yet tend to be unable to provide adequate reasons in support of these distinctions. (It is apparently common for chicken-sexers to explain their judgments in terms of some visible difference between the chickens, whereas their judgments are in fact based upon a difference in scent.) Most would grant that these sexers nevertheless count as *knowing* which chickens are which—would grant, on the usual tripartite analysis of knowledge, that they are *justified* in claiming of some chickens that they are female and of others that they are male—in spite of their inability *to justify* their knowledge-claims. By parity of reasoning, it would appear that a person can count as standing in the "right" relation to aspects of his or her attunement—they can count as "justified"—even if that person him- or herself cannot explicitly justify them. There is a crucial difference, in other words, between the possibility that a commitment could be explicitly justified and the actual provision of such justification, on the one hand, and a person's own ability to provide such justification, on the other: to require explicit justification of each commitment (by each person holding the commitment) would set off an infinite regress of justifications of the sort which spawned the worst sorts of foundationalist fantasy, which seems to suggest that one would be better off adopting a default-entitlement understanding of epistemic entitlement, on the one hand, and a "justificatory division of labor," on the other.[55] To be sure, this does not render

---

54   Schleiermacher's "populism" is well known. To take just one example, consider his characteristic remark to Dr. Lücke: "[W]ill one gainsay the poor person the possibility that his or her piety could be purer and better than his or her idea, even if that which is felt can relate only to the idea's object?" (*Sendschreiben*, 14).

55   The former phrase is borrowed from Brandom, *Making It Explicit*; the latter is from Hilary Putnam, "The Meaning of 'Meaning,'" in *Mind, Language, and Reality* (Cambridge: Cambridge University Press, 1975). It is worth noting that Schleiermacher himself seems to advocate a species of "permissive rationality," as when he claims, for instance, that "[f]ull agreement . . . is not necessary in the evangelical Church, since even at the same time different views may have currency for us, side by side. Thus, everything is to be regarded as having currency that is officially affirmed and

one unable to distinguish justified commitments from unjustified, or rational from irrational; it means simply that a set of such commitments (such as theology) "is rational, not because it has a *foundation* but because it is a self-correcting enterprise which can put *any* claim in jeopardy, though not *all* at once."[56]

*   *   *

In sum, then, Schleiermacher claims that attunement circulates through a process in which individual expressions are treated as carrying on the normative trajectory implicit in precedent expressions—and so as precedential for further expressions—inasmuch as other expressions "find their norm" in them; the latter expressions are treated as precedential for still further expressions, and so on; in this way, the conditions for judging a candidate expression are met: the expression is made explicit and so rendered potentially judgeable; the expression is made explicit in terms of its implicit commitment to go on in the same way as precedent expressions and to stand as precedent for subsequent expressions; and this relation to precedent supplies the norm in terms of which the expression may be judged (by its own lights, as it were).

4. Conclusion

I have argued that we can understand Schleiermacher's notion of *Gefühl* as one's non-inferential attunement to circumstances; that we can explain a good bit of this attunement as an internalization of that which circulates through custom; that this provides us with a way of understanding how Christ's own attunement is mediated to those who have no direct contact with him; and that theology renders attunement explicit, and so judgeable, by understanding it as carrying on and contributing to a normative trajectory of precedent expressions of that at-

---

officially heard without arousing strict official opposition" (KD [1830] §196, explanation).

56 Sellars, *Empiricism and the Philosophy of Mind*, 79. Further arguments to this effect can be found in Donald Davidson, "The Problem of Objectivity," in *Problems of Rationality* (Oxford: Clarendon Press, 2004); and Bas van Fraassen, *The Empirical Stance*. It is obligatory in this context to cite Otto Neurath's famous metaphor: "we are like sailors who must rebuild their ship on the open sea, without ever being able to disassemble it in dry-dock and build it anew out of the best materials." Neurath, "Protokollsätze," *Erkenntnis* 3 (1932): 206.

tunement. The basic strategy, accordingly, which I have identified as a species of pragmatism, is to take ordinary social practices as theology's explanatory primitive, that is, as that in terms of which to understand "higher" phenomena such as redemption, the indwelling of the Spirit, and so on, in order (a) to avoid the sort of explanatory gaps that characteristically arise when we try to explain theological phenomena in terms of something that is itself distant from everyday life, so as (b) to help us resist the temptation to posit "metaphysical" tertia by which to bridge such gaps, and (c) to provide us with explanations whose primitives we understand and are in the relevant sense "at home with." Naturally, this is not the only strategy one might pursue either in interpreting Schleiermacher or constructing a theology; I doubt such a strategy would be attractive to those who appreciate Schleiermacher's "mystical" tendencies, for instance. Let me end, however, with a final recommendation of the reading proposed here, namely, that it meets one of the key criteria by which Schleiermacher himself would assess it: its relevance to the contemporary situation. Two considerations speak in its favor. First, in view of the marked trend among recent philosophers and social theorists toward taking recognition-theoretic pragmatism as explanatory primitive, one of the distinct advantages of the present reading is that it provides several paths by which to navigate between theology and other disciplines (as well as between "analytic" and "Continental" philosophy).[57] Second, a reaction has been building over the past few years against overly particularistic theologies, and this seems to have sparked a renewal of interest in "public" theology: following the demise of foundationalism, theologians frequently claimed that Christian theology is answerable to Christian standards alone, that it is intelligible only to "insiders," and so on. More and more, though, theologians are recognizing that the particularity and integrity of Christian belief not only can, but in some sense must, be "publicly" intelligible, accountable, and relevant. A pragmatist reading of Schleiermacher might help address this need. For these and other reasons, accordingly, I take it that this reading may indeed have a future.

---

[57] Consider, for example, the work of W.V.O. Quine, Ludwig Wittgenstein, Wilfrid Sellars, Donald Davidson, Hilary Putnam, Richard Rorty, Robert Brandom, Mark Johnston, Bjørn Ramberg, Dagfinn Føllesdal, Jürgen Habermas, Axel Honneth, Stephen Darwall, Nancy Fraser, Cheryl Misak, Pierre Bourdieu, Michel Foucault, Terry Pinkard, Robert Pippin, Hubert Dreyfus, Cornel West, Arthur Fine, Bas van Fraassen, and Danielle Macbeth.

Schleiermacher on "The Roman Church"

Anti-Catholic Polemics, Ideology, and the Future of Historical-Empirical Dogmatics

JULIA A. LAMM

1. Introduction

One of the finest sessions ever sponsored by the AAR Schleiermacher Group was on "Schleiermacher and Roman Catholic Theology" in 1994, the last time the AAR was held here in Chicago. John Thiel traced Protestant criticisms of Schleiermacher as being too "Catholic," from Karl Bretschneider, through Brunner and Barth, to George Lindbeck. There were three presentations of Schleiermacher's influence on nineteenth-century Catholic theologians: Bradford Hinze presented on Drey, Michael Himes on Möhler, and William Madges on Kuhn.[1] Finally, Francis Schüssler Fiorenza—interestingly, the only presenter not employed by a Jesuit university—closed with "Schleiermacher and the Construction of a Contemporary Roman Catholic Foundational Theology."[2] More recently, the trend has shifted from the history of influence to comparative studies. I offer two quick examples of recently published dissertations: one, in German, compares the ethical theories of

---

1   These four papers were all published in *Heythrop Journal* 37, no. 1 (1996): John E. Thiel, "Schleiermacher as 'Catholic': A Change in the Rhetoric of Modern Theology," 61-82; Bradford E. Hinze, "Johann Sebastian Drey's Critique of Friedrich Schleiermacher's Theology," 1-23; Michael J. Himes, "'A Great theologian of our Time': Möhler on Schleiermacher," 24-46; William Madges, "Faith, Knowledge, and Feeling: Towards an Understanding of Kuhn's Appraisal of Schleiermacher," 47-60.
2   Francis Schüssler Fiorenza, "Schleiermacher and the Construction of a Contemporary Roman Catholic Foundational Theology," *Harvard Theological Review* 89, no. 2 (1996): 175-94.

Schleiermacher and Thomas Aquinas;[3] another, in English, compares the Christologies of Schleiermacher and Karl Rahner.[4]

What has yet to be done—and what very much needs to be done—is an investigation of Schleiermacher's portrayal of what he referred to as the "Roman Church." Attention, of course, has been given to his theory of religion and of religions; attention has been given to his views of Judaism, in particular;[5] but virtually no attention has been paid to his discourse concerning Catholicism. Whenever his assessment of Catholicism *is* addressed, it is usually done on a very formal level, with an unquestioning acceptance of Schleiermacher's definitions and assumptions. Such neglect is highly problematic, for many reasons. For now, let me just highlight three facts before us:

- Schleiermacher maintained that polemics (in particular, Protestant-Catholic polemics) is integral to the dogmatic method,[6] and part of why it is so integral is for the purpose of self-definition and identity;
- Schleiermacher described his dogmatic method as being historical-empirical—that is, he set out to describe the religious consciousness of the Evangelical Christian Church at a particular point in time;

---

3   Michael Feil, *Die Grundlegung der Ethik bei Friedrich Schleiermacher und Thomas von Aquin* (Berlin: Walter de Gruyter, 2005).

4   Allen G. Jorgenson, *The Appeal to Experience in the Christologies of Friedrich Schleiermacher and Karl Rahner* (New York: Peter Lang, 2007).

5   See, most recently, Richard Crouter and Julie Klassen, eds., *A Debate on Jewish Emancipation and Christian Theology in Old Berlin: David Friedländer, Friedrich Schleiermacher, Wilhelm Abraham Teller* (Indianapolis: Hackett, 2004). See also Richard Crouter, *Friedrich Schleiermacher: Between Enlightenment and Romanticism* (Cambridge: Cambridge University Press, 2005), chaps. 2 and 5; and Joseph W. Pickle, "Schleiermacher on Judaism," *Journal of Religion* 60, no. 2 (1980): 115-37.

6   See Friedrich Schleiermacher, *Der christliche Glaube nach den Grundsätzen der evangelischen Kirche im Zusammenhange dargestellt* (1830/31), in KGA I/13, §§23-25, henceforth CG; *The Christian Faith*, ed. H. R. Mackintosh and J. S. Stewart (Edinburgh: T. & T. Clark, 1928), henceforth CF. Also see Schleiermacher, *Kurze Darstellung des theologischen Studiums zum Behuf einleitender Vorlesungen* (1830), in KGA I/6, §§32-42, §217, henceforth KD; *Brief Outline of the Study of Theology*, trans. Terrence N. Tice (Atlanta: John Knox Press, 1977), henceforth BO. Francis Fiorenza explains, "In the *Glaubenslehre*, the elaboration of the distinctive reality of Christianity is developed in the propositions borrowed from apologetics, whereas polemics are a part of the method of dogmatic theology. Both are present within the Introductory section: one as a borrowed proposition, the other as an element of the method of dogmatics" ("Schleiermacher and the Construction," 184).

- and yet, Schleiermacher's portrayal of the "Roman Church" was anything but historical or empirical; it was instead ahistorical, a mere caricature.

Can these three be reconciled? How accurate can his description of the Evangelical Church be if his description of the "Roman Church" is ahistorical and inadequate?

My thesis is: Whatever advances Schleiermacher may have made with regard to religious pluralism and toleration, his anti-Catholic polemics was at times ideological, and this poses both methodological and ethical questions for anyone contemplating a future historical-empirical dogmatics. This general thesis can be broken down into three sub-theses. (1) Schleiermacher's portrayal of "the Roman Church" in the *Glaubenslehre* is too general and ahistorical to be credible or serviceable, and in fact it is inconsistent with his own methodological commitments. (2) More than being ahistorical, Schleiermacher's discourse about "the Roman Church" is ideological: it was informed by prejudices, fantasies, and deep-rooted animosities embedded in the specifically Prussian Protestant culture of his day; furthermore, it served not only to replicate these prejudices, but also to rationalize attitudes held by, as well as actions taken by, the Prussian government against Catholics.[7] (3) Polemics need not be ideological. Although he did not have this same language, this is what Schleiermacher was getting at when he relocated polemics from a territory of hostile warfare to a shop where bad ideas and worn-out paradigms are carved away. Any future historical-empirical dogmatics must therefore make very clear the criteria by which we are to judge the difference between polemics and ideology.

I shall argue this thesis in two steps, although limited time will allow only a sketch of a larger argument: I shall begin with *discourse analysis*,[8] looking at what Schleiermacher said about Protestant-Catholic polemics and examining how his polemics function in the *Glaubenslehre*. I shall then turn to *historical analysis*, relying on recent historiography of Catholicism and confessionalism in nineteenth-century Germany to suggest some new avenues of inquiry for Schleiermacher studies.

---

7 Here I am influenced by Arthur F. Marotti's study of anti-Catholic ideology in modern England: *Religious Ideology and Cultural Fantasy: Catholic and Anti-Catholic Discourses in Early Modern England* (Notre Dame: University of Notre Dame Press, 2005).
8 See Tim Murphy, "Discourse," in *Guide to the Study of Religion*, ed. Willi Braun and Russell T. McCutcheon (London: Cassell, 2000), 396-408.

2. Discourse: The Role of Anti-Catholic Polemics in Schleiermacher's Theology

a. Schleiermacher's Understanding of Polemics

In his *Brief Outline of the Study of Theology* (1830), Schleiermacher appeared to move beyond the entrenched ideologies of Protestant-Catholic polemics, striking a measured, even irenic, tone. Apologetics and polemics, he held, both belong to philosophical theology, "[a]pologetics tak[ing] a wholly outward, polemics a wholly inward, direction."[9] The purpose of polemics is to clear away "diseased aberrations" (*krankhafte Abweichungen*).[10] Schleiermacher distinguished his own approach from the "far more common usage"—namely, "the particular polemics of Protestants directed outwardly, e.g., against the Catholics, or the general polemics of Christians against the Jews or even against deists and atheists";[11] he insisted, "this has nothing in common with the polemics we are considering." *His* polemics was to be directed inward, to aberrations in Protestantism itself. When and if it would be directed against Catholicism, it would not be "against Catholicism as a whole, as it is nevertheless always intended to be, but only against that within it which is alien to its particular form and is thus to be regarded as a diseased condition of Christianity."[12]

This more irenic view stood in contrast to how he described anti-Catholic polemics in *On the Proper Value and Binding Authority of Symbolic Books* (1819). According to Schleiermacher, the Catholic-Protestant antithesis was necessarily heightened at that point in history because of the union of the Lutheran and Reformed Churches. We see clearly here the importance of polemics in forging a new kind of Protestant identity:

> In my opinion, the proper formula for this would be the following: "I declare that I find everything that is taught in our symbolic books against the errors and abuses of the Roman Catholic church, especially in the articles on justification and good works, on the church and ecclesiastical power, on the mass, on the function of the saints, and on vows, to be in complete

---

9   KD §41; BO, 32.
10 KD §40.
11 KD §41; BO, 32.
12 Ibid. Nevertheless, much later in the *Brief Outline* he also makes clear, "It is to be required of every evangelical student of theology that he be engaged in forming a personal conviction regarding every proper locus of doctrine: not only as these have been developed from the principles of the Reformation as such, and in opposition to Roman doctrines . . ." (KD §219; BO, 78).

agreement with Holy Scripture and with the original teaching of the church;...."[13]

(Note how specific Schleiermacher is about which dogmas were a matter of serious contention. I shall return to this point later.)

In his *Glaubenslehre*, Schleiermacher continued to stress the importance of Catholic-Protestant polemics for Christian dogmatics: "A system of doctrine drawn up at the present time within the Western Church cannot be indifferent to the antithesis between Roman Catholic and Protestant, but must adhere to one or the other."[14] He acknowledged that the Roman Church was "equally Christian," but he underscored that it was "equally alien to us"—indeed as a "spirit alien to ours, which repels us."[15]

b. The Definitions in §24

Let us turn our attention to that place in the *Glaubenslehre* where polemics is most explicit—his definitions of the Evangelical Church and of the Catholic Church in §24. These definitions are infamous, not because scholars have questioned how he defined the Catholic Church, but because in later propositions he purportedly revealed himself to be Catholic, not Protestant:

> In so far as the Reformation was not simply a purification and reaction from abuses which had crept in, but was the origination of a distinctive form of the Christian communion, the antithesis between Protestantism and Catholicism may provisionally be conceived thus: the former makes the individual's relation to the Church dependent on his relation to Christ, while the latter contrariwise makes the individual's relation to Christ dependent on his relation to the Church.[16]

How did he arrive at his definitions? Well, as he himself explained, he began with each church's accusation against the other. Whereas Catholics commonly accused Protestants of being fundamentally unable to build a communion, the result being "each individual standing by himself,"[17] Protestants regularly accused Catholics of the following: "in ascribing everything to the Church and tracing everything to the Church,

---

13 Friedrich Schleiermacher, *On the Proper Value and Binding Authority of Symbolic Books*, in *Friedrich Schleiermacher on Creeds, Confessions and Church Union: That They May Be One*, ed. and trans. Iain G. Nicol (Lewiston, NY: Edwin Mellen Press, 2004), 187.
14 CG §23; CF, 101.
15 CG §24.1; CF, 104.
16 CG §24; CF, 103.
17 CG §24.3; CF, 106.

it deprives Christ of the honour due to Him, and puts Him in the background, and even in a measure subordinates Him to the church."[18] Schleiermacher added, "and our opinion of the Roman Church is that, however fast it may hold this communion, it is nevertheless in danger of becoming un-Christian by neglecting the reference to Christ."[19]

Consider this carefully: not just polemics, but a certain kind of polemics, is being practiced here. The deepest mutual suspicions; what each side finds the most distasteful in the other; and the centuries of stubborn associations and prejudices that had fed and justified those suspicions — these were the tools used to arrive at definitions that play a crucial role in his dogmatics.

Schleiermacher's definition of "the Roman Church" is not nuanced, nor does it allow for self-definition on the Catholic side. It is not based on any careful description of the specifically Catholic Christian religious consciousness at a particular point in time. On the contrary, it is a borrowed discourse. There can be little doubt that his definition of the Catholic Church is a code for "papism," and it thus both expresses and feeds long-standing Protestant fears and fantasies. Evidence? Schleiermacher's Protestant detractors are content with showing how Schleiermacher by his own definition is Catholic, while Protestant defenders of Schleiermacher are careful to explain how mediation for him does not have to do with clerical hierarchies or ritualism. In short, more than being meta-doctrinal,[20] Schleiermacher's definition of the Catholic Church reiterates, and thereby perpetuates, Protestant ideology. Schleiermacher was certainly not unique in this, and he shows himself to be a person of his time — better than most.[21] The problem for us here

---

18 The passage continues, "To this add the fact, that ecclesiastical Protestantism is as little chargeable in the latter respect as Catholicism in the former; and consider how nevertheless each party is disposed to point out in the other chiefly what could most easily lead it astray from the common ground of Christianity."

19 CG §24.3; CF, 106.

20 Avery Dulles, SJ, writes, "For Schleiermacher the opposition between Catholicism and Protestantism is not doctrinal but rather metadoctrinal, not material but formal. Even if the two communions achieved total agreement on the controverted doctrines, said Schleiermacher, this would not bring about a reunion, for the two churches are governed by different spirits. They approach questions with different orientations." Dulles, "The Catholicity of the Augsburg Confession," *Journal of Religion* 63, no. 4 (1983): 340.

21 In the words of one historian of Catholic-Protestant relations in nineteenth-century Germany, "Catholics and liberals [were] locked in a rhetorically dependent relationship, promoting each other's cultural productivity of meaning by reappropriating vocabulary, symbols, and metaphors." Michael B. Gross, *The War Against Catholicism: Liberalism and the Anti-Catholic Imagination in Nineteenth-Century Germany* (Ann Arbor: University of Michigan Press, 2004), 168.

today is that Schleiermacher scholars have not acknowledged, much less examined, the ideological cast of his anti-Catholic polemics. What Catholics did Schleiermacher know?[22] What was the nature of his encounters with Catholics? What was he reading?

c. The Ethics of Polemics

The matter is not just methodological; it is ethical. *In engaging in polemics, most especially when the antithesis is heightened, how ought one to portray the "Other"?*[23] This is a question with which Schleiermacher himself wrestled. If dogmatic theology is "the knowledge of doctrine now current in the evangelical Church," then dogmatics needs the aid of church statistics, which Schleiermacher defined as "the knowledge of the existing social condition in all the different parts of the Christian Church."[24] Schleiermacher acknowledged that the problem is greatest when polemics at every level is so intense: "If, however, in times when the Church is divided, it is only possible for each larger community within the Church to work out its own doctrine in the form of dogmatics (see §98), this raises a problem. *How is the evangelical theologian to come to know the doctrine current in other communities of the Christian Church?*"[25] How, indeed?

Schleiermacher's extraordinary *Epilogue* to the second edition of his *Speeches on Religion* (1806)[26] provides an example of his being willing to set certain discourses aside. Despite his call, in the first edition of the *Speeches* (1799), to the cultured despisers to come over to Christianity (which he described in the fifth speech in terms of the polemical, purifying spirit of Protestantism), many had in fact converted to Roman

---

22 In 1817, only about three percent of the population of Berlin was Catholic.
23 How do you fairly portray the other, even as you admit an alien spirit there that repels you? And is that repulsion a product of a concrete, historical reality, or an inherited ideological fantasy? Ethicists working on Just War Theory have begun to take this self-critical stage into consideration, emphasizing the need for discernment about the human tendency to view "enemies" pejoratively. See, e.g., Richard B. Miller, "Just War, Civic Virtue, and Democratic Social Criticism: Augustinian Reflections," *Journal of Religion* 89, no. 1 (2009): 1-30. Constructive theologians, especially those claiming a historical-empirical approach, would do well to do the same.
24 KD §195; BO, 71-72.
25 Ibid., emphasis added.
26 *Nachrede*, in KGA I/12, 313-21; Schleiermacher, *On Religion: Speeches to Its Cultured Despisers*, 3rd ed., trans. John Oman (New York: Harper & Row, 1958), 266-74.

Catholicism.[27] Schleiermacher felt compelled to respond to that phenomenon. Shocked (perhaps), dismayed, sober, and somewhat chastened, Schleiermacher distinguished between two kinds of Catholic converts: on the one hand, those "children" who are "dazzled" "by glitter and show, or are talked over by monks"; on the other hand, those notable "poets and artists who are worthy of honour."[28] While he clung to the observation that many who had converted to the Catholic faith became "strong papists,"[29] and he condemned this as idolatry,[30] he also conceded, "It is hardly possible to avoid the conclusion that they have not apprehended the true character of the Catholic Church."[31] He continued: "[T]hey love in the Roman church *not what is in any way characteristic and essential*, but only its corruption—a clear proof that they know not what they wish. Consider this purely historically, that *the papacy is in no way the essence of the Catholic Church, but its corruption*."[32] Schleiermacher even granted that "many in the Romish church have rid themselves of her corruptions."[33] If here he acknowledged an essence of Catholicism that is contrary to "papism," that can appeal to the strength of one's nature and not simply one's spiritual immaturity or corruption,

---

27 The antithesis was heightened at this point in history because of Napoleon and the association of Napoleon and the French with Catholicism. As R. C. Raack has put it, "Schleiermacher saw Napoleon as the instrument of revived Catholic menace." Raack, "Schleiermacher's Political Thought and Activity, 1806-1813," *Church History* 28, no. 4 (1959): 377. Schleiermacher, however, makes clear the two needed each other, that each form of Christianity would be incomplete without the other: ". . . there has almost always been some pronounced antithesis in Christianity. As is natural, it always has a beginning, a middle, and an end. The hostile elements gradually separate, the division reaches a climax, and then gradually subsides until it fully disappears in another antithesis that has meantime [sic] been developing. This has marked the whole history of Christianity, and at present Protestant and Catholic are the dominant antithesis in Western Christendom. In each the idea of Christianity has characteristic expression, so that, only by conjoining both, can the historical phenomenon of Christianity correspond to the idea of Christianity. . . . Were I to interpret for you the signs of the time, I would say it has reached the turn of the tide, but has not appreciably diminished or disappeared" (Schleiermacher, *On Religion*, 3rd ed., 267-68).

28 Ibid., 268.

29 Ibid., 273 n. 3.

30 He acknowledged Protestantism has its own flirtations with idolatries, but "in a less gorgeous, and therefore less seductive form" (ibid., 269). Note the gender inflection here; such associations would also characterize anti-Catholic rhetoric in Germany in the mid- and latter part of the nineteenth century.

31 Ibid.

32 Ibid., emphases added.

33 Ibid., 270. Here I have purposely kept Oman's translation, "Romish," to underscore the point.

and thus that is to be honored, then why in the *Glaubenslehre* did he choose to define Catholicity according to its corruption?

d. The Choice of Dogmatic Material to Represent Catholicism

The question extends far beyond the definition of the church in §24. It touches also on the choice of material. We are all familiar with Schleiermacher's reasoning in emphasizing the Protestant symbolic books—and Walt Wyman has recently convinced us that we need to attend to how Schleiermacher used them.[34] Yet, what did Schleiermacher choose to represent the Catholic side? The answer is *The Roman Catechism*,[35] even though he notes in §19, "As for the popular presentation of doctrine, in catechisms and similar works, for the general instruction of the Church, this does indeed require completeness and coherence, but *it makes no claims to erudition and systematic arrangement and connexion; and therefore we separate this from the properly dogmatic field.*"[36] And yet, when it comes to the doctrine of grace and justification—at the heart, by Schleiermacher's own account, of Catholic-Protestant polemics—he chose a Catholic Catechism that "makes no claims to erudition and systematic arrangement and connexion." His choice of material to represent Catholic doctrine is therefore questionable. As far as I can recall, Schleiermacher scholars have not attended to this detail.

There is an added, more complicated problem. Take, for instance, Schleiermacher's propositions on conversion, justification, and sanctification. Schleiermacher scholars, when examining these doctrines at the center of Protestant-Catholic polemics, have taken Schleiermacher at his word, assuming that he was engaged in anti-Catholic polemics, even though the most intense polemics in these propositions are intra-Protestant. A more careful examination, however, reveals that in these propositions Schleiermacher was not, in fact, preoccupied with the Roman Catholic view, which is perhaps why he simply cites the *Catechism*. On this point I am defending Schleiermacher: here he stepped

---

34 See Walter E. Wyman, Jr., "The Role of the Protestant Confessions in Schleiermacher's *The Christian Faith*," *Journal of Religion* 87, no. 3 (2007): 355-85.

35 *Catechismus Romanus, ex decreto Concilii Tridentini et Pii V. Pont. Max. jussu primum editus* (Löwen, 1678); *Catechism of the Council of Trent for Parish Priests*, trans. John A. McHugh, OP, and Charles J. Callan, OP (New York: Joseph F. Wagner, Inc., 1934).

36 CG §19.4; CF, 90-91, emphasis added.

away from the typical anti-Catholic polemics, even admitting that the differences in the materials used made comparison difficult.[37]

So what happens when we begin to look at Schleiermacher's discourse about Catholicism in context? What did Catholicism look like in early nineteenth-century Germany, more particularly in Prussia, between 1799-1831? Here, Schleiermacher scholars can (and should) benefit from recent developments in historiography.

3. History: Catholicism in Prussia, 1799-1831

a. The Simple Fact of Pluralism and Particularity

The historiography on German Catholicism in the nineteenth century has exploded during the past two decades and has been transformed in the process.[38] One point of consensus is the plurality of *Catholicisms* during the "the long nineteenth century" and the need therefore of local and regional studies. Catholicism was anything but monolithic during Schleiermacher's time, as during any other time. To speak meaningfully of Catholicism, one must distinguish among social, intellectual, political, and institutional forms of Catholicism; one must be sensitive to the many different religious movements within Catholicism, to the role of religious orders, and to the tensions among these movements, religious orders, diocesan powers, and Rome; one must take into account differences between rural and urban Catholics, uneducated and educated Catholics; one must pay attention not only to location but also to milieu—to whether the Catholics in question are part of a minority or majority culture. In short, any general claims about Catholicism in German lands in the nineteenth century need to begin in the particular and concrete before moving to the general, and thus cannot avoid complexity.[39]

---

37 See CG §108.1; CF, 483. For elaboration on this point, see Julia A. Lamm, "Schleiermacher's Treatise on Grace," *Harvard Theological Review* 101, no. 2 (2008): 133-68.

38 Three important review articles highlight this shift in research. See Joel F. Harrington and Helmut Walser Smith, "Confessionalization, Community, and State Building in Germany, 1555-1870," *Journal of Modern History* 69 (1997): 77-101; Oded Heilbronner, "Review: From Ghetto to Ghetto: The Place of German Catholic Society in Recent Historiography," *Journal of Modern History* 72, no. 2 (2000): 453-95; and David Blackbourn, "The Catholic Church in Europe since the French Revolution: A Review Article," *Comparative Studies in Society and History* 33, no. 4 (1991): 778-90.

39 The move from the local to the general is being made in religious historiography. For example, Caroline Walker Bynum, a noted historian of medieval religion, reflects on shifts in methodology in the past quarter century and identifies in her more recent

Schleiermacher's own theory, of course, demands this. His principle of oscillation requires an almost continuous movement between the particular and the universal. (Indeed, in his review of Kant's *Anthropologie*, he had criticized Kant for not taking into account the particularity, therefore the humanity, of the native Australians.[40]) Schleiermacher's theory also insists that pluralism is necessary and good. And yet he did not take that into consideration in his own treatment of Catholicism. Whereas he portrayed Protestantism as a growing, vibrant thing precisely because of its pluralism, he portrayed Roman Catholicism (as he had Judaism) as dead or dying. Scholars have questioned his portrayal of Judaism but have left unquestioned his portrayal of "the Roman Church."

It is not, however, just a matter of bringing Schleiermacher's own theory back to him. We must go beyond that—for the issue is not just the simple fact of pluralism and the need to attend to the particular; it is also an issue of milieu.

b. The Status of Catholicism in Prussia

The status of Catholicism in Prussia was that of a minority religion in an emerging nation whose identity was intricately connected to Protestantism; in some areas of Prussia (Silesia and later Rhineland-Westphalia), Catholics were the conquered majority.[41] This in itself

---

    work a "simultaneous commitment both to specificity of starting point and to broad sweep. For I am not able to jettison either a 1990s sense that there are only particular stories and voices nor my 1960s conviction that somehow, behind it all, lie common assumptions" (*Wonderful Blood: Theology and Practice in Late Medieval Northern Germany and Beyond* [Philadelphia: University of Pennsylvania Press, 2007], xvi).

40 As Chad Wellmon argues, "For Schleiermacher, the problems and perils of Kantian anthropology are not merely metaphysical or theoretical; they are ethical: Kantian anthropology encourages a particular 'Denkungsart' that cultivates certain types of relationships with ourselves and others. . . . The isolation of individual observations and lack of context that Schleiermacher criticizes on a formal level emerge now as both an ethical and a theoretical problem. Kant's anthropology produces relationships between the observer and the objects of anthropological inquiry in which the object of observation is just another object of nature to be classified into a theoretical category." Wellmon, "*Poesie* as Anthropology: Schleiermacher, Colonial History, and the Ethics of Ethnography," *German Quarterly* 79, no. 4 (2006): 428.

41 On Silesia, see, e.g., Hans-Wolfgang Bergerhausen, *Friedensrecht und Toleranz: Zur Politik des preußischen Staates gegenüber der katholischen Kirche in Schlesien 1740-1806* (Berlin: Duncker & Humblot, 1999); on Rhineland-Westphalia, see, e.g., Jonathan Sperber, *Popular Catholicism in Nineteenth-Century Germany* (Princeton: Princeton University Press, 1984).

should give us pause and bid us to reconsider Schleiermacher's discourse concerning Catholicism. Did Schleiermacher's portrayal of Catholicism serve Prussia's political and social agenda? How and to what extent was his idea of Catholicism shaped by the fact that he grew up in Silesia, with its complex and contentious ethno-religious history?

One example should highlight the need for further investigation. Consider this passage from Schleiermacher's *Christmas Dialogue*, written in December 1805, as Napoleon's troops were making their way toward Halle. The character Leonhardt admits to his hosts concerns he has regarding their daughter Sofie's shows of piety:

> For heaven's sake, dear friends, do not give this feeling too much nourishment. Or can't you imagine her as vividly as I can, with withered colors, perhaps even wearing the veil and kneeling in front of the image of a saint performing the unfruitful rosary worship-service, or in a meager and feeble life in a Moravian Sisters' House, shrouded in the little repelling bonnet and in the charmless dress, excluded from the free and glad enjoyment of life? It is a dangerous time, many beautiful feminine hearts retreat to one of these contemptible aberrations, tearing asunder the family bond, and so, in any case, the most beautiful form and the richest happiness of the female identity is missed — not to mention the inner contortion, without which something like this cannot emerge.[42]

One might object that this is a dialogue, and here we hear the voice of a religious skeptic, not necessarily Schleiermacher's own voice. Well, a few paragraphs later another character, Karoline, expresses outrage that a comparison would be made between a Moravian "single sister" and a Catholic nun — the former being sensible, reasonable, and pious in a way that is not at all eccentric. The implication about the latter is clear. No one defends Catholic nuns or Catholic piety. Instead, it is taken for granted that Catholicism stems from an inner eccentricity, demands servility, smothers freedom, and is infertile and withering.[43] The only question is whether Sofie's early piety portends this kind of adulthood.

If we put this conversation in historical context, something else might strike us. In 1794, Prussia froze Catholic monasteries, forbidding

---

42 Friedrich Schleiermacher, *Die Weihnachtsfeier: Ein Gespräch*, in KGA I/5, 52-53.
43 Although in the *Reden* such gendered imagery had not been used, the charge of a withering and dying religion is clear: ". . . and I have nothing to do with the old-fashioned and barbaric lamentation with which they would like to clamor for the caved-in walls of their Jewish Zion and its Gothic pillars." Friedrich Schleiermacher, *On Religion: Speeches to its Cultured Despisers*, trans. Richard Crouter (Cambridge: Cambridge University Press, 1996), 78-79.

the admission of new novices;[44] in 1803, the *Reichsdeputationshauptschluß* dissolved "the monasteries and convents that were freeholds."[45] Moreover, compare Schleiermacher's language with an 1859 report from Aachen: "The vows of poverty, chastity, and unqualified obedience established under the abdication of all personal freedom and independence, impossible in a mere association, can only be realized in the polarized expression of the person."[46] As historian Michael Gross states, the assumption behind this report was that "monasteries represented a grotesque aberration of human life, entailing a suppression of the individual and a violent contortion of personality."[47] Keep in mind, too, that in 1875 the "Congregation Law," the capstone of the *Kulturkampf*, banned most religious orders; almost two hundred monasteries and cloisters were closed and the property appropriated by the state.[48] While these latter two events occurred long after Schleiermacher died, it does appear that Schleiermacher participated in a specific kind of ongoing discourse that served to rationalize specific actions taken by the government against Catholics.

c. Interconfessionalism

In addition to the fact of pluralism within Catholic Germany and the suppression of Catholicism in Prussia, there is the added insistence by historians that religions and religious denominations sharing a space, a history, a language, and a culture cannot be viewed as though they existed in a vacuum, isolated from each other. Historians are emphasizing, therefore, the necessity of studying the inter-confessional nature of any religious group or religious discourse in nineteenth-century Germany.

Our own Kurt Nowak stressed this in his 1995 work on the history of Christianity in Germany, where he argued that we must reject the

---

44 See, e.g., Heinz Hürten, *Kurze Geschichte des deutschen Katholizismus 1800-1960* (Mainz: Matthias Grünewald, 1986), 15-16.
45 Wolfgang Altgeld, "German Catholics," in *The Emancipation of Catholics, Jews and Protestants: Minorities and the Nation State in Nineteenth-Century Europe*, ed. Rainer Liedtke and Stephan Wenderhorst (Manchester: Manchester University Press, 1999), 103.
46 Landeshauptarchiv Koblenz, Bestand 403, Nr. 7532, "Betrifft die Niederlassung eines Franziskanerordens in der Stadt Aachen an den k. O.P. Pommer Esche zu Koblenz," 24 Nov. 1859, Bl. 113-22; cited and trans. by Gross, *The War Against Catholicism*, 72.
47 Gross, *The War Against Catholicism*, 72.
48 See ibid., 257.

assumption of "confessional monocultures"[49] and deal seriously with the fact that German lands have always been "tri-confessional."[50] Even so, he did not himself follow through on this imperative in his biography of Schleiermacher in 2002, at least when it came to Schleiermacher and Catholicism.[51]

4. Concluding Remarks

Two things drove me to write this paper. For years, I have sat through sessions on Schleiermacher at scholarly conferences and, not infrequently, have been caught off guard when presenters would iterate certain prejudices about Catholicism (e.g., that it is inherently superstitious, or its doctrine of grace Pelagian) as though these were clear facts without need of explanation or argument; even more disturbing was the lack of reaction on the part of the audience, the majority of which would inevitably be Protestant, of course. Also, in undertaking a translation of Schleiermacher's *Christmas Dialogue*, I have been struck by its strong anti-Catholic imagery and even more struck by the failure of previous editors and interpreters to critique this, or even take note of it. Such experiences have led me to question whether this dearth of criticism regarding Schleiermacher's understanding of Catholicism is due to the possibility that nineteenth-century prejudices remain under the surface of our own ecumenical currents.[52]

My hope is a simple one, whether or not you have agreed with my argument—namely, that the next time you are reading Schleiermacher and come across one of these passages, your eyes might not so easily glide over the words but might instead pause, and perhaps squint.

---

[49] Nowak, *Geschichte des Christentums in Deutschland: Religion, Politik und Gesellschaft vom Ende der Aufklärung bis zur Mitte des 20. Jahrhunderts* (Munich: C.H. Beck, 1995), 10.

[50] Ibid., 11.

[51] See Kurt Novak, *Schleiermacher: Leben, Werk, und Wirkung* (Göttingen: Vandenhoeck & Ruprecht, 2002).

[52] Jonathan Z. Smith has in several essays noted the role of Protestant anti-Catholic polemics in the history of the study of religion from early modern times to the present.

Schleiermacher's Original Insight

Infinite Inwardness as Consciousness of Freedom and its Consequences for Theology as Encyclopedia

ELISABETH GRÄB-SCHMIDT

A main concern of this conference is the relationship between theology and religious studies. In order to define this relationship in light of Schleiermacher's thought, it will be necessary to elucidate the role dogmatics plays in relation to philosophical theology. This question must be considered with respect to the concept of *ground*. We will need to consider Schleiermacher's conception of theology as a science (*Wissenschaft*), since the character of a theological science determines the status of religious studies (*Religionswissenschaft*) for theology. And the special status of history will be a key issue in this discussion, for Schleiermacher was well aware of the problematic situation of the theoretical status of Christian theology in the modern age. His *Brief Outline of the Study of Theology* (1811 and 1830; henceforth "Encyclopedia") is a product of this awareness.[1]

The systematicity of his Encyclopedia is the key to his modern understanding of theology as a science.[2] Its most remarkable feature is the understanding of theology as a positive science related to a fundamental task, namely, the governing of the church.[3] In view of this classification, my considerations will be concerned with the question of how the modern constellation of theory—and the position of culture and society in relation to religion—finds expression in the Encyclopedia. My thesis is that the *original insight* of Schleiermacher into the non-surpassable (*unhintergehbar*) constitution of religious consciousness, which precedes and determines all thinking and acting, is the hermeneutical key to his

---

1 Friedrich Schleiermacher, *Kurze Darstellung des theologischen Studiums zum Behuf einleitender Vorlesungen*, ed. Heinrich Scholz (Darmstadt: Wissenschaftliche Buchgesellschaft, 1982). Henceforth KD.
2 Heinrich Scholz, Introduction to KD, xii-xxxvii, esp. xvii.
3 KD §5.

theology. Given its importance, this insight must be taken into account, not only when interpreting his works in general, but also when interpreting his Encyclopedia in particular.

Schleiermacher's Encyclopedia is the result of the application of his epistemological principles to the conception of theology as a science. With this work, we encounter nothing less than the consequences of his "critical philosophy." Schleiermacher's critical philosophy—in contrast to Kant's—is not justified by reason alone, but rather by religious consciousness in its particular relation to freedom. It emerges from a peculiar constellation of the thinking of ground or basic principles (*Denken des Grundes*) developed by Schleiermacher in his Dialectics. According to the Dialectics, it is impermissible to seek the ground in a single "axiom" (*oberster Grundsatz*). Such a ground, Schleiermacher argues, can only be found in a totality (a whole), all individual elements of which can equally well serve as the beginning, and which can only be determined in infinite communication with one another. The key point here is the differentiation that takes into account the aspect of individuality as well as the coherence and interrelation of the different disciplines and therefore meets the necessary requirements of systematics.

It has been pointed out that Schleiermacher did not reflect on the systematicity of his Encyclopedia itself.[4] However, in my opinion, this systematicity can be derived from the starting point of his Dialectics, where he insists that a supreme science (*oberste Wissenschaft*) has to be developed. In the wake of the destruction of metaphysics, Schleiermacher had to establish a new theoretical framework, one that could take into account his conviction regarding the relation between being and reality—and thus allow for the development of a kind of cosmology. Even though this conviction stems from intuitions, that is, from subjective feelings, these nevertheless transcend the sphere of mere subjectivity.

I want to claim the following: A key term in this understanding of coherence and wholeness is the modern concept of infinity. The "oberste Wissenschaft" must focus on infinity as the one necessary "object" (*Gegenstand*).[5] This appeal to a fundamental principle, a fundamental science, reveals the persistence of a metaphysical interest in Schleiermacher's thought. However, this metaphysical interest must nonetheless be exposed to critique. As a result, the ground is withdrawn from a purely ontological and metaphysical sphere. Nevertheless, this metaphysical sphere still shines through as a dimension of wholeness—of

---

4 Martin Rössler, *Schleiermachers Programm der Philosophischen Theologie* (Berlin: Walter de Gruyter, 1994), 70.
5 Friedrich Schleiermacher, *Grundlinien der Kritik einer bisherigen Sittenlehre*, vol. III/1 of *Sämmtliche Werke* (Berlin: G. Reimer, 1834), 18.

totality and unconditionality—not in the realm of the "universal" but in the realm of the individual. Schleiermacher's construction of the relation between immediate and mediate consciousness was an attempt to cope with the new post-metaphysical situation while still providing a concept of a coherent knowledge of reality.[6] This was possible for him through a conception of infinity as a realm of infinite possibilities and therefore of freedom. With this conception of freedom, Schleiermacher was able to connect the individual and the universal within the subject as well as in the totality as a whole. This unique critical approach to the connection between the individual and the universal leads Schleiermacher to the idea of the centrality of history, which finds expression in his subsumption of dogmatics under the historical disciplines. This subsumption of dogmatics has often been seen and criticized as a depreciation of its importance and its reference to truth. But it is exactly this historical understanding that can be related to a possible truth in a modern way: because of the re-categorization of dogmatics as a historical discipline, a new understanding of history also emerges. Theology does not have a speculative starting point, but a *historical* one. This does not mean that it is removed from the sphere of the universal or of "truth." It rather means that any "universal" sphere must henceforth reflect on its historical basis. This new understanding of history conforms to Schleiermacher's concept of Encyclopedia. I would thus like to make the following claim: the hidden key to understanding the epistemological foundation is the modern concept of infinity, which itself leads simultaneously to the concept of theology as Encyclopedia and to dogmatics as a historical discipline.

These observations and conjectures provide the background to my reflections in this paper, which center on the following themes:

1. The presuppositions in the history of theory of Schleiermacher's new foundation of theology:
    a. Kant's critical philosophy:
    b. The new dimension of infinity in the modern age
2. Theology as Encyclopedia and its practical task
3. The new outlook of dogmatics as a historical, hermeneutical, and ecclesiastical discipline
4. The significance of philosophical theology for practical theology
5. The significance of the historical, hermeneutical, and ecclesiastical function of dogmatics in view of the question: Is practical theology a religious theory or indeed theology at all?

---

6   Friedrich Schleiermacher, *Der christliche Glaube nach den Grundsätzen der evangelischen Kirche im Zusammenhange dargestellt* (1830/31), in KGA I/13.1, §3, §5. Henceforth CG.

1. The Theoretical-Historical Presuppositions of Schleiermacher's New Foundation of Theology

a. Kant's Critical Philosophy

Schleiermacher's revolutionary critical insight emerged from Kant's destruction of metaphysics, with which Schleiermacher was confronted in the deep, yet narrow, religious life of the community of Herrenhut. A fundamentally new task now came into view: how was orientation possible, conceivable and justifiable under the conditions of a theory of consciousness?

According to Schleiermacher, a modern constellation of the ground is based upon religious consciousness. Portraying this is the task of a philosophical theology. A philosophical theology of this kind had not been necessary before, for its task had been included in dogmatics. This new discipline of philosophical theology, moreover, gives rise to a form of theology appropriate to modernity by replacing the previous metaphysical grounds with the thought of interrelation and coherence.

But after the abandonment of metaphysics, how can interrelation and coherence be philosophically guaranteed? In order to ensure such interrelation and coherence it is first necessary to take into account the modern thinking of infinity. The infinity Schleiermacher refers to in his *Speeches*[7] (especially the second) not only reflects the disposition of immediate self-consciousness but also — and this is the core of my argument — has theoretical validity. This is because the dimension of infinity became capable of taking over the function that the thinking of coherence had previously held. This argument can be supported by looking at the modern interpretation of infinity. For Schleiermacher, the modern determination of infinity seems to be decisive for his genuine insight into the determination of religious consciousness as intuition (*Anschauung*) and feeling (*Gefühl*).

b. The Philosophical-Historical Background of the New Determination of the Dimension of Infinity and its Consequences for the Question of Freedom

Long before Kant's critique of metaphysics and ontology and also before the Cartesian focus on the *cogito* as *"fundamentum inconcussum,"* a drastic turn arose at the beginning of the modern era, specifically in the

---

7 Friedrich Schleiermacher, *Über die Religion* (1806), in KGA I/12.

form of the new determination of infinity—primarily in physics and mathematics. From this point on, infinity no longer simply meant mere negation, as was the case in antiquity. On the contrary, it now signified the inexhaustible fullness of actuality and the unrestricted capacity of the intellect.[8] The interesting aspect of this for our purpose is the fact that with this new interpretation of infinity, freedom was given a new position in relation to theory. And it is precisely this combination of infinity and freedom that leads to the central role of history.

That Schleiermacher adopts this particular motif of freedom implied in the thinking of infinity can be seen in §4 of the *Glaubenslehre*. He does so, however, by taking into account a limitation of freedom— more precisely a *total* limitation—namely, the experience of freedom within the experience of utter dependence (*schlechthinnige Abhängigkeit*). The pre-critical sphere of wholeness and totality is now reflected in this conception of total dependence. By means of the combination of freedom and dependence or spontaneity and passivity within the experience of total dependence, Schleiermacher achieves nothing less than the inauguration of a post-metaphysical theory. The basis of this achievement is the possibility of a unity. And in the religious feeling of total dependence a kind of unity is present in a pre-predicative way. The distinctively modern feature of this quasi-metaphysical foundation consists in the fact that it is not the "universal" that is regarded as a unity. Following the emancipation of the subject, together with its irreducible value of individuality, the universal can no longer exist, nor can unity be situated in the individual subject. Instead, both the universal and the individual are conceived of in terms of an interconnection that can be grasped as a totality only in infinity. However, in order to conceive such infinity as totality, it is necessary to include the role of freedom and contingency. In other words, according to Schleiermacher, a reference to infinity as totality is already present within the very constitution of the self. As a totality, this reference is not given in terms of a teleological sum of possibilities, but rather is presented in an experience, namely, the experience of contingency. Contingency is itself characterized as the givenness of freedom within immediate self-consciousness as utter dependence.[9] At the same time, the infinite inwardness of the consciousness of freedom is transformed into the consciousness of contingency.

---

8   Ernst Cassirer, *Versuch über den Menschen* (Hamburg: Felix Meiner, 1966), 33-37. Cassirer emphasizes the peculiar transformation of the concept of infinity from antiquity to modernity. As I see it, it is this modern conception of infinity that can be seen in the thinking of Schleiermacher.
9   CG §4.

This contradictory constellation of freedom and dependence within contingency—which constitutes the modern constellation of ground as an interconnection of the individual and the universal—is precisely what leads to an emphasis on history in the modern era. History becomes the site of a symbolical manifestation of the infinite and thus of a contingent consciousness of freedom. It reflects on the foundation of the inwardness of freedom as something infinitely unobtainable—or as obtainable only in infinity.[10] Thus, it is now history, emerging from the self-manifestation of contingent freedom, that constitutes the reference to totality and unity. History comes to the fore as a reflective constitution of immediate self-consciousness in terms of a performative act.[11] As a performative act of this kind, it symbolizes, if only as contingency, what once was metaphysical ground. It is precisely this performative reflection of the ground that is the reason for the connection between the functional and substantial determinations of religion and theology.

This is Schleiermacher's genuinely new and ingenious approach. The foundation itself cannot be defined as concept, but only encountered as contingency. Thus, foundation still represents a unity, but it also includes differences by means of a form of freedom that is released into history. And by turning to a functional determination of theology, it also allows us to maintain a substantial relation to it, insofar as this functional determination is specified substantially as the *essence* of Christianity (*Wesen des Christentums*).[12]

Through this new constellation of thinking of the ground in reference to nothing beyond contingency, history is assigned the theoretical role of providing grounds. However, this theoretical function of history implies that both subjectivity and individuality attain an indispensable status. Indeed, coherence as the "universal" is not merely "there"; it depends upon the performance of a subject. Such interconnection between individuality and universality constitutes the critical procedure that must be applied from now on.

2. Post-Metaphysical Theology as Encyclopedia and its Practical Task

Schleiermacher's original insight into the presence of the foundation as total dependence is the hermeneutic key to his theology and especially

---

10   KD §14.
11   KD §26.
12   KD §24.

to his theology as Enyclopedia. The theoretical place of religion as foundation is thus maintained by virtue of a reflection on its historical forms of manifestation. It is this kind of reflection itself which guarantees coherence, and which thus enters into the perspective of foundation in a heuristic way.[13] Schleiermacher argues that theology and the church come into being in an equiprimordial way. The former comes into being as a form of reflection upon the historical development of Christianity, the latter as a form of its performance. That is, theology and the church do not denote two separate spheres: they are necessarily and equiprimordially related to one another as dimensions of knowledge and appropriation. Theology does not relate to its historical development in terms of theory and contemplation only. With regard to practice, it represents a "positive" science, which is to say that it consists of a fundamental task: the task of leading the church.

It is exactly this interpretation of theology as a task that leads to the central status of practical theology as the "crown of theology," as Schleiermacher put it in the first edition of the *Brief Outline*. However, as a technical discipline, practical theology remains highly dependent upon the appropriation of a critical reflection on historical reality in order for it to be capable of fulfilling its task of leading the church.[14] Schleiermacher develops a critical procedure in the *Speeches on Religion* that frees religion from metaphysics and morality. Corresponding to this delimitation of piety from metaphysics and morality, dogmatics is accompanied by philosophy of religion and practical theology. However, the critical procedure here requires dogmatics, for both philosophy of religion and practical theology cannot do without dogmatics as a reflection on piety/religion if they are to avoid ending up mired in pure speculation or merely "going through the motions." Thus critical reflection on the historical is itself the task of philosophical theology[15] and dogmatics,[16] and practical theology is obliged to refer to these disciplines. To understand this correctly, we must keep in mind the new status of the historical in its interconnection with the principle—and thus the new definition—of dogmatics. We have seen that the interconnection between the historical and the ground has consequences for the historical as such: the historical is itself now conceived of as a basic principle. And for practical theology this means that all of its principles of practice must become historically fluid. So, on the one hand, one

---

13 KD §2, §3, §6.
14 KD §336 and §2 (note 2).
15 KD §24.
16 KD §27.

must understand the basic principles in terms of their development. On the other hand, however, they have to be understood as a whole, as oriented towards coherence.

The critical-philosophical crux of Schleiermacher's thinking consists in the view of dogmatics as historical, but also in its peculiar conception of history and freedom. This is because it is the peculiar understanding of freedom that both emphasizes practical theology as the crown of theology and makes dogmatics indispensable. Dogmatics is indispensable because freedom as grounded in the immediate self-consciousness of a subject is nevertheless diagnosed as already given and thus as contingent.[17] And it is exactly this value and structure of freedom that throws light upon the systematic relevance of dogmatics as a historical discipline.[18] Thus it is history that attests to the coincidence of freedom and dependence as grounded in a contingent totality. History thus reflects upon the relation of immediate self-consciousness to the whole, the totality in its symbolizing processes and its manifold manifestations. Insofar as this totality as impulse and vision is made legitimate through religious feeling, it takes up the systematic role of what once was the metaphysical foundation. We must, moreover, take into account the intricate complexity of the relation of philosophy to practical theology and dogmatics. Such a ground in immediate self-consciousness can only function in philosophy as an empty placeholder. In dogmatics, however, it manifests itself in terms of a reflection of the historical performances of practice. It is precisely by not being assigned a (metaphysical) place, but through its revealing itself in terms of *acts* of religious consciousness that the transcendental ground is historicized and thereby tied hermeneutically to dogmatics. Hermeneutics here functions as a representation of historical acts in their reference to unity and totality, which both come together in infinity.

Thanks to this constellation of thinking the ground, which entails thinking of religion historically, Schleiermacher's theology meets the conditions of modern thought. The Encyclopedia views theology as practical—that is, as a theory of performance (*Vollzugstheorie*)—and as ecclesiastical—namely, as stemming from a vision of a whole. An understanding of theology of this kind is safeguarded by:

---

17 CG §4.
18 KD §§252-54.

3. The Modern Character of Dogmatics as an Historical and Hermeneutical Discipline and its Ecclesiastical Function

At this point we can say that despite its continuity with traditional and metaphysical thinking, Schleiermacher's understanding of theology is indeed different from the theologies of antiquity, the Middle Ages, and of the Reformation, and does exhibit a new and identifiably modern character. Moreover, the relation of practical theology to the church is not orthodox in character. The dogmatic striving towards unity and its ecclesiastical consequences for communication are not experienced as necessity, but as freedom, due to the fact that this striving is not deducible from a given being, but is situated historically. Indeed, the relation to unity is part of the contingent ground of freedom, because unity is an infinite entity that is present as a range of never-ending possibilities.[19] This interrelation of unity and freedom (possibility) bears consequences for the place of dogmatics and the church: dogmatics represents the orientation toward unity and coherence. Yet unity cannot be conceived as something given and presupposed: at best it can be grasped through the experience of coherence and through historical communication.

This can be accomplished only if a ground that unifies differences is presupposed, one which provides orientation for communication in this way. Communication as such experiences itself as freedom. The task of dogmatics implies a peculiar theory of freedom: the theory of freedom built upon the modern determination of infinity. Through its character as possibility, the dimension of infinity maintains unity within the manifold. The church is such a community of communication oriented toward unity. The ecclesiastical dimension of theology encounters nothing less than a transcendental and theoretical task with respect to the coherence of religious consciousness, to which theology must relate in its rational comprehension of the various forms of religious consciousness. This coherence is now established by virtue of the vocation of the church. And this coherence needs to be identified by dogmatics time and again. It is here that the task of hermeneutics comes into view, a task that is safeguarded by dogmatics. This is because understanding requires a relation to unity, and it is on this fact that the enduring importance of theology, as opposed to a mere religious studies, is based. Communication and understanding remain bound to the church as a community of communication. At the same

---

19   KD §§71-74.

time, the latter refers to a dimension of performance, which is now the only means by which a unity may be constituted.

It is this interrelation of possibility (within infinity) and unity that makes hermeneutics possible in the first place. Without unity there cannot be any hermeneutics, but within infinity the endeavor of understanding turns hermeneutics into an infinite task.

The interrelation of unity and freedom has consequences for the respective roles of dogmatics and the church: it is only if we place emphasis on both—on the infinite but contingent thought of freedom, and on communication as oriented towards unity—that the task of theology will be appropriately acknowledged. This indicates its ecclesiastical function. Dogmatics represents the orientation toward unity and coherence. Unity can no longer be presupposed as something ontological, but it can be experienced by means of coherence in historical communication. The church is a community of historical communication, stemming from and oriented toward unity.[20] The philosophical relevance of the thought of unity requires holding on to dogmatics as well as holding on to the church as an institution. This fact has significant consequences for the character of philosophical theology.

4. The Meaning of Philosophical Theology for Practical Theology

As mentioned above, philosophical theology may be seen as the successor of metaphysics, but—and this marks its difference from the theology of the metaphysical age—it cannot authenticate unity and truth by means of its intellectual achievements. This is because these criteria have to be handed over to history. They cease to be merely rational and relate to the domain of action and performance, which is now the only sphere in which it is possible to constitute a unity. This change of position and metaphysical function is reflected in the peculiar position of philosophical theology in the Encyclopedia. Philosophical theology does determine the structure and the connection between the disciplines,[21] but this does not take place on the basis of pure conceptual thinking. Instead, this is achieved on the pure basis of a reflection on the symbolizing and organizing expressions that grow at the heart of immediate self-consciousness, which are what ultimately give rise to

---

20 Conversely, it is only by means of dogmatics that the doctrines of the church are capable of being established.
21 KD §24.

history. This means that a philosophical theology is structurally dependent upon these expressions, which are themselves archived, interpreted, and reformulated by dogmatics.

This makes it clear that dogmatics remains irreplaceable for theoretical and systematic reasons—not only for practical, but also for philosophical theology. If philosophical theology bears normative force in relation practical theology,[22] this does not mean that this occurs in isolation from dogmatics: dogmatics has always already imposed itself upon the reflections of philosophical theology[23]. Philosophical theology is not informed by metaphysical transcendence, but it is informed by a critical investigation of what mediates unity in history. And this is exactly what takes place in the reflections of dogmatics.

With this, the technical task of practical theology as well as the critical task of philosophical theology become inevitably dependent upon the historical knowledge of dogmatics. For this reason, philosophy of religion is not, in fact, a standard for dogmatics.[24] If this were the case, then dogmatics could indeed be circumvented and could give way to religious studies. Dogmatics offers the necessary knowledge that is inevitable for the transactions of practical theology and safeguards it from a regression into a mechanical and ritualized procedure.[25] It delivers to philosophical theology exactly those references to unity that are required for a critical reflection and that are hermeneutically established by means of historical performance. In other words, dogmatics establishes a concrete freedom for practical theology (and all criteria for philosophical theology, which itself is related to hermeneutics).[26] Theology is not immune to the danger of loss of concrete freedom, especially when it turns away from the church as a community of communication of the inner infinity of freedom. For it is the unifying character of the church that preserves not only hermeneutical coherence, but also freedom—and, indeed, the specific understanding of relative freedom (which is to say, finite, human freedom) through which individuals can prove their worth.

However, this also means that dogmatics as a historical discipline and primarily as a historical discipline retains its still new but ever-indisputable theological function. Its function is to grasp communication and place it into a system, that is, those utterances that are directed toward coherence, toward understanding. Dogmatics, so to speak,

---

22 KD §140.
23 KD §28.
24 Cf. KD §255.
25 KD §2.
26 KD §30.

functions as a snapshot of a historically given time. In this way it has only historical validity. It does not have eternal validity in its concrete form and *Gestalt*, but in its impulse of purpose and orientation.

It is thus important to realize that, precisely in its historical significance, dogmatics has metaphysical value and therefore remains indispensable. It is the task of dogmatics to emphasize and to remain aware of the relevance of the historical in all its symbolization and organization. The appropriate form of its function is thus a hermeneutics that represents the infinite but purposeful task of understanding.

This means that for theoretical and systematic reasons dogmatics remains irreplaceable, not only for practical theology, but also for philosophical theology. But this indispensability is tied to the acceptance of the qualitative understanding of the historical. Moreover, it is not a diminishment of dogmatics to be subsumed under the various historical disciplines, but rather its considerable enhancement. This is accomplished by the achievement of a form of coherence that, as contingency, is capable of simultaneously visualizing transcendence and freedom. Through this retaining of coherence, dogmatic propositions are transformed into theological propositions. This, however, is possible only in virtue of the coherence of infinity and freedom in religious consciousness. And this coherence itself comes to the fore heuristically and hermeneutically only in relation to the task of governing the Church. Even though the governing body of the Church is the task of practical theology, this task is rendered hermeneutically possible by means of dogmatics.[27]

Against this background, we can now attempt to answer to our main question: Does practical theology remain theology or will religious studies take its place? This will be done in the final section of this paper, by means of a summary.

5. The Meaning of the Historical, Hermeneutical, and Ecclesiastical Function of Dogmatics in View of the Question: Is Practical Theology a Religious Theory or Indeed Theology at All?

The Encyclopedia is the theoretical program of a theology that aims to assert itself in modernity. The modernity of this program is due to a number of factors: the transformation of dogmatics into a historical discipline, the establishment of philosophical theology as an independent

---

27 KD §40.

discipline aside from dogmatics, and an increase in the value of practical theology as an ecclesiastical discipline. These are themselves made possible by the principle of functionalization, which in modern history has to determine the "universal" as such—now that the metaphysics of substance has been given up. That the Encyclopedia nevertheless remains faithful to metaphysics is demonstrated by its program of differentiation. And it is by means of this differentiation that the Encyclopedia remains oriented towards the whole of theology. From now on, differences are not obstructions to unity and coherence, but presuppositions of their constitution. Anything that can be represented as an object—Schleiermacher here follows Kant—emerges from the principles of construction in our consciousness. These, however, orient themselves towards difference. Even though unity both precedes and is transcended by means of difference, it will never be possible to represent unity conceptually. However it *does appear* in terms of the coherence and systematicity of the principles of construction.[28] The aspect of wholeness without which theology cannot remain theology, is heuristically kept in view in terms of the performance of principles of hermeneutics. We might understand this differentiation in terms of what Ricoeur was later to refer to as the "metaphysics of performance." The dialectical form of reasoning characterizes all thinking from now on and makes the generation of contradictions into a measure of the authenticity of experience and knowledge.

Schleiermacher does not give up knowledge of validity, but does acknowledge ontological discontinuity, and thus transfers validity to the sphere of the historical. The peculiar relatedness of empirical knowledge and knowledge of validity is expressed by subsuming dogmatics under the historical disciplines. And the hermeneutical structure of dogmatics in its historical task of infinite understanding consequently makes an infinite increase in the value of the historical as such. This new hermeneutical function of dogmatics, which conceives of hermeneutics not only in terms of a task for dogmatics, but which understands dogmatics itself as hermeneutics from now on, is rendered possible by the modern concept of infinity. Schleiermacher qualifies this modern concept of infinity by relating it to the subjective ground of freedom. But this also leads to an unavoidable attention to all knowledge and therefore to the necessity of including religious studies within the encyclopedic program. It is only through including all the knowledge of the world in its relations to past and present phenomena, that it

---

28 This determines Schleiermacher's conception of religion as transcendental in view of its consequences for the construction of the Encyclopedia as well as for dogmatics as a historical discipline.

becomes possible to lead the church. It is in this sense that theology needs to encompass religious studies. However, this must be done with an awareness of the subjective—and contingent—ground of freedom that has its intellectual roots in the modern thinking of infinity. Such a viewpoint is no longer rendered as a representation from outside, but has to be executed with reference to the inner, individual experience of being certain of inwardness—especially in view of its groundedness, its relatedness to the whole, to humanity, to the infinite universe, to the "One and All." It is precisely this idea of the thought of infinity from which contingency of freedom emerges, and which represents the structure of the thinking of a metaphysical foundation. Such thinking of foundation has not been abandoned as such, but has been purified in a critical way and corresponds to the intellectual determinations of modernity. Accordingly, Schleiermacher's understanding of theology is characterized by means of eight different positions, all which are in harmony with modernity:

1. The specific interrelatedness of empirical knowledge and knowlege of validity, which is given expression to by means of the subsumption of dogmatics under the historical disciplines. Schleiermacher does not give up knowledge of validity, but acknowledges ontological discontinuity and thus transfers the former to the historical sphere.
2. This leads to the development of the Encyclopedia as such. This follows from the new understanding of religion, which, from the point of view of its ground and with regard to a theory of consciousness, is predicated upon theoretically challenging "groundings" per se, especially those of a theological nature.
3. Theology ceases to be a rigid doctrinal system, but turns out to be in fact concerned with the determinations of the performance of Christian belief. In other words, theology ceases to be a conceptual description of the truth of belief, but becomes a science dedicated to investigating the parameters of the effectiveness of Christian piety.
4. This leads to an emphasis on history and the ecclesiastical function of theology. The historical manifestations of piety emerge from communication just as much as they elicit it. In this respect, Schleiermacher sees the becoming of a community, the way in which the church is organized, as a necessary aspect of religion.[29]

---

29 KD §22.

5. Dogmatics is, accordingly, transformed into hermeneutics, due to the requirement of the coherence of religious consciousness in the face of the diversity of its historical interpretations.
6. This new hermeneutical function of dogmatics, which conceives of hermeneutics not only in terms of a task of dogmatics, but which from now on understands dogmatics per se as hermeneutics, is rendered possible by means of the modern concept of infinity. Schleiermacher qualifies this modern conception of infinity by relating it to the subjective ground of freedom.
7. It is precisely this idea of the thought of infinitude from which the contingency of freedom emerges that constitutes the structure of the thinking of a metaphysical foundation. Such thinking of ground has not been abandoned as such, but has been purified in a critical way such that it is in keeping with the intellectual determinations of modernity.
8. With regard to our basic question this means that religious studies and theology must be related to one another. The former cannot be played off against the latter.[30] It is the hermeneutical structure of dogmatics in its historical task of infinite understanding that infinitely increases the value of the historical as such and replaces it with a "metaphysics of performance."

Translated by Ulrich Knappe and Martin Rodden

---

30 KD §240, §243.

Schleiermacher and the Hermeneutics of Culture

Schleiermacher's "Essentialist" Hermeneutics of Culture

BRENT W. SOCKNESS

The terms "hermeneutics" and "culture" are today dominant categories through which scholarship throughout the humanities or the *Geisteswissenschaften* understands itself. They are also terms that for anyone familiar with the full range of Schleiermacher's intellectual endeavors call to mind a good number of sciences, disciplines, and arts that Schleiermacher sought to reconstruct and ground philosophically. Naturally I have in mind here his hermeneutics proper, for which he is best known outside of theological studies, as well as his philosophical ethics, which has repeatedly been characterized in twentieth-century German secondary literature as a philosophy or theory of culture. But elements of, and contributions to, a "hermeneutics of culture" in our sense of the term—namely, a theory informing the practice of understanding diverse human communities—can be found throughout Schleiermacher's corpus. For this reason it is only appropriate that this conference devote a session to some regions of the significant terrain in Schleiermacher's oeuvre lying beyond his impact/reception in religious studies, his theory of religion proper, and his revisionary program in dogmatics. Hence the rather generous rubric of this, our fourth, session: "Schleiermacher and the Hermeneutics of Culture."

The question I have chosen to explore is itself a hermeneutical one, namely, how might Schleiermacher have understood the idea of a "hermeneutics of culture?" The attempt to answer it, moreover, nicely illustrates the concerns expressed by Richard Crouter in his keynote address regarding the precariousness of "translating" Schleiermacher into idioms other than those of his own time and place, for the rubric and the question are, of course, ours, not his. A doggedly historical answer to this question—one that "leaves the author in peace, as much as possible, and moves the reader towards him"[1]—might reply: Schleier-

---

1 Crouter, "A Precarious Journey: The Art of Translating Schleiermacher," ch. 1 of this volume.

macher would have looked upon the term "Kulturhermeneutik" with considerable puzzlement, even incomprehension. This is because in his usage both of our terms, culture and hermeneutics, had far more limited scope than they do today. Especially in the second half of the twentieth century both terms underwent considerable expansion in the discourse of the human sciences. The reasons for this are complex and fall well beyond the scope of this paper. Suffice it to recall that for Schleiermacher hermeneutics is a "technical" discipline, the aim of which is to formulate guidelines for the art of interpreting linguistic expressions, especially the written word. By contrast, after Heidegger and Gadamer the act of interpretation comes to characterize the entire fate of *Dasein*, and philosophy in this tradition (and in fields such as cultural anthropology) comes to understand itself as profoundly "hermeneutical." So what began as a *Kunstlehre* devoted to the exegesis of written artifacts is now widely understood to constitute the character of humanistic studies per se.[2]

What about the term, culture? It, too, has ballooned into a global category, this time indicating not the method, but rather the entire subject matter of the humanities and social sciences. Many of us no longer speak of culture as something distinct from and coordinate with society, politics, and economics; rather, culture is the umbrella term under which these various institutions and forms of human association fall; at the very least it is their "software." And if I understand contemporary German academic politics: *Geisteswissenschaften* are out, *Kulturwissenschaften* are in. As with hermeneutics, Schleiermacher's use of the term *Kultur* was more circumscribed than ours. A strict reading of his philosophical ethics shows that he reserved the term almost exclusively for those activities of embodied reason—in other words, *human* activities—involved in the cultivation and organization of nature: both our own natural organism in the form of physical and intellectual self-cultivation and that of our environment through such practices as agriculture, trade, and technology. Thus *Kultur* in Schleiermacher's strict sense refers to just *two* of the four modalities of rational activities that constitute the highest good in a comprehensive moral theory, which, more often than not (and not without its price) has been read as a theory of culture.[3]

The upshot of this foray into what Schleiermacher might have made of our rubric is that he would have likely found it an odd combi-

---

[2] See Gunter Scholtz's excellent *Ethik und Hermeneutik: Schleiermachers Grundlegung der Geisteswissenschaften* (Frankfurt: Suhrkamp, 1995).

[3] See Sockness, "Cultural Theory as Ethics," in *Christentum—Staat—Kultur*, ed. Andreas Arndt, Ulrich Barth, und Wilhelm Gräb (Berlin: Walter de Gruyter, 2008), 524.

nation of words. Why, he might ask, would one want to apply a technical discipline devoted exclusively to understanding the written and spoken word (*symbolisirende Vernunft*) to those corporate activities and social institutions through which nature is appropriated and shaped toward human ends (*organisirende Vernunft*)? Surely this is a category mistake. More precisely, it is an application of hermeneutics to the wrong object.

In what follows I would like to extricate us from this admittedly self-inflicted confusion by exploring a different construal of the notion of a "hermeneutics of culture," and one entirely within the spirit, if not the letter, of Schleiermacher's thinking. My thesis is that he was indeed concerned with the hermeneutics of culture in our sense of the term, that the so-called "critical disciplines" within his system of the sciences lie at the very heart of it, and that the best exemplification of Schleiermacher's general *Kulturhermeneutik* is to be found in a surprisingly familiar place: the opening propositions (§§1-11) of the *Glaubenslehre*, where a "critical procedure" (in Schleiermacher's peculiar sense of "kritisch" to be discussed below) is adopted to identify the "essence" of Christianity. Moreover, I want to suggest that the mediation between empirical history and speculative ethics, which Schleiermacher held to be necessary for a truly "scientific" apprehension of the Christian religion, applies mutatis mutandis to the determination of any other "historical totality" (Troeltsch) or cultural whole. While this argument for the best candidate for the title "hermeneutics of culture" in Schleiermacher's philosophical system is by no means the last word on the subject, it is an important first word intended to provide a basic orientation to our session's theme.

1.

Perhaps the quickest entrée into my proposal is to call to mind Schleiermacher's frequent polemic against two opposing approaches in his day to understanding the Christian church: the "purely scientific" approach, on the one hand, and the "merely empirical" approach, on the other. This polemic makes an appearance already in the second proposition of the *Glaubenslehre* and is developed in the introduction and first part of the *Brief Outline*. A third, related and fascinating source from which I draw is David Friedrich Strauss' lecture notes from Schleiermacher's course on Theological Encyclopedia of 1831-1832.[4]

The purpose of proposition 2 of *The Christian Faith* is three-fold: First, to call to mind the *Brief Outline's* understanding of theology as a "positive science" directed toward the understanding and maintenance of an object given in history, namely, Christianity as a distinctive "way of believing" or being conscious of God. As is well-known, theology for Schleiermacher is an assemblage of heterogeneous disciplines organized for the practical goal of effectively leading the Christian community. Second, to defend the thesis that a conception of dogmatics — understood as a branch of historical theology — waits upon an understanding of the *concept* of the Christian church. And third, to introduce those disciplines that must come into play — ethics, philosophy of religion, and apologetics — if one is to correctly grasp the "idea," the "concept," or the "essence" of Christianity. In our haste to debate the theory of religion developed in propositions 3-6, it has been a perennial temptation to pass over proposition 2 casually, as if Schleiermacher was just warming up his quill. This is unfortunate, since the *logic* of the controversial paragraphs that follow is contained in a nutshell in proposition 2. Far from being a philosophical proof for the truth of Christianity, the opening chapter of the *Christian Faith* follows what we would today call a hermeneutical procedure aimed at understanding one religious culture, the Christian, among and in relationship to others. In polemicizing against the Scylla of a speculative deduction of Christianity and the Charybdis of mindless (*geistlos*) empiricism towards it, proposition 2 announces Schleiermacher's intent to build his dogmatics upon a "critically" constructed concept of historic Christianity's "essence." Propositions 3-11 carry out this construction and provide us with a prime example of Schleiermacher's "hermeneutics of culture."

Schleiermacher's talk of "essences" will strike most of us as quite traditional, and in some respects it is. Echoing classical theories of definition, whereby a thing is to be placed in its genus and assigned its specific difference, Schleiermacher seeks first to secure a general concept of a church (i.e., religious association per se) and only then to identify whatever it is about the Christian faith that makes it distinctive from other religious communities. Less traditional, indeed post-Kantian, is the attention paid to concept-formation and the recognition, we might

---

4   Friedrich Schleiermacher, *Der christliche Glaube nach den Grundsätzen der evangelischen Kirche im Zusammenhange dargestellt* (1830/31), in KGA I/13.1 (henceforth CG); *Kurze Darstellung des theologischen Studiums zum Behuf einleitender Vorlesungen* (1830), in KGA 1/6; and *Theologische Enzyklopädie (1831/32): Nachschrift David Friedrich Strauß*, ed. Walter Sachs (Berlin: Walter de Gruyter, 1987). All translations are my own.

say, of the constructed character of the essence of any historical-cultural phenomenon. This is not to say—in radically historicist or postmodern fashion—that there are no actual and permanent features constituting the sine qua non of historic Christianity. It is rather only to admit that all of our knowledge and understanding of it consists of vast web of concepts and judgments produced by the active and unifying powers of the mind—what the *Dialektik* refers to as our intellectual function— and refined endlessly in communication with others.

It is against this background that Schleiermacher's attacks on a purely scientific deduction of Christianity and a merely empirical description of it make sense. Because *Wissenschaft*, strictly speaking, trades in universals, it can never "arrive at or produce something individual via mere thoughts." Try as one might to construct history a priori *von oben nach unten*, science—here understood as *speculative* knowing via the division of high-order concepts—will always "come to grief" when confronted by the facticity (*Irrationalität*) of concrete individuals in the realm of life.[5] In this respect, the individual is indeed ineffable.[6] On the other hand, "merely empirical conceptions of historical phenomena" are said to "lack a criterion or formula for distinguishing what is essential and permanent from what is variable and accidental" in some cultural whole.[7] And if Strauss' lecture notes are accurate, Schleiermacher took special pleasure in the classroom deflating empirical history's claim to possess real knowledge (*Wissen*) or be genuine historical apprehension (*eigentlich historische Anschauung*).[8] Here we

---

5   CG §2.2.
6   Dilthey chose this 1780 aphorism from Goethe's correspondence to Lavater as the epigraph to his famous and influential biography of Schleiermacher. As we shall see presently, it epitomizes just one side of Schleiermacher's approach to understanding historical-cultural entities, a fact frequently overlooked by admirers of Schleiermacher's sensitivity to human historicity.
7   CG §2.2.
8   On the contrast between a merely empirical grasp of the stuff of history and real knowledge or understanding of it, see Schleiermacher, *Theologische Enzyklopädie*, §21, §29, §65, §66; and *Kurze Darstellung*, §65. The intriguing expression "eigentlich historische Anschauung" appears in both sources and invites a word concerning Schleiermacher's mature usage of the term *Anschauung* as an epistemological concept. In the *Dialektik* lectures of 1814/15, *Anschauen* is carefully defined as the balanced integration of our intellectual and organic functions, i.e., thinking proper and perception (KGA II/10.1, 96 [§§115-17]). To have an *Anschauung* of something, then, is just to have a successful *cognitive* grasp of it. Indeed, the propositions cited treat *Anshauen* as a species of *Denken* and equate it with *Wissen* proper. This is clearly a departure from the 1799 *Speeches*, in which the term is plausibly understood with reference to (which is not to say equivalent to) Kant's definition of intuition in the Transcendental Aesthetic, with its strong ties to *Sinnlichkeit* (cf. Theodore Vial's and Peter Grove's contributions to this volume). Even less is *Anschauung* in Schleier-

confront a significant and general problem in the hermeneutics of culture that should give any reflective student in the human sciences pause. How is it that we can pick out of the complex and ever changing skein of human activities, practices, and institutions that make up the realm of human history something we call the Christian religion? Or Manchester capitalism? Or Renaissance art? Schleiermacher's conception of a "critical procedure" performed by various "critical disciplines" is meant to answer to just this question.

2.

In the *Glaubenslehre* and the *Brief Outline*, Schleiermacher argues that any "truly scientific" understanding of the *proprium* of Christianity will follow a "critical operation" that calls into play three distinct disciplines: ethics, philosophy of religion, and apologetics. For the sake of my reconstruction and because the texts themselves invite it, I am going to modify this trio slightly so as to bring out the logic of Schleiermacher's hermeneutic of Christianity. What we need to examine is the division of labor Schleiermacher consistently sets up among speculative ethics, philosophy of religion, and empirical history.

Ethics' job is to put forward (*aufstellen*) a general or generic *concept* of "church" qua religious association.[9] As the "speculative presentation of reason in its total effectiveness"[10] upon nature, it falls to philosophical *Sittenlehre* to identify that which all genuinely religious associations share (*Frömmigkeit* or piety), to define religious activity in relation to other elemental forms of free communal action (such as commerce and education), and to show that religious community (*fromme Gemeinschaft*) is a fundamental good grounded in human nature.[11] To be sure, speculative ethics cannot demonstrate the rational necessity of Christianity, but it can "deduce" the individual-symbolizing activity of reason that underlies the natural human impulse to form religious associations and thereby deflect the charge that being religious is pathological.[12] Empirical history's job is to attend to actuality and supply the extant material, the factual appearances of religion in histo-

---

macher's mature thought some vague premonition or intimation attained by extraordinary means. To the contrary, *Anschauung* is the goal (never fully attained) of the human drive to know.

9   CG §2.2.
10 CG §2, Zusatz 2.
11 Schleiermacher, *Theologische Enzyklopädie*, 33.
12 Cf. Schleiermacher, *Kurze Darstellung*, §22 and *Theologische Enzyklopädie*, §22.

ry. With respect to Christianity, this is the realm of historical theology, although Schleiermacher is insistent that without a "formula," "idea," "principle," or "criterion" (all synonyms for the "Wesen des Christentums") supplied by the philosophy of religion (or philosophical theology), historical theology is blind.[13] Philosophy of religion's job is twofold and involves a movement between the abstract science of ethics and the concrete facts of history: on the one hand, it divides the *concept* of religious community into a classificatory scheme; on the other hand, it assigns the historical faiths discovered by empirical history their place among the *conceptually possible* ways of being religious.[14] Such a "balance" (*Gleichgewicht*)[15] between the speculative and the historical is Schleiermacher's alternative to one-sidedly positivistic and one-sidedly philosophical approaches to Christianity. Let's take a closer look at this quite original conception of the philosophy of religion in the history of modern European religious thought.

"Balance" is not quite the right word for what Schleiermacher actually has in mind for the philosophy of religion and its close cousin philosophical theology. Rather, a twofold movement of "division" and "subsumption" better characterize a critical discipline's mediational role in rendering corporate human practices intelligible.

Division: Once philosophical ethics (in its *Güterlehre*) has "deduced" the human good instantiated in religious associations and thereby tendered a generic concept of a church as a community dedicated to the cultivation of piety, it is the task of philosophy of religion to "develop" this concept by dividing it into a classificatory scheme that captures *all* of the conceptually possible types of religion that could put in an appearance in history. I stress "all" because Schleiermacher intended this first moment in the philosophy of religion to produce "an integral whole exhaustive of the concept" church.[16] Put differently, Schleiermacher stresses that this act of ramification performed on the concept of religion is not dependent on historical or factual data, but rather arises somehow naturally out of the concept of a church. In keeping

---

13   CG 2.2; *Kurze Darstellung*, §29 (explanation); and *Theologische Enzyklopädie*, §26, §29, and §65. Because the differences in scope and aim between the philosophy of religion and philosophical theology are not significant for my argument, I treat them in tandem.

14   "Conceptually possible" is my way of construing such locutions as we find at *Kurze Darstellung*, §23: "Die weitere Entwikkelung des Begriffs frommer Gemeinschaft muß auch ergeben, auf welche Weise und in welchem Maaß die eine von der andern verschieden sein *kann* . . ." (emphasis added). This turn of phrase appears in all three sources under examination here.

15   CG §2.2

16   Ibid. Cf. CG §2, Zusatz 2.

with this moment's turn toward speculative science, the trick is to identify a "principle of distinction" (*Teilungsgrund*) residing in the concept itself.[17] In the *Encyclopedia* lectures, the logical distinction between the one and the many provides the basis for the contrast between polytheism and monotheism as possible ways of construing our relation to the highest being (*das höchste Wesen*).[18] The *Glaubenslehre*, recall, adds a third possibility—idol worship or "fetishism"—to round out a theory of stages of religious development,[19] and then proceeds to distinguish between basic kinds of religion, the aesthetic and the teleological. In this latter case as well, the search for a "Teilungsgrund" that is not merely empirical is a prominent feature of the argument.[20] Admittedly this first conceptual moment of philosophy of religion will strike us more historicistic late-moderns as something of a pipe dream. Yet one can hardly accuse Schleiermacher of lacking methodological sophistication or self-reflexivity: on the contrary, he is among the very first in a long line of nineteenth-century German thinkers such as Ranke, Droysen, Dilthey, Weber, and Troeltsch, to theorize the principles underlying the historical-cultural sciences.

Subsumption: Once the concept "church" has been carved up, as it were, so as to display the complete array of possible forms of piety, the philosopher of religion must look to the factual appearances of religion in human history and assign them their place among the essential forms of religious life. This, too, is hardly a hermeneutically innocent matter. Here we arrive at the core of Schleiermacher's distinctive understanding of the "critical operation" or "procedure" required for historical understanding. Strauss' lecture notes show Schleiermacher struggling for clarity regarding what he admits is a very multivalent term.[21] Two aspects of his conception of "Kritik" emerge: First, "the critical" for Schleiermacher involves just this *juxtaposition* of the historically given and the natural distinctions inherent in the concept of a re-

---

17 Schleiermacher, *Theologische Enzyklopädie*, §23: "Aus dem Begriff der frommen Gemeinschaft muß sich auch die Möglichkeit der Differenzen ergeben. D.h. es muß in diesem Begriff selbst ein Theilungsgrund vorhanden seyn. Die Entwicklung eines Begriffs muß auf eine Mehrheit von Merkmalen zurückgehen, die in diesem Begriff vereinigt sind."
18 Ibid., §24.
19 CG §8.
20 See CG §9.1. With respect to co-ordinate types of religion, the principle of distinction is discovered through an analysis of the two possible ways in which the utterly simple feeling of absolute dependence can relate to the passive and active moments of the subject's sensible self-consciousness. Here it is worth noting that the ground of the distinction is not purely logical, but rather philosophical-anthropological.
21 Schleiermacher, *Theologische Enzyklopädie*, §32.

ligious community. Second, it also involves an important *comparative* aspect. For the subsumption of more than one concrete individual under a universal category establishes for the first time a cognitive (*geistig*) relationship between facts, which opens the possibility for discriminating their similarities and differences. "To the expression 'critical' belong comparison and contrast—the determination that takes place via comparison."[22]

3.

It remains to make good on my claim that the "critical procedure" I have been analyzing with respect to understanding the Christian community's essence—the *Glaubenslehre*'s proposition 11 is the culmination of the procedure set in motion in proposition 2—applies mutatis mutandis to all the cultural sciences envisioned by Schleiermacher and is therefore representative of a general *Kulturhermeneutik* and not merely an ad hoc feature of his prolegomena to dogmatics. This is not difficult.

The explanation to proposition 23 of the *Brief Outline* reads: "The name [philosophy of religion] . . . designates a discipline that relates to ethics with respect to the idea of church precisely as another discipline relates to the idea of the state and yet another to the idea of art." And sure enough, when one turns to Strauss' lecture transcripts, we find Schleiermacher assigning familiar names to these additional critical disciplines: political theory (*Politik*) and aesthetics. Moreover we are told that just as ethics was charged with the task of demonstrating the "necessity" of communal religious life in the development of the human spirit, so too must it demonstrate the necessity of an order of justice institutionalized in the state and the cultivation of art embodied in various schools. Drawing an exact parallel between philosophy of religion and political theory, Schleiermacher instructs his students: "If the rule of law (*Rechtszustand*) and state have been shown to be necessary, then we must also ask what kind of essential differences with respect to the state are possible? This is a purely philosophical question [conceptual division!]. But if we then ask how actual states relate to these [essential differences], this [involves] a referring of what has been grasped empirically to that which has been grasped philosophically [subsumption and comparison!]." In precisely the same way, Schleiermacher continues, Christianity is assigned its place (by the philosophy of religion or philosophical theology) among the religions "by referring the histor-

---

22   Ibid.

ical existence of Christianity to the general existence of religious communities in different forms."²³

Like so much else in Schleiermacher's published writings, the hermeneutics of the Christian religion pursued in the opening propositions of the *The Christian Faith* represents merely the exposed tip, as it were, of the large and largely hidden iceberg that is Schleiermacher's philosophy. Further elaboration and defense of the claim that the critical disciplines constitute the core of Schleiermacher's "hermeneutics of culture" would require detailed analyses of Schleiermacher's far less user-friendly lectures on *Ethik* and *Dialektik*.²⁴ Suffice it to say that proposition 109 of the 1816 introduction to the lectures on philosophical ethics provides the formal rationale for an array of critical disciplines standing midway between speculative ethics and empirical history, but belonging to neither. Moreover, this same proposition lays down the rationale for a set of practical disciplines, which likewise mediate between speculative ethics and empirical history, but whose purpose it is to formulate prescriptive guidelines for bringing actuality into conformity with an "idea."²⁵ And this reminds us that for Schleiermacher to determine the essence of something—be it of a human good such as religion per se or of a historic religious tradition such as Christianity—is eo ipso to lay down a norm or criterion for judging and shaping history.²⁶

---

23 Ibid., §23.
24 Much of this difficult work has been done brilliantly by Markus Schröder in *Die kritische Identität des neuzeitlichen Christentums: Schleiermachers Wesenbestimmung der christlichen Religion* (Tübingen: J.C.B. Mohr, 1996), to my argument owes a considerable debt.
25 Friedrich Schleiermacher, *Ethik (1812/13)*, ed. Hans-Joachim Birkner (Hamburg: Meiner, 1990), 217-18.
26 Cf. his carefully worked out definitions of *Kraft* and *Erscheinung*, on the one hand, and *Wesen* and *Dasein*, on the other, in the introduction to the 1816 *Ethik* lectures just cited (201-2). Applied to theology see, e.g., *Theologische Enzyklopädie*, §26, where Schleiermacher explains that "three elements" alone make up Christian theology as a positive science: "Habe ich die Principien wonach ich den gegenwärtigen Zustand beurtheile, habe ich den gegenwärtigen Zustand selbst neben seiner Genesis begriffen, und habe ich die Regeln für die Geschäftsführung: so bin ich mit Allem ausgerüstet, was zur Kirchenleitung gehört." See again *Kurze Darstellung*, §29, where Schleiermacher explains that "[o]hne die fortwährende Beziehung auf ethische Säze, kann auch das Studium der historischen Theologie nur unzusammenhängende Vorübung sein, und muß in geistlose Ueberlieferung ausarten." At this point in Strauss' notes—and significant for the third, generalizing step of my argument—Schleiermacher explains: "Was hier nur von der historischen Theologie gesagt ist, gilt von der Geschichte überhaupt. Es ist zu unterscheiden das blose Auffassen einer räumlichen und zeitlichen Erscheinung und die eigentlich geschichtliche Auffassung, die immer auch ein Urtheil über die Erscheinung in sich schließt. Dieß wird recht klar wenn man sich vergegenwärtigt, daß nichts was eigentlich Geschichte ist,

To pursue this line of thought further would land us in a discussion of the "sources of normativity in Schleiermacher's interpretation of culture," the topic of our next paper by Professor Scheliha. In closing, permit me instead to call to mind and underscore the remarkable extent to which Schleiermacher thought through the epistemological conditions of a hermeneutics of culture. Not only can the notion of a critical procedure undertaken by the philosophy of religion and the other *Kulturwissenschaften*[27] be traced back into, and thereby grounded upon, the speculative derivation (*Ableitung*) of the critical disciplines sketched out in the lectures on philosophical ethics. The *Dialektik* lectures, in turn, pursue the conditions of Schleiermacher's *Kulturhermeneutik* one final step further. For there, in Schleiermacher's answer to the post-Kantian dispute over the modern heir to "first philosophy," a theory of empirical and speculative concept-formation is developed that corresponds precisely to the critical mediation between history and ethics required to achieve any real historical understanding.[28] In the final analysis, then, Schleiermacher's hermeneutics of culture finds its ultimate justification in his still largely neglected epistemology.

---

ohne Urtheil seyn kann, denn der Inhalt wird aufgenommen auf geistige Weise nur vermittlest eines Urtheils, indem ja der Inhalt auf Begriffe zurückgeführt werden muß. Die Principien dieses Urtheils sind aber immer ethischer Natur" (*Theologische Enzyklopädie*, §29).

27 I am here, of course, "disturbing Schleiermacher's peace" by employing the preferred contemporary German nomenclature. Heeding Crouter's stern warning, I won't even venture an English equivalent.

28 See footnote 7 above and part three of David Klemm's contribution to this volume.

Sources of Normativity in Schleiermacher's Interpretation of Culture

ARNULF VON SCHELIHA

For a long time it was common practice in German Schleiermacher scholarship to characterize Schleiermacher's philosophical ethics as a theory of culture.[1] The tendency was to view Schleiermacher's ethics as a speculative and fundamental science that provides the concepts for empirical studies in human culture and for historical analysis. Recently, some scholars, especially Brent Sockness, have emphasized the normative assumptions and implications of Schleiermacher's ethical thought.[2] This article picks up on that thesis and explores sources of normativity operating at different levels of Schleiermacher's thinking. First, I will discuss Schleiermacher's concept of science. Second, on the level of philosophical ethics, the relation between doctrine of the good and doctrine of duty will be surveyed. Third, the doctrine of virtue will be taken as a site for investigating the relation between philosophical and Christian ethics. Finally, I will examine Schleiermacher's political theory as field in which his normative assumptions are applied. In what follows, Schleiermacher's addresses to the Royal Prussian Academy will serve as my primary reference point because these texts provide us with the most reliable sources for his mature ethical thought.[3]

---

1 See the overviews of Hermann Fischer, *Friedrich Daniel Ernst Schleiermacher* (Munich: C.H. Beck, 2001), 78-83; and Kurt Nowak, *Schleiermacher: Leben, Werk und Wirkung* (Göttingen: Vandenhoeck & Ruprecht, 2001), 292-304. For the state of recent Schleiermacher research, see Ulrich Barth, "Schleiermacher-Literatur im letzten Dritten des 20. Jahrhunderts," *Theologische Rundschau* 66 (2001): 408-61.
2 See Brent Sockness, "Was Schleiermacher a Virtue Ethicist?: *Tugend* and *Bildung* in the Early Ethical Writings," *Zeitschrift für neuere Theologiegeschichte/Journal for the History of Modern Theology* 8 (2001): 1-33; Brent Sockness, "The Forgotten Moralist: Friedrich Schleiermacher and the Science of Spirit," *Harvard Theological Review* 96 (2003): 317-48; and Brent Sockness, "Cultural Theory as Ethics," in *Christentum—Staat— Kultur: Akten des Kongresses der Internationalen Schleiermacher-Gesellschaft in Berlin, March 2006*, ed. Andreas Arndt, Ulrich Barth, and Wilhelm Gräb (Berlin: Walter de Gruyter, 2008), 517-25.
3 "On the Concepts of the Different Forms of the State" (1814); "On the Scientific Treatment of the Concept of Virtue" (1819); "On the Scientific Treatment of the Con-

1. The Function of Science

Instead of expounding Schleiermacher's entire system of sciences, I will focus on the function of science in the life of reason, the latter understood as a power that penetrates and shapes nature.

Schleiermacher assumes "a step-like progression in the development of the living."[4] After "vegetation"[5] (first step) and "animalization"[6] (second step), human life with its rationality constitutes a third, higher level. On this level, an "intellectual process"[7] enters earthly life, which initiates the moral process of the unification of reason and nature. Initially, this occurs in an unconscious and unsystematic way; Schleiermacher calls it "a result formed by unconscious necessity."[8] One of its basic elements is a description of nature driven by a natural desire to put the variety of shapes of life into order and to classify them into genus and species.[9] The author of this "intellectual process" is the human species as a whole, not any individual. Its product is empirical knowledge in the form of everyday experience.

Reason is able to reflect upon ordinary empirical knowledge and analyze it, and, insofar as it does so self-consciously, the development of life achieves a new (fourth) level. Schleiermacher defines "science" generally as the methodically conscious mode of the rational cultivation of nature, and hence nature's self-reflexive elevation. The specific features of science are "circumspection" and the "artful construction" of knowledge.[10] Next to the scientific knowledge of nature stand those disciplines that describe the great spiritual formations brought forth by human reason and technology. Since the nineteenth century, these have been called the *Geisteswissenschaften* or humanities. Among them, indeed, one of their oldest disciplines, is the theory of the state, in which Schleiermacher took a very early interest.

---

cept of Duty" (1824); "On the Difference Between the Natural and Moral Law" (1825); "On Plato's View of the Practice of the Art of Healing" (1825); "On the Concept of the Permitted" (1826); "On the Concept of the Highest Good" (1827 and 1830). These lectures are available in Friedrich Schleiermacher, *Akademievorträge*, KGA I/11. Subsequent references to this volume supply page numbers followed by line numbers in parenthesis.

4 Michael Moxter, *Güterbegriff und Handlungstheorie: Eine Studie zur Ethik F. Schleiermachers* (Kampen: Kok Pharos, 1992), 6.
5 KGA I/11, 448 (24).
6 KGA I/11, 449 (9).
7 KGA I/11, 449 (23-24).
8 KGA I/11, 98 (9-10).
9 See KGA I/11, 97 (3-13).
10 See KGA I/11, 97 (9-12).

The scientific formation of knowledge is, however, not uniform. Rather, the "great abundance of scientific life"[11] continually undertakes "new examinations and reconfigurations of the system of nature."[12] One might say that science is, on the one hand, strongly guided by reason because it claims to bring forth general and valid knowledge. On the other hand, science is always conducted from a specific perspective, is often mistaken, and thus always requires supplementation and correction.

In his treatise "On the Difference Between Natural and Moral Law," Schleiermacher consolidates this thought. His basic insight is that laws describing nature and laws describing human acts have the same structure, namely, they contain rules that analyze real events in the world. Natural laws refer to the "is" in nature, to what is actually the case. Yet they also claim that reality ought to be as it is described by the rule. These rules are generally correct, yet they occasionally differ from reality.[13] Such discrepancies are occasions either for correcting an established rule or for identifying "diseases as deviations in the course of some or another life function."[14] Challenging the bifurcation of "is" from "ought," Schleiermacher holds that natural laws serve a critical aim.

The reverse applies to the moral law. It formulates not only an imperative or counterfactual "Sollen," but also refers to an established reality or a "Sein." Schleiermacher puts this thesis forward as an explicit challenge to the deontological ethics of Kant and Fichte.[15] The "is" or actuality entailed in the moral law is the disposition (*Gesinnung*) that has brought forth the moral law and enforced it. Schleiermacher says that "respect for the law . . . first constitutes the law and is the reality [*Wirklichkeit*] of the law."[16] He argues further that the "determining force of the disposition is the essential and original moral 'is.'"[17] In other words, the "ought" of the moral law is founded on the recognition of the moral law, and it refers critically to the assessment of any immoral acts in historical life.[18]

---

11 KGA I/11, 97 (12-13).
12 KGA I/11, 97 (30-31).
13 See Moxter, *Güterbegriff und Handlungstheorie*, 73.
14 KGA I/11, 448 (14-15).
15 For the details of Schleiermacher's criticism of Kant's and Fichte's ethics, see Moxter, *Güterbegriff und Handlungstheorie*, 64-107; and Eilert Herms, "Sein und Sollen bei Hume, Kant und Schleiermacher," in *Menschsein im Werden: Schleiermacher-Studien* (Tübingen: Mohr Siebeck, 2006), 296-319.
16 KGA I/11, 444 (12-13).
17 KGA I/11, 445 (6-7).
18 See KGA I/11, 448 (17-18).

To execute the task of ethics, Schleiermacher constructs, on the one hand, a "cycle of critical disciplines which build on ethics" in order to "judge the individual manifestations as depictions of the idea."[19] On the other hand, he envisions a set of the technical disciplines, which serve to optimize the moral process.[20] As examples, Schleiermacher mentions critical political science (*Staatslehre*) and technical statesmanship (*Staatsklugheit*).[21]

To summarize: through the optimization of methods and the rational justification and differentiation of the scientific self-disclosure of the human spirit, reason brings itself forth as the normative source of its self-actualization and thereby becomes a critical standard for assessing the evolution of culture. The goal of science consists in demonstrating norms residing in reason itself and applying these norms to what is historically given.

2. The Relation of the Doctrine of the Good to the Doctrine of Duty

It is indisputable that the priority of the doctrine of the good is a distinguishing feature of Schleiermacher's ethical system. Schleiermacher shared with his colleague Hegel the basic insight that the morality of an individual depends on the socially constructed morality in the established culture. Their common criticism of Kant's practical philosophy led them to a theory of culture, which Hegel calls "the doctrine of objective spirit" and Schleiermacher calls the "doctrine of the good." But Schleiermacher scholarship has not always given proper weight to the fact that within Schleiermacher's overall conception of ethics, the doctrines of duties and of virtue are of abiding, if subordinate, significance.[22] An examination of the interrelation between the doctrine of the

---

19 Friedrich Schleiermacher, *Lectures on Philosophical Ethics*, ed. Robert B. Louden, trans. Louise Adey Huish (Cambridge: Cambridge University Press, 2002), 8 (General Introduction, §§57-58).

20 As Sockness puts it, "The critical disciplines employ the knowledge of ethics to grasp the 'essences' of concrete historical individuals and judge these empirical appearances against their ideal. The technical disciplines draw on ethical knowledge as well, but for a different purpose: to prescribe guidelines for prospective historical praxis" (Sockness, "The Forgotten Moralist," 347).

21 See Schleiermacher, *Lectures on Philosophical Ethics*, 9 (General Introduction, §61).

22 Exceptions are Eilert Herms, "Reich Gottes und menschliches Handeln," in *Friedrich Schleiermacher: 1768-1834. Theologe—Philosoph—Pädagoge*, ed. Dietz Lange (Göttingen: Vandenhoeck & Ruprecht, 1985), 163-92; Moxter, *Güterbegriff und Handlungstheorie*; and Sockness, "The Forgotten Moralist."

good and the doctrine of duty can provide some important answers to the question of the sources of normativity in Schleiermacher's theory of culture.

For Schleiermacher, the highest good is the result or product of all moral actions and the aim of human history: "Everything which has become moral is a good, and the totality of that [process] a single entity, hence the highest good."[23] This highest good is the cultural manifestation of all moral acts and the goal of every single action. The task of the "Güterlehre" is to provide a differentiated presentation of the moral productions of reason and its institutions: family and free sociality, nation and state, knowledge and schools, religion and church. Whereas in the doctrine of the good Schleiermacher takes a collective perspective, in the doctrines of virtue and of duty he focuses on individuals and their contribution to the realization of the highest good. The doctrine of duty "formulates prescriptions governing discrete moral acts."[24] Schleiermacher emphasizes the "critical interest" of the doctrine of duty because "it distinguishes what is to be regarded as ethically real from what is ethically empty."[25] The doctrine of duty provides normative orientation to the individual in the form of imperatives that tie in with the basic concerns of the moral community. Thus, the *first imperative* says: "Using his whole moral power, every single individual should bring about the maximum possible for the solution of the overall moral task within the community of all individuals."[26]

This appears to imply that the individual becomes nothing more than the mechanical executor of the common task. But this implication is blocked by Schleiermacher's complex conception of the highest good. For as Schleiermacher conceives it, the highest good just *is* the coexistence and cooperation of collective and individual actions. Moreover, it simultaneously represents the aim of all free acts and makes them possible. Thus, the voluntary contribution of every single person is an element of the highest good and a duty for everyone. As a result, the imperative of duty acquires two qualifications: "While taking part in the community by sharing its identity, endeavor to act in your own particular manner."[27] This formulation prescribes a regard for individuality, which presupposes the possibility of nurturing individuality along with the social conditions that make it possible. On the other hand, the pursuit of individuality must not cut ties with the community. The

---

23 Schleiermacher, *Lectures on Philosophical Ethics*, 11 (General Introduction, §83).
24 Sockness, "The Forgotten Moralist," 344.
25 Schleiermacher, *Lectures on Philosophical Ethics*, 12 (General Introduction, §95).
26 KGA I/11, 425 (35-38).
27 KGA I/11, 426-27 (41-1).

third imperative thus says: "While being different from the community [or: by acting in your own particular manner], never act in such a way that your acting is not consistent with the acting of the community."[28] The balance between community and individuality is thus a moral norm,[29] and this norm can also be characterized as a duty of mutual recognition. Every joining of a community requires the individual's consent to the communal aims and, conversely, every community must grant its members moral independence, i.e., freedom. Presupposed in this balance is the normative idea of a community of independent human beings.

Schleiermacher puts the normative significance of this balance in concrete terms as can briefly be shown with reference to the sphere of law (*Recht*). Entrance into a political community (*Rechtsgemeinschaft*) requires of an individual the duty to follow the law and recognize that society's aims. But this duty of right (*Rechtspflicht*) has two limits. First, the society must provide space for the moral contributions of its individual members. This is the sphere of professional life. Second, it must respect the consciences of individuals. Thus the complete duty of right is summed up in the formulation: "Do not submit to a system of law without securing yourself a profession and without reserving the domain of conscience for yourself."[30] The normative intent of the doctrine of duty is clear. It aims at the mutual recognition between the community and individual freedom. This means that "every action [must] always remain open to its . . . counterpole."[31] Locating this balance is the essence of morality.

3. The Doctrine of Virtue, and Christian Faith as a Source of Historical Normativity

But just how does the realization of the highest good occur? Is it an evolutionary development that carries out some higher natural necessity? Or does history include contingency, variation, and setbacks? In other words, is there a guarantee for achieving the highest good or is it tied to historical conditions that are not to be taken for granted?

---

28 KGA I/11, 427 (12-14).
29 See Herms, "Reich Gottes und menschliches Handeln," 169; Moxter, *Güterbegriff und Handlungstheorie*, 235; and Claus Müller, *Ist theologische Ethik philosophisch möglich?: Zum Verhältnis von philosophischer Ethik und christlicher Sittenlehre im philosophisch-theologischen System F. Schleiermachers* (Frankfurt: Peter Lang, 2002), 19-21.
30 KGA I/11, 428 (24-27).
31 Müller, *Theologische Ethik*, 21.

Schleiermacher was convinced that Christianity was an important dynamic factor in history, and that it had a great influence on achieving the aim of history.[32] He took into account both the steady expansion of civilization fostered by Christianity and the errors and setbacks that occur in the process of realizing the aim of history—a *Humanitätskultur*.[33] Given this outlook, Christian morality is an important source for the normative assessment of history. Yet it is not altogether clear how this historical criterion is to be applied to the experience of historical contingency and crisis.

This question leads to the problem of the relationship between philosophical and Christian ethics, a puzzle in Schleiermacher scholarship that has still not been completely solved. In the introduction to his lectures on Christian ethics, Schleiermacher alludes to this problem. Regarding content, Christian and philosophical ethics are said to be "completely the same"; with respect to their form, however, they are "completely different."[34] That these conceptions of ethics are not to be considered rivals is certain.[35] But against Jörgensen's early opinion that Christian ethics is only a translation of philosophical ethics into Christian language,[36] scholarship has for a long time emphasized the formal distance between the disciplines.[37] Indeed, there is no direct path from one discipline to the other. Philosophical ethics is a formal and speculative science that identifies religion as a rational operation of human spirit and, in a general sense, identifies the religious community (the church) as a necessary domain of religious activities (in Schleiermacher's words: representational deeds). The doctrine of Christian morality is, by contrast, a historical subfield of theology, one that refers to empirical facts and has a practical aim—namely to standardize acts within a Christian denomination. But two recently published books by Brandt

---

32 Schleiermacher saw humane culture primarily as the consequence of the influence of Christianity; he neglected other factors, e.g., the Jewish ethos. See Wilhelm Gräb, *Humanität und Christentumsgeschichte: Eine Untersuchung zum Geschichtsbegriff in Schleiermachers Spätwerk* (Göttingen: Vandenhoeck & Ruprecht, 1980).
33 The most important example of such setbacks is war. See, for example, Friedrich Schleiermacher, *Die christliche Sitte nach den Grundsätzen der evangelischen Kirche im Zusammenhang dargestellt*, ed. Wolfgang Erich Müller (Waltrop: Spenner, 1999), 484-85.
34 Ibid., 75.
35 See Hans-Joachim Birkner, *Schleiermachers christliche Sittenlehre im Zusammenhang seines philosophisch-theologischen Systems* (Berlin: Walter de Gruyter, 1964), 87.
36 See Poul Henning Jörgensen, *Die Ethik Schleiermachers* (Munich: Kaiser, 1959).
37 See Birkner, *Schleiermachers christliche Sittenlehre*, 87; and Sockness, "The Forgotten Moralist," 336 n. 66.

and Müller[38] set forth the "significant correspondence between the two structures."[39] According to these authors, it is true that the difference between the disciplines is grounded in the different sources of morality, namely, reason on the one hand and religious feeling on the other. Nonetheless, they also find "direct points of contact . . . between the two ethics."[40] One of these direct points of contact can be found in the treatise "On Scientific Treatment of the Concept of Virtue." This is no coincidence, of course, since faith or piety resides in the self-consciousness of an individual. In what follows I intend to show that in Schleiermacher's eyes the Christian virtues make an important contribution to the overcoming of the experience of moral crisis and historical contingency.

The doctrine of virtue focuses on "reason in the human individual"[41] as a "generative power . . . for the good."[42] The virtues represent the presence of a given moral substance in the individual and are the inner pre-condition for a dutiful fulfilling of the moral norms. Schleiermacher describes the presence of moral substance from two perspectives. On the one hand, morality is given as a steady disposition (*Gesinnung*) that Schleiermacher calls "animating virtue" (*belebende Tugend*). On the other hand, virtue must fight against attractions caused by sensory self-consciousness. From this perspective, virtue is a "fighting virtue" (*bekämpfende Tugend*) and is considered a proficiency (*Fertigkeit*). By combining this distinction between steady disposition and struggling proficiency with the more familiar distinction in his philosophical ethics between reason's symbolizing and organizing activities, Schleiermacher constructs a scheme of four virtues: wisdom, love, prudence, and steadfastness. Wisdom and love are the qualities of the moral disposition, while prudence and steadfastness are proficiencies that help to overcome the attractions caused by the lower or sensible self-consciousness. The virtues that refer to moral action in its strictest sense are love and steadfastness. The virtue of love governs "the striving to produce community."[43] It therefore stands above the state and its

---

38   See James M. Brandt, *All Things New: Reform of Church and Society in Schleiermacher's Christian Ethics* (Louisville: Westminster John Knox Press, 2001); and Müller, *Theologische Ethik*.
39   Brandt, *All Things New*, 77.
40   Müller, *Theologische Ethik*, 58.
41   Schleiermacher, *Lectures on Philosophical Ethics*, 100 (Doctrine of Virtue, Introduction, §1).
42   Sockness, "The Forgotten Moralist," 344.
43   KGA I/11, 333 (12-13).

legal system and realizes itself in the coexistence of a multiplicity of different communities.[44]

Towards the end of this treatise, Schleiermacher turns to the relation between the rational virtues of wisdom and love and the Christian virtues of faith, hope, and love. Schleiermacher demonstrates their correspondence by referring to his concept of God. The aim of ancient philosophy—he has Plato and Aristotle in mind—was "to become similar to God according to capacity," and this was to be attained by cultivating the rational virtues.[45] This goal is achieved in the Christian faith because in it, God's most essential attributes—the identity of love and wisdom—are transferred to us as our own capacities and are efficacious here on earth under the conditions of our "divided spirit."[46] Faith is "the innermost aspect of consciousness"; it is the "religious term for what in science we call . . . wisdom."[47] It is also the "lively source of good works" and identical to practical reason, containing love as a steady disposition or animating virtue.[48] Only the virtue of hope transcends human rationality, and Schleiermacher reserves it for the personal experience of contingency and crisis. Hope is not a rational emotion that refers to religion within the limits of reason alone, but rather an element of the Christian religion. It reflects the unpredictability and the risk of all actions and imagines success in a religious way. As a religious feeling, it assures us of the success of our actions, a success that is otherwise "uncertain for the individual."[49]

Schleiermacher restricts the Christian doctrine of virtue to the disposition and says nothing about Christian virtues as proficiencies. The task of Christian virtue is to make us ready for outward action, to give us an aim, and to make this disposition steady. The need for steadiness or constancy alludes to the struggle rational agents undergo in having to wrestle with the inclinations of the sensible self-consciousness. Schleiermacher dealt with such vices in the academy addresses "On Plato's View of the Practice of the Art of Healing" and "On the Concept of the Permitted."[50] In these addresses, pleasure-seeking, sleep, and

---

44 "[W]e have to say that everywhere love brings forth law, and if love ends law will be lost" (KGA I/11, 332-33 [39ff]).
45 KGA I/11, 335 (2).
46 KGA I/11, 335 (20).
47 KGA I/11, 334 (31-36).
48 KGA I/11, 334 (32).
49 Schleiermacher, *Lectures on Philosophical Ethics*, 104 (Doctrine of Virtue, Introduction, §26).
50 KGA I/11, 459-78, 491-513.

disease are given as examples of things that prompt people to neglect their moral duties, to indulge in leisure, and to be loveless.[51]

It is however impossible for the individual to stabilize morality single-handedly, for the moral life can only thrive within the framework of an already existing spiritual sphere, which first produces the necessary conditions for it. For Schleiermacher the Christian religion in history serves this purpose by disseminating in the human race the higher self-consciousness that confers upon the will the strength to determine the lower-consciousness. The moral struggle is thereby fundamentally resolved in the Christian disposition and vices are seen as fading transitional phenomena. In this respect, Christian faith overcomes the crises of pure reason.

This steadiness is also the reason why the presentation of Schleiermacher's Christian ethics does not follow the structure of his philosophical ethics. Rather it analyzes the religious activities such as prayer or worship under the rubric of "representational actions" and then focuses on the actions that are necessary because of the social embeddedness of the church. These "effectual actions" are, on the one hand, directed inward to members of the Christian community under the title "restoring or purifying actions." On the other hand, they are directed to the church's social environment under the title "broadening action." This revised structure indicates that Christian ethics is in fact richer with regard to content than is suggested by the treatments of "religion" and "church" in the philosophical ethics. This is because Christian ethics thematizes action under the condition of social complexity and the experience of historical contingency.

It should be clear by now that Christian faith is an important source for the normative assessment of history. For it reveals that reason-based morality is unsteady and vulnerable. Because in its broadening action Christian morality is tied to its social environment and influences it, Christianity is an important factor within the historical realization of the highest good. Faith creates the steadiness of the higher self-consciousness, which is often hindered in its purely rational state. It thus becomes clear that history is not the unfolding of some eternal necessity, but a sphere in which reason and contingency must be put in equilibrium by the power of faith.

---

51 On vices such as "error," "lovelessness," "arrogant unscrupulousness," "dullness," "unwholesome softness," "lethargy," "sensory desire or reluctance," and "routine," see the marginal additions in Schleiermacher, *Lectures on Philosophical Ethics*, 106-7, 109-10, 121-22 (Doctrine of Virtue). They indicate the fundamental tension in rational morality because it is exposed to the stimulus given by the lower self-consciousness.

4. The Application of Moral Norms to Schleiermacher's Theory of the State

In this final section, I will provide a few examples of the application of norms in Schleiermacher's theory of culture to his political theory. This will enable us to take into account the different levels at which heretofore identified sources of normativity operate.

a. The State Is No "State of Emergency" But a State of Culture

Against the grain of mainstream of Protestant tradition, Schleiermacher assigns a fundamentally positive role to the state as a full-fledged moral good. The state is the manifestation of the self-consciousness of a nation, and it serves the nation's vital interests. If certain conditions are fulfilled (the unification of several families into a nation, common territory, common education via common language, a shared history, etc.), the building of legal and, therefore, state structures belongs to the essential tasks of the rational development of common life.

b. Freedom as a Normative Foundation of the State

The constitution of a state does not, however, take place by natural necessity. There is a gap between a nation's pre-political and its political existence, and the overcoming of this gap is an act of absolute contingency, which Schleiermacher construes as freedom. Indeed, the precondition of every state is freedom, for the transformation from a pre-political condition, dominated by family ties and custom, to political life proper, in which rulers and subjects are clearly distinguished and the law expresses the common will and compels individuals, occurs only through the voluntary act of the nation.[52]

Thus the act that establishes a state is performed collectively. And once the state is established, the political sphere ought to strive to make room also for the freedom of individuals by differentiating itself from the social sphere. Here, the normative aspect of Schleiermacher's concept of political freedom becomes apparent. "Politics" is defined as the "lively interaction" between government and citizens to arrive at the

---

52 "Having power and yielding to power is subjected to the common will; power is grounded upon the will of totality, so the subjugation is only done voluntarily" (Schleiermacher, *Vorlesungen über die Lehre vom Staat*, KGA II/8, 329 [18-22]).

common will, which takes the form of laws.[53] This "mediation of difference is the real conscious life of a state."[54] For Schleiermacher, then, politics are the procedural form of reflection of the life of a state in which citizens actively take part.[55] Significantly, this interpretation of politics is employed by Schleiermacher as part of an evaluation of the functionality or dysfunctionality of historical state institutions. Accordingly, he does not simply take over the classical theories of the types of state (monarchy, aristocracy, and democracy) or more modern theories of the separation of powers, but instead treats them as temporary stages in the development of a state. Indeed, only those states that succeed through political processes in involving their citizens in the life of the state have a future.

Again, the normative core of this conception of politics is a "concept of civic freedom," because it demands "a minimum of constraint of the subject by [state] authority."[56] Freedom makes state actions possible and restricts them at the same time. It transforms the opposition of ruler and subjects into a functional relationship based on the mutual recognition of each other's responsibilities.[57] The task of politics is to promote the vibrant interaction of government and citizens. Hence, for Schleiermacher, political freedom is a rational norm that can be used to evaluate the level of civilization of a state. Yet this norm cannot be taken for granted, for the success of its realization depends on historical conditions that are linked intimately to Christianity.

c. The Christian Transformation of the Idea of the State and the Idea of Equality

In spite of the difficulties of determining the formal connection between philosophical and Christian ethics, it is possible to identify fur-

---

53 Schleiermacher, *Lectures on Philosophical Ethics*, 74 (Highest Good, On the State, §104).
54 KGA I/11, 108 (26-27).
55 See Arnulf von Scheliha, "Religion und Gemeinschaft und Politik bei Schleiermacher," in Arndt, Barth, and Gräb, *Christentum—Staat—Kultur*, 317-36.
56 Schleiermacher, *Lectures on Philosophical Ethics*, 75 (Highest Good, On the State, §111).
57 To the extent this mutual recognition does not occur, the state is in fact cancelled. Law that is incompatible with the people's ethical life dissolves the state and enslaves its citizens, for a genuine state is constituted by the assumption of a voluntary submission to its authority (see Schleiermacher, *Die christliche Sitte*, 484). The institutions of political freedom are: representative assemblies, the public expression of opinion, freedom of the press, and local governments that involve the citizens in the state administration.

ther norms provided by the Christian faith, which serve to evaluate the historical condition of a state. Christianity did not, of course, invent states but rather acknowledged, adopted, and also modified them via its participation in them.[58] Indeed, the Christian religion initiated a critical and innovative transformation of the state that took place through the inner conviction and disposition of Christian people, on the one hand, and through the institutional deeds of the church, on the other. The church's "broadening actions" helped develop the rational idea of equality, which places *all* people on the same level.[59] Under the condition of inequality one "class" of people remains "outside of public life."[60] The Christian idea of equality demands participation of *all* citizens in political issues. Accordingly, the task of political life is to organize the freedom of the state as a freedom for *all* people. This combination of equality and freedom is critical of feudal society, the Indian caste system, and any kind of slavery, and restricts the use of state power; the idea of human worth (*Menschenwert*), moreover, places an absolute limit on state action.

The political task of Christian education and of preaching is, on the one hand, to reinforce the virtue of love as obedience to the government and, on the other hand, to encourage people to participate in state life.[61] In this regard the Christian faith is an essential contributor to the formation and stabilization of political virtues, and Schleiermacher regarded himself as a political preacher.[62]

The final normative implications of Christian faith concern the international community. From the perspective of reason and philosophical ethics, the nation-state is an individual that acts in the world of states. Christianity transcends the boundaries of nation-states and constitutes, as does science, the consciousness of a cosmopolitan community among all people. A moral limit is transgressed if a state violates equality of freedom or stirs up hostility between people. From this perspective, war is a cultural setback. Schleiermacher takes up Kant's idea of perpetual peace and gives it a Christian foundation. He deems

---

58 Schleiermacher, *Die christliche Sitte*, 241, 441, 481.
59 Ibid., 483-84.
60 KGA II/8, 149 (28).
61 For examples of this, see Schleiermacher's sermons: "Die Gerechtigkeit ist die unentbehrliche Grundlage des allgemeinen Wohlergehens," in *Predigten von protestantischen Gottesgelehrten*, ed. Wichmann von Meding (Darmstadt: Wissenschaftliche Buchgesellschaft, 1989), 231-56; and "Ueber das rechte Verhältnis des Christen zu seiner Obrigkeit," in *Friedrich Schleiermachers Sämmtliche Werke* II/4 (Berlin: Reimer, 1835), 1-13.
62 See Hans-Joachim Birkner, "Der politische Schleiermacher," in *Schleiermacher-Studien*, ed. Hermann Fischer (Berlin: Walter de Gruyter, 1996), 137-56.

the idea "purely Christian" because its foundation is the cosmopolitan disposition, which is spread by the broadening action of the Christian faith, by global interaction, and by the exchange of scientific knowledge. These global networks are important elements for peace between the nations and for the global civil society that gives international law a moral basis. Thus, the international community is not only to live under "the rule of a formal contract," but also under the "general peaceful interaction of all nations."[63]

In conclusion, permit me to summarize my results as follows: Schleiermacher's theory of culture is not only a doctrine of categories to understand history, it also contains moral criteria for the assessment of historical development. Moreover, it takes account of the experience of historical contingency and social complexity, which are judged in terms of the balance between community and individuality. For Schleiermacher, the Christian religion first established and subsequently broadened a culture of universal freedom based upon mutually supportive social institutions and individual virtues.

---

63 Schleiermacher, *Die christliche Sitte*, 485. For details of Schleiermacher's vision of international law, see Arnulf von Scheliha, "Die Beziehungen der Völker nach Schleiermachers Staatslehre," *Zeitschrift für neuere Theologiegeschichte/Journal for the History of Modern Theology* 12 (2005): 1-15.

Schleiermacher and Contemporary Theories of Culture

MICHAEL MOXTER

In the following, I shall stick to the proposed title, which was part of the friendly invitation to participate in this conference. It was indeed so agreeable that I did not hesitate to dive into the matter, despite the obvious fact that with a theme this broad it is easy to lose one's way. Looking for a compromise between gratefulness and honesty, one might spell out the proposed title in a narrow and strictly historical sense. Then "contemporary theories of culture" would indicate philosophical reflections on the concepts of culture held by Schleiermacher's contemporaries, such as Kant, Herder, Hegel, and Humboldt, and perhaps Jean Paul and Adam Müller as well. But none of these authors, even Schleiermacher himself, would have called their reflections on human culture "a theory of culture." Not even the term "philosophy of culture" was available, since it is an offspring of the second half of the nineteenth century, a concept that came to dominate Germany's philosophical scene only during the Weimar Republic and then again more recently in the debates of the last two decades. Moreover, there remains to this day a gap between "philosophy of culture" and "theories of culture." Leafing through the twelve volumes of the well-known German *Historisches Wörterbuch der Philosophie*, the reader will not come across the latter term. One finds articles on "Gesellschaftstheorien," "Wissenschaftstheorien," "theories of games," "theories of learning," "cultural anthropology," "cultural history," and "Kulturprotestantismus," but nothing like "theories of culture." Even though "Kulturwissenschaft" is mentioned from time to time, it does not receive an entry of its own. Turning to the English-speaking world, the situation changes entirely. Compared with its German counterpart, the article on "culture" in *The Oxford Companion to Philosophy* is very short; nonetheless, the term "theories of culture" is mentioned twice. Having gathered these statistics myself, I will not hesitate to suggest that "theories of culture" belong to our present-day discourse. If this is so, then the invitation to comment on "Schleiermacher and Contemporary Theories of Culture" gives me license to interpret Schleiermacher's ethics in light of recent philosophical theories of culture such as those launched by such authors as Ernst Cassirer, Peter Winch, Susan Langer, and Hans Blumenberg. For this reason, the following remarks are divided into three parts. Part one queries Schleiermacher's descriptive ethics from the perspective of the is/ought-distinction. The second part contextualizes Schleiermacher's ethics within its time, while the third part ventures into more systematic reflections.

1.

The aforementioned article on "culture," written by Professor Kim from Brown University, opens with the significant remark: "The word [culture] may be used in a wide sense to describe all aspects characteristic of a particular form of human life, or in a narrow sense to denote only the system of values implicit in it."[1] This quotation indicates the important task of distinguishing between normative claims and empirical statements. "Culture" might be the name for everything that makes our activities human in an emphatic sense, but it is also used as a common dominator for just about everything that human beings bring about in and through their activities. The gap between the two deepens as soon as it is related to the is/ought- or fact/value- distinction. Human "Culture" with a capital "C" represents ideas about a "good life" or a "good society," in light of which we ought to choose our conduct, whereas "culture" in the broad sense denotes everything mediated by mankind, that is to say, everything that is not given by nature as such. The former leads Schleiermacher to talk about an ultimate unity, a harmony integrating all human goods, whereas the latter is nothing but the totality of social acts, including crime as well as art, and violence as well as activities opposing it.

The problem, however, is that Schleiermacher does not seem to pay real attention to this distinction. Indeed, his ethics claims to be merely descriptive and narrative. It describes the "laws of human actions,"[2] and in this respect it opposes the Kantian classification in which ethics is organized around the ought-scheme and based on the concept of du-

---

1 Jaegwon Kim, "Culture," in *The Oxford Companion to Philosophy*, ed. Ted Honderich (Oxford: Oxford University Press, 1995), 172.
2 "Beschreibung der Geseze des menschlichen Handelns." Friedrich Schleiermacher, *Brouillon zur Ethik (1805/06)*, ed. Hans-Joachim Birkner (Hamburg: Felix Meiner Verlag, 1981), 4.

ty.³ Schleiermacher's ethics includes "every authentic human action" (*alles wahrhaft menschliche Handeln*)⁴ and interprets its totality as "the life of reason as acting upon nature." In contrast to physics, which describes finite beings according to the possibilities of their nature, ethics describes the same finite beings as they are seen from the angle of reason, i.e., according to the human capability to transform nature into something rational. Ethics becomes a description of the unity of reason and nature under reason's performative power—what I would like to call *the recognition of embodied reason*. Schleiermacher called this type of ethics "the science of history" (*die Wissenschaft der Geschichte*).⁵ This discipline characterizes the process of unification, beginning with simple forms of initial unity between reason and nature and leading continuously and progressively to expanded and more sophisticated versions of this unity. Human history, seen from this perspective, is the evolution of reason according to an ultimate end, a telos that already inheres in (human) nature, but is not actualized automatically. Only through our own activities does the latent goal become manifest. As long as it is not completely realized, it remains external, and is still remote from our present lives and behavior. But insofar as it is already an efficient power, a potency embodied in finite beings, it is internal to human activity. As a consequence, it reveals its capacity to transform society as a whole in the way it already has transformed the life of smaller communities or of the individual. "Reason" is already present and active, but not yet completely manifest. Viewed from the perspective of Schleiermacher's Christian ethics, one might say that the spirit of a new social life is among us, but not every promise has been fulfilled.⁶

The descriptive method and the concept of realized goods raise the question of whether Schleiermacher is running into a naturalistic fallacy by converting social facts into norms and—even worse—by concealing his prescriptive attitude. What is proclaimed to be nothing but "mere description" of human culture might in the end be dismantled as an attempt to establish a substantialistic concept of reason—not to mention the idealistic optimism underlying Schleiermacher's idea of human's progress through history.

---

3   "Die Formel des Sollens ist ganz unzulässig" (ibid.).
4   Friedrich Schleiermacher, *Ethik (1812/13)*, ed. Hans-Joachim Birkner (Hamburg: Felix Meiner Verlag, 1990), 6.
5   Ibid., 11.
6   Friedrich Schleiermacher, *Christliche Sittenlehre: Einleitung (Wintersemester 1826/27)*, ed. Hermann Peiter (Stuttgart: Verlag W. Kohlhammer, 1983).

Some have claimed that Schleiermacher's definition of ethics seems to blend together two concepts that should be sharply distinguished. According to this criticism, Schleiermacher begins with a conceptual confusion and ends up with a normative description of German culture in the early nineteenth century. In a word: his philosophical ethics operates in a manner that lacks philosophical justification. This means its significance for contemporary theories of culture is mainly negative: Schleiermacher's ethics seems to be an outstanding example of what can no longer be done.

If we do not want to close our examination with a farewell that would relegate the interpretation of Schleiermacher's work to the history of ideas, something has to be done. It seems to me insufficient to simply blame contemporary ethics for leading us into relativism. Even if this strategy were more than a mere suggestion, it would not provide us with convincing arguments to rebut the charge that Schleiermacher has committed the naturalistic fallacy. What we have to ask is whether there is some good reason to reintroduce Schleiermacher's theoretical account into our contemporary systematic discussions. My answer to this question is positive, but the price we have to pay for an affirmation is a critical re-reading of Schleiermacher.

The first thing to be done is to question the Is/Ought-distinction. The debate about naturalistic fallacies has shown the impossibility of identifying a real logical fallacy without already presupposing Hume's law.[7] If (and only if) we use "nature" and especially "human nature" as a plain empirical concept, it is indeed impossible to draw normative conclusions from descriptive presuppositions. But as soon as the concept of human nature is conceived as an element of human self-understanding, or, let us say, as soon as it is imbued with significance, the shift from "is" to "ought" conceals no logical faults. According to MacIntyre's interpretation, there is nothing wrong (in a logical sense of the word) to conclude that Mr. Smith ought to do what a sea-captain is obliged to do, just because the statement 'Mr Smith is a sea-captain' is in fact true. Such a descriptive proposition is internally linked with our understanding of social roles and institutions. Analogously, the fact that someone has made a promise is a good reason to believe that he ought to act accordingly. A general denial of this relationship will undermine any understanding of "making a promise." Calling a certain action "a promise" means precisely to affirm a generally justified rule of expectation, even if "keeping a promise" might sometimes run into

---

7   See, for example, Philippa Foot, "Moral Arguments," *Mind* 67 (1958): 502-13; and Alasdair MacIntyre, *After Virtue: A Study in Moral Theory* (Notre Dame: University of Notre Dame Press, 1981), 54ff.

conflict with other normative rules and therefore could be overruled by more general norms. This point was already made at the beginning of the twentieth century by the German philosopher Adolf Reinach, Husserl's first assistant, who from a phenomenological point of view developed a speech-act philosophy *avant la lettre*.[8]

I do not want to suggest that every description of human life is guided by a set of general norms. Something less sophisticated is meant, namely, that the total exclusion of substantial statements about the human condition will render the phenomena of culture unintelligible. Any description of human activities presupposes an understanding of the meaning and significance that is already part of human culture, and is therefore beyond naturalism. Only from common ground, only from the perspective of an agent, do cultural behavior and cultural forms come into sight.

The descriptive method of Schleiermacher's ethics rejects the purported complete disjunction between facts and norms. In contrast to behavior in general, a concept of human action always bridges the gap between factual statements and normative claims (however concealed). Human agency is always identified between the limits of rational nature, on the one side, and natural reason, on the other. This is why, in describing human culture, Schleiermacher invokes the concept "organism" and refers to "organic reason."[9] It is true, of course, that his key statement in this regard—"Since pure nature and pure reason are not to be found in ethics, everything we can find in it is rational nature or natural, that is, organic reason"[10]—belongs to a speculative background, to a metaphysics in which knowledge and being, ideality and reality, and unity and difference structure the relationship between physics and ethics. But I think it is both illuminating and helpful to transform this metaphysical claim into what I would call an insight into the necessary conditions for any understanding of human culture. The cash value of Schleiermacher's position is closer to a set of methodological observations concerning a cultural theory than it is to some of the metaphysical extravagancies of his time. Schleiermacher hints at the fact that any understanding of culture or human activity in general always has to refer to "existence plus meaning," to something given that

---

8   Adolf Reinach, *Zur Phänomenologie des Rechts: Die apriorischen Grundlagen des bürgerlichen Rechts* (Munich: Kösel, 1953), 35ff.
9   Michael Moxter, *Güterbegriff und Handlungstheorie: Eine Studie zur Ethik Friedrich Schleiermachers* (Kampen: Kok Pharos, 1992), 137ff.
10 "Indem nun reine Natur und reine Vernunft in der Ethik selbst nicht vorkommen, so ist alles in ihr Vorkommende vernünftige Natur und natürliche oder organische Vernunft" (Schleiermacher, *Ethik*, 13).

already bears significance, and this means: to meaningful facts. Therefore the dichotomy of existence versus reason is transformed into a gradual arrangement of human goods that are more or less rational. To draw a distinction between more advanced and less appropriate cases is the normative task of ethics. Its starting point, however, is the acknowledgement of a reason incarnate, of "something given" that is already more than just a fact.

2.

The second part of my paper focuses on contemporary theories of culture in the historical sense of referring to Schleiermacher's contemporaries. It highlights Kant's *Critique of Judgment*, which proved so important for the development of German Idealism, and explores the question of whether the third critique also sheds light on Schleiermacher's ethics.

In the second part of the *Critique of Judgment*, one of Kant's final comments on teleological ideas is concerned with the relationship between nature and culture. In contrast to the physico-theological tradition, Kant holds that the ultimate purpose of nature can no longer be described as an intention to foster human happiness. Were this the goal, nature could have attained it far more easily in the absence of human freedom, since the abuse of freedom would have thereby been excluded in principle. Enclosed in paradise without self-awareness or freedom, human beings would have enjoyed a happiness guaranteed by nature. Provided, however, that the human condition is characterized by finite freedom, our longing for happiness remains unsatisfied—at least in some, perhaps even most respects. Therefore, an end-in-itself and a purpose of nature are to be identified in a slightly different way: human freedom is the outstanding presupposition of talking about natural ends. This restriction leads to at least three different aspects of Kant's concept of "culture."

With regard to the idea of a teleology of nature, only "culture," not happiness, deserves the title of an *ultimate end* of nature. Therefore, "culture" comes into view as an abandonment of, and substitution for, happiness, since the attempt to fulfill human desires in an immediate manner always fails. Kant and Freud agree on this point. Instead of making us happy, culture enables us to use our freedom. The capacity of human beings to choose their own means in accord with their existence as ends-in-themselves is the basic and most characteristic feature of Kant's concept of culture. The ability to choose means according to one's ends establishes a cultural sphere, a realm of man-made signs and objects. This established sphere reinforces and strengthens the use of freedom. We may call works of culture "goods" in a Schleiermacherian sense. They are ethical goods even if they are not, strictly speaking, "moral goods." As products of human activity, they enable human beings to perform certain actions which otherwise would remain impossible. Institutions such as a common market, a school system, and the "community of scientific investigators" are examples of activities that mold and transform the modes of action: they depend on social activities and modify them in such a way that new possibilities of interaction come to the fore. Thus the communication of knowledge and ideas leads to insights that a sheerly solipsistic life can never afford. From the perspective of individuals, institutions are already established. They are based on intersubjective performances and they challenge us to act in a particular way. Even if we are going to change them, the ability to act in a certain way still depends on them. For this reason, culture is a mediator and a symbol for the ability of human agents to use nature according to rules. Culture in general, like language in particular, is a result of human activity—*ergon* as well as *energeia* (to use Humboldt's distinction).[11] As a consequence, culture cannot be reduced to an outer world of facts or given circumstances. Therefore it would be misleading to conceive of the social order by analogy with the natural order, i.e., as something agents must merely take into account in order to achieve their purposes. On the contrary, it is a sphere within which actions are formed and made possible.

The second aspect is a methological one: statements about culture as the "ultimate end of nature" are not empirical propositions, which can be falsified or justified according to standards of theoretical or scientific knowledge. They do not refer to objects or the way things are determined by our faculty of cognition in general. Such statements are judgments that are not deduced by logical procedures and not justified by general premises. Nor do they depend upon definitely determined concepts. No proof can be given and no standards of objectivity are at hand. Nonetheless a judgment is put forward, to which an exemplary validity is ascribed.[12] In Kant's terms, such statements are "reflecting" (*reflectierende*) judgments, whose status is not to be confused with "determining" (*bestimmende*) judgments. Even though they are subjective

---

11 Wilhelm von Humboldt, *Über die Verschiedenheit des menschlichen Sprachbaues*, vol. 3 of *Werke in fünf Bänden*, ed. Andreas Flitner and Klaus Giel (Darmstadt: Wissenschaftliche Buchgesellschaft, 1963), 418.

12 Immanuel Kant, *Critique of Judgement*, ed. Nicholas Walker, trans. James Creed Meredith (Oxford: Oxford University Press, 2007), 113.

statements, they are not based upon private reason or arbitrariness. On the contrary, they refer to common sense and obtain their significance only within communication. Far from being just private statements, reflective judgments solicit the consent of others, even though they cannot compel agreement by means of rational argumentation—or we might say, precisely because they cannot constrain others to agree.

This brings us to a third dimension, to the internal relationship between Kant's definition of aesthetic judgments and the "sphere of culture." According to Kant, culture serves as a *purgatorium* for aesthetic judgments. Education (in the broad sense of *Bildung*) plays an important role in any judgment concerning the beauty of nature (and art). Although aesthetic judgments cannot be determined by concepts, precepts, or general rules, they require examples—"examples of what has in the course of culture maintained itself longest in esteem."[13] A regression or a relapse into crudity can only be avoided by keeping those examples present as elements of a living culture. A person who does not share an aesthetic sense that has been developed within a cultural context will be unable to participate in this peculiar form of communication. Turning to the sublime, this connection between aesthetic judgment and culture becomes even more obvious: Kant explicitly states that "culture is requisite for the judgment upon the sublime in nature" and that, compared to judgments concerning beauty, "a far higher degree of culture" is presupposed.[14] It is quite clear that this remark does not declare such judgments to be nothing but cultural products introduced into society by convention. Such an interpretation would undermine everything Kant argues for in the third critique. Aesthetic judgments are, rather, grounded in the character of human consciousness and the interplay of its capacities, and thus in human nature itself. Cultural processes, however, are involved here, indeed required, since the susceptibility to ideas depends highly on communication. Common sense, according to which aesthetic judgments are made, is distinguished from social or quasi-natural facts. The former is constituted by the way we refer to it, and therefore cannot be compared to ready-made substantial forms waiting to be applied.[15] The power of judgment develops only insofar as it is practiced within a cultural community. It is continuously modified by its usage and mediated by the performance and communication of aesthetic judgments. It is thus not by accident that the third critique became the turning point at which Kant's

---

13 Ibid.
14 Ibid., 95.
15 This was, to be sure, Hannah Arendt's main idea in interpreting Kant.

transcendental philosophy obtained a more pragmatic and historical outlook. Kant discovered that there are judgments without foundation, without general validity, that nonetheless claim our consent and entitle us to expect their general affirmation. They possess a kind of necessity that is not to be confused with theoretical or practical truth claims.

I have argued elsewhere in several papers that some of Schleiermacher's main ideas about leadership in the church and its dependence on communication are linked up with genuine insights into the logic of judgments in a Kantian sense.[16] As I see it, Schleiermacher's ethics is structured by correlating different types of social communities to varying forms of social action and social communication. In the final part this paper I will briefly comment on this.

3.

In his *Brief Outline of the Study of Theology*, Schleiermacher introduces the term "Kunstlehre" in order to highlight his understanding of hermeneutics: "The full understanding of a discourse or piece of writing is a kind of artistic achievement and thus requires an 'art doctrine' or technology." The term "art" suits this definition, since "understanding" (*Verstehen*) is characterized as a process in which "we are conscious of certain general rules [I would translate: in which we are well aware of certain general rules], the application of which to particulars cannot be reduced to still other rules."[17] The crucial point is that theoretical knowledge consists in knowledge of general rules, which is not automatically applicable to new or previously unknown situations, because rules can never be totally specified with regard to particular circumstances. There are no general rules for the application of rules. There are only rules, the application of which remains a practical task requiring "competence" and acquaintance. Schleiermacher's remark clearly shows the impact of Kant's third critique on his methodology and on his understanding of theology as a positive science. Without the virtue of judg-

---

16 Michael Moxter, "Urteilskraft und Intersubjektivität: Zur Eigenart theologischer Reflexion," in *Subjektiver Geist: Reflexion und Erfahrung im Glauben*, ed. Klaus-Michael Kodalle and Anne M. Steinmeier (Würzburg: Königshausen & Neumann, 2002), 25-36; and Michael Moxter, "Kirchenleitung und Kulturaufgabe," in *Sine vi, sed verbo: Die Leitung der Kirche durch das Wort Gottes* (Leipzig: Evangelische Verlagsanstalt, 2005), 101-16.

17 Friedrich Schleiermacher, *Brief Outline of Theology as a Field of Study*, trans. Terrence Tice (Lewiston, NY: Edwin Mellen, 1990), §132; *Kurze Darstellung des theologischen Studiums* (1830), in KGA I/6, 375.

ment, without wisdom gained through experience, the governing of the church cannot succeed. Whoever wants to exercise leadership in the church, or more modestly, whoever intends to participate in the ongoing reform-processes of the church must come to grips with the present situation in light of his understanding of the essence of Christianity.[18] However, this "essence of Christianity" is never given as such, and Schleiermacher does not make a plea for essentialism. An understanding of the essence of Christianity is needed to figure out new forms of ecclesiastical life in order to shape and form a better future. Discerning the essence of Christianity is a critical task that depends greatly on both historical knowledge and general rules. It is impossible to deduce specific measures of church leadership from *a priori* knowledge, which transcends the history of Christianity. On the contrary, a creative act embedded within practice is always required. Grasping Christianity's essence is a process of clarification involving a specific reaction to Christianity's actual appearance. Or, as Troeltsch put it a century later: "Wesensbestimmung ist Wesensgestaltung."[19]

What is true for the church should be kept in mind as we return to the theme of culture in general, i.e., to other forms of human practice. To act upon nature (to organize nature according to reason) presupposes an understanding of what has already been done by former generations or other agents. Acting as a human being always implies forms of recognition, not only of other persons, but also of human traditions, institutions, and cultural forms, which is done by reconstructing their significance and meaning. The question at stake is whether the already established cultural traditions deserve to be acknowledged as "reasonable traditions," which would give us good reason to continue them in our own practices. From this it follows that organizing activities (*organisierendes Handeln*) do depend highly on symbolic representation: we have to understand, reconstruct, and sometimes simply decide to what extent cultural traditions symbolize human reason, and whether we will take the responsibility to act according to this understanding. Cultural forms make good practice possible as long as they are understood as symbolic forms. Following Ernst Cassirer, I want to call the genuine productivity of symbolic forms in shaping more advanced forms and fostering rational practices "symbolic pregnance."[20] Since understand-

---

18 Schleiermacher, *Brief Outline*, §259; *Kurze Darstellung*, 417-18.
19 Ernst Troeltsch, "Was heißt 'Wesen des Christentums'?" in *Zur religiösen Lage, Religionsphilosophie und Ethik*, vol. 2 of *Gesammelte Schriften* (Tübingen: J.C.B. Mohr, 1913), 431.
20 Ernst Cassirer, *The Philosophy of Symbolic Forms*, vol. 3, trans. Ralph Manheim (New Haven: Yale University Press, 1957), 202.

ing the meaning of historically given forms seems to be its constitutive condition, culture can only proceed by identifying "sense in sensibility." Schleiermacher's use of the term "symbolic action" (*symbolisierendes Handeln*), therefore, is his legacy for contemporary theories of culture.

Let me conclude by summarizing my view on Schleiermacher's ethics. I take it for granted that neither a substantialistic concept of reason nor a normative concept of culture lies at the heart of Schleiermacher's thinking. One might, of course, read him in this way and argue that his view of culture is inspired by a naive optimism concerning the development of human societies and is shaped by a general belief in cultural progress. One might even accuse him of believing in a Kingdom of God that is established by human activities and will be furthered by and through cultural achievements. At the end of this progress, each and every part of nature will bloom as a symbol of human reason while human beings appear as "maîtres et possesseurs de la nature."[21] But if we really stick to Schleiermacher's texts, a quite different perspective is possible: As long as finite human beings are performing finite actions, they will continue to engage in practices in a world that does not completely unite reason and nature. And the differences between social institutions, the plurality of communities, and the gap between the Supreme Good (*das höchste Gut*) and the contingencies of cultural forms and historical traditions are always relevant and at risk. Whatever is *symbolized* within culture is not yet totally *realized*. From this angle, no one can identify "reason in history" by classifying stages of cultural development, in which the *status quo* appears as the fulfillment of what our predecessors were longing for. The difference between organizing and symbolizing activities is always at work within the human condition. Because of his sense for finitude, Schleiermacher always regarded the point in history at which everything appears as sublated to be nothing but a passageway, a point of transition for further cultural activities.[22]

---

21 René Descartes, *Discourse de la Méthode*, ed. Lüder Gäbe (Hamburg: Felix Meiner Verlag, 1960), 100.
22 Many thanks to Dr. Christian Polke and Anne-Kathrin Peters, who improved various drafts of this paper.

Interpretation of Culture in Schleiermacher's *Christian Ethics*

JAMES M. BRANDT

The purpose of this paper is to contribute to thinking about sources of normativity in Schleiermacher's hermeneutics of culture by attending to his *Christian Ethics* (*Die christliche Sitte*). I will begin by showing how the *Christian Ethics* can be understood as a theology of culture. Then I will argue that the *Christian Ethics*, and thereby theology of culture, can be seen as the culmination and telos of Schleiermacher's system of doctrinal theology, fulfilling the role usually assigned to eschatology. While eschatological themes in the *Christian Faith* are qualified almost to the point of non-existence, Schleiermacher's eschatological vision comes to vivid expression in the *Christian Ethics*. The idea of "the Reign of God on earth" as the highest good provides the goal toward which all of cultural life is directed. The distinctively Christian character of the *Christian Ethics* is here most evident, since all of cultural life is taken up and put in service of the Reign of God as the absolute community of all with all. Another key eschatological theme—the "blessedness" that comes to expression in Christian worship and symbolizes "eternal life"—is identified as representing the completion of the human moral task. Thus in terms of eschatological themes, the *Christian Ethics* giveth what the Dogmatics taketh away. In different ways the eschatological themes of the Reign of God and the blessedness of eternal life provide the goal for all cultural life and thus the most significant norm for the theology of culture in the *Christian Ethics*.

Structured in a way that gives considered attention to a broad array of cultural life forms, the *Christian Ethics* has long been seen as containing a theology of culture.[1] Analysis of life in the "outer sphere," social and cultural life that occurs beyond the bounds of the Christian com-

---

[1] Wolfgang Trillhaas called the *Christian Ethics* "die erste große Kulturtheologie des Protestantismus." Cited in Hans-Joachim Birkner, *Schleiermachers christliche Sittenlehre im Zusammenhang seines philosophisch-theologischen Systems* (Berlin: Töpelmann, 1964), 113. See also my *All Things New: Reform of Church and Society in Schleiermacher's Christian Ethics* (Louisville: Westminster John Knox Press, 2001), esp. 67-78, 116-30.

munity, includes diverse areas ranging from criminal justice to economic production to art and play; this indicates the comprehensive scope of the *Christian Ethics*. In addition, even the analysis of life in the "inner sphere" of the Christian community with its focus on practices of the life of faith—ranging from discipline and church betterment to education and missions to worship—might be identified as reflection on the cultural life of the Christian community. The *Christian Ethics* revolves around reflection on diverse communities of social practice that are constitutive of cultural life.

The focus on cultural life results from Schleiermacher's understanding that the task of ethics is to identify the structures, dynamics, and goals of human historical life.[2] In his view the moral task is the appropriation of nature by reason or spirit; progress in the fulfillment of this task is ongoing and never-ending in human history. While Schleiermacher acknowledges that an ethics of virtue, ethics of duty, and ethics of the highest good would all need to be integrated to form a comprehensive ethical system, in both his philosophical ethics and *Christian Ethics* he shows a clear preference for an ethics of the highest good.[3] This is so because an ethics of the good considers the moral task of humanity as a whole and the forms of communal life in which the task is carried out, and it also attends to the uniqueness of individuals and the distinctive place each has in the overall moral task in a way that an ethics of duty or virtue cannot.

An ethics of the good is teleological in character. It identifies the goal of the moral task and the social and cultural arenas in which the moral task is pursued. The philosophical ethics, which provides a speculative philosophy of culture, identifies four distinct spheres of cultural life: the state, encompassing economic and political life; "free sociality" (*freie Geselligkeit*), including social relationships and hospitality; knowledge, including the academy and schools; and the church, the great social form in the realm of art and religion.[4] Thus for Schleiermacher ethics, both in its philosophical form and even in its Christian form, is a descriptive enterprise. Working at a general, speculative level, philosophical ethics names the moral goal and describes the human

---

2   See Friedrich Schleiermacher, *Entwürfe zu einem System der Sittenlehre*, vol. 2 of *Schleiermachers Werke: Auswahl in vier Bänden*, ed. Otto Braun and Johannes Bauer, 2nd ed. (Leipzig: Meiner, 1927).

3   See Friedrich Schleiermacher, *Grundlinien einer Kritik der bisherigen Sittenlehre*, vol. III/1 of *Sämtliche Werke* (Berlin: G. Reimer, 1846), 261ff.

4   Schleiermacher, *Entwürfe*, 252, 365-67, 549-56; and Birkner, *Schleiermachers christliche Sittenlehre*, 34-36.

actions and communities—the goods of human life—that, if integrated and brought to perfection, would constitute the highest good.

Christian ethics, which provides an empirical theology of culture, is similarly teleological and descriptive. Schleiermacher does allow that Christian ethics can take on an imperative mode when Christian individuals or communities fail to live in accord with the rules for the Christian life, but these rules are understood to be analogous to scientific rules that describe how processes unfold.[5] Only secondarily are rules considered imperatives to be followed. Christian ethics is descriptive because it describes what is already given: faith and the life that flows from it. Methodologically faith is the given since theology does not seek to prove it, but presumes its existence and reflects on it. Theologically faith is given because it is a gift, a new creation that no human effort can produce.

Schleiermacher's Christian Ethics derives its structure from the different determinations of Christian self-consciousness or piety that are possible. Christian piety is grounded in redemption given by Christ; it is participation in the Redeemer's perfect communion with God mediated by the church; it is a sense of blessedness, an "emerging blessedness";[6] it is dominion of Christian spirit over flesh. When negation of communion with God comes into consciousness, it is felt as displeasure and this feeling becomes an impulse to restoring action. When a drawing near to absolute blessedness—a heightening of communion with God—comes into consciousness, it is felt as pleasure and is the basis of broadening action. These two forms of action Schleiermacher calls efficacious actions because each seeks to bring about a change in God-consciousness, its restoration or expansion. Between moments of pleasure and lack of pleasure there must also be a moment of relative blessedness that includes within itself an impulse to action, but not an action that produces change. There is a sense of rest that accompanies this blessedness. This action, which produces no change, Schleiermacher calls presentational action, action that sets forth or manifests what is inner in an outward way (CS, 38-55).

---

5   Friedrich Schleiermacher, *Die christliche Sitte nach den Grundsätzen der evangelischen Kirche im Zusammenhange dargestellt*, vol. I/12 of *Sämtliche Werke*, ed. Ludwig Jonas (Berlin: G. Reimer, 1843), 31-34. Henceforth cited parenthetically in text as CS. All translations of this work are my own.

6   I am indebted for this rendering of "werdender Seligkeit" to Jacqueline Mariña and Christine Helmer, the translators of Eilert Herms' "Schleiermacher's *Christian Ethics*," in *The Cambridge Companion to Friedrich Schleiermacher*, ed. Jacqueline Mariña (Cambridge: Cambridge University Press, 2005), 209-28.

Restoring actions in the Christian community include discipline and church betterment, broadening actions include education and missions, and presentational action is worship in broad and narrower senses. Schleiermacher fills out the structure of the *Christian Ethics* by identifying corresponding forms of action in the outer or civil realm. Restoring action includes criminal justice and warfare; broadening action includes education and economic development; and presentational action includes all forms of sociality, art and play. The way these areas of cultural life are divided separates elements that belong together and brings together odd bedfellows. Nonetheless, the whole range of cultural life (with the exception of knowledge and the academy) receives considered attention in the *Christian Ethics*. The question addressed in terms of the outer sphere is how Christian conviction is to be expressed, how the Christian is to participate in the various forms of social life. Taken together then, this reflection on Christian involvement in the whole range of human social activity constitutes a comprehensive theology of culture.

Important to the *Christian Ethics* and the theology of culture within it is its striking recognition of the historically conditioned character of theology itself. One of Schleiermacher's most significant contributions to theological self-understanding is the way he acknowledges its historical relativity. There is no final or fixed way to embody or to assess Christian engagement with cultural life, for any practices or claims about those practices must be appropriate to a particular historical and ecclesial location. Schleiermacher claims that Christian teaching "includes only what is valid in the church" at a particular time; universal Christian teaching that is valid for all times and places is impossible (CS, 8-9). This means that ongoing engagement with and reflection on cultural life in all its diversity is a necessary moment in the work of Christian ethics.[7]

The initial question I want to pose about the *Christian Ethics* as theology of culture has to do with its place in Schleiermacher's system of doctrinal theology (or dogmatics in the broad sense) as a whole. Given the profoundly practical and this-worldly character of Schleiermacher's theology, it makes sense that ethics would be its culminating moment. While eschatological claims are qualified to such an extent that they

---

[7] In his introduction to the reprint edition of CS, Wolfgang Erich Müller notes that the descriptive approach corresponds to the need to reflect on the current cultural situation. A biblical ethics or an imperative ethics would not meet this requirement. Friedrich Schleiermacher, *Die christliche Sitte nach den Grundsätzen der evangelischen Kirche im Zusammenhange dargestellt*, Theologische Studien-Texte 7.1 (Waltrop: Spenner, 1999), xviii.

bear minimal theological weight in Schleiermacher's dogmatic system (his *Glaubenslehre*), his *Christian Ethics*' appropriation of eschatological themes provides the completion and culmination of doctrinal theology.

Schleiermacher's discussion of eschatological themes in the *Glaubenslehre* is part of the analysis of the church. He first considers the origin and maintenance of the church; then the perfection or consummation (*Vollendung*) of the church completes the ecclesiological material. Reflection on "the continuation of personal existence" and "the perfection of the church" are the centerpieces of the *Glaubenslehre*'s eschatological discussion.[8]

Significant affirmations of traditional eschatological claims are present in the *Glaubenslehre*'s analysis.[9] The claims for the church's perfection and the continuation of personal existence after death are grounded in doctrinal loci of utmost importance: doctrines of the Holy Spirit and of Christ. There is no question of letting them go altogether. Schleiermacher's revisionism is about re-interpretation; it remains engaged with the tradition and its theological claims seeking to identify the current significance they have for life in the church.

In the realm of distinctively Christian God-consciousness "it may well be claimed that belief in the continuation of personal existence is bound together with our faith in the Redeemer" (CG §158.2). Schleiermacher's reflection on the claim that Christ's survival grounds survival for the rest of humanity is characteristic of the way he engages eschatological matters. Here, there is clear affirmation of traditional understanding of Jesus' continued existence grounding ours because of Jesus' sayings reported in the New Testament. Alongside this moment of affirmation there is equally clear qualification regarding this claim: it is framed conditionally (e.g., "Thus, nothing remains but to expect the continued existence of the whole human race *if* we take the Redeemer's sayings to be perfectly true as his disciples undeniably did" [CG §158.2, emphasis added].) and, importantly, no notion of individual life after death is necessary to Schleiermacher's own position. A coherent version of Christian faith could persist nicely without it. However, this

---

8   Friedrich Schleiermacher, *Der christliche Glaube nach den Grundsätzen der evangelischen Kirche im Zusammenhange dargestellt* (1830/31), in KGA I/13. Henceforth cited parenthetically in text as CG. Translations are my own. See §§113-63 for the analysis of the church and §§157-63 for "The Perfection of the Church."

9   For considerations of Schleiermacher's eschatology see Eilert Herms, "Schleiermachers Eschatologie," *Theologische Zeitschrift* 46 (1990): 97-123; Martin Weeber, *Schleiermachers Eschatologie: Eine Untersuchung zum theologischen Spätwerk* (Gütersloh: Christian Kaiser, 2000); and Bernd Oberdorfer, "Schleiermacher on Eschatology and Resurrection," in *Resurrection: Theological and Scientific Assessments*, ed. Ted Peters et al. (Grand Rapids: Eerdmans, 2002), 165-82.

highly qualified traditional claim is not thrown to the theological scrapheap, for that would alter the historic character of Christianity too drastically. Finally, in addition to the moments of affirmation and qualification there is a moment of transformation in thinking about life after death. Notions of reprobation or damnation are called into question, and Schleiermacher asserts that a milder, universal view "traces of which are also to be found in scripture, that there will one day be a universal restoration of all human souls resulting from the power of redemption" (CG §163, Postscript) should be given standing along with traditional views.

Thus the *Glaubenslehre*'s analysis of the continuation of individual human existence is complex. In relation to traditional claims it includes moments of affirmation, qualification, and transformation. Schleiermacher positions himself in relation to the tradition in this multifaceted way. Clearly, individual life beyond the grave is not the unqualified culmination or telos of his theological system.

There is less tension in the *Glaubenslehre*'s consideration of the church's perfection; the qualifications are less sharply drawn. The idea of the church's perfection stands much nearer to the heart of the *Glaubenslehre*'s eschatological thinking. Knowing that the Spirit animates the church is an indispensible aspect of Christian consciousness. The church lives, grows, and expands in the way that other human societies do, for even the work of the Spirit is "subject to the laws of temporal life" (CG §157.1). Since this growth and expansion is observable, the church's perfection can be imagined, but it cannot be realized under the conditions of temporal life, for the opposition between church and world cannot be overcome in a final way as long as human procreation continues.

Thus together with this strong affirmation of the notion of the church's perfection there is an equally strong qualification. In a strict sense there can be no doctrine of the church's perfection "since our Christian consciousness can have absolutely nothing to say about this state that is completely unknown to us" (CG §157.2). The positive meaning that perfection does have is that it is "always the object of our prayer" (CG §157.2). It represents "unbroken fellowship of human nature with Christ," a hope to which Christian consciousness looks and a hope that animates Christian activity. Along with this affirmation comes the qualification that this state is conceivable "under conditions completely unknown to us and only vaguely imaginable" (CG §157.2). In this way the analysis of the church's perfection in §157 confirms its opening claim: "the representation of [the church's] perfected state is directly useful only as a pattern to which we are to draw near" (CG

§157). The real significance of the most important eschatological theme in the *Glaubenslehre*, the perfection of the church, lies in ethics. It provides a vision that motivates Christian action.

Ethics' role as the culmination of the doctrinal system is evident as it develops an aspect of piety that is crucial to the distinctiveness of Christianity as presented in the *Glaubenslehre*: its teleological character. As teleological "the pious disposition's basic type has a predominant intention toward the moral task. . . . In Christianity all pain and all joy are pious only in so far as they are intended for activity in the Reign of God" (CG §§9.1-9.2). "In light of the teleological character of Christianity we cannot imagine any completely developed pious moment that does not pass over into activity or that does not contribute to activities already in progress in a definite way and combine with them" (CG §56.2, Postscript). Christian piety culminates in activity. This supports our contention that ethics provides a culmination for dogmatics. The system of doctrinal theology culminates in ethics as its crowning moment, just as Christian piety culminates in activity.

In the *Christian Ethics* the eschatological theme of the "Reign of God" names the highest good toward which all Christian action aims. In one sense, the Reign of God on earth is nothing more than a way to name Christian ethics. "[T]he Reign of God on earth is nothing other than the way of being Christian that must always come to be recognized through actions. The presentation of the idea of the Reign of God on earth is therefore nothing but the presentation of the way for Christians to live and act, and that is Christian ethics. . . ." (CS, 13). The Reign of God is established by the action of Christ and all Christian action is to be a continuation of Christ's action. So in another sense, the Reign of God names the goal of all Christian action. Broadening action in the inner sphere seeks to expand the sway of the Christian disposition (formation of the capacities for knowing and willing) and the formation of talent for the sake of disposition. This expansion is to occur both within individual persons and to persons who are not yet within the Christian communion. The endpoint of this process is the "perfection of the whole of the human race in Christ" (CS, 330).

For Schleiermacher the highest good must encompass the integration and perfection of all goods of human life. The goal then of human historical life from the perspective of Christian ethics is cultural life in all its manifestations, appropriated and brought together to be in service of the Reign of God—that is, the perfection of the Christian disposition in all persons—and, secondarily, the perfection of all nature and talent formation. Thus Schleiermacher's *Christian Ethics* is at once distinctively Christian and includes within itself an ethics based in the doctrine of creation that affirms all the "natural" goods of cultural life.

Schleiermacher's reflection on the relationship between the Christian and the state is particularly illuminating of his understanding of the Reign of God as the highest good. Note that the state in Schleiermacher's view is the custodian of the general human process of reason's appropriation of nature—i.e., of broadening in the outer sphere. The question is whether "religious ethics [is] only to sanction what can already be demonstrated to be natural or is religious ethics also to transform it?" (CS, 459) Schleiermacher holds that Christian ethics and philosophical ethics are identical as regards content and different as regards form. This will provide the answer to the question.

Schleiermacher appeals to Romans 13:5, "where Paul says it is necessary to subject oneself to the authorities, not only for the sake of avoiding punishment, but also the sake of conscience" (CS, 460). In Schleiermacher's view the conscience of an individual is to be subject to the conscience of the community to which the individual belongs. Civil conscience, then, might well subject itself to the state. But religious conscience knows that the divine will is not defined by an individual people, but by the relationship of "an individual people to the universal relationship among all persons" (CS, 461).

"The Christian can only intend the whole sphere of the processes of nature and talent formation for the broadening of the Reign of God according to the Christian idea" (CS, 461). The focus of Christian broadening is the expansion of the Christian disposition and the expansion of talent and nature formation for the sake of that disposition. In terms of nature and talent formation (general human expansion of the dominion of reason over nature) the Christian and the citizen intend the same thing. However while the citizen may will this as an end in itself, the Christian "intends all of civil virtue for the sake of [the] broadening of the Reign of God" (CS, 462). Thus we have identity of content and difference in form. That is, the Christian and the citizen participate in identical moral processes, but toward a different end.

All the goods of human cultural life are included and taken up in the Christian vision of the highest good, the Reign of God on earth. The Christian vision of the highest good affirms all natural goods found in human culture. All these goods are taken up and intended for the expansion of the Reign of God. In this sense the Christian does everything for the glory of God.

As Eilert Herms points out, Schleiermacher's specification of the Reign of God being "on earth" indicates that it has to do with "morality in life that is not yet perfected."[10] The perfection of the Reign of God cannot be attained in this world; while growth is possible, the perfected Reign remains an ever-beckoning but unattainable ideal. However, the notion of "eternal life" represents perfect blessedness, the complete dominion of spirit over flesh. "This will be a state that can only be symbolized in worship in an exemplary way: the eternal presentation of the dominion of spirit over flesh."[11]

The concept of "eternal life" is not developed to the extent that the Reign of God is. However, Schleiermacher says that the completion of purifying and broadening actions is what "underlies the expression 'eternal life'" (CS, 508). Then "no further action whatsoever can be conceived except one that has no function in relation to a result . . . only the sign and expression of the completed process" (CS, 508). This is presentational action—the pure outward expression of blessedness. Thus we can say that presentational action as expression of emerging blessedness is analogous to and symbolizes the perfected blessedness of eternal life.

While the Reign of God represents the goal toward which Christian life aspires, eternal life represents the ground of that life and activity. Christian consciousness of emerging blessedness "is the true and basic feeling for a Christian, a feeling that there is some power of spirit over flesh" (CS, 516). This feeling is presupposed by restoring action and broadening action, receives an increase by means of restoring and broadening action, and finds expression in presentational action. Schleiermacher says that "presentational action rests upon community and produces community." Community and presentational action are "equally original" (CS, 510). Community and presentational action stand at the basis of Christian faith. Or Schleiermacher can say that "in the Christian realm community rests purely in the fact that the divine Spirit is one and the same in all and for all and in the fact that all individuals are only its instruments" (CS, 516). But there is no resting here, for this includes a consciousness of the fact that all other members of the community are also instruments of the Spirit. And this comes about only as a person takes the self-consciousness of others into his or her own, which, in turn, requires that the self-consciousness of others come into appearance. For "this inner necessity for the continual joining of self-consciousness separated by personal existence is the essence of brotherly love and conditions both presentational action and the continuity

---

10 Eilert Herms, "Reich Gottes und menschliches Handeln," in *Friedrich Schleiermacher 1768-1834: Theologe—Philosoph—Pädagoge*, ed. Dietz Lange (Göttingen: Vandenhoeck & Ruprecht, 1985), 187.
11 Ibid.

of community" (CS, 518). Presentational action in the inner sphere, which for Schleiermacher is worship (in broad and narrower senses), represents a real but emerging blessedness. From this perspective Christian worship is the highest form of cultural expression.[12] The culminating role of presentational action is evident in the way that the brief, compact introduction to presentational action in the inner sphere shows the inner connection among the theological convictions at the heart of Schleiermacher's system. We have already identified the inner connections among community, presentational action, and blessedness. In addition, the "absolute eminence" (*absolutes Erhabensein*) of Christ (CS, 518), the presence of the divine Spirit in all community members, and the love that binds all community members together are woven together around the themes of blessedness. Not only these themes, but also the equality of all Christians, the community of all persons in Christ to be realized in time—a signal difference (for Schleiermacher) between Roman Catholic and Protestant ecclesiology and worship—and the equality between men and women in the Christian community are all intimately linked together at the heart of his understanding of Christian faith: blessedness made manifest through presentational action that at the same time constitutes community.

Most important for our consideration is the other eschatological theme included here—the ultimately universal character of the Christian fellowship of love. Noting that presentational action cannot be separated from the other forms of action, if broadening and presentational actions are considered together, love must be seen to include all persons.

> No one can be conscious of the divine Spirit except insofar as one is conscious at the same time that the whole human race belongs to this Spirit; the distinction among individuals is only temporal, that is to say that some already have the πνεῦμα ἅγιον, others do not yet have it, and Christian brotherly love is entirely universal, some are included as already partaking of the divine Spirit and others included to whom the Spirit is to be communicated. (CS, 514)

Christian worship, then, is grounded in a blessedness that partakes of eternal life, extends love to all persons, and anticipates the inclusion of

---

12 It is worth noting that in his essay, "On the Concept of the Highest Good," Schleiermacher allows that any of the four basic forms of human community—state, academy, "free sociality," or church—could develop a vision of the highest good that would include all the others within it and would represent the whole. Thus we may say that "Christian worship represents the highest form of cultural expression" from one point of view. See "Über den Begriff des höchsten Gutes," in vol. III/2 of *Sämtliche Werke*, ed. Ludwig Jonas (Berlin: G. Reimer, 1843), 466.

all persons in the perfection of Christ. In that way worship has a deeply eschatological sense as a "foretaste of the feast to come" and as the pinnacle of cultural life—from the Christian perspective. At the same time, Christian worship makes use of the means of artistic expression developed by the κοινὸς λόγος—speech, music, drama, and the plastic arts. Once again Christianity takes up the goods of human life and appropriates them for it own purposes.

Eschatological themes so muted in the *Glaubenslehre* have tremendous ethical purchase in the *Christian Ethics*. Eschatological themes provide the culmination and telos to Schleiermacher's theological system, not as hope for fulfillment beyond this world but as they animate the ethical vision that is the system's climax. Eschatological themes of the Reign of God and eternal life are the norms that function as ground and goal for the theology of culture in the *Christian Ethics*. Christian ethical action is grounded in the sense of blessedness/eternal life that constitutes Christian piety. Similarly presentational action, which is the outward manifestation of that blessedness in community, represents the pinnacle of human cultural life. And finally, the Reign of God as the highest good is the goal toward which all Christian action, indeed all of human historical action, aims. Eschatological themes are rendered this-worldly and become the ground and goal for Schleiermacher's theology of culture.

Schleiermacher's Ethics

Humanistic Premise and Ecological Promise

WILLIAM SCHWEIKER

1.

The last decades have witnessed scholarly engagements with Friedrich Schleiermacher's ethical thought, its relation to his theology, and possible contributions to current philosophical and theological ethics. The basic contours of his ethics are well-known: it is related to physics as "real aspects" of knowledge and, additionally, both ethics and physics are related to dialectics, the art of thinking. Further, his philosophical ethics explores the relation of reason and nature and systematically orders three great themes: the doctrines of the good, duty, and virtue. The highest good is constituted by the state, free sociality, academy, and church as forms of embodied reason. Ethics is a hermeneutics of the highest good embodied in objective social realities. Thanks to this scholarship we have a better grasp of the development of Schleiermacher's thought and the central importance of ethics in it.

Recent scholarship has then complicated earlier assessments of Schleiermacher's corpus that were often marked by rancor and misunderstanding. Of course, because of the entrenched character of theological opinion, it is doubtful that the assessment of his work held by some theologians will change. In a time when post-liberal thinkers insist on the priority of the Christian story in theological thinking, Schleiermacher's concern for consciousness and the coordination of philosophical and Christian ethics seems wrongheaded and dated. That is true even though he insisted that "narration" was the proper style for a descriptive ethics. In an age when the voices of peoples around the world seek expression in their own terms, he will seem too modern, Western, and Christian. This is the case even though Schleiermacher considered the distinctiveness, the individuality, of persons and communities to be central to ethics and disavowed the possibility of a universal synthesis in ethics. Further, his willingness to accept and then to think beyond the Kantian critiques of reason is roundly rejected by those who attack things modern. Here too the criticism endures despite Schleiermacher's early and persistent criticism of an overly rationalistic account of faith. Finally, in a time when the battle-lines in moral theory are drawn between utilitarianism, deontology, and virtue theory, Schleiermacher's attempt to mediate theories will seem foolish, at best, or impossible, at worst.

One must be honest about the prospects of widespread appreciation of Schleiermacher's ethics even if we also witness renewed interest in his corpus. Rather than entering into the historical and exegetical task of sorting out his complex moral vision, its relation to his whole corpus, or responding to his critics, I want here to explore his ethics' resonance with, and possible contribution to, current reflection. Let me explain the specific focus of the reflections that follow.

2.

Contemporary moral problems and challenges are endless. Not surprisingly, scholars have found a number of points of contact between current thought and Schleiermacher's ethics.

1. Schleiermacher's concern for *Bildung* resonates with work in virtue theory. It also continues a tradition of *paidiea* that could be explored in terms of the interest in spiritual practices and the legacy of humanism.

2. His criticism of Kantian rationalism and a focus on the concept of the good dovetails with current conceptions of human flourishing and a widened conception of ethics beyond ideas about duty and right.

3. Scholars have noted that he rejects the typical "modern" pattern of thought that begins with subjectivity and self-identity and then explores relations to encompassing environments. His conception of free sociality and various forms of human community (state, church, academy) relates to current interest in community and new ideas about the nature of moral subjectivity in a pluralistic world.

4. Schleiermacher's broad definition of ethics as a theory of culture and history relates well to contemporary attempts to articulate the moral space, worldview, or moral atmosphere of a

society. And because of his distinction and yet relation between philosophical and Christian ethics, Schleiermacher's thought should also be drawn into the current debate about "secularism."

Despite the numerous and entrenched criticisms, Schleiermacher continues to hold resources for addressing pressing questions of our time.

One of those questions is the focus of the present inquiry. There is great debate in ethics about the possibility and desirability of linking a humanistic premise with an ecological outlook. By humanistic premise I mean a focus in ethics inseparable from the affirmation of the place and distinctive worth of human action in the formation of social worlds and also the specific task of rightly cultivating good character and just communities. That premise, some now argue, too easily devolves into an anthropocentric outlook that negates the possibility of a robust ecological ethics for the protection and flourishing of non-human life. How to relate a humanistic premise with ecological promise in ethics? That is the question at the root of these reflections. In order to show Schleiermacher's contribution to its resolution, one must attend to the zone between physics and ethics, in his sense of the terms. Exploring that zone invites historical and exegetical research already begun by some scholars—especially about Schleiermacher's connection to Heinrich Steffens, his colleague at Halle—on the philosophy of nature. I hope that work continues, of course. Yet my questions are systematic and constructive ones.

In this essay I want to attend to the zone between physics and ethics because I believe that a pressing issue of our day—maybe *the* pressing issue of our day—are the manifold endangerments to human, non-human, and planetary life. These endangerments arise in large part because of the extension of human power to enfold worldly-existence into its kingdom, what we can call "the overhumanization of the world."[1] It might seem, then, that Schleiermacher's ethics is the problem and not the answer. His insistence that the highest good is described as the product of reason turning nature into its organ seems to betray a profoundly "technological" outlook that endangers environments necessary to sustain present and future life. Those who understand Schleiermacher's ethics in this way must reject his focus on human action, and hence his humanistic commitments about the place of "culture" or *Bildung* in a conception of the good. Yet precisely because of the profound entanglement of human action and natural systems, it is

---

1   See David E. Klemm and William Schweiker, *Religion and the Human Future: An Essay on Theological Humanism* (Oxford: Wiley-Blackwell, 2008).

not at all clear that we can simply reject a humanistic premise in current moral and political thinking. Psychic, social, and natural sciences are more deeply intertwined than some theorists like to hold, and this fact, I suggest, was grasped by Schleiermacher in ways that are of use to current ethics. My task in what follows is to sustain that claim by exploring interlocking "logics" in his moral theory.

In adopting this strategy of reading Schleiermacher's ethics we must acknowledge the deficiencies in his thought with respect to contemporary reflection on the relation of science and ethics. His account of life is simply not complex enough to address the advances in modern biology and the life sciences. What is more, his contention that there is an essential connection between reason and nature could imply a claim about the fundamental rationality, perhaps design, of the natural world difficult to square with current evolutionary thought. This is not to foreclose the discussion or to assume that science wins the day, as it were. A full engagement with Schleiermacher's ethics that seeks points of resonance with contemporary concerns would have to engage developments in science which have transpired well after his time and also clarify the relations between disciplines of thought. His capacity to link a humanistic focus with a naturalistic conception of the highest good as the organization of life is fecund for contemporary theological and philosophical ethics.[2]

Again, I aim to demonstrate that Schleiermacher's ethics holds resources for developing a genuinely humanistic and yet also deeply ecologically moral outlook by uncovering two "logics" in the ethics. In other words, I want to engage Schleiermacher at a systematic and theoretical level in order to disclose the possible contribution to a range of more practical issues about genetics and ecological ethics. Addressing those practical questions is beyond the scope of this essay. Let me turn next, then, to his thought, and, with that in hand, attempt constructive suggestions within the zone between "science" and "ethics."

3.

In his *Brouillon zur Ethik* (1805/1806) and elsewhere too, Schleiermacher argues that ethics is a description of the laws of human action. Further, the guiding intuition is about personal existence (*Persönlichkeit*) because, as he says, one "must present what the human spirit produces

---

2   See William Schweiker, "Consciousness and the Good: Schleiermacher and Contemporary Theological Ethics," *Theology Today* 56, no. 2 (1999): 180-96.

when it is ensouled in this manner by the higher faculty [of reason]." More generally, the basic intuition is that "reason should be soul." Lastly, the "whole of organized life is to be presented as the highest good."[3] These claims are neatly summarized in the *Ethics 1812/1813: Introduction and Doctrine of Goods*. Schleiermacher writes:

> Reason is to be found in nature, and ethics does not depict any action in which it arose originally. Ethics can only depict the possibility of penetrating and forming nature to an ever-increasing degree, of spreading as broadly as possible the unification of reason and nature, taking as its starting-point the human organism, which is part of general nature in which, however, a unification with reason is already given.[4]

As John Wallhausser has summarized, "Schleiermacher's own [ethics is] in company with Plato, is the ethics of *Bildung*... Reason (spirit) enters into and forms nature, making nature into something new through which humanity orders and reveals itself... Nature is transformed into 'world,' and moral 'world' is itself a new mode of human consciousness."[5] Several points need to be examined. First, "reason is found in nature" and yet ethics can only depict "the possibility of penetrating and forming nature to an ever-increasing degree." This places a metaphysical claim at the core of the ethics: nature is always and already rational and the law of human action must therefore be to increase the "ensoulment" of reason in human life and thus the moral world. Nature is not pre-rational or non-rational. The moral task of human beings is the further "ensoulment" of reason by making reason—rather than some other force—the formative principle of nature, their own and by extension non-human nature as well. The moral task is not about constraining or coercing the natural realm but the ordering of nature by its ownmost principle. The basic moral intuition and the metaphysical claim it entails are profoundly at odds with the methodological reduction of evolutionary biology, because natural selection is not directed or "rational" in his sense of the term. Yet in terms of the ethics, the construal of the moral task places it squarely within the kind of naturalism usually associated with the teleological outlooks of Plato and Aristotle. The moral task is to order and direct capacities to their fulfillment rather than to constrain or override appetites by a higher, non-natural,

---

3 Friedrich Schleiermacher, *Brouillon zur Ethik/Notes on Ethics (1805/1806)* and *Notes on the Theory of Virtue (1804-1805)*, trans. John Wallhausser and Terrence N. Tice (Lewiston, NY: Edwin Mellen Press, 2003), 36, 38, 40.
4 Friedrich Schleiermacher, *Lectures on Philosophical Ethics*, ed. Robert B. Louden (Cambridge: Cambridge University Press, 2002), §39.
5 John Wallhausser, "Schleiermacher's Critique of Ethical Reason: Towards a Systematic Ethics," *Journal of Religious Ethics* 17, no. 2 (1989): 31.

duty or command of God. This is why Schleiermacher rejects purely empirical and purely formal ethics: empirical positions are trapped in the contingent and have not grasped—intuited—the "rationality" of nature and the law of action; a formal ethics, such as Kant's, falsely disrupts the relation of ideal and the real, reason and nature. Given the intuition of the ethics that "reason should be soul," neither of those theories is right.

Second, life (*Leben*) is to be organized, and life rightly organized is the *summum bonum*. This suggests a Platonic aspect in the ethics. Whereas Plato articulates the goods of the polis on analogy to the soul, Schleiermacher derives goods from the work of reason in nature. More profoundly, recalling that Plato's concern was a substantive conception of *justice*, one might ask if there is an analogue in Schleiermacher's ethic. That conception would be the normative formulation of the basic intuition of the ethics. It would clarify why reason *should* be soul. I will return to this point at the end of this paper; it is crucial for retaining a humanistic premise and the ecological promise of ethics. It is enough here to note that while it is not a kind of *Lebensphilosophie* or vitalism, and knowing that both Nietzsche and Schopenhauer scorned the theologian, there is still reason for a second look at Schleiermacher's conception of life and its organization.[6]

The distinction between life and the organization of life is critical. Scheiermacher, unlike Nietzsche or later vitalists, is not claiming that life *qua* life is the good. The good, for Schleiermacher, is not the release of power in self-overcoming through the relentless increase of power, as it is for Nietzsche, nor is the moral good the cessation, no matter how fleeting, of the fruitless and tireless drama of suffering, as Schopenhauer, and later Albert Schweitzer, would have it. Life, for Schleiermacher, is a dynamic oscillation of abiding-in-self and passing-beyond-self in relation to some environment. "Life" for him is the medium and dynamic of interaction between an entity and its environments. I note, again, that this is hardly as complex an account of "life" as found in standard evolutionary biology since we have nothing about reproduction, selection, equilibria, and so on.

Whatever the science, philosophically the point, as some note, is that Schleiermacher rejected the typically modern form of thought that begins with the identity of the self with itself and then asks about interactions and community with others.[7] Entity and environment are co-

---

6 See Brent W. Sockness, "The Forgotten Moralist: Friedrich Schleiermacher and the Science of Spirit," *Harvard Theological Review* 96, no. 3 (2003): 317-48.

7 See Michael Welker, "We Live Deeper than We Think: The Genius of Schleiermacher's Earliest Ethics," *Theology Today* 56, no. 2 (1999): 169-79.

constitutive and this means, already in very early writings like the comments on Aristotle's account of friendship, that there will be moral shifts given the specific relation between individual and environment. As he puts this in the *Notes*, "[t]o exhibit this relation of individual function and the whole correctly, we must proceed from the vision of life: self-contained existence and community with the whole; the more developed such existence is, the more distinctly self-contained it is and the freer the community."[8] This means that "original life," so called in the *Dialectic*, is confused, and the project for any entity is to individuate itself in relation to an undifferentiated environment. There can be, as he puts it in the *Notes*, an organic bonding and inorganic deposits, and in higher, human forms these become perception and production. The human moral project centers on self-formation in community with others and the forms that constitute the highest good. This is because human action and the consequences of human action are always intertwined with the actions of others. Further, changes in the agent (e.g., through age) and the environing community (e.g., from church to state) will alter the morality of an action. The point is that the increase of self-contained life, individuality, is interdependent with the development of freer community. The importance of this insight for ecological and humanist thought has not yet been exploited.

Finally, the organization of life and thus the formation of a moral world interrelating academy, state, church, and free sociality is presented as the highest good. This means a principled rejection of hedonism, whether personal or utilitarian, since the highest good entails the rational organization of life. Morality is the formative process, the *Bildung*, of human and historical development. The rational organization of life links Schleiermacher's focus on the ethical subject to his equal concern for cultural goods and institutions. The doctrines of duty and virtue thus ensure that the highest good is not simply the maximization of life *qua* life, but, rather, the rational organization of life. This point could take us, if space allowed, into his discussions of state, free association, the academy, and also the church. Theologically, we would explore the church and also the Kingdom of God. Those topics, together with his schematics of organ-forming and organ-using with respect to the individual and community, are beyond the scope of this inquiry.

---

8   Schleiermacher, *Brouillon zur Ethik*, 41.

4.

For my purposes there are conclusions to be drawn from the points just noted about Schleiermacher's moral theory. The intuition that founds the ethics—the intuition that reason should be soul—is a grasp of the metaphysical relation of reason and nature but as the law of human action. Schleiermacher's metaphysical claim is not postulated, as with Kant, on the free legislative power of pure practical reason. The moral intuition apprehends that there is no ultimate gap between reason and nature even if this intuition also entails the imperative to further permeate nature with reason, to realize the good by becoming more of what is ultimately the case. Yet Schleiermacher is not arguing that the "laws" of human action can be read off a supposed natural teleology, as some forms of traditional natural law ethics and also hedonistic ethics argue. Since reason "should" be soul, the laws of action—or at least the most basic imperative—are not the workings of natural processes *simpliciter*. The moral intuition secures the place of "duty" within his ethics, but, importantly, secures it within the wider conception of the highest good. Whether or not a case can be made for a metaphysical ethics of this or any other sort is of course hotly debated in our avowedly post-metaphysical age. I cannot enter that debate here. Yet with respect to the global endangerments to life and the demand of human responsibility for the integrity of life, reflection on the zone between physics and ethics seems unavoidable. Schleiermacher's ethics anticipates this question.

Ironically it is this primary intuition and the metaphysical assumption and moral demand it carries that might signal the most profound problem with Schleiermacher's ethics in postmodern and global times. That is true no matter what updating is needed in his account of life and natural science. At issue, I submit, is the fact that two different "logics" intersect in this ethics, as do the problems they each entail. These logics have not been previously noted or explored. So, first, Schleiermacher subscribes to a teleological outlook drawn within the distinction of the ideal and the real, of reason and nature. This distinction is grasped from the perspective of reason. The highest human good is given some pride of place. His conceptions of culture and history, as well as his account of the moral formation of the individual, are both teleological in character. A theory of virtue is thereby crucial to the ethics, since a moral agent must be able to attain moral ends—and yet, likewise, a eudaemonistic conception of the good, as we have seen, cannot capture the meaning of the highest good.

One of the legacies of Schleiermacher's ethics is teleological in this sense and rests on the distinction between the ideal and real and its overcoming in history. The generation of so-called liberal theologians who followed him, thinkers like Ritschl and even Troeltsch, insisted, despite various criticisms of Schleiermacher's thought, that the moral task was to realize the ideal in the real, specified in different ways. The progressive transformation of society and history—an impulse of Social Gospel theologians in the USA—was the hallmark of what was called "moral idealism." After World War I, this line of thought came under searing criticism from "crisis" or "dialectical" theologians and, in the USA, from forms of "Christian realism." The same "logic" is now under attack from a different angle by thinkers concerned with endangerments to life. Any teleological conception of ethics formulated from the perspective of the human good alone must be widened to include non-human life, and yet in doing so we confront metaphysical questions that seem difficult to sustain in our current situation. How can one isolate a moral telos for non-human life on strictly scientific grounds?

Second, the co-constitutive relation between individual and environment, wherein distinctiveness increases with free community, signals a different logic, one drawn on the distinction—but not the separation—between "parts and wholes." This logic is developed from the perspective of some sense or apprehension of the "whole" given expression in his overtly Romantic writings and in his claims about free sociality. Importantly, a good deal of contemporary ecological ethics, whether in ecological holism or even the so-called land ethics, insists on this logic of parts and whole. The same is found among theologians who advocate theocentrism and ecofeminism. This logic comes to expression in part through Schleiermacher's doctrine of duties, since these are about obligations among selves and communities. The problem here is whether or not forms of ethical holism that give moral priority to the whole over the parts do not, in fact, endanger the rights and goods of the parts, i.e., of individuals.

The reason to isolate these two logics and the distinctions they dialectically relate (ideal/real, part/whole) is central to the possible contribution of Schleiermacher's moral thought to our current situation. Why is that so? Without holding the *tension* between these logics, the teleological aim of forming nature by reason too easily supports the project of the over-humanization of the world. The many critiques of a technological mindset would then fall harshly on his project. Conversely, neglect of the teleological logic in favor of the part/whole logic, while attractive to ecological reasoning, endangers individuals and undercuts the moral task of free self- and world-formation. Recent attempts to find some resonance between Schleiermacher's ethics and current thought have not addressed the possible tension between the two logics found in his ethics. I turn now to address that challenge.

5.

Schleiermacher's ethics has points of resonance with current reflection. Two worth enumerating draw together suggestions made throughout these reflections. First, Schleiermacher makes the question of organization of life basic to his conception of the highest good, and this can be extended beyond the scope of the highest good of human life, since, on his terms, human communities are part of a wider community of life. Correlatively, while he uses the highly idealistic vocabulary of the relation and distinction between "reason" and "nature," it is clear that for Schleiermacher the natural world is not void of purpose or status. Theologically construed, "nature" is part of creation and has a place in the Kingdom of God. The law of human action is rooted in the wider compass of life and therefore no insurmountable gap is found between human ethics and environmental concerns. The moral ought is not rooted in human rational freedom, as it is for Kant, but arises from an intuition consistent with the relation of reason and nature: reason should be soul. While history is the focus of his ethics, "history" must include human interactions with their environments. That "reason should be soul" cannot mean, then, that human beings should dominate the natural world. The inverse is the case. Human freedom is constitutively related to the whole realm of the natural world. A good human world requires right relations with other environments. Of course the question remains whether in our technological age the idea of "nature" is salient or if we need to think about the "end of nature." That is not a matter that can be addressed here.

The second point of resonance between Schleiermacher's ethics and current concerns, and I believe the most profound one, is that by keeping in tension two moral logics—a teleological logic of the ideal and real and a systemic logic of parts and wholes—he provides the conceptual means to affirm ideas that are often at odds. The teleological logic enables one to insist on a humanistic premise in ethics: the moral task is the proper formation of a genuinely humane world and cultivated selves. This preserves the idea that the interpretation of history and culture requires, methodologically speaking, some account of human agency. Of course there are various so-called postmodern theories—deconstructionism, systems theory, and discourses of power—that reject the humanistic premise. Further argument is thereby needed in order to redeem a humanistic position. Yet it is important that Schleiermacher insists on this point and that is why "ethics" is so central to his theological and philosophical project.

It is equally important to see that by coordinating a systemic logic of part/whole—or system/environment—with his teleological and humanistic outlook, Schleiermacher provides some means to counter a runaway technological outlook that would reduce the realm of the "non-human" to the formation and extension of the human kingdom. From this perspective, our present ecological crisis is the overhumanization of the world and is a crisis in which we are also endangering ourselves. The imperative that reason should be soul has been violated. Of course, here, too, much more work needs to be done. Insofar as this systemic logic of part/whole is often expressed in emotional and aesthetic Romantic terminology—just as the teleological logic adopts the discourse of high idealism—work needs to be done to make sense of it for contemporary sensibilities. Still, the genius of his ethics is to articulate the co-constitutive relation of individual and community and how the respect and enhancement of each reciprocally respects and enhances the other.

Only one question remains. How does Schleiermacher conceptualize the relations between reason and nature with respect to these divergent logics that I have isolated in order to sustain the tension between them? In my judgment, that is precisely the point of his conception of the highest good. The "whole of organized life is to be presented as the highest good." This formula just means that the highest good coordinates the intuition that reason should be soul arising from within natural life with the co-constitutive relation of individual and community, including—we must add—the community of non-human life. Stated otherwise, if Plato conceived of the Good as justice, meaning the proper ordering of the soul and the polis, Schleiermacher, on my reading, articulates the highest good as organized life itself. The idea of the highest good is the conceptual and substantive linchpin for the entire ethics and the point at which Schleiermacher might contribute to current thought. That is the case only if, as I have argued, we see that his conception of the highest good not only relates duty and virtue in the actualization of objective social relations but also the two logics isolated above. In order to sustain itself, his contribution requires new concepts, a deeper engagement with current science, and an insistence on expanding the conception of life beyond the human realm. On these points, we must think with but also beyond the brilliant insights of Schleiermacher's ethics.

6.

One might ask what this re-working and extension of Schleiermacher's thought—one that preserves its humanistic premise but also its ecological promise—might look like in detail.[9] In terms of the conception of the highest good, we would need to drop an idealistic conception of the "organization" of life and speak rather of the "integrity" of life. This is important in order to ensure the balance between teleological and systemic logics and the values and obligations they entail, a balance too easily lost once the highly teleological concept of "organization" is made central in ethics. We would need likewise to engage developments in the life sciences in order to provide a robust conception of "life." In order to sustain the humanistic premise about the place of human action in a conception of culture and history, one would have to address anti-humanistic arguments as well as re-engage the question of the relation between humanism and a theological outlook drawn from Christian sources. I think the idea of "responsibility" would be important in both of those tasks, because Schleiermacher's ethics lacks a synthetic concept for relating virtue and duty in an account of moral action that is coordinated to the highest good. Finally, one would have to engage the problem of ethics within a global age of immense cultural and religious diversity. Doing so would require, I judge, addressing basic questions in moral theory without too quickly retreating to the discourse of a particular religious community or culture. That is why, in fact, I have explored Schleiermacher's ethics with an eye to issues in moral theory. The challenge, I believe, would be to show that, in fact, something like the intuition that "reason should be soul" can again resonate and make sense in times of profound endangerments to life.

Admittedly, much would need to be done to re-work and extend Schleiermacher's ethics for our day. The point of this essay has been to demonstrate that this re-working and extension is possible because of the profundity of his insight into life and the highest good, an insight that preserves a humanistic premise and yet also ecological promise.

---

9 I have tried to develop something like this theological ethics elsewhere; see my *Responsibility and Christian Ethics* (Cambridge: Cambridge University Press, 1995); *Power, Value, and Conviction: Theological Ethics in the Postmodern Age* (Cleveland, OH: Pilgrim Press, 1998); and *Theological Ethics and Global Dynamics: In the Time of Many Worlds* (Oxford: Blackwell, 2004).

Schleiermacher's Conception of Theology and Account of Religion as a Constitutive Element of Human Culture

WILHELM GRÄB

1. Academic Theology in the Modern University

The founding of the University of Berlin in 1810, which became for many the archetypal modern university, was a formative event in the shaping of the modern academic tradition of Christian theology in the nineteenth and twentieth centuries. When Hans Frei made this assertion in *Types of Christian Theology*, he was referring to the considerable debate circa 1800 about whether theology ought to be included in the university.[1] Some, first and foremost the philosopher J.G. Fichte, argued that it had no place in a university committed to modern standards of rationality.[2] The position that won out, however, was that of the theologian Friedrich Schleiermacher. Schleiermacher affirmed the role of rationality in the university, yet allowed it neither to dictate to theology its content nor to be in competition with it. He saw theology as a "positive" science or discipline (*Wissenschaft*), by which he meant that it was not included within any single theoretical discipline but was rather related to several of them and directed towards the practical task of educating those who would lead the Christian Church.[3]

---

1   Hans W. Frei, *Types of Christian Theology*, ed. George Hunsinger and William C. Placher (New Haven: Yale University Press, 1990), 34-38.
2   Johann Gottlieb Fichte, "Deduzierter Plan einer in Berlin zu errichtenden höheren Lehranstalt," in *Die Idee der deutschen Universität* (Darmstadt: Hermann Gentner, 1956), 125-218.
3   "Theology is a positive science, the parts of which join into a cohesive whole only through their common relation to a particular mode of faith, that is, a particular way of being conscious of God." Friedrich Schleiermacher, *Brief Outline of Theology as a Field of Study*, trans. Terrence N. Tice (Lewiston, NY: Edwin Mellen, 1990), §1. Henceforth BO. One should note that the German word "Wissenschaft" is much broader than the English "science." *Wissenschaft* includes any academic theoretical research based on rational argument and presented in the context of the other *Wissenschaften*. The opposition is not that of science vs. humanities, but of *Wissenschaft* vs. *Praxis*.

According to this conception of theology as "positive Wissenschaft," theology is a field held together not on the basis of theoretical reasons but by the professional tasks that were being undertaken by theology departments at German universities in the nineteenth century. The usual pattern of theology departments at German universities became that of the state overseeing and paying for a faculty that owed allegiance to general standards of rationality (*Wissenschaft*) and academic freedom, on the one hand, and was committed to training clergy for the state Protestant church, on the other. Schleiermacher's conception helps to demonstrate that theology and religious studies need not oppose, but rather can complement each other. Three consequences follow that make Schleiermacher's understanding of theology a good lens through which the discipline in its modern context can be studied. Firstly, theology was carried on in an environment where it was continually engaged with and informed by other academic disciplines in their most advanced forms. Secondly, the attempt to hold together the requirements of the academy and the church necessitates that theology bridge the gap between reason and faith. Thirdly, theology therefore considers itself obligated to give reasons for the meaning and truth of faith, i.e., it needs a reasonable justification of its object. While the Christian religion cannot be deduced from philosophical premises, it can be shown that being religious is a meaningful element of human culture.

This German pattern of theology, first established by Schleiermacher in the context of the founding of the university in Berlin, might be described as confessional theology, implying that the practical goal of theology refers it strictly to the practice of a religious community or "confession" of faith. This does not entail, however, that theology is inevitably a narrowly ideological endeavor. The close relationship of confessional theology to other academic disciplines, together with its high critical and hermeneutical standards, ensures that in all of its subdisciplines theology fulfils the highest standards of an academic discipline. Such a university theology is, moreover, also oriented toward other religions and based on an anthropology in which religion is theorized as a constitutive element of human culture.

The practical aims of theology do require that the Christian religion remain the primary object of its theoretical endeavors. Yet this need not prevent theology from understanding the Christian religion as one religion among others. On the contrary, theology must integrate fundamental questions about the essence and meaning of religion within society with specific inquiries into the distinctions between different religions. In fact, following Schleiermacher's paradigm of theology, most theology departments at German universities also teach the history of religions or religious studies (*Religionswissenschaft*). These disciplines are either integrated into theology departments or they cooperate with them. Being well coordinated with theology departments, they take other religions as their subject matter and likewise reflect upon the essence, meaning, and truth of different religious systems of belief. And despite their confessional status, all theological disciplines perform their work—in teaching as well as research—just like any other discipline within the humanities: through the employment of historical and critical, hermeneutical methods.

Nevertheless, theologians in Germany frequently confront the suspicion that their work is ideologically driven. This is an unjustified bias based upon the false assumption that the teaching and learning of theology requires one to be a believer or that being a Christian means that one is ipso facto incapable of attaining critical distance on one's personal religious standpoint. Anyone familiar with the research and teaching that goes on today in theology departments can attest that both assumptions are false. The Schleiermacherian model of theology requires that all branches of the theological disciplines, including practical theology, follow scientific methods such as historical criticism, hermeneutics, and empirical research. Most theologians, moreover, adopt a highly critical distance to their own confession. Furthermore, in this paradigm historical and practical theology are based on a form of philosophical theology or philosophy of religion that secures the rational basis of the entire discipline.

Schleiermacher maintained a distinction between the discourse surrounding the term "religion" and the specific propositions or doctrines articulating the peculiar content of the Christian faith. He emphasized that "philosophical theology," which is responsible for developing the general understanding of religion, must take a higher standpoint than the various confessions and religions. A Schleiermacherian theology promotes the integration of the philosophy of religion or—why not?—today's religious studies into theology departments. The key assumption enabling this integration is that religion be understood as a constitutive element of human culture in general.

In this broader perspective, theology is a speculative, critical, and empirical theory of religion, specifically concerned with Christian traditions, churches, and communities. What makes this ensemble of disciplines theological is not their distinctive method. There is no theological hermeneutics or special kind of theological thinking. Theology uses the same methods as all of the other humanities. Speculative, critical, or empirical disciplines can and must become theological disciplines because they are needed both for understanding the Christian religion and for fulfilling the practical tasks of leadership within the Church.

Nevertheless, from the perspective of contemporary debates about the relationship between religious studies and theology, Schleiermacher represents a position that allows for a differentiation between *Religionswissenschaft* (i.e., the philosophy of religion or religious studies) and theology—but without entirely separating them. Theology is a combination of heterogeneous disciplines. The same is true of the *Religionswissenschaften* or religious studies. Today, both ensembles of disciplines integrate sociology, psychology, history, ethnology, and anthropology. The only difference is that religious studies departments are not obligated to function within or otherwise foster church leadership. As a consequence, they do not focus primarily, if at all, on the Christian religion. But this difference does not of itself impugn theology's standards of rationality or academic credentials. Theology and *Religionswissenschaft*/religious studies are both ensembles of diverse scientific disciplines that employ empirical, critical, and speculative methodological procedures.

Indeed, they have more in common than their scientific methods. In Schleiermacher's paradigm, the object of theology is religion as a dimension of human life. The object of theology is not "God in his revelation in Jesus Christ." Rather, theology is a positive discipline in the double sense that its object is empirically given and that it has to solve practical tasks. I want to go a bit further into this conception of theology before explaining how, on the basis of a philosophical anthropology, Schleiermacher makes his case that religion is a constitutive element of human culture.

2. Theology as a Praxis-Oriented Theory of a Profession

In Schleiermacher's view, theology lives on its subject matter. Its content is represented in the praxis of human life. This content is the Christian religion, which includes the entire history of Christianity and its continuation into present-day Christian communities, the church, and, last but not least, church leadership. With this as its content, theology as a whole is also committed to the practical challenges facing "leadership in the Christian church."

This understanding of theology—that theology in its essence is a positive and a praxis-oriented science—does not presuppose a special definition of scientific studies that would apply to theology and not to other disciplines. In his 1808 proposal concerning the plans for the founding of a new university in Berlin, *Occasional Thoughts Concerning the Universities as They are Understood in Germany*), Schleiermacher wrote about the three so-called "higher" departments of the traditional university—theology, law, and medicine—as the "positive faculties" because a connection to practical tasks is constitutive for all of them.[4] In theology such practical tasks call for the development of a special "methodology of church leadership." Schleiermacher employed the concept of leadership in a rather broad sense. It can mean leadership one level above that of the parish, i.e., on the organizational level of the regional church (*Landeskirche*). For this, Schleiermacher mostly used the term "government of the Church" (*Kirchenregiment*).[5] But the term "church leadership" (*Kirchenleitung*) also includes all of the forms of leadership that operate in local congregations. Schleiermacher generally described these local tasks with the term "service of the church" (*Kirchendienst*)—meaning liturgy, preaching, education, and pastoral care. All of these endeavors belong to the life of the congregation and receive treatment in the first part of his practical theology.[6] According to Schleiermacher, church leadership includes two institutionally structured forms: the "binding" (*gebundene*) element and what he calls the "discretionary" (*ungebundene*) element. The latter comprises the "free influence upon the whole, which may be undertaken by any individual member of the church, who believes him or herself call to it"; this is "the free spiritual power."[7] Evidently, Schleiermacher wanted to strengthen the participation of laity in the church so that they too were involved in theological learning.

At the same time, Schleiermacher understood practical theology and theology as a whole to be distinct from the life of the church. Moreover, he defined practical theology as "the theory of practice."[8] The practical life of and within the church is not yet practical theology as an academic discipline. Only if this practical life is being reflected upon methodologically, if "technical rules" or "rules of the craft" (*Kunstlehren*) are being developed that can be applied to support and help church life to fulfill its purpose, can we speak of practical theolo-

---

4 Friedrich Schleiermacher, *Gelegentliche Gedanken über Universitäten in deutschem Sinn: Nebst einem Anhang über eine neu zu errichtende*, in KGA I/6, 15-100.
5 See BO §§309-34.
6 See BO §§277-308.
7 BO §312, §328.
8 Friedrich Schleiermacher, *Die Praktische Theologie nach den Grundsäzen der Evangelischen Kirche im Zusammenhange dargestellt*, ed. Jacob Frerichs, *Sämtliche Werke* I/13 (Berlin: G. Reimer, 1850), 12.

gy.[9] Only those who accept responsibility for shaping church life and contributing to it in these ways, those who are called and trained, will make use of practical theology. These persons, however, need not exclusively be ministers of the church in the sense of professional clergy. The decisive point is whether one merely participates in the life within the church—its worship services, pastoral care, and education—or takes on a role of responsibility for shaping the life of the church, thus serving Christian life. What people need in this latter instance is practical knowledge: a familiarity with and competence in the methods for organizing worship, preparing a religious discourse or sermon, teaching classes about religion, providing pastoral counseling, and governing and directing the church as a large organization in society. This is what church leaders—all of those people with special responsibilities for Christian life within Christian communities—have to do. Assumed in all of this, however, is Schleiermacher's distinction between theology as a whole (including practical theology) and the practical life of Christianity and its churches, i.e., the Christian religion as it is actually lived out. Practice is not theology; it is religion. Lived religion is, however, the object of all theological reflection, ranging from practical theology to the philosophy of religion.

3. Theology as a Historical and Empirical Theory of Christian Religion

For Schleiermacher, theology as a theory of Christian religion includes questions that belong to philosophical and historical theology—the latter of which includes dogmatics and ethics—as well as those concerned with Christian life as it is lived in practice and in the activities of church leadership. The former disciplines have to provide "the right conception of these tasks" so that practical theology can proceed to consider the "correct [i.e., appropriate] procedure" for accomplishing them.[10] The specific task of practical theology is thus to develop methods that promote forms of religious practice in the church.

Christianity is a historical phenomenon. In its institutionalized form as the church, it is a significant factor in culture and society. As an organized communal body, it requires support and strengthening. Therefore, it is necessary that theology in general, and practical theology in particular, be taught at universities as an academic subject.

---

9 BO §265.
10 BO §260.

Theology is not the science of God, as the rational theology of the Enlightenment still claimed. It is, rather, the science of Christianity. And Christianity is a form of lived religion, "a particular mode of faith, that is, a particular way of being conscious of God."[11] Hence theology is the science of God in an indirect sense only: it communicates the specifically Christian way of being conscious of God. Put differently: it is reflection upon the religious faith of human beings as expressed in and through Christianity. For this reason theology presupposes the historical and empirical facts of the Christian religion. As the science in which reflection upon the Christian religion takes shape, it is, moreover, internally self-differentiating. While practical theology represents one way of doing theology, another way is represented by philosophical theology or the philosophy of religion, and yet a third by historical theology.

Because Christianity is a historical phenomenon, historical theology for Schleiermacher constitutes "the actual corpus of theological study."[12] It supplies the knowledge of the historical whole: from the historical beginnings of Christianity through the course of its history to the present day. *Glaubenslehre* (or dogmatics) and Christian *Sittenlehre* (or ethics) are part of historical theology because they are likewise concerned with Christianity in its historically given form and with the religious practice of Christianity as we actually find it in the Christian church. Dogmatics and ethics for Schleiermacher explicate what Christianity—Christian faith as it is being lived—has to say about human beings, God, and the world, and also what implications this has for the practical life of the church and for the life of the family, society, culture, and politics.

Theology requires and is the product of a certain level of reflexivity—reflection upon a religion that has been handed down in history and is alive in contemporary practice. The critical and reflective work of theology provides self-clarification for a specific religion, and whether or not theology as a science is needed will depend upon the level of development in a given religious community.[13] A religion that is alive primarily in symbols and rituals, or that belongs to "a community of small scope," or that is not institutionally organized, has little need for theology as an academic discipline. Such a theology will be in demand, however, as soon as the meaning of symbols and rituals is questioned, as soon as people no longer agree about what these symbols have to do

---

11 BO §1.
12 BO §28.
13 BO §2.

with their lives. Whenever a church develops into a religious organization, a theology will develop. Theology's task then is to provide conceptual explication of the basic beliefs articulated at the roots of religious life; it must show how these beliefs and life practices cohere with each other. Moreover, it will have to establish a connection with the tradition and give new expression to old beliefs so that they can be understood and communicated in the context of a new situation.

Schleiermacher developed this theory of theology in view of the challenges confronting Christianity at a time of great intellectual and cultural upheaval. With this new conception of theology as a theory of lived religion, he sought to guard against the decline of religion. For in the wake of the Enlightenment, many of his contemporaries were questioning the meaning and purpose of religion in general and Christianity in particular: What did religion stand for in the social and cultural context of their world? And what value did it have to offer a humanity come of age? Schleiermacher's conclusion was that theology could address these questions and become a "theology of religion" only if it combines a variety of theological disciplines—practical, historical, and above all, philosophical theology—with an anthropological theory of religion as a constitutive element of culture. Indeed, it was left to philosophical theology—with its foundation in a philosophy of culture—to work out the most basic understanding of religion within Schleiermacher's conception of theology.

4. Philosophical Theology and the Task of Theology

The task of philosophical theology is to define the "essence" of Christianity as well as the essence of Protestantism.[14] In order to define the essence of Christianity, it is not enough simply to describe Christianity in its factual existence. It is not enough to go back to its Biblical beginnings and trace the course of its history, or to study what its more or less qualified proponents claim it to be. It is not enough merely to repeat its own claim to divine revelation and Holy Scripture, or even to support such claims by means of a supernaturalistic doctrine of revelation. While Schleiermacher was not willing to develop a theology based upon supernaturalistic revelation, neither could he approve of a rationalist or a speculative theology. To repeat: for him, Christianity is a historical phenomenon unfolding in history, an empirical religion, a par-

---

14   BO §24.

ticular mode of faith, a specific shape and form of religious consciousness.

Christianity is one religion among other religions. The acknowledgement of this fact requires philosophical theology to be a critical philosophy of religion. Such a philosophy is critical in the sense that the "distinctive nature of Christianity" can only be "defined critically . . . by comparing what is historically given in Christianity with those contrasts by virtue of which various kinds of religious communities can be different from one another."[15] The fact that no historical phenomenon in its particular individuality can be deduced from general concepts is also true of the Christian religion. On the other hand, the specific particularity of Christianity—its history and its world of thoughts and ideas—cannot be defined without a general concept of religion and, in addition, a concept of how religions are to be categorized.

Schleiermacher was already aware in his time of the modern situation of Christianity with respect to religious pluralism and the relationship between religion and society. This is one reason why he saw theology as a whole, including practical theology, as being built upon a foundation of the philosophy of religion. Theology is not simply there; in fact, it did not even exist at the beginnings of the Christian faith.

By Schleiermacher's time, the demands upon the church had increased in complexity due to socio-cultural changes and a general awareness of those changes, which had developed with the Enlightenment and continued to grow in the second half of the eighteenth century. Here I am thinking of the religious wars and the experience of religious pluralism that followed in their wake. Christianity no longer held the position of the one and only true religion, proven by appeal to divine revelation. It no longer functioned as the prime integrating force in society; it was becoming a dividing force instead. And it no longer sanctified the whole of the social world, but was increasingly regarded as one social phenomenon among others. Closely related, the new historical consciousness had a strong influence. Christianity, which had once enjoyed the status of an absolute in many parts of the world by claiming divine authority as its foundation, now stood as one religion beside others. Possessing only relative validity and being tied to a particular culture, Christianity ceased to dominate the whole society and was reduced to one of its segments. As a consequence of these historical changes, theologians had an increasingly difficult time affirming the absolute priority of scripture.

---

15   BO §32.

On the other hand, the rational religion of much Enlightenment theology was not producing very convincing results. The same period, moreover, witnessed the uncovering of the human origins and historical contexts of the Christian scriptures by historical criticism. This issued in more probing questions about theology, including the question of whether theology was concerned directly with the nature of God or rather with the nature of Christianity and its distinctive understandings of God. Schleiermacher tried to meet this challenge with a conception of theology in general that is grounded in an anthropology in which religion forms a constitutive element of human culture.

5. The Account of Religion as a Constitutive Element of Human Culture

Religion as a "feeling of absolute dependence" (*schlechthiniges Abhängigkeitsgefühl*) is an essential element of human nature, which is to say, of human culture. This basic statement of proposition 6 of the "Glaubenslehre" refers to the anthropological foundation of theology as a theory of Christian religion.[16] The feeling of absolute dependence is the presence of the transcendent ground of the human capacities of knowing and willing. My conscious relationship to the world, to other human beings, and even to my own self is characterized by oppositions because in my consciousness of the world, of others, and no less in my self-consciousness, I am distinct from the object of my consciousness. In self-consciousness I am at once an object to my self and subject who is conscious of me. Nevertheless, I have confidence in my identity and in the correspondence of my thinking with the reality of the world. I am conscious of my identity throughout the course of my life, and I have the feeling that my knowledge and my will fit into the world. This feeling of personal identity as well as the confidence that I do know what is real and that I can be successful in my endeavors in the world are constitutive moments of my self-consciousness. Where does this self-consciousness come from? This fundamental question led Schleiermacher to the notion of an *immediate* self-consciousness (*unmittelbares Selbstbewußtsein*), which human beings find in themselves in a pre-reflective and pre-verbal form. In this self-consciousness we are think-

---

16 Friedrich Schleiermacher, *Der christliche Glaube nach den Grundsätzen der evangelischen Kirche im Zusammenhange dargestellt*, ed. Martin Redeker (Berlin: Walter de Gruyter, 1960), 41. On this anthropological argument for becoming religious, cf. also §4 of the *Glaubenslehre*, 23-30.

ing being and being thinking, Schleiermacher says in his "Dialektik."[17] Such self-consciousness emerges immediately and, precisely for this reason, is the constitutive factor of our awareness that our thinking is real and our willing meaningful. Yet we cannot know the ground of this unity because all forms of knowing and acting are determined by oppositions or polarities. Within our cognition and conduct, we can never overcome the oppositions between thinking and acting, idea and reality, universality and individuality. The consciousness of unity and, with it, the confidence of being free to act according to our will, based on our knowledge, only emerges within a pre-reflective experience of the self. The consciousness of unity is a passively constituted moment in our self-relationship. It emerges as a feeling of the self, but we cannot achieve access to it through our knowing and acting. This condition of our ability to know and act therefore remains transcendent to our knowing and acting. It is present in us and accessible in the self's pre-reflective moments of "feeling."[18]

As a consequence, Schleiermacher argues, this immediate self-consciousness of our identity is the actual presence of the transcendent ground of our activity of knowing and acting and, as such, the feeling of absolute dependence. We are not the agents in becoming free and self-determined in a world of oppositions and under the finite conditions of relative dependence and relative freedom. We do not make ourselves into free human beings, but we do have the ability to modify our acts in correspondence to our knowledge and our will. This is what we feel. We are conscious of being constituted as free beings from outside ourselves. This is what the feeling of absolute dependence is about. Due to its passivity, it can also be called a religious feeling. The feeling of absolute dependence or of immediate self-consciousness of identity is passively constituted through our bodily existence, a relationship to ourselves through our body. Thus the transcendent ground of our ability to know and act is given to us and becomes present for us. It is the transcendent ground of our freedom, and it gives us the confidence that we are able to know and act in a self-determining way, despite the oppositions of a world in which only a relative freedom is possible. We can self-confidently move through these worldly relativities because our feeling of absolute dependence makes us conscious of not being completely absorbed in these oppositions.

---

17 See KGA II/10.1, 143-44 and KGA II/10.2, 572-73.
18 See Ulrich Barth, "Der Letztbegründungsgang der 'Dialektik': Schleiermachers Fassung des transzendentalen Gedankens," in *Aufgeklärter Protestantismus* (Tübingen: Mohr Siebeck, 2004), 353-85, esp. 380-85.

Schleiermacher calls the feeling of absolute dependence a religious feeling because it connects us as human beings with the transcendent and absolute ground of our finite freedom. Both the theory about the conditions of the capacity of knowing (*Dialektik*) and the theory of the types of activities that constitute human culture (*Philosophische Ethik*) have to refer to this feeling. Thus, as a consequence of the philosophical anthropology sketched briefly above, Schleiermacher argues that being religious is a constitutive aspect of human existence. Religion, however, does not primarily fulfill this constitutive function through the use of its doctrines, symbols, and rituals, but by representing and interpreting the immediate experience of the self.[19]

One of the most important consequences of this argument is that in Schleiermacher's conception of theology all expressions and articulations of religious self-consciousness have a functional meaning. Religious doctrines, symbols, and rituals are external signs of bodily mediated modes of self-consciousness; they must be acknowledged as such signs in order to be valued as religious signs. Therefore we can indeed analyze religious doctrines, symbols, and rituals without being involved with our own personal existence. However, we have to recognize that to deal with religious doctrines, symbols, and rituals requires reflection upon the way in which human beings express their self-consciousness together with their needs, world-views, faith, and hopes. Again we see that Schleiermacher's anthropological theory of religion permits the academic to deal with religious phenomena with critical distance. In examining the objective expressions of the Christian faith, neither theologians nor researchers in religious studies are necessarily involved as believers in the religious objects—doctrines, symbols, and rituals—that they study. Yet they must acknowledge that these religious phenomena can be or are in fact expressions of a basic human self-understanding. The differences between religions, which are treated by the *Religionswissenschaften* or religious studies, express diverse human self-understandings and therefore different worldviews and cultural concepts. Understanding a religion is linked throughout with understanding human conceptions of the self. It therefore also requires the scholar to examine his or her own self-understanding. We cannot understand any religion without examining our own self-understanding and, consequently, our own religious standpoint—be it explicit or implicit.

---

19 See Wilhelm Gräb, "Religion als Praxis der Lebensdeutung: Zu Schleiermachers Bestimmung des Verhältnisses von Philosophie, Religion und Theologie," in *Protestantismus zwischen Aufklärung und Moderne: Festschrift für Ulrich Barth*, ed. Roderich Barth et al. (Frankfurt: Peter Lang, 2005), 147-62.

This merely means that each human being and also each researcher in theology or religious studies finds in themselves the potential to develop a religious self-consciousness or to deny self-interpretation in religious terms. It does not mean that everyone must belong to a religious community or denomination or that researchers in religious studies have to be believers who affirm their own religious standpoint, specific doctrines, or symbolic and ritual systems. In Schleiermacher's thinking, an articulated religious position, religious doctrines, rituals, and the like are secondary elements within a given religion that is based on a cultural-anthropological, transcendental structure of subjectivity. Nevertheless, such secondary elements are historically and culturally mediated expressions and articulations of how human beings most fundamentally understand themselves. In the end, understanding not our own religion but a foreign one demands a complicated hermeneutics. It is impossible to describe the meaning of the doctrines, symbols, and rituals of other religions as if they were our own without going back to the basic elements of the self-understanding and worldviews of those who were educated in the doctrines of the religion concerned.

One last remark: it should be obvious that this conception of religion as the expression of the deepest human self-understanding is based on the Christian notion of the *conditio humana*. Schleiermacher understands religion as the feeling of absolute dependence, and for him the feeling of absolute dependence is the condition of the possibility of human self-consciousness, including the self-understanding of freedom. This understanding of religion as the conception of the self as free coheres with the Christian faith's concentration on Jesus as the redeemer. The individual who belongs to Jesus and his community of faith is not completely absorbed—such is the confession of a Christian—by the oppositions of his or her worldly existence. Jesus is the redeemer because he communicates the feeling of absolute dependence and therefore the presence of the ground of freedom and self-determination in the oppositions of finite human existence. To follow Jesus is to actualize personal freedom.

There is a circle in Schleiermacher's theory of religion, but this circle is necessary. Because religion in the form of the expression of the deepest human self-understanding is a constitutive element of human culture, we cannot develop a theory of religion while at the same time bypassing our own self-understanding and therefore our own religious standpoint. But this does not have to be an impediment to attempts to understand other religions. On the contrary, the better we understand our own religious standpoint and its religious doctrines, symbols, and rituals as a more or less fitting expression of our self-understanding, the better we are able to understand other religions, their doctrines, rituals, and symbols as articulations of the worldviews and cultural constructs of believers of other faiths.

Schleiermacher Studies in Germany:
New Avenues and Vistas

Schleiermacher

Dialectic and Transcendental Philosophy, Relationship to Hegel

ANDREAS ARNDT

1.

In my remarks I would like to concentrate on Schleiermacher's stance towards the classical German philosophy of his time, with his *Lectures on Dialectic* forming a central point of reference. My approach here is by no means as obvious as it may seem. Scheiermacher's stance towards the philosophy of his time has in fact not yet been fully explained. This is largely due to the fact that Schleiermacher is still not seen, and is perhaps instead increasingly less seen, as an independent philosopher of his era. Whoever speaks of so-called "German Idealism" can do so very easily without mentioning Schleiermacher at all. Two reasons in particular may be responsible for the fact that Schleiermacher has been and continues to be overshadowed by Kant, Fichte, Schelling, and Hegel. First: within his own lifetime and long afterwards, Schleiermacher was perceived by many as a philosopher of religion and faith, one who—as formulated by Heinrich Ritter in his review of Ludwig Jonas' *Dialectic* edition—attempted to "win philosophical ground for theology." With the post-Hegelian critique of religion, which was to commit philosophy largely to a "methodological atheism" (Heidegger), Schleiermacher's concerns seemed to have become anachronistic. That Schleiermacher could have been interpreted in this way relates, secondly, to the fact that he was only present as a literary force during his lifetime through his early-Romantic theory of religion, and later as a theological dogmatician, but not through the groundwork of his philosophy, which he presented exclusively in his Berlin *Lectures on Dialectic*. The posthumous and relatively late publication of these lectures in 1839 was, moreover, aimed at creating the exact impression that Ritter formulated in his review.

Since this time, we have not only seen the publication of the 2002 critical edition of the *Dialectic*, which may now serve as the basis for a new evaluation of Schleiermacher's philosophical intentions and works; substantial interpretations, such as works by Ulrich Barth, Manfred Frank, Johannes Michael Dittmer, Peter Grove, and Sarah Schmidt have also come out.[1] Significantly, only the interpretations of Frank and Schmidt are works by philosophers, the others focusing on theology or philosophy of religion. Worth mentioning in particular is the anthology *Schleiermachers Dialektik*, edited by Christine Helmer, Christiane Kranich, and Birgit Rehme-Iffert, which not only unites philosophical and theological perspectives, but is also representative of international research.[2] Again, however, this volume was published in a series devoted to the problems of religion. Within philosophy Schleiermacher has not yet found his place as an independent and equally esteemed thinker of classical German philosophy.

2.

My introductory remarks raise the question of the relationship of Schleiermacher's philosophy to his theology. This issue has been discussed extensively in the past and, in my view, has been essentially explained. The interpretation of Schleiermacher in terms of theology or philosophy of religion has provoked varying reactions. In 1910 Schleiermacher was depicted by Ernst Troeltsch and others as a "philosopher of faith,"[3] while Karl Barth and Emil Brunner later attempted to discover philosophy rather than faith in his theology.[4] Schleiermacher

---

1   Ulrich Barth, *Christentum und Selbstbewußtsein* (Göttingen: Vandenhoeck & Ruprecht, 1983); Manfred Frank, "Einleitung des Herausgebers," in *Friedrich Schleiermacher: Dialektik*, vol. 1 (Frankfurt: Suhrkamp, 2001), 10-136; Johannes Michael Dittmer, *Schleiermachers Wissenschaftslehre als Entwurf einer prozessualen Metaphysik in semiotischer Perspektive: Triadizität im Werden* (Berlin: Walter de Gruyter, 2001); Peter Grove, *Deutungen des Subjekts: Schleiermachers Philosophie der Religion* (Berlin: Walter de Gruyter, 2004); and Sarah Schmidt, *Die Konstruktion des Endlichen: Schleiermachers Philosophie der Wechselwirkung* (Berlin: Walter de Gruyter, 2005).
2   Christine Helmer et al., eds., *Schleiermachers Dialektik: Die Liebe zum Wissen in Philosophie und Theologie* (Tübingen: Mohr Siebeck, 2003).
3   Ernst Troeltsch et al., *Schleiermacher der Philosoph des Glaubens: Sechs Aufsätze* (Berlin: Buchverlag der "Hilfe," 1910).
4   Karl Barth, *Die protestantische Theologie im 19. Jahrhundert*, 3rd ed. (Zürich: Evangelischer Verlag, 1960), 379-424; Emil Brunner, *Die Mystik und das Wort: Der Gegensatz zwischen moderner Religionsauffassung und christlichem Glauben dargestellt an der Theologie Schleiermachers* (Tübingen: Mohr, 1924).

would have rejected both views. He took a clear stance in a letter to the philosopher Friedrich Heinrich Jacobi on March 30, 1818. He was, he wrote, "with the understanding a philosopher, as this is the independent and original activity of the understanding, and with feeling I am ... a Christian," because religiosity was the cause of feeling, which the understanding, so to speak, translates or interprets (*verdolmetscht*).[5] It follows from this, on the one hand, that religious content has to take on a philosophical form, which, however, must remain external to it, and, on the other hand, that in Schleiermacher's view philosophy and religion do not contradict each other: "My philosophy and my dogmatics are firmly resolved not to contradict each other."[6]

This resolve, however, evidently depended on the fact that Schleiermacher, as he formulated it in the *Speeches on Religion*, regarded religion as a separate "province" in the human mind (*Gemüt*)—that is, a domain that eludes philosophical comprehension (*Begreifen*) in the strict sense and can only be "translated" by philosophy, but never dealt with originally. Due to religion's exceptional position in being withdrawn from philosophy, for Schleiermacher there can be no "true atheism," as it is put in his *Dialectic*.[7] Were philosophy to reject this limit to it drawn by Schleiermacher, however, the harmony (*Zusammenstimmung*) of philosophy and religion or theology would no longer be certain.

Schleiermacher himself could not rule this out, because—as he emphasizes in the second *Letter to Lücke* (1829)—philosophy is no longer *ancilla theologiae*, that is, theology and philosophy have "become free" from each other.[8] This means above all that philosophy is autonomous in the sense that it develops and establishes its own procedures and is responsible for its own results. And this is what Schleiermacher carries out. Thus in his draft of the *Dialectic* lectures in 1814/15, with regard to religious feeling as the becoming conscious of the transcendental ground, he writes: "If, then, the feeling of God is the essence of religion [*das Religiöse*], then religion thus seems to stand over philosophy ... this is not the case, however. We have come here on a purely philosophical path, without having proceeded from feeling."[9] This means that the limit of philosophical comprehension must be drawn in philosophy and through philosophy itself, not through recourse to religious

---

5 "Schleiermacher to Jacobi, 30 March 1818," ed. Andreas Arndt and Wolfgang Virmond, in *Religionsphilosophie und spekulative Theologie*, ed. Walter Jaeschke (Hamburg: Meiner, 1994), 395.
6 Ibid., 396.
7 "Aufzeichnungen zum Kolleg 1811," in KGA II/10.1, 38.
8 See KGA I/10, 390.
9 KGA II/10.1, 143.

convictions. The harmony (*Zusammenstimmung*) of philosophy and religion or theology, their non-contradiction, can thus only be the *result* of an independent philosophical development of thought. In his philosophical argumentation Schleiermacher is thus a philosopher and nothing else. This is formulated precisely in the *Dialectic* lecture of 1818-19: "The philosopher thus needs religion not for his trade, but as a human being, and the religious need philosophy not in and for itself but only in communication."[10]

In connection with this problem I have been accused by Michael Moxter of a "marginalization of theology" that would lead to the separation of "that which Schleiermacher only wanted to distinguish."[11] Uncontroversially, Schleiermacher does not see a contradiction between theology and philosophy. Moxter, however, is silent about the fact that in Schleiermacher's view philosophy can only establish an agreement of this kind through itself and only by philosophical means. In my view this insight is the precondition for Schleiermacher being regarded as a philosopher in his own right at all, and for the necessity of a philosophical engagement with him on the part of philosophers.

3.

In what relationship, then, does Schleiermacher stand to his contemporaries? Michael Theunissen has recently argued that Schleiermacher's philosophical significance consists in his "getting post-Idealist thought off the ground in the midst of Idealism."[12] Schleiermacher's *Dialectic* did in fact exert an influence on philosophy as a whole until the mid-nineteenth century that cannot be underestimated,[13] on the critique of Hegel especially—as in, for example, Trendelenburg and also Feuerbach.[14] Whether this impact can be sufficiently captured in the idealism/post-idealism schema is questionable, however. Those who, like Manfred Frank recently, have been searching for "ways out of German

---

10   KGA II/10.2, 242.
11   Michael Moxter, "Philosoph ohne Leser," *Frankfurter Allgemeine Zeitung*, October 24, 1996.
12   Michael Theunissen, "Zehn Thesen über Schleiermacher heute," in *Schleiermacher's Philosophy and the Philosophical Tradition*, ed. Sergio Sorrentino (Lewiston, NY: Edwin Mellen Press, 1992), iv.
13   See Klaus Christian Köhnke, *Entstehung und Aufstieg des Neukantianismus* (Frankfurt: Suhrkamp, 1993).
14   See Andreas Arndt, introduction to *Dialektik (1811)*, by Friedrich Schleiermacher (Hamburg: Meiner, 1986), xxxviff.

Idealism"[15] must first explain what this idealism is supposed to be. Walter Jaeschke has demonstrated not only that the concept "German Idealism" is a later (neo-Kantian) product, but also that the label "idealism" does not meet the self-understanding of the philosophers subsumed under it.[16] Kant, who described himself as a "transcendental" or "critical" idealist had nevertheless not only made a "criticism of idealism" the subject matter of the *Critique of Pure Reason*; he also described critical idealism at the same time as "empirical realism."[17] Fichte too, who defended a practical idealism of the ought, attempts in the theoretical part of the *Wissenschaftslehre* to demonstrate a "middle course between idealism and realism."[18] Behind the "critical" or "practical" idealism, therefore—as in the transcendental idealism of Schelling too—there lies a program for an overcoming of the alternatives of idealism and realism, and this, in my view, is the leading program for the whole post-Kantian epoch, which I would thus like to refer to as "classical German philosophy," and not as German Idealism.

In the dispute with Kant and in particular with Fichte, then, it is above all the insufficiency of the unification of idealism and realism that is emphasized. Schelling's question concerning the "subjectobjectivity" beyond the opposition of subjectivity and objectivity that is constitutive of the alternatives of idealism and realism belongs in this context as much as Hegel's turn against the "subjective idealism" of Kant and Fichte, with Hegel ultimately declaring in his *Science of Logic* that the "opposition of idealism and realism" is "without meaning."[19] In programmatic terms Schleiermacher also takes his place in this movement. I quote from a letter from March 1801: "The unification of idealism and realism is what all my endeavors are geared towards, and I have hinted at this where I have been able to do so in the *Speeches* as well as in the *Soliloquies*. The basis of this does lie very deep, though, and it will not be easy to open the sense for this to both parties. Schlegel, who has already said so much that was aimed at this, is not under-

---

15 Manfred Frank, *Auswege aus dem Deutschen Idealismus* (Frankfurt: Suhrkamp, 2007).
16 Walter Jaeschke, "Zur Genealogie des Deutschen Idealismus: Konstitutionsgeschichtliche Bemerkungen in methodologischer Absicht," in *Materialismus und Spiritualismus: Philosophie und Wissenschaften nach 1848*, ed. Andreas Arndt and Walter Jaeschke (Hamburg: Meiner, 2000), 219-34.
17 KrV B274ff/A371. See also Andreas Arndt, "Ontologischer Monismus und Dualismus," in Arndt and Jaeschke, *Materialismus and Spiritualismus*, 1–34.
18 Johann Gottlieb Fichte, *Werke*, ed. Immanuel Hermann Fichte (1834-35; repr., Berlin: Walter de Gruyter, 1971), 1:173.
19 Georg Wilhelm Friedrich Hegel, *Die Wissenschaft der Logik, Teil 1: Die objektive Logik, Band 1: Die Lehre vom Sein (1832)*, ed. Friedrich Hogemann and Walter Jaeschke, vol. 21 of *Gesammelte Werke* (Hamburg: Meiner, 1984), 142.

stood, and my works have probably not yet been looked at in this way elsewhere."[20]

In Kant empirical realism stands in a relationship of tension towards critical or transcendental idealism. This involves an unacknowledged dualism that Kant wants to avoid at all costs on the foundational level of transcendental philosophy. Here he makes pure self-consciousness the "highest point" of theoretical philosophy,[21] but the affirmation of this self-consciousness can itself only take place at the empirical level. The sentence "I think," writes Kant, expresses an "indeterminate empirical intuition, i.e., perception."[22] In these formulations dualism recrudesces at the transcendental foundation level.

It is of particular importance to recall that a connection exists between the foundation problem of transcendental idealism in Kant's theory of self-consciousness and the theory of the empirical certainty of reality. This is so for two reasons. First, primarily under the influence of Dieter Henrich's research on the genesis of so-called "German Idealism," this connection was largely neglected in favor of a one-sided emphasis on the theory of subjectivity and the problem of self-consciousness.[23] The discussions that took place in the wake of Kant, however, are completely impossible to understand if they are reduced to the problem of self-consciousness.[24] Second, the epistemological turn in post-classical philosophy, and in Neo-Kantianism in particular, ultimately disguised this problem by extensively stripping Kant's philosophy of its metaphysical program and the problems connected to it—for example, ontology and realism. In pointed terms: the fact that the transcendental philosophy that Kant gave rise to was, after Kant, combined with Spinoza, and that in this manner a point of unity between subject and object (which also means: beyond the opposition of self and world-consciousness) came into view, is a consequence of the Kantian approach itself and not a relapse into pre-critical thought. It is thus with some justification that Frederick Beiser has described the early history of "German Idealism" as a "struggle against subjectivism."[25]

---

20 Schleiermacher to F.H.C. Schwarz, 28 March 1801, in KGA V/5, 73.
21 KrV B134.
22 KrV B422.
23 See Dieter Henrich, *Selbstverhältnisse: Gedanken und Auslegungen zu den Grundlagen der klassischen deutschen Philosophie* (Stuttgart: Klett-Cotta, 1982); Dieter Henrich, *Konstellationen: Probleme und Debatten am Ursprung der idealistischen Philosophie (1789-1795)* (Stuttgart: Klett-Cotta, 1991).
24 See Walter Jaeschke, "Selbstbewußtsein: II. Neuzeit," in *Historisches Wörterbuch der Philosophie*, vol. 9 (Darmstadt: Wissenschaftliche Buchgesellschaft, 1995), 352-71.
25 Frederick Beiser, *German Idealism: The Struggle against Subjectivism 1781-1801* (Cambridge: Harvard University Press, 2002).

It is also in this respect that Schleiermacher stands in the center of the movement of post-Kantian philosophy—indeed, he must even be seen as one of its protagonists. In his early studies on Jacobi's Spinoza book he had already attempted, in full separation from and independent of the discussions in Jena, to combine Kant and Spinoza, an effort that was very much in keeping with the philosophical debates of his day. This position was maintained by Schleiermacher up to and throughout the *Dialectic*, where he quotes Spinoza's parallelism of the connection of ideas and things in terms of the "parallelism of being and thought,"[26] which has its ground in an "absolutely highest being"[27]: "The ideal and the real run parallel to each other as modes of being."[28] Schleiermacher is in fact convinced, like Spinoza, that it is only by means of a return to a common ground (of the highest opposition of the ideal and the real or of thought and being) that knowledge, as the agreement of thought with the object of thought, can be secured. Because knowledge always presupposes an opposition of thought and the object of thought, however, this ground cannot be known. Schleiermacher thus distinguishes between a possible knowledge of things (within the opposition of the ideal and the real) and an impossible knowledge of the ground itself.[29] The issue then is how we can nonetheless have a consciousness, if not an objective knowledge, of this ground—that is, in what way we have the transcendental ground, as Schleiermacher calls it at least, in us.

This is one of the most vehemently discussed problems of Schleiermacher's philosophy. Scheiermacher's answer, briefly put, is that the immediate unity of the ideal and real in the transcendental ground—immediate because they are thought without opposition and thus without *relata*—must have an analogy in us. This analogy, according to Schleiermacher, is feeling, which, in the *Dialectic* lecture of 1822 he refers to as "immediate self-consciousness."[30] In my view this corresponds structurally to what functioned in the *Speeches* (1799) as intuition of the universe. On closer examination this does indeed involve feeling more than mere self-consciousness. Feeling, that is, stands for the indifference of thinking and willing, or knowing and acting. According to Schleiermacher, the being of things is posited in us in think-

---

26 Baruch de Spinoza, *Ethica*, in vol. 2 of *Opera-Werke*, ed. Konrad Blumenstock (Darmstadt: Wissenschaftliche Buchgesellschaft, 1980), part 2, proposition 7.
27 "Notizen zur Dialektik (1811)," in KGA II/10.1, 5.
28 "Ausarbeitung zur Dialektik, (1814/15)," in KGA II/10.1, 100.
29 See Andreas Arndt, "Die Metaphysik der *Dialektik*," in Helmer et al., *Schleiermachers Dialektik*, 139-40.
30 KGA II/10.1, 266.

ing, and in willing we posit our being in things—i.e., in acting we will the realization of a purpose posited by us. Self-consciousness is thus equally consciousness of the world. In Schleiermacher's words: the consciousness of God as the transcendental ground is given "as a component of our self-consciousness as well as of our consciousness."[31] It may also be said that in feeling, empirical realism (in Kant's sense) and practical idealism (in Fichte's sense) are united, because the "positedness" of things in us is realism, while the positing of our being in things is (practical) idealism.

At any rate, an interpretation of the presence of the transcendental ground in us that is merely subjectivist and focused on the problem of self-consciousness alone is, in my opinion, inadequate. This is because it involves a relative unity of the subjective and the objective, or the ideal and the real, in a unity of self and world-consciousness. What is controversial here is whether the immediate unity for which the expression "feeling" stands can be regarded as self-differentiated and as such internally structured, as Peter Grove, in agreement with Ulrich Barth, has emphasized.[32] It may be beyond question that immediacy—be it that of the transcendental ground itself or that of its analogy in us—has mediating functions. It is disputable, though, whether this can be satisfactory in theoretical terms, or whether immediacy in Schleiermacher does not merely operate as a black box of mediation.

With regard to the assumption of a conceptually unknowable Absolute, Schleiermacher argues that knowledge is permanently in a process of becoming and can never be brought to a conclusion by us. Given this fact, Schleiermacher stands in a critical relationship to the system-thinking of Kant and his followers. For Kant, the system is no longer objectively presented to thought—as in, for example, a system of nature. Instead thinking itself—reason—forms a system that also allows us to behold the manifesting reality in a systematic way. In short, "[t]he unity of reason is the unity of the system."[33] Hegel's program of a conclusion of thought in itself is also based on this view. Schleiermacher does assume, with Spinoza and Hegel, that thought and being correspond to each other, but for him a systematic conclusion can only be gained if being is also entirely comprehended in its inner systematic structure, and not only in categories in terms of which we refer to it reflectively.

Schleiermacher's conception of dialectic must be regarded in general as a working out and continuation in essential points of an early-Romantic conception that originally goes back to Friedrich Schlegel.

---

31   KGA II/10.1, 143.
32   This is the position of Peter Grove in *Deutungen des Subjekts*, 519.
33   KrV B708.

I have attempted to demonstrate this in several works, and have been followed here by Peter Grove, Sarah Schmidt, and others.[34] It can at any rate be maintained that Schleiermacher is not the antipode of a development culminating in an absolute idealism, but rather someone who maintained standpoints on the battleground of post-Kantian philosophy that link him to the early Romantics and others, standpoints that he was also able to introduce into the post-Hegelian debates. In so doing, however, he moved within the spectrum of positions that the post-Kantian philosophy had developed to solve the problems of Kant's philosophy; Schleiermacher's philosophy is an integral component of classical German philosophy.

4.

To conclude my necessarily incomplete remarks I would like briefly to treat of the relation of Schleiermacher's philosophy to the philosophy of Hegel. I will begin by highlighting what they have in common.[35] No differently from Hegel in the *Science of Logic*, Schleiermacher in his *Dialectic* pursues the program of a unity of logic and metaphysics.[36] It is not the renunciation of a philosophy of the Absolute that distinguishes Schleiermacher from Hegel, as is often claimed, but rather the view that there is no knowledge of the Absolute that can be consummated conceptually. However, for Schleiermacher, there is no knowledge without a metaphysical foundation.[37] Logic, as he claims, can only "be based on metaphysics. If it is not based on this, it is based on feeling. It is then supposed to found all other knowledge, though it is itself based on a non-knowledge."[38] Metaphysics here is the knowledge of being, and as such for Schleiermacher is also a science.

Schleiermacher here essentially draws on Kant's program for a transcendental logic in the *Critique of Pure Reason*, which in the Transcendental Analytic deals with the former *metaphysica generalis* (ontology) and which in the Transcendental Dialectic deals with the former

---

34 Andreas Arndt, "Zum Begriff der Dialektik bei Friedrich Schlegel 1796-1801," *Archiv für Begriffsgeschichte* 35 (1992), 257–73; Andreas Arndt and Jure Zovko, introduction to *Friedrich Schlegel: Schriften zur Kritischen Philosophie 1795–1805* (Hamburg: Meiner, 2007).
35 See Andreas Arndt, "Schleiermacher und Hegel: Versuch einer Zwischenbilanz," *Hegel-Studien* 37 (2004), 55-67.
36 See KGA II/10.1, 77 (§16).
37 For more detail see Arndt, "Die Metaphysik der *Dialektik*," in Helmer et al., *Schleiermachers* Dialektik, 135-49.
38 KGA II/10.2, 110.

metaphysica specialis (rational psychology, cosmology and rational theology). The structure of the transcendental part of the *Dialectic* also clearly follows Kant: in parallel to the Kantian Analytic, ontology is discussed in the theories of the concept and of judgment, which are related to knowable being. Then, with the presence of the transcendental ground in (immediate) self-consciousness and with the ideas of the world and God, the traditional objects of reason come into play. This involves a far-reaching revision, insofar as Schleiermacher awards a systematic primacy to rational psychology as the becoming-conscious of the transcendental ground. This also subsumes ontology "because this construction of finite being is given to us at all only in the basic condition of our being."[39] The object of rational psychology is the "development of the idea of knowledge and the idea of action, how both lead to the idea of God and the world as a constitutive principle of human existence."[40] Cosmology and theology are thus also allocated to rational psychology.

In short, Schleiermacher's *Dialectic* draws on the program of transcendental logic in Kant's *Critique of Pure Reason*. This also means that it does not entail—just as Hegel's *Science of Logic* does not do so—a relapse into pre-critical metaphysics. This becomes clearer still when we bring to mind a further basic feature of the *Dialectic*: it is a theory of the *coming into being* of knowledge, specifically, as *the art of achieving a science*. It is therefore essentially a procedure or method, and not an ensemble of propositions concerning what, at the metaphysical level, is the case.

That such propositions are disputable, and that there is no secure ground here on which to build philosophically, but rather only the rubble of all prior metaphysics, is in fact the point of entry of the *Dialectic*, which can assume nothing outside of the will to know. Here too Schleiermacher meets with Hegel, for such a will also forms the only presupposition of the *Science of Logic*: "only the resolve—which can also be regarded as arbitrariness—that one wishes to consider *thinking as such* is present."[41] And for Hegel too the *Logic* ultimately culminates in the Absolute Idea as Absolute Method. It is this as the unity of the idea of the true and the idea of the good, that is, of the theoretical and the practical. The practical moment includes its self-operationalizing in relation to the real practice of cognition and acting in the world, that is, the work of Spirit in the broadest sense of the term. In the same way we

---

39 KGA II/10.1, 152-53. (§228).
40 Ibid.
41 Hegel, *Die Lehre vom Sein (1831)*, 56.

find in the second, technical, part of Schleiermacher's *Dialectic* an operationalizing of the transcendental presuppositions of knowing with regard to the construction of real knowing that includes the historical, that is, the ethical process. This operationalizing is, in my opinion, also based in the fact that Schleiermacher, as mentioned above, finds the ground of knowing—in this respect the equivalent of the Absolute Idea—in the transition from knowing to willing, that is, in the unity of the theoretical and the practical.

Both Schleiermacher's *Dialectic* and Hegel's *Science of Knowledge* discuss the traditional elements of metaphysics from the perspective of a thinking that understands itself internally through its conditions in the process of knowledge-oriented thinking. Internal here means that it is exclusively subject to the logic of this process and cannot draw its presuppositions from anywhere else. From the perspective of prior metaphysics this means for Schleiermacher that being only comes into play as something known, i.e., as the correlate of knowledge in the process of the coming into being of knowledge, and not as an immemorial being in-and-for-itself.

"Knowing and being exist for us only in relation to one another. Being is the known, and knowing knows that which is."[42] I thus cannot see how—as Manfred Frank claims—Schleiermacher should be compared to the late Schelling. He certainly does speak of an absolute being that cannot be understood consciously and thus also cannot be understood as concept. Nonetheless, he describes this as the unity of thought and object. It is thus unthinkable precisely because it is not only being (as such it would only be the correlate of consciousness), but rather unifies thought and being in a non-relational way. Schleiermacher therefore, as far as I can see, also does not hold the view that the ontological in Absolute Being should have a priority in relation to thought in some form or another; on the contrary, the thought of a non-relational, absolute identity of both excludes any asymmetry of this kind.

In contrast to Schleiermacher, Hegel characterizes the absolute unity as the absolutely self-related Concept, that is, as the Idea. Being, as presented in the *Science of Logic*, is "passing-over into Other" (*Übergehen in Anderes*) and cannot be grasped, but only understood as relation. What exist in truth are not self-identical entities, but rather relations, for Hegel, a conceptual structure. True knowing is thus the Concept's knowing of itself, of how it completes itself in the Absolute Idea as Absolute Method. Hegel would also philosophically accuse Schleiermach-

---

42 Friedrich Schleiermacher, *Ethik (1812/13)*, ed. Hans-Joachim Birkner (Hamburg: Meiner, 1981), 192.

er of what he had already charged him with in relation to his doctrine of faith:[43] reference to a sphere that cannot be deduced conceptually would involve abandoning the radicalness of critique in favor of an ultimately subjective opinion. Conversely, Schleiermacher would claim against Hegel that the Concept, irrespective of the unity of thought and being, can only constitute and complete itself in distinction from that which is conceived or thought. Hegel, however, escapes this objection in that he thinks the absolute Concept as contradiction, which constitutes the called-for difference from within itself. For Schleiermacher, on the other hand, a unity of contradictions, which he refers to as the idea of the world, is just as transcendent and conceptually unachievable as unity without contradiction, which he refers to as the idea of God. Beyond all of the polemics in relation to immediacy, feeling, and the omnipotence or impotence of the Concept, the dispute between Schleiermacher and Hegel is at its core primarily a dispute over the concept and status of "identity" in the process of knowledge. This was never to truly get off the ground, but it was a dispute on a shared field of inquiry first opened up by Kant.

Friedrich Nietzsche negatively underlined Schleiermacher's belonging to this field of inquiry by making his very name into a synonym for the errors of German philosophy: "The Germans have been recorded in the history of knowledge with exclusively ambiguous names, they have always produced only 'unconscious' forgers (—Fichte, Schelling, Schopenhauer, Hegel, Schleiermacher deserve this word, as do Kant and Leibniz; they are all mere Schleiermacher ['veil makers']."[44] Perhaps, however, Schleiermacher's *Dialectic* can—like Hegel's *Logic* and in confrontation with it—contribute to a consideration of whether philosophy really is able to abstractly negate the elements of metaphysics, or whether it is not rather obliged to reflect explicitly on these if it is not to be blind to its own presuppositions, and thus, to effectively relapse into an unacknowledged, unreflected, and thus pre-critical, metaphysics of the understanding.

Translated by Martin Rodden

---

43   See Eric von der Luft, ed., *Hegel, Hinrichs, and Schleiermacher on Feeling and Reason in Religion: The Texts of Their 1821-22 Debate* (Lewiston, NY: Edwin Mellen Press, 1987).
44   Friedrich Nietzsche, *Ecce homo*, vol. 6 of *Sämtliche Werke: Kritische Studienausgabe*, ed. G. Colli and M. Montinari (Berlin: Walter de Gruyter, 1980), 361.

Schleiermacher's Encyclopedia, Philosophical Ethics, Anthropology, and Dogmatics in German Protestant Theology

EILERT HERMS

You invited me to offer some observations concerning the impact of Schleiermacher's anthropology, philosophical ethics, *Kurze Darstellung,* and dogmatic theology (both the *Glaubenslehre* and the Christian *Sittenlehre*) upon recent German Protestant theology. Before undertaking this task, I want to call to mind the fact that from the beginning there has been a continuous awareness of the epoch-making status of Schleiermacher's oeuvre in German Roman Catholic theology. Already in 1819, the *Kurze Einleitung in das Studium der Theologie* by Johann Sebastian Drey (1777-1853), head of the early Roman Catholic Tübingen School, deeply and expressively breathes Schleiermacher's influence.[1] Some decades later, a prominent member of the second generation of the Catholic Tübingen School, Johann Evangelista von Kuhn (1806-1887), stated with reference to Thomas Aquinas, that "among all the theologians of subsequent times until today, as concerns scientific power and influence, there is only one comparable to him: Schleiermacher."[2] A revival of this Roman Catholic interest, parallel to the new Schleiermacher renaissance among Protestants, can be observed in the last decades of the twentieth century and is manifest in important and comprehensive monographs, the latest of which is a University of Mainz dissertation by Michael Feil on the foundations of ethics in Schleiermacher and Aquinas.[3]

---

1   Johann Sebastian Drey, *Kurze Einleitung in das Studium der Theologie mit Rücksicht auf den wissenschaftlichen Standpunct und das katholische System: Tübingen 1819,* vol 3. of *Nachgelassene Schriften,* ed. Max Seckler (Tübingen: Francke, 2007).
2   Cited in Robert Stalder, *Grundlinien der Theologie Schleiermachers* (Wiesbaden: Franz Steiner, 1969), ix.
3   Michael Feil, *Die Grundlegung der Ethik bei Friedrich Schleiermacher und Thomas Aquin* (Berlin: Walter de Gruyter, 2004). Also especially important are Stalder, *Grundlinien;* and Michael Eckert, *Gott—Glauben und Wissen: Friedrich Schleiermachers philosophische Theologie* (Berlin: Walter de Gruyter, 1987).

I propose that we take a methodological lesson from this repeated comparison between Aquinas and Schleiermacher: Roman Catholic Theology has invested a lot of historical study in discovering and elaborating what can be judged to be the genuine intention of Thomas himself within his own historical context. Yet this immense amount of historical research was never undertaken merely for its own sake. Rather, it was always aimed at making the unrestrained richness of this heritage available to the present and preventing contemporary theology from falling beneath the level of insight and reflection already reached by former generations. It seems to me that Protestant Theology, too, should study its own history and classics with just such an attitude, if such study is to be fruitful and reasonable.

This is all the more urgent in light of the fact that the enormous expansion of attention to nineteenth-century theology in general[4] and to Schleiermacher in particular[5] has been motivated and propelled by a sense of deficit and narrowness in the theological positions that survived the troubles between 1914 and 1945. The harsh criticism during these years of so-called "liberal" or "idealistic" prewar and nineteenth-century theology—as a whole and directed at Schleiermacher in particular—came to seem unjust and marred by prejudice. Moreover, there was a vivid impression that the mainstream schools of German Protestantism in the 1960s had failed to reach a solid understanding of—let alone anything like a solution to—the fundamental problems facing Christianity and challenging its theology since the Enlightenment. From such dissatisfaction arose the demand to re-read the great authors since the end of the eighteenth century with the intention of taking seriously the horizon of problems that drove their work and of capturing the full scope of the solutions they set forth for their contemporaries and posterity. A leading venue of this interest—already during the 1950s and then in the 1960s—was the Göttingen Faculty of Theology, where prominent teachers like Emanuel Hirsch and Wolfgang Trillhaas, as well as the young Hans-Joachim Birkner and Hans-Walter

---

4   As representative of this interest, see the opus magnum of Jan Rohls, *Protestantische Theologie der Neuzeit*, 2 vols. (Tübingen: Mohr Siebeck 1997).

5   On the situation until 1999, see the outstanding article by Hermann Fischer, "Schleiermacher," in *Theologische Realenzyklopädie* 30 (Berlin: Walter de Gruyter, 1999), 143-89; and by the same author, *Friedrich Schleiermacher* (Munich: C.H. Beck, 2001). A review of recent literature is given by Ulrich Barth, "Schleiermacher-Literatur im letzten Drittel des 20. Jahrhunderts," *Theologische Rundschau* 4 (2001): 408-61.

Schütte, promoted research to rediscover the genuine intention of prominent figures in nineteenth-century theology.[6]

Already during this earliest phase of the Schleiermacher renaissance there was a felt need for a solid edition of texts, which eventually prompted the heroic undertaking of the *Schleiermacher Kritische Gesamtausgabe* (KGA).[7] The first division (in fifteen volumes) is now completed.[8] Completion of all five divisions may still take a number of decades.[9] But what has appeared already has triggered an ever growing number of historical studies in search of the true beginnings and exact steps of development in Schleiermacher's thinking,[10] on the one hand, and the genuine *intentio auctoris* in the different parts of his philosophical and theological work—together with the genuine structure underlying the coherence of these parts—on the other. Whoever wants an impression of this kind of intense and detailed "problemgeschichtliche" interpretation of Schleiermacher need only glance at two recent examples: Peter Grove's *Deutungen des Subjekts: Schleiermachers Philosophie der Religion* (Berlin: Walter de Gruyter, 2004) and Christof Ellsiepen's *Anschauung des Universums und Scientia Intuitiva* (Berlin: Walter de Gruyter, 2004). My own experience with this sort of research,[11] however, entitles me perhaps to underscore a simple fact: between the text and

---

6   See in particular Hans-Joachim Birkner, *Schleiermachers christliche Sittenlehre im Zusammenhang seines philosophisch-theologischen Systems* (Berlin: Walter de Gruyter, 1964). This *Habilitationsschrift* marks the starting point of the new Schleiermacher research in Germany after World War II, which asked about Schleiermacher's own intentions and their systematic structure. See also Hans-Joachim Birkner, *Schleiermacher-Studien* (Berlin: Walter de Gruyter, 1996).

7   As is well known, it was the merit of H.-J. Birkner to have inaugurated this immense endeavor.

8   This was the occasion for a symposium held June 2, 2005 at the University of Kiel. For these papers, see Günter Meckenstock, ed., *Schleiermacher-Tag 2005: Eine Vortragsreihe* (Göttingen: Vandenhoeck & Ruprecht, 2006). Especially noteworthy in this collection is Hermann Fischer's "Schleiermachers Neuentdeckung im 20. Jahrhundert: Beobachtungen eines Zeitzeugen," 35-44.

9   Work is carried out at two cooperating Schleiermacher research centers: one is at the University of Kiel in the Faculty of Theology and is led by Günter Meckenstock (who is presently occupied with the edition of the sermons); the other is at the Berlin-Brandenburg Academy of Sciences and is led by Andreas Arndt (who is presently occupied with further work on the edition of letters).

10 See, e.g., Günter Meckenstock, *Deterministische Ethik und kritische Theologie: Die Auseinandersetzung des frühen Schleiermacher mit Kant und Spinoza 1789-1794* (Berlin: Walter de Gruyter, 1988). This was the first study after the critical edition of the *Jugendschriften* in KGA I/1 (1984).

11 Eilert Herms, *Herkunft, Entfaltung und erste Gestalt des Systems der Wissenschaften bei Schleiermacher* (Gütersloh: Gütersloher Verlagshaus, 1974). This book was written before the publication of KGA I/1, but it seems to me not wholly superseded.

what an author has in mind there always exists a gap that the interpreter must bridge constructively by way of a divinatory act. This is especially true in Schleiermacher's case. The majority of his texts are of the sort that requires readers who do not refuse the challenge to put themselves in relation to the reality referred to by the author and to reconstruct at their own risk the entire structural complex of the real phenomena to which the texts refer—often briefly, sketchily, and with variant terminologies. Schleiermacher's texts demand not only "Nachdenken," but also "Selbstsehen" and "Selbstdenken." On the one hand, this means that the historical search for the true *intentio auctoris* is confined to demarcating some fixed reference points that, through ordinary exegesis and attention to context, can be placed beyond dispute; within these parameters one can then go on to develop and consider the various possibilities of meaning that exist within this space. The expectation that the expansion of research along the lines of "Problemgeschichte," "Begriffsgeschichte," and "Überlieferungsgeschichte" could eventually lead to a definitive and objective identification of *the* meaning of the author and that the history of such research unerringly moves toward this telos should be given up as the product of a misconception concerning what historical research is good for and what it can achieve at all. On the other hand, it can then be left to systematic consideration to decide what the historically identified parameters, together with the different views and insights attained within the space defined by them, might mean for an understanding of the present situation of Christianity, its problems and its challenges.

The legacy of Schleiermacher's oeuvre presents us with just such a mixture of firm reference points and open space for variant interpretative possibilities—a mixture that gives rise to quite fruitful insights for coping both theoretically and practically with various problems facing an adequate understanding of contemporary Christianity. This shall be shown in what follows.

One of the fixed points beyond dispute is that the *Kurze Darstellung des theologischen Studiums* characterizes theology as at once a member of a larger "cosmos" of sciences and as an internally coherent system of three essential elements or sub-disciplines: Philosophical, Historical and Practical Theology. Also beyond dispute is the fact that this triad of disciplines is a consequence of Schleiermacher's view of the essence of Christianity, which he regarded as a distinct corporate religious life, whose identity in history demands its practice, and therefore a leadership praxis that is faithful to the historic origins of Christianity as well as the challenges of its current situation. Last but not least, it is beyond dispute that this view of the essence of Christianity has two key points:

First, that the practice of leadership involved in historical Christianity must be circumspect and judicious (*besonnen*)—guided by adequate knowledge of the enduring essence and changing presence of Christian life, which, as knowledge of a specific totality of historical life and practice, has *in itself* a practice-leading scope. Consequently, theology as the whole of this knowledge, is a "positive science," a science with a functional character, existing only on the ground of this specific sort of social life and practice and in support of it. Second, the knowledge necessary for every activity of church leadership must be historical knowledge—knowledge not only of the past career of the Christian community, but of its present reality in the flux of history. Such knowledge, however, is obtainable only in a philosophical framework, namely, the framework of Philosophical Theology.

For the contemporary German situation the impact of this conception is a double one: In its indubitably clear main features, the concept has become a sort of fixed consensus within theological faculties and departments,[12] helping them quite effectively to clarify their relation to the public by showing that theology not only *studies* religion scientifically, but at the same contributes to the practical cultivation of religion and prevents it from becoming fundamentalistic. Secondly, the Schleiermacherian conception has enabled the theology faculties to clarify their relations to the churches.

At the same time, however, two vital elements of this conception are particularly open to question and have caused fruitful debates indeed. One is the position of Practical Theology within the cosmos of theological disciplines. Surely Practical Theology is not an appendix to scientific theology; Schleiermacher's view integrates Practical Theology into theology as a whole. But what, then, is its special task and contribution to the whole, as distinct from the theoretical task and output of the philosophical and historical disciplines? Schleiermacher's answer— Practical Theology is the technical doctrine (*Kunstlehre*) for guiding congregational service and church leadership—is on the face of it clear, but just what this means for Practical Theology, and whether it is acceptable, are heavily debated issues.[13] The other point of debate is the

---

12 On this see the 1994 declaration of the Evangelisch-Theologischer Fakultätentag, in *Studium der evangelischen Theologie: Zur Vorbereitung auf den Pfarrberuf* (Hannover: Kirchenamt der Evangelischen Kirche in Deutschland, 2008), 16-19.

13 The comprehensive study by Ralf Stroh, *Schleiermachers Gottesdiensttheorie: Studien zur Rekonstruktion ihres enzyklopädischen Rahmens im Ausgang von Kurzer Darstellung und Philosophischer Ethik* (Berlin: Walter de Gruyter, 1998), argues that, although Practical Theology is avowedly the "crown of theology," Schleiermacher assigns it no specific *theoretical* task.

status of Philosophical Theology and its relation to Historical Theology. When the second edition of *Kurze Darstellung* says (§33) that Philosophical Theology starts "above" Christianity, this surely means that its starting point is not the concept of the essence of Christianity, which is fundamental for theology as such, but rather the concept of religion taken universally as a constant trait of human existence, a concept belonging in the context of philosophical ethics (and arguably psychology). But does this mean that this philosophical reflection takes place on neutral ground and, as such, is indifferent to Christianity? Or does it tacitly imply that philosophy is and can only be done at all on the basis of certain historical conditions (which, for Schleiermacher, are the conditions of Christianity)? And if one holds the second view,[14] does this then mean that philosophy in general is *not* a performance of "pure" reason, but of historically conditioned reason? And what does it mean for theology that one of its essential disciplines is a philosophical one? Does it mean that theology, insofar, moves on foreign ground? Or is theology *in itself* and because of *its own object* bound to philosophize? And what then would be the conditions and the outcome of such theological philosophizing? What are its relations to the philosophizing of representatives of other religions and worldviews, and of other sciences—for example, law, medicine, and the natural sciences?

What is beyond dispute, as Schleiermacher's *Kurze Darstellung* shows, is that these sorts of questions cannot be avoided in theology. Some sort of answer must be given, and conventionally clear-cut boundaries between academic and cultural spheres—as, for example, between the scientific and the religious—are no longer beyond dispute.[15] In my opinion, to show how this bundle of problems is indispensable for any concrete self-understanding of theology and science in general

---

14 In his introduction to the lectures on philosophical ethics and in his *Dialectics*, Schleiermacher always stresses that real knowledge—the speculative as well as the empirical—exists within history and thus is continuously in the making (*im Werden*). Therefore, only this second view can be the right one. This I hold against the lucid dissertation by Martin Rössler, *Schleiermachers Programm der Philosophischen Theologie* (Berlin: Walter de Gruyter, 1994).

15 Such considerations, strange as they may feel to the modern mind, are forced upon us simply by the undeniable fact that, for Schleiermacher, religion (conceived as "eine Bestimmtheit des unmittelbaren Selbstbewußtseins") is the basic and mediating sphere for organizing and symbolizing activities of every kind. For this see Eilert Herms, "Religion, Wissen und Handeln bei Schleiermacher und in der Schleiermacherrezeption," in *200 Jahre "Reden über die Religion": Akten des 1. Internationalen Kongresses der Schleiermacher-Gesellschaft, Halle, 14.-17. März 1999*, ed. Ulrich Barth and Claus-Dieter Osthövener (Berlin: Walter de Gruyter, 2000), 142-66; also published in Eilert Herms, *Menschsein im Werden: Studien zu Schleiermacher* (Tübingen: Mohr Siebeck, 2006), 272-97.

is more important than supplying a historical answer to the question of what Schleiermacher himself really thought about all these points.

Similarly beyond debate is the fact that what Schleiermacher calls Philosophical Theology is a material part of what he calls philosophical ethics, and that the later, in turn—understood as a theory of the universally possible forms of human life in history, i.e., of the activity of reason towards nature—is conceptualized by Schleiermacher as an essential element of the complete system of all possible spheres of knowledge. With respect to the project of philosophical ethics, certain points are once more beyond debate, while others remain open for discussion. Beyond debate are: 1) the threefold form of Schleiermacher's philosophical ethics as *Tugendlehre, Pflichtenlehre,* and *Güterlehre,* and 2) that this last—as a theory of all possible forms of human interaction and therefore of all possible forms of human social life—provides a philosophy of culture or a conceptual theory of society, whose basic approach and general outlook is yet to be surpassed by any proposal in the nineteenth or twentieth century. This was seen already by Albert Reble between the wars and recently underscored by Michael Moxter's study, *Güterbegriff und Handlungstheorie.*[16] Yet the following issues remain continuously debated: 1) just what the indissoluble connection of *Güterlehre* to *Pflichtenlehre* and *Tugendlehre* really means for the conception of human goods, i.e., social systems, and 2) what it is that constitutes the final basis from which the possibilities of human living together are to be conceptually deduced: whether the basis lies in a general theory of action (as Moxter suggests) or whether it lies at the deeper level of a conception of human nature, i.e., a "fundamental anthropology" conceived as a transcendental theory of finite, that is, innerworldly, rational beings (as I myself have argued on several occasions).[17]

This discussion is closely related to that other one concerning the systematic connection among all possible spheres of knowledge. Beyond dispute is the fact that the basic plan of this system is determined by the four distinctions between: 1) the action of nature towards reason and the action of reason towards nature (together with the corresponding theories of physics and ethics), 2) conceptual knowledge versus empirical knowledge, 3) the identical (or common) versus the individual symbolizing function of reason, and 4) theoretical (critical)

---

16   Albert Reble, *Schleiermachers Kulturphilosophie: Eine entwicklungsgeschichtlich-systematische Würdigung* (Erfurt: Kurt Stenger, 1935); Michael Moxter, *Güterbegriff und Handlungstheorie: Eine Studie zur Ethik Friedrich Schleiermachers* (Kampen: Kok Pharos, 1992).

17   See my collection of essays, *Menschsein im Werden.*

disciplines versus technical ones. But what is the basic fact that calls for all these distinctions in knowledge and makes them unavoidable? In other words, what according to Schleiermacher is the "highest science" (*höchste Wissenschaft*)? Is it the conceptual discipline having for its object the first principle of knowledge behind which no finite rational being can go and unsurpassable by any possible act of finite knowledge? Again, something here is beyond dispute: namely, that Schleiermacher's first lectures on *Dialectics* had something like a Fichtean *Wissenschaftslehre* in mind. But what remains controversial is whether this was Schleiermacher's original and enduring intention or whether it was simply a temporary deviation from his actual original view (guiding the presentation not only of the *Reden* of 1799 but also of the *Broullion zur Ethik* of 1805-06) that "Menschheit" as "Beseelung der Natur" (animation of nature) is the whole of the fundamentally given, factual, and unsurpassable conditions of finite rational beings, including all their knowing and acting and, therefore, the object and theme of the highest science—a view he resumed in 1818, when for the first time he lectured on psychology (one essential part of anthropology, the other being physiology).[18]

Again, it is beyond dispute that what Schleiermacher conceives and describes as the first and unsurpassable principle of all possibilities of finite rational being is the facticity of immediate self-consciousness in its continuously varying forms of innerworldly determinacy. It is also indisputable that this fact, because it contains all of the original conditions of all possible forms of human life (i.e., organizing and symbolizing activities), must be and is thematized in the transcendental part of the theory of knowledge (*Dialektik*), in the introductory parts of the theory of action, and in the lectures on psychology. And finally, it is beyond dispute that in the introduction to the second edition of *The Christian Faith* the concept of this original fact is exposed—nota bene as a lemma from psychology[19]—as the concept of the factual essence of religion as a universal feature of human nature. Still controversial,

---

18 So while Andreas Arndt, for example, holds that the transcendental part of the *Dialectics* is for Schleiermacher the highest science (see the introduction to his edition of the *Dialektik*, KGA II/10.1, viiff.), I remain convinced that it can be demonstrated that, beginning in 1818, psychology enjoys the status of the highest science. See Eilert Herms, "Die Bedeutung der 'Psychologie' für die Konzeption des Wissenschaftssystems beim späten Schleiermacher," in *Schleiermacher und die wissenschaftliche Kultur des Christentums*, ed. Günter Meckenstock and Joachim Ringleben (Berlin: Walter de Gruyter, 1991), 369-401; also published in Herms, *Menschsein im Werden*, 173-99. On this issue see also Fischer, *Schleiermacher*, 83ff.

19 Friedrich Schleiermacher, *Der christliche Glaube nach den Grundsätzen der evangelischen Kirche im Zusammenhange dargestellt* (1830/31), in KGA I/13.1, §3.3. Henceforth CG.

however, is the question regarding how this immediate self-consciousness in its respective forms of determinatedness[20] is related to the whole activity of human symbolizing and organizing—i.e., whether religion in its respective positive forms is the *determining basis* of all possible forms of rational activity (a notion highly offensive to conventional Enlightenment convictions!), or whether it is only an essential feature of the self *alongside* the functions of knowing and doing, each of which can go its way and do its work without being bound to some religious basis and horizon. Obviously, at stake in this dispute is not only what Schleiermacher really meant, but also what sort of claims human reason as finite and innerworldly reason may be entitled to at all.[21]

Likewise, an important area of debate is the question of how the immediacy of self-consciousness allows us to reflect on it and to catch its own content in thought and language. The thesis of Falk Wagner and his follower Jörg Dierken that the so-called immediacy of self-consciousness is only a presupposition made by reflection itself—i.e., a secondary, reflection-mediated immediacy—represents one position.[22] An alternative is the thesis that 1) the conditions that make it possible and unavoidable for finite reason to reflect actively are received by reason in a radical passivity that underlies and accompanies all relative passivity characteristic of our relation to the sensible environment, and 2) these utterly passively received conditions contain in themselves the double immediate reflexivity[23] that confer upon feeling the distinct content that presents itself as the determinate object of reflective thought and language, including the transcendental distinction between world (as the sphere of all possible relative dependence between innerworldly reason and its environment) and God as the Absolute (which, as such, is the transcendent ground of the existence of this worldly sphere as a whole).

Here we arrive at a truly critical point, which not only determines what the original relations between all sorts of possible *objects* of our knowing are (transcendentally, the relationship between world and God; within the world, the interaction between nature and reason), but

---

20 CG §5.
21 On this disputed question, again see note 18 above.
22 See Falk Wagner, *Schleiermachers Dialektik: Eine kritische Interpretation* (Gütersloh: Gütersloher Verlagshaus, 1974); and Jörg Dierken, *Glaube und Lehre im modernen Protestantismus: Studien zum Verhältnis von religiösem Vollzug und theologischer Bestimmtheit bei Barth und Bultmann sowie Hegel und Schleiermacher* (Tübingen: Mohr Siebeck, 1996), 308-416.
23 See the concept "unmittelbarste Reflexion" in CG §4.4.

also what the original relations between all possible *forms* of knowing (knowing und symbolizing empirically versus speculatively; knowing and symbolizing individually versus identically). It is of the greatest importance, especially for theology, to bring sufficient clarity to the relationships between these original forms of knowing and symbolizing. For only then will it be possible to *distinguish* not only between Philosophical and Historical Theology, but also to see how the whole enterprise of Historical Theology depends entirely on clear-cut perspectives from Philosophical Theology:

- Only then can it be seen that (and why) all religious life in history, including the Christian life as well, is faith as a determinatedness of immediate self-consciousness resulting from the historical and social communication of that very faith, whose determinate content shapes and motivates determinate practice across all fields of human interaction.
- Only then can it be seen that (and why) all religious life, including Christian life as well, is a communal reality indissoluble from institutional forms.[24]
- Only then can it be seen that (and why) amidst the changes of history the identity of all religious life, including the Christian life as well, depends upon the enduring presence of the historical beginning and origin—in the Christian case, the spiritual presence of the absolutely potent God-consiousness of Christ—within all historical communication of this faith.
- Only then can it be seen that (and why) all religious life, including the Christian life as service to God in a general sense, is and must be centered around the service to God in the specific form of a *cultus*.
- Only then can it be seen that (and why) all religious cult, including the Christian cult as well, contains not only a non-verbal, but also a verbal communication of faith.
- Only then can it be seen that (and why) this verbal communication of faith requires both an adherence to the original form of religious discourse (*Glaubenssprache*), which is a kind of symbolizing in individualized style, and an attempt at a doctrinal description of the real phenomena to which religious language refers, which always is and must be symbolizing in the identical style.

---

[24] This must be emphasized against a widespread view that regards Schleiermacher as the classic father and founder of Protestant "individualism."

- And only then can it be seen that (and why) the identity of any religious life in history, including the Christian, demands both 1) a fixed body of texts that testify to and hold present (at the level of individual symbolization) the real beginning and origin of the faith, which is canonical for the form of religious life in question and, 2) a body of doctrine that represents the communal consensus concerning the direction in which doctrine is to look for the real phenomena referred to in the original language of faith.[25]

An adequate understanding of Schleiermacher's program in dogmatics and its realization in the two editions of his *Glaubenslehre* and the lectures on Christian ethics should be aware of all of these systematic presuppositions as they stem from Schleiermacher's conception of theology—its basis, its context, and its implications. It must be said, however, that the way in which German systematic theology typically treats Schleiermacher's dogmatics rarely fulfills this condition adequately. One still finds numerous references in the literature to Schleiermacher's dogmatics that tacitly take *one* part (*Der christliche Glaube*) as the whole, neglecting the second part (*Die christliche Sitte*), and that confront it with alien questions, censuring it from the outside and rejecting its basis without understanding it. This holds especially for arguments rejecting his dogmatics as "subjectivistic." With some Barthians the situation remains just as it was with Karl Barth himself: They honor Schleiermacher as a great theologian (see Eberhard Jüngel's entry on Schleiermacher in *Religion in Geschichte und Gegenwart*, 4th ed.), but still have reason to ask themselves: "Did I understand him rightly?" On the other hand, a sort of a natural link is constituted between Schleiermacher and the so-called hermeneutic theology (following Rudolf Bultmann) by the fact that both conceive Christianity within an anthropological framework. It is symptomatic of the situation that Gerhard Ebeling, the last leader of this hermeneutic school, joined the editorial board of the KGA.[26] This fact shows that although the renewed interest in Schleier-

---

25 For Schleiermacher's conception of canonical scripture and exegesis, see my "Welt—Kirche—Bibel: Zum hermeneutischen Zentrum und Fundament von Schleiermachers Verständnis der Christentums- und Sozialgeschichte," in Herms, *Menschsein im Werden*, 250-71 and, in the same volume, "Schleiermachers Verständnis der exegetischen Theologie," 427-82.
26 For Ebeling's work on Schleiermacher, see "Schleiermachers Lehre von den göttlichen Eigenschaften," in Gerhard Ebeling, *Wort und Glaube*, vol. 2 (Tübingen: Mohr Siebeck, 1969), 305-42; as well as the following essays in *Wort und Glaube*, vol. 3 (Tübingen: Mohr Siebeck, 1975): "Frömmigkeit und Bildung," 60-95; "Beobachtungen zu Schleiermachers Wirklichkeitsverständnis," 96-115; and "Schlechthinniges

macher started mainly within the aforementioned Göttingen Group—fueled by a dissatisfaction with the theological mainstream of the 1960s and a newfound interest in nineteenth-century theology and its roots in Kantian and post-Kantian philosophy—the recognition of such fixed reference points as those sketched above transcended the boundaries of any such school and has been an incentive to reexamine the whole spectrum of problems in systematic theology.

Let me conclude by summarizing the main themes:

First, in contrast to the German theological mainstream of the 1960s, it is now widely accepted that theology cannot avoid philosophizing. For only in this way can it make plausible that and how religion is an unmistakable attitude toward the entirety of the shared, real world of humankind, and that religion's God-talk is more than merely a relatively coherent language game (*Sprachspiel*); it is, rather, a discourse about our common phenomenal reality, i.e., about the dynamic essence, origin, and destination of the common world and our lives within it.

Second, we can observe a growing awareness and acknowledgement that Schleiermacher's conception of religion, Christianity, and theology enables one to show that and how the indispensable concepts of *revelation* as the origin of Christianity and *the authority of Holy Scripture* as testimony to the original, and therefore canonical, traits of the essence of Christianity can be made plausible in a way that takes seriously and works through each moment of truth in the radical criticism leveled against them by the Enlightenment.

Third, the path taken by Schleiermacher to identify the phenomenal reality referred to by the religious distinction between the world and God has attracted a great deal of attention. I can here only mention Ebeling's early study "Schleiermachers Lehre von den Eigenschaften Gottes" and Claus-Dieter Osthövener's recent dissertation, *Die Lehre von Gottes Eigenschaften bei Friedrich Schleiermacher und Karl Barth*.[27] Schleiermacher's proposal requires us to ask whether we can have a concept of God without a concept of the world that refers to the same reality dealt with by the natural sciences—a pivotal question in debates about the place of religion and theology in modern culture, which has

---

Abhängigkeitsbewußtsein als Gottesbewußtsein," 116-36. Also noteworthy is the influence of Schleiermacher on the structure of Ebeling's *Dogmatik des christlichen Glaubens*, 3 vols. (Tübingen: Mohr Siebeck, 1979).

27 Claus-Dieter Osthövener, *Die Lehre von Gottes Eigenschaften bei Friedrich Schleiermacher und Karl Barth* (Berlin: Walter de Gruyter, 1996).

been answered with a "Yes" by Ulrich Barth[28] and with a "No" by the present speaker.[29]

All of these are incentives provided by Schleiermacher to overcome weaknesses and deficits in German Protestant theology between the 1920s and 1960s. Yet there are also features in the heritage of Schleiermacher's oeuvre that prompt the critical questioning of certain tendencies in some forms of recent liberal theology that have emerged since the 1960s.

First, Schleiermacher stresses that in and through all historical change there remain overarching moments of continuity that serve as the condition for the identity of Christian life in history. Indispensable and central among these moments of continuity is the doctrinal consensus of the church, which orientates pastors and church leaders in their service to the community. In *Schleiermacher und die Bekenntnisschriften*, Martin Ohst has shown how Schleiermacher respected this binding consensus in a manner that avoids both the abstract neglect of the confessional writings and their thoughtless, literalistic abuse.[30] Thus Schleiermacher recognizes the effective function of these doctrinal writings in sustaining the identity of Protestantism through the ages. This permits him to distinguish between the new and the old Protestantism, while at the same time precluding any abstract opposition between the two.

Second, Schleiermacher insists that Christian faith—as felt conviction with unmistakable content regarding the origin, dynamic essence, and final destiny of world and mankind—inspires a certain kind of conduct of life in every sphere of interaction. This, in turn, provokes a critical reconsideration of abstract claims concerning the so-called "Eigengesetzlichkeit" of all social systems espoused by classical figures such as Friedrich Naumann and Max Weber. It also calls into question the flat-out negation of a specific content for Christian ethics at all, found, for example, in Wilhelm Herrmann and Emanuel Hirsch.

Third, and finally: for Schleiermacher the reality of Christian faith is essentially—whatever the historic circumstances may be—a communal,

---

28 See Ulrich Barth, "Abschied von der Kosmologie: Welterklärung und religiöse Endlichkeitsreflexion," in Ulrich Barth, *Religion in der Moderne* (Tübingen: Mohr Siebeck, 2003), 401-26.

29 See Eilert Herms, "Freiheit Gottes—Freiheit des Menschen: Schleiermachers Rezeption der reformatorischen Lehre vom servum arbitrium in seiner Abhandlung 'Über die Lehre von der Erwählung besonders in Beziehung auf Herrn Dr. Bretschneiders Aphorismen,'" forthcoming (2009) in a Festschrift for Oswald Bayer.

30 Martin Ohst, *Schleiermacher und die Bekenntnisschriften* (Tübingen: Mohr Siebeck, 1989).

and as such, an experiential affair of visible loyalty to the visible church as the only sphere of the origin and effective communication of faith. In this light, one may really ask whether this position or the more recent one set forth by some sociologists who entertain the possibility of an essentially individualistic, informal, and invisible form of religion, is truer to the facts. Thanks to Schleiermacher, we may at least doubt the truth of the latter thesis. And here, as at so many other points, we may honor the complex heritage of Schleiermacher's œuvre as a lively spring of fruitful questions.

Friedrich Schleiermacher

Symbol Theory, Hermeneutics, and Forms of Religious Communication

CORNELIA RICHTER

Although it stands last in the title of this paper, religious communication is the first theme I must address, for it is the main concern and focus of Schleiermacher's entire theology and parts of his philosophy as well. In their excellent anthology on Schleiermacher's philosophy, Dieter Burdorf and Reinhold Schmücker chose the title *Dialogische Wissenschaft* to denote not only research into dialogue as a form, but also scholarship that is itself dialogical. They claim that Schleiermacher, like Plato, chose dialogue as philosophy's essential form. Yet Schleiermacher was not simply imitating Plato, for in his decisively *theoretical* approach to modern dialogical research Schleiermacher incorporated the dialogical principle into the constitution of knowledge itself.[1] Although Burdorf and Schmücker recognize that Schleiermacher tried to put his theoretical reflections to the test in sermons, educational programs, and academic lectures, I would like to underscore this point even more strongly: Schleiermacher not only *declares* theology to be communicative and provides us with theoretical reflections on this conception, he also *performs* communicative theology and philosophy throughout his works. Beginning with the early *Speeches* in 1799 and continuing up to his last introduction to the *Dialectics* in 1833, Schleiermacher stresses the fundamental importance of communicative acts, owing to the inescapable difference between individuals and their divergent opinions. Hence, it is not only a philosophically or academically interesting task to reflect on dialogue and dialectics, it is also a prerequisite for all knowledge and action among people.[2]

---

1   Dieter Burdorf and Reinhold Schmücker, "Streitgespräche: Schleiermachers Konzept einer dialogischen Wissenschaft," introduction to *Dialogische Wissenschaft*: *Perspektiven der Philosophie Schleiermachers* (Paderborn: Schöningh, 1998), 7-18, esp. 7.
2   In 1984, the University of Göttingen organized lectures to commemorate the 150th anniversary of Schleiermacher's death. I highly recommend these lectures as a pri-

In the first section of this paper I will treat Schleiermacher's early and, of course, most famous work, *On Religion: Speeches to its Cultural Despisers* from 1799. Here, in an *act* of religious and theological communication, Schleiermacher offers basic reflections on why religion is inextricably bound to religious communication. This is, of course, also true for Schleiermacher's *Soliloquies* (1800), *Christmas Celebration* (1806), and his *Sermons*, but time and length constraints permit me to provide only some brief comments on these in a classical German footnote.³ In

---

mary introduction to Schleiermacher's works. Dietz Lange, ed., *Friedrich Schleiermacher 1786-1834: Theologe—Philosoph—Pädagoge* (Göttingen: Vandenhoeck & Ruprecht, 1985). See Burdorf and Schmücker, *Dialogische Wissenschaft*, 13.

3   At first glance, the *Soliloquies* and *Christmas Celebration* may appear somewhat antiquated. This is true especially of the latter, in which Schleiermacher portrays a bourgeois family and friends on Christmas Eve in a very Romantic manner and develops some rather unlikely characters—especially the women. Yet in the way these four women, four men, and one child talk about Christmas, the meaning of Christian belief—its value and comforting power—becomes visible. Whereas the *Christmas Celebration* is set up as a play, the *Soliloquies* of 1800 evolved from a sermon Schleiermacher delivered on New Year's Eve in 1792, which was subsequently expanded to include broader self-reflections on the value of life. Here, too, we find that theology is embodied in communicative acts: his discourse about religion is performed in a way that incorporates emotion as well as intellect, and implies a loving and caring way of acting. It is no surprise that an author who made the connection among intellect, emotion, and action his central concern was also an impressive preacher. Churches were overflowing when Schleiermacher was to preach and the congregants were deeply moved by his words. See Wolfgang Trillhaas, "Der Berliner Prediger," in Lange, *Friedrich Schleiermacher*, 9-23. Schleiermacher's outstanding success, however, was not only due to his rhetorical talent, but also to the homiletic program that the sermons expressed. Wilhelm Gräb thus takes Schleiermacher to be the founder of modern homiletics in the sense of self-reflective acts of Christian consciousness that avoid pedagogical-missionary claims as well as a proclamatory or kerygmatic approach ("Predigt als kommunikativer Akt: Einige Bemerkungen zu Schleiermachers Theorie religiöser Mitteilung," in *Internationaler Schleiermacher-Kongreß Berlin 1984*, ed. Kurt-Victor Selge [Berlin: Walter de Gruyter, 1985], 2:643-59, esp. 643). As an act of self-reflection, preaching is not simply about delivering a speech, but is bound up with the active appropriation and interpretation on the part of each person involved. In "Die unendliche Aufgabe des Verstehens," (in Lange, *Friedrich Schleiermacher*, 47-71), Gräb draws on the universality of hermeneutics as a never ending story of subjectivity: "Schleiermachers Hermeneutik zielt auf diesen produktiven, sinndeutenden, ja sinnstiftenden Verstehensvorgang, der ohne die unmittelbare Selbsterschlossenheit der verstehenden Subjektivität nicht zustande kommen kann"(68). Theodor Jørgensen likewise tried to defend Schleiermacher's idea of preaching as self-presentation because for him it was a question of a sermon being trustworthy or not ("Predigt als Selbstdarstellung," in *Schleiermacher und die wissenschaftliche Kultur des Christentums*, ed. Günter Meckenstock [Berlin: Walter de Gruyter, 1991], 173-85, esp. 174). Despite the fact that this conception of preaching seems to be completely at odds with the position of Karl Barth (we should speak of God, not of man!), Jørgensen nonetheless argues that Barth and Schleiermacher share a modern perspective (176), one in which God must not become an object of theology, but rather must remain its subject, and in which the reference to Christ is

section two I will turn to Schleiermacher's *Hermeneutics*, in which he theoretically develops the problem of understanding and the inevitability of communication in detail and outlines criteria for a better understanding of texts and oral discourse. In the third section, I will show how these hermeneutical considerations extend to symbol theory in its various forms, be it in cultural theory, in the arts, or in practical theology, and how this brings us back to the issue of communication. All of this will be done in light of recent research on Schleiermacher and thus in accord with the charge given to our panel.

1. Forms of Religious Communication

Richard Crouter once said that Schleiermacher is always communicative, but that *"On Religion* stands as primary example of this extensive rhetorical process."[4] The reason for this primacy is not only Schleiermacher's special interest in rhetorical or hermeneutical processes as we might discuss them today. Rather, Schleiermacher's interest is based on a profound theological idea. In the first speech, the *apologia,* he confesses that he is driven by divine necessity, by natural force, and by divine vocation. Life as a whole, he says, is determined by two essential and reciprocal forces, attraction and repulsion (*Aneignen und Abstossen*).[5] Every individual constantly seeks to perceive and to share what is perceived, to confide in and open up to others. Thus, in the second speech on the essence of religion Schleiermacher calls religion "the necessary and indispensible third" complement to metaphysics and morality; religion is "Sinn und Geschmack fürs Unendliche," and in religion we have an "Anschauen des Universums."[6] The aim, however, of all those who seek religion is humankind, since love strives to be

---

pronounced and constant. I cannot go into detail here, since this topic would lead us further into practical theology and ecclesiological reflections, but it is important to recall not only Schleiermacher's rhetorical power but also the almost natural way in which he publicly performed what he penned. In this regard Martin Nicol was right to call Schleiermacher a virtuoso of conversation. See Martin Nicol, *Gespräch als Seelsorge: Theologische Fragmente zu einer Kultur des Gesprächs* (Göttingen: Vandenhoeck & Ruprecht, 1990), 23-44.

4   Richard Crouter, "Schleiermacher's Theory of Language: The Ubiquity of a Romantic Text," in *Friedrich Schleiermacher: Between Enlightenment and Romanticism* (Cambridge: Cambridge University Press, 2005), 201. Chapter eleven of Crouter's book, entitled *"On Religion* as a Religious Classic: Hermeneutical Musings After Two Hundred Years," offers an excellent typology of interpretations of the *Speeches.*
5   Friedrich Schleiermacher, *Über die Religion: Reden an die Gebildeten unter ihren Verächtern* (1799), in KGA I/2, 190-91.
6   Ibid., 212-13.

enacted and answered.[7] The third speech explains how this can be obtained: the path to religion is a question of self-education (*Bildung zur Religion*), and any single step must be enacted by oneself, thereby revealing again that we have been born with a natural predisposition for religion.[8] So, on the one hand, all religious ideas and impressions can and must be shared. On the other hand, they cannot be taught like natural sciences; rather, they must be performed, felt, and enacted. It does not come as a surprise, then, that in the fourth speech, before proceeding to characterize the different religions in the fifth and last speech, Schleiermacher declares religion to be bound to community, for it is the nature of religion to express itself, to be expressed, and to share deep impressions, perceptions, and feelings.[9] All of this is to be carried out, however, not in academic monographs and papers, but by actually talking to each other and using all efforts, arts, and means of language in order to substantiate our vague and fleeting words.[10]

The fascinating power of the *Speeches*—especially their insistence on putting religion on par with metaphysics and morality and their strong emphasis on feeling—had an enormous impact in Schleiermacher's time. The focus on "Gefühl" has subsequently stimulated an extensive interdisciplinary debate on feeling and emotion, which to this day remains unsettled. Within theology, a re-orientation towards his position in the German-speaking countries of Europe in the 1970s caused a change of perspective that is often called the "Schleiermacher-Renaissance" and is closely tied to the name of Hans-Joachim Birkner. After decades of the dominance of dialectical theology, *religion* became once again the focus of theological reflection, spurring on immense and still ongoing research on the concept of religion, the relation between religion and culture, and the theory of religion in classical German philosophy. This flurry of scholarly activity thereby established Schleiermacher as a philosopher of stature equal to Kant, Fichte, Schelling, and Hegel. Pursuing these topics within the context of recent German theology inevitably means surveying the works of Ulrich Barth, Friedrich Wilhelm Graf, Dietrich Korsch, Jan Rohls, Wilhelm Gräb, Jörg Dierken, Michael Moxter, and Georg Pfleiderer, among others. Unfortunately, going down this road on this occasion would surely exceed the limitations of this paper.

For many years research on the *Speeches* focused on Schleiermacher's concepts of intuition (*Anschauen*) and feeling (*Gefühl*), proceeding

---

7 Ibid., 228.
8 Ibid., 252.
9 Ibid., 267-68.
10 Ibid., 269.

from there to Schleiermacher's other writings and to the general discourse on subjectivity and emotion. In 1984, Robert R. Williams discussed the differences between Schleiermacher and Hegel and came to the conclusion that Schleiermacher's

> Gefühl is not a transcendental subjectivity in the foundationalist Cartesian-Kantian sense . . . not a self-sufficient foundation prescribing structures to and legislating for experience. Rather Gefühl is the original disclosure of the pre-given life-world, the immediate presence of whole undivided being. Gefühl then is not a transcendental foundation of experience, but only the medium of access to the foundation. But in this case the foundation turns out to be the world (Lebenswelt) as the ultimate horizon of consciousness.[11]

I mention Williams here because it is interesting to see how close his interpretation is to Dieter Henrich's theory of subjectivity, which takes immediate self-consciousness as a pre-reflexive familiarity (*präreflexive Vertrautheit*) prior to any reference of the subject to herself.[12]

Jan Rohls has stressed the fact that the notion of feeling, which in the *Speeches* is closely tied to the notion of intuition, was later developed by Schleiermacher in the *Glaubenslehre* in such a way that notion of intuition was gradually dropped in favor of feeling as "immediate self-consciousness." Rohls then extended the theory of feeling as "immediate self-consciousness" to a theory of piety by drawing upon analytical philosophy, and defended this theory against objections raised by the critique of religion.[13]

In 1994, Christian Albrecht published an extensive study of Schleiermacher's theory of piety, which, he claimed, could be understood as a general theory of the relation between consciousness and reality, whether we look at the *Speeches*, the *Glaubenslehre*, or the *Dialectics*.[14] Given the size of his topic, Albrecht confined himself to an analy-

---

11 Robert R. Williams, "Immediacy and Determinacy in Schleiermacher's Phenomenology of Self-Consciousness," in Selge, *Schleiermacher-Kongreß 1984*, 213.
12 Dieter Henrich, "Selbstbewusstsein: Kritische Einleitung in eine Theorie," in *Hermeneutik und Dialektik: Aufsätze I*, ed. Rüdiger Bubner, Konrad Cramer, and Reiner Wiehl (Tübingen: Mohr Siebeck, 1970), 257-84, esp. 260. Also see Henrich's famous studies, *Selbstverhältnisse: Gedanken und Auslegungen zu den Grundlagen der klassischen deutschen Philosophie* (Stuttgart: Reclam, 1982).
13 Jan Rohls, "Frömmigkeit als Gefühl schlechthinniger Abhängigkeit: Zu Schleiermachers Religionstheorie in der 'Glaubenslehre'," in Selge, *Schleiermacher-Kongreß 1984*, 221-52, esp. 222-23. For a more general discussion, see Rohls' "Religion—jenseits von Metaphysik und Moral?" in *Reden über Religion I*, ed. Jutta Höcht-Stöhr and Michael Schibilsky (Stuttgart: Kohlhammer, 1999), 9-26.
14 Christian Albrecht, *Schleiermachers Theorie der Frömmigkeit: Ihr wissenschaftlicher Ort und ihr systematischer Gehalt in den "Reden," in der Glaubenslehre und in der Dialektik* (Berlin: Walter de Gruyter, 1994). Cf. Fred Lönker, "Religiöses Erleben: Zu Schleier-

sis of the texts mentioned above and refrained from relating Schleiermacher to his historical and philosophical context. He thereby not only followed much contemporary research on Schleiermacher, which was and still is focused on the new critical edition of Schleiermacher's works, but also presented Schleiermacher as a versatile author, who not only thought in an inter- and transdisciplinary way, but also encouraged theology to enlarge its research programs to topics far beyond what was expected, e.g., to hermeneutics and symbol theory.

Before we discuss the latter, allow me to return for a moment to Schleiermacher's relation to the classical German philosophy and theories of subjectivity of his day. In a major 2004 study, Peter Grove pursued both of these topics simultaneously via a systematic interpretation of Schleiermacher's philosophy of religion, which focused mainly on the *Speeches* and the later *Glaubenslehre*.[15] This wide-ranging work investigates Schleiermacher's relation to the Enlightenment, Kantianism, the so-called "Spinoza Renaissance," and early German Romanticism. His detailed analysis of Schleiermacher's writings through 1803 demonstrates the strong impact of authors such as Wolff, Eberhard, Reinhold, Kant, Jacobi, Fichte, and Friedrich Schlegel. Particularly noteworthy are Grove's new insights into Schleiermacher's relationship to Reinhold and Kant. And while the idea that Schleiermacher neither simply followed nor rejected Kant's dualisms is not new,[16] Grove has provided us with a more nuanced understanding of the specific differences between these thinkers.

This brings me to one of the most recent debates concerning Schleiermacher's *Speeches*, namely, his relation to Spinoza and the question of whether the *Speeches* are pantheistic or not. In 1999, at a Schleiermacher Gesellschaft conference in Halle commemorating the *Speeches*, Konrad Cramer argued for a significant difference between Spinoza and Schleiermacher, despite the fact that both employ the notion of intuiting the Universe. Cramer concluded that while in Spinoza this notion denoted rational comprehension (*denkendes Begreifen*), in Schleiermacher it was bound to feeling qua "sense and taste" (*Sinn und Geschmack*).[17] Christof Ellsiepen has pursued this topic a step further by

---

machers zweiter Rede 'Über die Religion'," in Burdorf and Schmücker, *Dialogische Wissenschaft*, 53-68.

15 Peter Grove, *Deutungen des Subjekts: Schleiermachers Philosophie der Religion*, Theologische Bibliothek Töpelmann 129 (Berlin: Walter de Gruyter, 2004).

16 See Cornelia Richter, *Die Religion in der Sprache der Kultur: Schleiermacher und Cassirer — Kulturphilosophische Symmetrien und Divergenzen* (Tübingen: Mohr Siebeck, 2004).

17 Konrad Cramer, "'Anschauung des Universums': Schleiermacher und Spinoza," in *200 Jahre "Reden über die Religion": Akten des 1. Internationalen Kongresses der Schleier-*

relating Schleiermacher's notion of intuiting the Universe to Spinoza's idea of *scientia intuitiva*.[18] Ellsiepen was able to build upon two previous studies of the relationship of Schleiermacher to Spinoza—those of Günter Meckenstock and Julia Lamm—both of which drew support from the critical edition of Schleiermacher's *Jugendschriften* on Spinoza published in 1984.[19] Distinctive of Ellsiepen's study is its deeper investigations into Schleiermacher's reading and commentary on Jacobi's *Letters on Spinoza*, which Ellsiepen considers the basis for understanding Schleiermacher's notion of religious intuition. Interpreting the latter as grounded in the relationship between individuality and universality and viewed from the perspective of finite human consciousness, Ellsiepen clearly rejects all interpretations of the *Speeches* that suggest an immediate and somehow revelatory relation between the human subject and the divine.[20] Instead, Ellsiepen suggests, it was exactly this complex tension between the non-concrete "Universum" (as the Absolute) and our vivid and embodied relation to it that was determinative for Schleiermacher's theology.

With respect to the *Speeches*, then, we are back to where we started, namely, to the enormous influence of Spinoza, or let us say of Jacobi's Spinoza, on Schleiermacher. It is intriguing to see how—at least in the *Speeches*—the philosophy of Spinoza meets communication theory. Given the absoluteness of the Universe, hermeneutical efforts are the very least that finite subjects need! So let's proceed to section two on Schleiermacher's hermeneutics.

---

    macher-Gesellschaft Halle, 14.-17. März 1999, ed. Ulrich Barth and Claus-Dieter Osthövener (Berlin: Walter de Gruyter, 2000), 141.

18 Christof Ellsiepen, *Anschauung des Universums und Scientia Intuitiva: Die Spinozistischen Grundlagen von Schleiermachers früher Religionstheorie*, Theologische Bibliothek Töpelmann 135 (Berlin: Walter de Gruyter, 2004).

19 Günter Meckenstock, *Deterministische Ethik und kritische Theologie: Die Auseinandersetzung des frühen Schleiermacher mit Kant und Spinoza 1789-1794* (Berlin: Walter de Gruyter, 1988); and Julia Lamm, *The Living God: Schleiermacher's Theological Appropriation of Spinoza* (University Park: Pennsylvania State University Press, 1991). The critical edition of the *Jugendschriften* has also been of importance to historical studies, such as Dorette Seibert's *Glaube, Erfahrung und Gemeinschaft: Der junge Schleiermacher und Herrnhut* (Göttingen: Vandenhoeck & Ruprecht, 2003).

20 Here Ellsiepen distances himself from Albrecht's notion of "Uraffektion" and from Lönker's concept of religious experience of totality (see note 14 above), as well as from Gunther Wenz's idea of intuition or the feeling of totality. On the latter, see Gunther Wenz, *Sinn und Geschmack fürs Unendliche* (Munich: Verlag der Bayerischen Akademie der Wissenschaften, 1999).

2. Hermeneutics

This is a perfect opportunity to highlight the value of the new critical edition of Schleiermacher's works (KGA), keeping in mind what Wolfgang Virmond wrote in 1984 about the complex processes of identifying the individual manuscripts and reconstructing their history.[21] So far, the new edition contains some relatively unknown texts on hermeneutics and philology, which until now have been familiar only to scholars working in the archives.[22] Moreover, thanks to their excellent historical introductions and principled organization, the KGA volumes provide us with a coherent picture of the development and relations of these texts for the first time.[23]

Schleiermacher's different forms of religious communication and his reflections on them have deeply influenced all kinds of academic discourse on communication, hermeneutics, linguistic theory, and symbol theory—not only within theology, but also far beyond, e.g., in linguistics and rhetorical studies.[24] Within contemporary German the-

---

21 Wolfgang Virmond, "Neue Textgrundlagen zu Schleiermachers früher Hermeneutik: Prolegomena zur kritischen Edition," in Selge, *Schleiermacher-Kongreß 1984*, 575-90.
22 See, for example, Schleiermacher's "Entwurf zur Abhandlung über den Stil" (1790/91) and "Über den Stil" (1790/91) in KGA I/1, lix-lxii, 357-390, as well as "Sprachphilosophische Untersuchungen" (ca. 1809) in KGA I/14, xlix-li, 107f.
23 The way in which the new edition will make things much easier can be seen in Hendrik Birus' very helpful study of Schleiermacher's notion of "technical interpretation," in which the author still had to contend with many different manuscripts, some of them still unpublished ("Schleiermachers Begriff der 'technischen Interpretation'," in Selge, *Schleiermacher-Kongreß 1984*, 591-99). Like so many others, Birus refers to Peter Szondi's early essay, "Schleiermachers Hermeneutik heute" (in Peter Szondi, *Schriften II*, ed. Jean Bollack et al. [Frankfurt: Suhrkamp, 1978], 106-30). The new critical edition of the *Hermeneutics* was well under way but unfinished in 1986 when Werner Jeanrond reexamined the *Hermeneutics* on the basis of Heinz Kimmerle's (1959) and Manfred Frank's (1977) respective editions ("The Impact of Schleiermacher's Hermeneutics on Contemporary Interpretation Theory," in *The Interpretation of Belief: Coleridge, Schleiermacher and Romanticism*, ed. David Jasper [Houndmills: Macmillan, 1986], 81-103). Jeanrond saw the impact of Schleiermacher's hermeneutics on contemporary interpretation theory in a) the problem of a theory of text, b) the dialectic of text and reading, c) the theory of style, d) hermeneutics and criticism, e) the aims of interpretation, and f) the fact of pluralism in interpretation (89-95). See also Peter P. Kenny, "Correcting the History: The Significance of Schleiermacher's Early Hermeneutics Manuscripts," *New Athenaeum/Neues Athenaeum* 3 (1992): 43-65.
24 This is particularly true for the more philosophical and pedagogical disciplines in linguistics, which are called "Sprechwissenschaft" and "Sprecherziehung" in Germany. These disciplines are based on ideas developed by Humboldt, Schlegel, and Schleiermacher, and proceed from the insight that understanding is not self-evident, but is rather tied to various conditions of (inter-)subjective interaction and expres-

ology, Schleiermacher's hermeneutical and communication-theoretical insights have even inspired some of the most popular approaches in exegetical or dogmatic theology. As far as I can see, there is no philosophically or linguistically oriented introduction to hermeneutics today that would not regard Schleiermacher as a turning point in the hermeneutic tradition. In saying this, I do *not* mean to imply that hermeneutics before Schleiermacher was worthless. According to Wolfgang Hübener's able reconstruction,[25] this was the verdict of Dilthey.[26] What I *do* wish to say is that Schleiermacher's idea that all understanding is based on misunderstanding has opened new perspectives in a rather crucial way. Hence it is quite astonishing that Jürgen Habermas, famous for his models of intersubjective communication, had yet to refer to Schleiermacher in 1989, when Gunther Wenz argued that Schleiermacher's theory of communication is not only close to Habermas' conception, but could even help strengthen it, thanks to its strong claim not to neglect the religious foundations of modernity.[27]

Having broached the question regarding the originality of Schleiermacher's hermeneutics, I should note that this issue has become a major focus of ongoing research. I would first mention Lutz Danneberg, who has put enormous effort into relating Schleiermacher's hermeneutics to the earlier hermeneutic tradition.[28] His scholarship is im-

---

sion. See, for example, the works of Hellmut Geißner and the various publications of the *Deutsche Gesellschaft für Sprechwissenschaft und Sprecherziehung* (DGSS). For a theological perspective, see Joachim Ringleben, "Die Sprache bei Schleiermacher und Humboldt: Ein Versuch zum Verhältnis von Sprachdenken und Hermeneutik," in Meckenstock, *Schleiermacher und die wissenschaftliche Kultur*, 473-92. Within theological and philosophical discourse it is always safe to refer to Manfred Frank, *Das individuelle Allgemeine: Textstrukturierung und Textinterpretation nach Schleiermacher* (Frankfurt: Suhrkamp, 1977); and to Gunter Scholtz, *Ethik und Hermeneutik: Schleiermachers Grundlegung der Geisteswissenschaften* (Frankfurt: Suhrkamp, 1995).

25 For his attempt to reintegrate Schleiermacher into the history of hermeneutics, see Hübener, "Schleiermacher und die hermeneutische Tradition," in Selge, *Schleiermacher-Kongreß 1984*, 561-74, esp. 561. Hübener also accuses Manfred Frank of a faulty reading of the old traditions (568). Also pertinent from the Selge volume (631-40) is Ulrich J. Schneider's "Die Geschichtsauffassung des hermeneutischen Denkens," which describes Schleiermacher's turn to historicity (*Geschichtlichkeit*) as an important development in the hermeneutic tradition.

26 Wilhelm Dilthey, *Leben Schleiermachers*, vol. 14, bk. 2 of *Gesammelte Schriften* (Göttingen: Vandenhoeck & Ruprecht, 1966), 698.

27 Gunther Wenz, "Verständigungsorientierte Subjektivität: Eine Erinnerung an den Kommunikationstheoretiker F.D.E. Schleiermacher," in *Habermas und die Theologie*, ed. Edmund Arens (Düsseldorf: Patmos, 1989).

28 Lutz Danneberg, "Schleiermachers Hermeneutik im historischen Kontext—mit einem Blick auf ihre Rezeption," in Burdorf and Schmücker, *Dialogische Wissenschaft*, 81-105. Even more historically detailed is his "Schleiermacher und das Ende des Ak-

portant because he tries to carefully distinguish between continuities that have simply been overlooked, on the one hand, and Schleiermacher's innovative moves, on the other. According to Danneberg, there is one problem in particular that continuously and deeply troubles Schleiermacher and which might be the reason why his hermeneutic program was never finished—namely, the relation between hermeneutics and theology, particularly the latter's close relation to the New Testament.[29] For in the discourse of his contemporaries, especially in a tradition called *hermeneutica sacra*, the idea of accommodation (as put forward by Ernesti) was involved—that is, the idea that the interpretation of texts is not only tied to the author's intention, but also to the possibilities of reception and understanding of the first readers. To what extent did the authors of the biblical texts simply follow (and have to follow) the then common use of language? How did they express their individual, and thus new, Christian ideas?[30] This became a problem for Schleiermacher because he held that any intellectual revolution, any paradigmatic shift in tradition, is tied to a linguistic revolution. New ideas need new forms of expression, new words, and new arguments. Such issues were closely related to the question, crucial at the time, concerning the relation between the Old and New Testaments.

In a similar manner, Harald Schnur claims that many interpreters see Schleiermacher's position as a turning point in the tradition of hermeneutics, but they do so with insufficient knowledge about the history of that tradition.[31] He therefore retrieves and explores the hermeneutical writings of Johann August Ernesti, Johann Georg Hamann, Johann Gottfried Herder, and Friedrich Schlegel. Another such effort to relate Schleiermacher to his predecessors (e.g., Leibniz, Wolff, Baumgarten, Herder, and Schlegel) was made by Reinhold Rieger, who interprets Schleiermacher's hermeneutics to be a hermeneutics of "Sinn" (sense/meaning), because understanding aims at texts containing sense—this, in contrast to the merely referential hermeneutics found

---

komodationsgedankens in der hermeneutica sacra des 17. und 18. Jahrhunderts," in Barth und Osthövener, *200 Jahre "Reden,"* 194-46.

29 Danneberg, "Schleiermachers Hermeneutik," 85. Danneberg harshly criticizes Peter Szondi for not having understood the theological problem inherent in Schleiermacher's hermeneutics (ibid., 95-96).

30 Ibid., 97-98.

31 Harald Schnur, *Schleiermachers Hermeneutik und ihre Vorgeschichte im 18. Jahrhundert: Studien zur Bibelauslegung, zu Hamann, Herder und F. Schlegel* (Stuttgart: Metzler, 1994), 3.

especially in semiotics.³² According to Rieger, the notion of *Sinn* provides the missing link in Schleiermacher's attempt to understand the relationship between subject-constituted spontaneity and object-related receptivity, and Schleiermacher's principle of oscillation between identity and difference furnishes the philosophical backdrop: Whatever *it* is that makes sense *to me*, there will always remain a difference, however small, in what is supposed to be identical.³³ Over time, Schleiermacher developed this basic idea into a hermeneutics of difference, determination, and development.³⁴ Although I concur in the main with Rieger's reconstruction, I think it incorrectly reduces Schleiermacher's import for hermeneutics to textual hermeneutics.

Let me therefore conclude this section by referring to Wolfgang H. Pleger, who stresses Schleiermacher's ability to connect rhetoric, hermeneutics, and dialectics within his philosophical thinking.³⁵ Pleger is absolutely right in pointing out the fact that Schleiermacher did not confine himself to textual exegesis but was interested in all sorts of communication. What we first understand is something someone actually said. Indeed, all understanding is part of this understanding, since each text is human speech in a fixed form. Even a formal speech (*eine Rede*), Pleger argues, is no monologue but an act of dialogical communication. So, in fact, dialectics, which Schleiermacher from 1822 on interpreted as the art of communication, would structure the outer framework of hermeneutics—not in the sense of being just one philosophical discipline among others, but as the universal way of building knowledge in general.³⁶ The notions of the "art of understanding" and "general knowledge" are bound to such diverse concepts as arts, semiotics, and symbol theory. Remarks on the first two of these concepts have made for some nice footnotes.³⁷ Symbol theory will occupy us in my third and final section.

---

32 Reinhold Rieger, *Interpretation und Wissen: Zur philosophischen Begründung der Hermeneutik bei Friedrich Schleiermacher und ihrem geschichtlichen Hintergrund* (Berlin: Walter de Gruyter, 1988), 332.
33 Ibid., 333-34.
34 Ibid., 339.
35 Wolfgang H. Pleger, "Die Kunst der Gesprächsführung: Zu Schleiermachers Hermeneutik und Dialektik," in Burdorf and Schmücker, *Dialogische Wissenschaft*, 125-36.
36 Ibid., 132.
37 One of the most prominent scholars of the theme of art in Schleiermacher was Thomas Lehnerer, who pointed out the fact that Schleiermacher not only understood art as genuine communicative medium of feeling, but also tried to integrate this idea into the aesthetic tradition. Lehnerer holds that Schleiermacher finally based his theory of art not on the idea of beauty but on the idea of individual self-manifestation ("Selbstmanifestation ist Kunst: Überlegungen zu den systematischen Grundlagen

3. Symbol theory

It is noteworthy that research on Schleiermacher and Ernst Cassirer has run parallel during the last few years. Critical editions of both authors are underway (or in the case of Cassirer have just been finished), both authors are invoked in interdisciplinary discourse, and both are studied in order to raise crucial questions for a better understanding of religion. In 2000, Dietrich Korsch and Enno Rudolph organized a conference on Cassirer in theology and invited Martin Laube to give a lecture on Schleiermacher and Cassirer.[38] Even though Schleiermacher and Cassirer seem to be rather close at first sight, Laube's conclusion was disillusioning: the closer they seem to get, the further they drift apart.[39]

---

der Kunsttheorie Schleiermachers," in Selge, *Schleiermacher-Kongreß 1984*, 409-22, esp. 409-10, 422). Similar conclusions are to be found with Rainer Volp, although he took semiotics to be fundamental to Schleiermacher's notion of art. For Volp, the function of art lies in its ability to express religion, since both art and religion share the same kind of subjective cognition, but are—just like language itself—conscious and not at all irrational (*unvernünftige*) acts ("Kunst als Sprache von Religion: Ein Beitrag zur Semiotik Friedrich Schleiermachers," in Selge, *Schleiermacher-Kongreß 1984*, 423-38, esp. 425, 427, 429). Reinhold Schmücker, to name just a third example, acknowledges Schleiermacher's contribution to aesthetics as a very distinct approach to the philosophy of art, which focuses not on the perfection of the artistic work but on the process of producing art—a process constituted by emotional excitement (*Erregung*), mental prefiguration, and finally by productive expression or manifestation. Every work of art is thus an autonomous subjective expression which is nevertheless bound to intersubjective interpretation ("Schleiermachers Grundlegung der Kunstphilosophie," in Burdorf and Schmücker, *Dialogische Wissenschaft*, 241-65, esp. 246, 254-55, 258).

Semiotics in the German-speaking context refers mainly to Peirce, but there are at least two other versions worth mentioning here. First, there are the early works by Rainer Volp, who reads Schleiermacher as an originator of relational logics and, as such, even regards him a predecessor of Peirce ("Praktische Theologie als Theoriebildung und Kompetenzgewinnung bei F.D. Schleiermacher," in *Praktische Theologie heute*, ed. Ferdinand Klostermann and Rolf Zerfaß [Mainz: Kaiser/Grünewald, 1974], 52-64). Second, there is the extremely detailed study by Johannes M. Dittmer of Schleiermacher's *Dialektik*, which also contains a large chapter on semiotic perspectives. Dittmer concedes that Schleiermacher did indeed use triadic relations but, in contrast to Peirce, was unable to work it out in detail. Schleiermacher's achievement, nonetheless, was to prioritize the relation over what is related. On the whole, he was so surprisingly close to Peirce that studying the one complements the other. (*Schleiermachers Wissenschaftslehre als Entwurf einer prozessualen Metaphysik in semiotischer Perspektive: Triadizität im Werden*, Theologische Bibliothek Töpelmann 113 [Berlin: Walter de Gruyter, 2001], 456-57).

38 Martin Laube, "Kultur und Individuum: Aspekte ihrer gegenläufigen Verhältnisbestimmung bei Friedrich Schleiermacher und Ernst Cassirer," in *Die Prägnanz der Religion in der Kultur*, ed. Dietrich Korsch and Enno Rudolph (Tübingen: Mohr Siebeck, 2000), 139-61.

39 Ibid., 139.

While Cassirer sought to extend the Kantian critique of reason toward a general critique of culture, Schleiermacher sought to found culture entirely upon the transcendental principle of knowledge. While Cassirer kept his distance from all integrative systems of symbolic forms, Schleiermacher aimed precisely for a systematic construction.[40] In the same volume, Dietrich Korsch argued that for Schleiermacher the relation between culture and religion is based on an implicit theological premise, namely that religion is not just one sphere or form of culture among others, but that the two are in some sense equivalent and culture is itself religious—an idea Korsch considered to be incorrect.[41] Wilhelm Gräb, in turn, proposed that any comparison between Schleiermacher and Cassirer must focus on Schleiermacher's philosophical *Ethics*, not on his *Hermeneutics*.[42] According to Gräb, Schleiermacher had already formulated an idea of culture close to that of Cassirer; both were even based on the idea of symbolization. But in contrast to Cassirer, Schleiermacher had not yet formulated this idea of symbolization as a process of "reflexive self-transparency" (*reflexive Sich-Durchsichtigkeit*) or through the notion of "sense" (*Sinn*).[43] In the wake of this debate, I decided to attempt an extensive comparison of Schleiermacher and Cassirer myself, aiming at a clarification of their similarities and differences.[44] With respect to Schleiermacher's corpus, I chose the *Dialectics* and *Ethics* as basic texts for my twofold examination. First, I tried to determine the internal relation between transcendental philosophy and cultural phenomenology, with the problematic result that the latter is determined by the former. Second, I inquired into how the transcendental structures we find in the *Dialectics* also shape the position of religion within cultural phenomenology. This examination led me to the firm conclusion that for Schleiermacher all culture is ultimately bound to its absolute transcendent foundation as the unifying perspective of everything ideal and real. This is, however, an ambivalent result. For now it becomes obvious that Schleiermacher's constant reference to something absolute—no matter whether he calls it

---

40 Ibid., 140.
41 Dietrich Korsch, "Religion und Kultur bei Hermann Cohen und Ernst Cassirer," in Korsch and Rudolph, *Prägnanz*, 166.
42 Wilhelm Gräb, "Religion in vielen Sinnbildern: Aspekte einer Kulturhermeneutik im Anschluss an Ernst Cassirer," in Korsch and Rudolph, *Prägnanz*, 229.
43 Ibid., 230.
44 See note 16 above as well as Cornelia Richter, "Feeling and Sense, Ethics and Culture: Perspectives on Religion and Culture in Schleiermacher and Cassirer," in *Schleiermacher and Kierkegaard: Subjectivity and Truth: Proceedings from the Schleiermacher-Kierkegaard Congress in Copenhagen, October 2003*, ed. Niels Jørn Cappelørn et al. (Berlin: Walter de Gruyter, 2006), 159-77.

the Universe (*Speeches*), the transcendental foundation (*Dialectics*), or the "whence" of all our dependence (*Glaubenslehre*)—implies the danger of an asymmetrical and pre-reflective determination of cultural phenomena, processes, and interpretations. Hence, it is all the more important to connect this transcendental line of thinking in Schleiermacher to his other basic idea, namely, that one ought constantly to seek to understand and formulate religious and theological issues in the language of culture.

This can be achieved in a prominent way in the arts, as Inken Mädler has shown. By synthesizing Schleiermacher and Cassirer, Mädler has found a way to analyze the products of art and their use that is both intellectually satisfying as well as artistically challenging. In 1999, she presented a study of Schleiermacher's well-known idea of "religious style" in the context of art as a religious act.[45] Mädler pointed out the inherent mathematical connotations of this concept and thus demonstrated that the idea of unity (*Einheit*) that Schleiermacher aimed at constantly must not be understood in the sense of a static figure but in the sense of constancy and continuity. She also draws on Cassirer, who championed the notion of progression over that of substantial concepts. "Einheit" in Schleiermacher accordingly means a principle of progression *ad infinitum*.[46] In subsequent work, Mädler has extended this concept to objects of emotional importance for people—i.e., objects people set their hearts on. Using a phenomenological approach, she explored the way in which such objects create a dense network of spatial, temporal, social, and religious relations. For this reason, her study is highly illuminating for pastoral care and educational theory.[47]

What was implicit in Mädler became the explicit program of Martina Kumlehn, who inquired into the relevance of Schleiermacher's theory of religious communication for present educational theory.[48] She began her study by citing Schleiermacher's remark to Lücke to the effect that those who wished to hear nothing of God rarely contended

---

45 Inken Mädler, "Ausdrucksstil und Symbolkultur als Bedingungen religiöser Kommunikation," in Barth and Osthövener, *200 Jahre "Reden,"* 897-908.
46 Ibid., 904.
47 Inken Mädler, *Transfigurationen: Materielle Kultur in praktisch-theologischer Perspektive*, (Gütersloh: Gütersloher Verlagshaus, 2006).
48 Martina Kumlehn, *Symbolisierendes Handeln: Schleiermachers Theorie religiöser Kommunikation und ihre Bedeutung für die gegenwärtige Religionspädagogik* (Gütersloh: Kaiser/Gütersloher Verlagshaus, 1999). Cf. Dietrich Korsch, "Leibhaftes Verstehen: Grundzüge der Hermeneutik Friedrich Schleiermachers im Blick auf die Situation kirchlicher Beratungstätigkeit," *Zeitschrift für Evangelische Ethik* 36 (1995): 262-78. Also highly recommended are the writings of Michael Meyer-Blank, who frequently discusses Schleiermacher, Cassirer, and Peirce.

with the idea of God itself, but rather attacked the way the idea of God was generally *treated*, i.e., its prevailing expression.[49] Her point was that this remark is still valid today and applicable to understanding contemporary difficulties in teaching and speaking about religion. In order to demonstrate this, she examined and drew upon Schleiermacher's idea of "individual symbolization," as well as his reflections on language and hermeneutics. She concluded that Schleiermacher's special merit was that he did not restrain himself to forms of religious communication, but instead understood them as part of interpersonal communication in general.

And with this, the stage for my own concluding remarks is set. Current research on Schleiermacher is widespread and promising, opting for interdisciplinary and—as shown by this conference—international discourse. I would identify the main currents of this growing research in two areas: First, completion of the critical edition and advancing historical research enables us to read the well-known texts anew, to understand their historical context, and see them in "full view." Reading hitherto unknown texts or familiar ones in new constellations sometimes even changes the discourse overall (e.g., Walter Jaeschke's edition of Hegel's *Lectures on the Philosophy of Religion*). Yet, Schleiermacher's full potential will not be revealed through more thorough historical research alone, for this would run the risk of becoming an exclusively internal scholarly debate. I would therefore, second, stress the idea that we must not only read Schleiermacher, but also adopt his way of practicing theology. Scholarly reflections on various theories and concepts of religion are extremely important and must not be neglected. Yet in the fourth *Speech* Schleiermacher left us with this word of warning: academic theology must not cling to lifeless reflection but must be carried out through vivid perceptions. This implies not only addressing our papers to a broader public, even though these efforts to communicate—like the *Speeches*—might lack conceptual clarity and precision. It means above all not forgetting to talk about basic experiences and needs that relate the Christian dogmatic tradition to what we consider relevant for human life. So let us—or, at least the theologians among Schleiermacher's heirs—speak about hate and despair, trust, hope, and responsibility, as well as about those symbols still held to be central to Christian belief. Let us speak about the Universe, about God, and about the narratives told about Jesus Christ; about emotion and self, about misunderstanding and understanding. In short, let us speak about religion.

---

49 Mädler, *Transfigurationen*, 17.

Contributors

Andreas Arndt, Schleiermacher Research Center of the Berlin-Brandenburg Academy of Sciences; Free University, Berlin
James M. Brandt, St. Paul School of Theology, Kansas City
Richard Crouter, Carleton College, Northfield
Jörg Dierken, University of Hamburg
Andrew Dole, Amherst College
Franklin I. Gamwell, University of Chicago
Wilhelm Gräb, Humboldt University, Berlin
Elisabeth Gräb-Schmidt, Justus Liebig University, Gießen
Peter Grove, University of Flensburg
Kevin W. Hector, University of Chicago
Eilert Herms, Eberhard Karls University, Tübingen
David E. Klemm, University of Iowa, Iowa City
Dietrich Korsch, Philipps University, Marburg
Volkhard Krech, Ruhr University, Bochum
Julia A. Lamm, Georgetown University, Washington, D.C.
Jacqueline Mariña, Purdue University, West Lafayette
Arie L. Molendijk, University of Groningen
Michael Moxter, University of Hamburg
Georg Pfleiderer, University of Basel
Wayne Proudfoot, Columbia University, New York
Cornelia Richter, Philipps University, Marburg
Arnulf von Scheliha, University of Osnabrück
William Schweiker, University of Chicago
Notger Slenczka, Humboldt University, Berlin
Brent W. Sockness, Stanford University, Palo Alto
Sergio Sorrentino, University of Salerno
Theodore Vial, Iliff School of Theology, Denver
Walter E. Wyman, Jr., Whitman College, Walla Walla

Index of Authors

Adams, Robert Merrihew 33-36, 123, 125, 126
Albrecht, Christian 379, 381
Apel, Karl-Otto 137
Aquinas, *See* Thomas Aquinas, Saint
Arendt, Hannah 306
Aristotle 293, 327, 329
Arndt, Andreas 363, 368

Barth, Karl 88-90, 93, 94, 203, 208, 210, 243, 350, 371, 372, 376
Barth, Ulrich 112, 118, 350, 356, 373, 378
Bastow, David 17
Baumgarten, Alexander Gottlieb 384
Beiser, Frederick 354
Bellah, Robert 53
Berger, Peter L. 74
Berkhof, Hendrikus 211
Bernhardt, Reinhold 52
Bigler, Robert 22
Birkner, Hans-Joachim 1, 209, 362, 363, 378
Birus, Hendrik 382
Blair, Hugo 4
Bloom, Paul 20
Blumenberg, Hans 300
Brandt, James M. 292
Brandt, Richard B. 112
Bretschneider, Karl 243
Brunner, Emil 243, 350
Bultmann, Rudolf 371
Burdorf, Dieter 375
Bynum, Caroline Walker 252
Byrne, Peter 15, 18

Capps, Walter 15, 25, 40
Cassirer, Ernst 261, 300, 308, 386-388
Collins, David 4
Cramer, Konrad 380
Crossley, John 132
Crouter, Richard 43, 45, 273, 283, 377
Cupitt, Don 128

Danneberg, Lutz 383, 384
Davidson, Donald 220, 221, 226
Descartes, René 167, 171, 173, 200, 260, 379
De Wette, Wilhelm Martin Leberecht 22, 24
Dierken, Jörg 369, 378
Dilthey, Wilhelm 13, 40, 43, 277, 280, 383
Dinkel, Christoph 95
Dittmer, Johannes Michael 350, 386
Dohna, Wilhelm 100
Dole, Andrew 32, 40, 190, 191, 201
Dorner, Isaak August 70
Drey, Johann Sebastian 243, 361
Droysen, Johann Gustav 280
Dulles, Avery 248
Durkheim, Émile 70, 77

Ebeling, Gerhard 371, 372
Eberhard, Johann Augustus 380
Eco, Umberto 3, 6, 8
Eliade, Mircea 40-42, 48
Ellsiepen, Christof 115, 116, 363, 380, 381
Ernesti, Johann August 384

Feil, Michael 361
Feuerbach, Ludwig 48, 352
Fichte, Johann Gottlieb 41, 43, 91, 122, 155, 183, 287, 335, 349, 353, 356, 360, 368, 378, 380
Fiorenza, Francis Schüssler 40, 243, 244
Frank, Manfred 31, 124, 350, 352, 359, 383
Frei, Hans 335
Freud, Sigmund 304
Fries, Jacob Friedrich 39, 40

Gadamer, Hans-Georg 274
Gerlach, Ludwig von 23
Gerrish, B. A. 42, 191, 194
Gesenius, Wilhelm 23
Glotz, Peter 86

Goethe, Johann Wolfgang von 2, 7, 10, 117, 277
Gogarten, Friederich 88, 378
Gräb, Wilhelm 376, 378, 387
Graf, Friedrich Wilhelm 85, 92, 95, 378
Gross, Michael 255
Grove, Peter 350, 356, 357, 363, 380

Habermas, Jürgen 383
Hamann, Johann Georg 384
Harnack, Adolf von 88
Hartshorne, Charles 147
Hector, Kevin 34, 36, 37
Hedley, Douglas 99
Hegel, Georg Wilhelm Friedrich 2, 39, 41, 91, 155, 162, 177, 224, 235, 236, 239, 288, 299, 349, 352, 353, 356-360, 378, 379, 389
Heidegger, Martin 11, 170, 175, 177, 274, 349
Helmer, Christine 350
Hengstenberg, Wilhelm Ernst 22, 23
Henrich, Dieter 354, 379
Herder, Johann Gottfried 39, 41, 46, 299, 384
Herms, Eilert 89, 318
Herrmann, Wilhelm 373
Herz, Henriette 4
Hick, John 51, 52, 54-56, 132
Hilgenfeld, Adolf 23
Himes, Michael 243
Hinze, Bradford 243
Hirsch, Emanuel 362, 373
Hölderlin, Friedrich 8
Honneth, Axel 236
Huber, Wolfgang 88
Hübener, Wolfgang 383
Humboldt, Wilhelm von 8, 41, 299, 305, 382
Hume, David 72, 146, 302
Husserl, Edmund 303

Inwagen, Peter van 20

Jacobi, Friedrich Heinrich 351, 355, 380, 381
Jaeschke, Walter 353, 389
James, William 42, 70, 89
Jaspers, Karl 53
Jeanrond, Werner 382
Jonas, Ludwig 349

Jörgensen, Poul Henning 291
Jørgensen, Theodor 376
Jüngel, Eberhard 88, 92, 371

Kant, Immanuel 2, 27-30, 41, 44-47, 70, 97, 102, 103, 109, 112-117, 122, 129, 135, 139-141, 147, 151-155, 161, 162, 173, 189, 190, 192, 195, 196, 200, 215-218, 220, 222-224, 226, 230, 253, 258-260, 269, 277, 287, 288, 297, 299, 300, 304-307, 324, 328, 330, 332, 349, 353-358, 360, 372, 378, 380, 387
Kim, Jaegwon 300
Korsch, Dietrich 378, 386, 387
Kranich, Christiane 350
Kuhn, Johann Evangelista 243
Kuitert, Harry 211
Kumlehn, Martina 388

Lamb, Charles 6
Lamb, Mary 6
Lamm, Julia 184, 381
Lang, Andrew 70
Langer, Susan 300
Laube, Martin 88, 386
Lehnerer, Thomas 385
Leibniz, Gottfried 360, 384
Lindbeck, George 40-44, 47, 49, 190, 194, 243
Locke, John 62
Lonergan, Bernard 42
Lönker, Fred 381
Lübbe, Hermann 95
Luckmann, Thomas 74, 77
Luhmann, Nicklas 77
Luther, Martin 181

MacIntyre, Alasdair 302
Mackintosh, Hugh Ross 190, 191, 201
Madges, William 243
Mädler, Inken 388
Magnus, Albert 33, 127
Matthes, Joachim 94
McCutcheon, Russell 39, 40
McDowell, John 216
McFague, Sally 217
Meckenstock, Günter 363, 381
Mensching, Gustav 52
Milbank, John 221
Möhler, Johann Adam 243
Moxter, Michael 352, 367, 378

Müller, Adam 299
Müller, Claus 292
Müller, Friedrich Max 70
Müller, Wolfgang Erich 314

Napoleon 250, 254
Naumann, Friedrich 373
Nicol, Martin 377
Nietzsche, Friedrich 2, 165-169, 171-173, 328, 360
Novalis 41, 116
Nowak, Kurt 255

Ohst, Martin 373
Otto, Rudolf 17, 32, 39-44, 48, 70, 71, 112

Pals, Daniel 40
Pannenberg, Wolfhart 89, 90
Panikkar, Raimon 52
Parsons, Talcott 70
Paul, Jean 299
Percy, Walter 6
Pfleiderer, Georg 378
Pickstock, Catherine 221
Pierce, Charles 386
Pierson, Allard 203, 211
Pinkard, Terry 216
Plato 9, 168, 293, 327, 328, 333, 375
Pleger, Wolfgang 385
Proudfoot, Wayne 15, 16, 40-44, 49, 125, 126, 228

Raack, R. C. 250
Rahner, Karl 244
Ranke, Leopold von 280
Reble, Albert 367
Rehme-Iffert, Birgit 350
Reinach, Adolf 303
Ricœur, Paul 175, 269
Rieger, Reinhold 384, 385
Ringmüller, Joseph 69
Ritschl, Albrecht 331
Ritter, Heinrich 349
Rohls, Jan 379
Rorty, Richard 234
Rössler, Martin 7
Rudolph, Enno 386

Sack, Friedrich Samuel Gottfried 4
Schelling, Friedrich Wilhelm Joseph 43, 91, 117, 224, 349, 353, 359, 360, 378

Schiller, Friedrich 41
Schlegel, August Wilhelm 8
Schlegel, Friedrich 41, 116, 117, 356, 380, 382, 384
Schmidt, Sarah 250, 357
Schmidt-Leukel, Perry 52, 56
Schmücker, Reinhold 375, 386
Schnur, Harald 384
Scholz, Heinrich 90
Schopenhauer, Arthur 328, 360
Schröder, Markus 94
Schütte, Hans-Walter 363
Schweitzer, Albert 328
Sellars, Wilfrid 36, 228, 242
Semler, Johann Jakob 86, 87
Sharpe, Eric 39, 40, 46
Simmel, Georg 70, 74-77, 79
Slone, D. Jason 17
Smith, Jonathan Z. 256
Smith, Wilfred Cantwell 52, 55, 56
Sockness, Brent 285, 288
Söderblom, Nathan 71
Spencer, Herbert 72
Spinoza, Baruch 102, 115, 123, 157, 354-356, 380, 381
Steffens, Henrich 50, 325
Strauss, David Friedrich 276, 277, 280-282
Strenski, Ivan 40
Stroh, Ralf 365
Szondi, Peter 384

Taylor, Charles 41
Tenbruck, Friedrich 94
Theunissen, Michael 352
Thiel, John 243
Thomas Aquinas, Saint 33, 122, 127, 142, 143, 244, 361, 362
Thrower, James 15, 16
Tieck, Ludwig 8
Tiele, Cornelius Peter 73
Tillich, Paul 88, 92, 117, 118, 143, 175, 192
Timm, Hermann 85
Trendelenburg, Friedrich Adolf 352
Trigg, Roger 133
Trillhaas, Wolfgang 311, 362
Troeltsch, Ernst 70, 77, 79, 88, 161, 201, 204, 207-210, 212, 275, 280, 308, 331, 350

Vial, Ted 28, 29
Virmond, Wolfgang 382

Volp, Rainer 386
Voss, Johann Heinrich 8

Wagner, Falk 369
Wallhausser, John 327
Weber, Max 70, 73, 77, 280, 373
Wegscheider, Rudolf 23
Wellmon, Chad 253
Wenz, Gunther 381, 383
Whitehead, Alfred North 147

Wieland, Christoph Martin 7, 8
Wildman, Wesley 16, 17
Williams, Robert R. 379
Winch, Peter 300
Wittekind, Folkart 87, 89
Wolff, Christian 380, 384
Wyman, Walter E., Jr. 207, 251

Zöller, Günter 122

www.ingramcontent.com/pod-product-compliance
Lightning Source LLC
Chambersburg PA
CBHW050848160426
43194CB00011B/2080